SCHOOL LAW

SCHOOL LAW

Theoretical and Case Perspectives

Julius Menacker

University of Illinois at Chicago

PRENTICE-HALL, INC., ENGLEWOOD CLIFFS, NEW JERSEY 07632

Library of Congress Cataloging-in-Publication Data
Menacker, Julius.
  School law.

  1. Educational law and legislation—United States—
Cases. I. Title.
KF4118.M46   1987   344.73'07   86-8889
ISBN 0-13-793753-9   347.3047

Editorial/production supervision and
  interior design: Debbie Ford
Cover design: Edsel Enterprises
Manufacturing buyer: Barbara Kittle

© 1987 by Prentice-Hall, Inc.
A division of Simon & Schuster
Englewood Cliffs, New Jersey 07632

Printed in the United States of America

10 9 8 7 6 5. 4 3 2 1

ISBN   0-13-793753-9   01

Prentice-Hall International (UK) Limited, *London*
Prentice-Hall of Australia Pty. Limited, *Sydney*
Prentice-Hall Canada, Inc., *Toronto*
Prentice-Hall Hispanoamericana, S.A., *Mexico*
Prentice-Hall of India Private Limited, *New Delhi*
Prentice-Hall of Japan, Inc., *Tokyo*
Prentice-Hall of Southeast Asia Pte. Ltd., *Singapore*
Editora Prentice-Hall do Brasil, Ltda., *Rio de Janeiro*

Dedicated with love to my sisters

Janet Brier

and

Frances Kalin

Contents

THREE

Religious Controversies in Public-School Policy   57

FOUR

Defining the Limits of First Amendment Rights of Expression   100

FIVE

The Concept of Due Process: Fairness in Educational Administration   147

Cases   177

SIX

Equal Protection: Concepts of Equality in Education   208

Cases   232

Table of Cases

Preface

Many books devoted to school law can be characterized primarily as case-books that provide the reader with an appropriate scope and variety of edited court decisions, or theoretical, didactic works that explain school law from the author's understanding of the major cases that form this body of information. I have combined these two approaches, giving roughly equivalent emphasis to each. Both the edited cases chosen for inclusion and the didactic and theoretical information provided conform to several organizing principles that have guided the development of this work.

After an introductory chapter explaining the rationale of the book and the legal framework for education, subsequent chapters are organized around the major legal concepts (for example, freedom of expression, due process) that occupy school-related litigation. This approach is intended to give the reader a firm understanding of the theory and principles related to the legal concepts before they are applied to representative issues that follow. This enables the reader to better understand the manner in which legal principles are applied to current as well as future issues.

Another objective is to focus attention on the flexibility of interpretation inherent in the judicial process. I use the liberal-conservative and judicial activism-judicial restraint paradigms as frameworks for understanding the variations possible in judicial resolution of legal controversies in education. The selection

of edited cases has been guided by the intention to show a balance in the expression of these paradigms in the school law arena. Numerous dissents have been included with edited cases to further elaborate on contrasting views.

Finally, since the liberal-conservative and activist-restraintist paradigms explore the flexibility possible in judicial interpretation of the law applied to education, each chapter contains a summary review of policy implications related to the major concepts studied. School law is an aspect of the broader area of education policy studies. The policy implications at the end of each chapter focus attention on this, and help the reader to better understand the interaction of the schools and the judiciary in the formulation of educational policy.

I have been fortunate in receiving needed assistance and support in this project, and I want to acknowledge those who have helped. My son, Mark Menacker, provided extensive research assistance that added considerable substance to most of the chapters. He also contributed critical reactions and constructive advice, as well as continual encouragement. He did this while attending to the demands of his own law school education. Attorney Scott Silzer provided valuable case editing and criticism. Professors Edward Wynne and Van Cleve Morris read a number of draft chapters and contributed useful editing and criticism. Professors Manny Hurwitz and Ward Weldon provided important assistance on numerous conceptual and theoretical matters. Merry Mastny and Renee Okonek were cheerful, helpful, and efficient performers in preparing the manuscript. Finally, my wife, Nadine, and daughters, Terri and Becky, encouraged and supported my work throughout the period needed to complete it.

Julius Menacker

SCHOOL LAW

ONE

The Judicial Context in Education:
Attitudes and Legal Framework

There are two important institutions in American government that are commonly considered to be least affected by partisan politics—courts and public schools. At the very least, when partisanship is discovered in either, the general reaction is that this is wrong. Yet both institutions are, and always have been, deeply involved in and sensitive to the passions and controversy of politics. The American mythology of nonpolitical evaluation of courts and public schools has served to obscure the nature of each, as well as the process involved when the two interact.

Courts make decisions important, at one time or another, to all segments of the political spectrum. Further, judges receive their appointments through a political process, whether they are elected or appointed. Even for federal judges with lifetime tenure, their past political experience and connections continue to play a role in their judicial decision making. Public schools, in their turn, are supported by public funds raised through referenda or otherwise within the political arena. Local board members reach office through public election or political appointment. Why, then, has this myth been perpetuated?

The answer is that both courts and public schools are expected to provide a very important service in an impartial way to all citizens, regardless of race, ethnicity, religious preference, sex, political attitude, or any other difference distinguishing one citizen from another. The very thought that either of these two

1

noble institutions might harbor biases against any class, group, or type of citizen, or engender attitudes that distort the equitable administration of the services of courts or schools, is anathema to the democratic foundations of our government.

The truth is that while most educators and jurists are good and just men and women, they are not provided with any special inoculation freeing them from holding particular political or social attitudes that creep into the execution of their professional roles. These political and social attitudes become evident when judges deal with issues for which there are no clear precedents, or when old issues are raised in the context of new or changing conditions. For example, the Supreme Court of the United States reflected the changed attitudes of the society when it overturned the nineteenth-century precedent established in *Plessy* v. *Ferguson* (1896) (that is, separation of races in public services is legal, provided segregated services are equal) in favor of the view that legal racial segregation in public schools is unconstitutional (*Brown* v. *Board of Education of Topeka* [1954]). In like manner, educators respond to opportunities to give vent to their personal sociopolitical attitudes regarding curriculum, textbook, and other decisions.

In order to understand the processes and considerations that attend adjudication of education issues, and to develop appropriate education policy based on court decisions, these cases must be understood within the framework of sociopolitical attitudes that have influenced them. This allows educators to be disabused of the notion that the law, as interpreted by courts, is fixed, clear, and inflexible. On the contrary, the diverse and changing attitudes of jurists insure the continuing underlying ambiguity and complexity of interpretations characteristic of legal decisions and resultant educational policy. Given the increased intervention of the courts in education, which shows no signs of abatement in the foreseeable future, a fuller understanding of the reasoning, attitudes, and potential impact of court decisions on education is necessary for school administrators and other educators. Addressing court decisions from the perspective of sociopolitical attitudes allows the consumer of education law to understand the decisions and their policy implications more fully.

Two analytical approaches can be used to illuminate the sociopolitical implications of court decisions affecting education. One is the liberal-conservative paradigm. The other is the more judicially oriented paradigm of court activism as opposed to court restraint. Taken together, they provide an analytical framework for evaluating the educational-policy implications of court decisions to a fuller extent than what may be revealed in the context of any one particular decision.

LIBERAL-CONSERVATIVE ATTITUDES

This model is so widely known and used that the meanings that differentiate one attitude from the other have become confused and obscured. Therefore, it is important to set down the principles and attitudes that best help to distinguish one attitude from the other, as relevant to education law. The seminal spokesman for the conservative position was the eighteenth-century British philosopher Edmund Burke. Here is his view of the essence of the conservative tradition: "The conservative . . . in any generation is influenced by his regard for the continuity of tradition, his resistance to uncontrolled social change, and his profound distrust of all Utopian reform movements that are based allegedly on reason."[1]

In contrast, consider the following view, expressed by a modern apostle of the liberal tradition, Charles Frankel:

> To hold the liberal view . . . meant to believe in "progress." It meant to believe that man could better his condition indefinitely by the application of his intelligence to his affairs; it meant, further, to measure the improvement of man in secular terms, in terms of his growth in knowledge, the diminution of pain and suffering, the increase in joy, the diffusion and refinement of the civilized arts; and it meant that such improvement . . . could be brought about by deliberately adopting legislative and judicial techniques which could gradually change the institutions that framed men's lives.[2]

These quotations suggest a fundamental distinction between the liberal and conservative attitudes. The liberal believes in the ability of people to progress, personally and through the institutions of society, toward continuing perfectibility through gradual change, and sees the promotion of individual liberty and progress as an important responsibility of government. For their part, conservatives prefer the "tried and true" status quo, and rely on government to maintain societal order and stability. They distrust unverified, extremist, novel solutions to societal problems. Another approach to distinguishing between liberals and conservatives was provided by the conservative political spokesman Barry Goldwater, who saw the distinction as follows:

> The root difference between the Conservatives and Liberals of today is that Conservatives take account of the *whole* man, while the Liberals tend to look only at the material side of man's nature. The conservative believes that man is, in part, an economic, an animal creature; but that he is also a spiritual creature with spiritual needs and spiritual desires. What is more, these needs and desires reflect the *superior* side of man's nature, and thus take precedence over his economic wants. Conservatism therefore looks upon the enhancement of man's spiritual nature as the primary concern of political philosophy. Liberals, on the other hand—in the name of a concern for "human beings"—regard the satisfaction of human wants as the dominant mission of society.[3]

If we disregard the frank bias of this conservative apostle in his espousal of the supremacy of conservatism over liberalism, we see how Goldwater distinguishes well between the greater concerns of liberals for the direct, immediate material welfare of the disadvantaged, as opposed to the more comprehensive view of human welfare held by conservatives, which places less emphasis on quick, concrete "fixes" for the needy. The conservatives, it would appear, are willing to wait for such problems to work themselves out in proven, if slower, ways. Generally, a conservative is someone who has something to conserve. The poor and disenfranchised might favor and welcome any change, on the theory that things could not get much worse for them.

This rich-poor influence on liberal-conservative attitudes can create different views on different issues. For example, Lipset observed:

> The poorer strata everywhere are more liberal . . . on economic issues; they favor more welfare and state measures, higher wages, graduated income taxes, support of trade unions and so forth. But when liberalism is defined in non-economic terms—as support of individual liberties, internationalism, etc.—the correlation is reversed. The more well-to-do are more liberal, the poorer more intolerant.[4]

Another general distinction that can serve to identify and differentiate between liberal and conservative positions is found in a more focused concentration on the issue of change, which allows for eliminating the confusion of changing positions and the emotional loading of particular issues. The following scheme provides a way of distinguishing between liberal and conservative positions according to three aspects of attitude toward change.

CRITERIA	LIBERAL	CONSERVATIVE
Rapidity of change desired	Rapid but considered change in problem areas; gradual in other areas	Cautious, gradual change only when the need is clearly demonstrated in a conceded problem area
Pervasiveness of change desired	Piecemeal to quite extensive	Piecemeal to none at all
Temporal orientation	Present and future	Present and past

This chart suggests that the conservative tradition would view change hesitantly and only when the need is incontrovertibly demonstrated. Even then, only the most clearly necessary changes should be made in limited areas of society. The conservative is influenced by the values of the past and the present, and would not attempt to influence future events along unaccustomed, unproven paths. In contrast, liberals are open to change in proportion to the seriousness of the problem, as judged by them. The time perspective of liberals is oriented to the present and future. Traditions of the past are less important to them.

The final general distinction to be made between liberals and conservatives has to do with educational philosophy. Conservative tradition extends as far back as Plato and his views of society being led by "philosopher kings." Today, this can be related to conservative allegiance to the concept of a "meritocracy," in which those showing the greatest competence in the serious aspects of schooling are rewarded and endowed with leadership. In the process, educational conservatives support clear, effective adult control of the curriculum, strong policies for control of students, and emphasis on following well-trod, proven paths to educational excellence. The "back to basics" movement of the early 1980s is an example of the conservative educational attitude. Finally, conservatives view the fact of being a student as evidence that one does not have the answers to school-related matters. It is far more reasonable to assume that those placed in positions of school authority do have them.

In contrast, liberals have an Aristotelian bent, believing in the capacity of each individual's power of reason. Liberals combine this with the Rousseauian belief in each person's innate goodness. Thus, the school should have an egalitarian emphasis, and students should participate in decisions affecting how they are taught, what they are taught, and how they are controlled. The school should nurture the development of students in their emotional as well as intellectual aspects, but should not impose its will too strongly on the unique nature of the individual.

Judicial Distinctions Regarding Liberalism and Conservatism

Judges, of course, do not come to their positions devoid of attitudes that brand them as liberals or conservatives in matters of economics, social relations, government authority, education, or any other matters of human involvement or interest. Indeed, it is well known that presidents appoint federal judges based on certain liberal or conservative leanings. As an example, President Eisenhower went on record as claiming that the worst decision he made as President was appointing Earl Warren as Chief Justice of the United States Supreme Court. The reason for his lament was that he thought he was appointing a conservative, but found a liberal on the bench after the appointment. The President has either misread Warren's philosophic preference or that preference changed once Warren found himself on the bench. When the Warren Court was in its prime, much rhetoric was directed against the "excessive liberalism" of those jurists who together controlled the Supreme Court during much of the fifties and sixties. By the seventies and eighties, enough liberals had died or resigned to allow the more conservative presidents of those years to appoint conservative replacements. This set in motion a gradual shift toward a more conservative Court stance. In its turn, the present Burger Court is sometimes criticized for its "excessive conservatism."

ACTIVISM AND RESTRAINT

The labeling of liberal or conservative for the decisions produced by the judicial process does not tell the whole story of the influence of court attitudes on education decisions. Also important is the attitude of jurists toward *judicial restraint* as opposed to *judicial activism*. Judges exercising judicial restraint are "strict constructionists," careful not to engage in "judicial policy making" through allowing their attitudes and notions of what is right or wrong to guide a decision where there is no clear constitutional, statutory, or legal precedent. Where the basis of law is unclear, they favor deference to legislative or executive authority rather than blazing a new trail of constitutional interpretation or developing novel legal theories to apply to an issue. These jurists are loath to overrule the constituted authorities in other branches of government, and do so only on strictly legal, unavoidable grounds. They are also careful to avoid dealing with political issues where the introjection of the court might swing the balance of democratic political controversy in one direction or another. Additionally, advocates of judicial restraint attempt to find the narrowest grounds for their ruling, as a statute rather than the Constitution, so as to limit the court's intervention into areas reserved for other processes of government. Also, practitioners of judicial restraint are cautious about granting "standing to sue" to litigants; that is, agreeing that the issue is serious enough to occupy the time of the court and that the individual bringing suit has established a sufficient legal basis for doing so. Related to this concept is that of the "ripeness" of the issue presented. If, in the judgment of an appellate court (particularly the Supreme Court), an issue has not sufficiently been developed or is for whatever reason not ready to be considered, it will not be accepted for adjudication. Those advocating judicial restraint are likely to reject a concept considered not yet "ripe."

As an illustration of the reasoning applied by restraintist justices, consider the following view, expressed by Justice Frankfurter in his dissent to the U.S. Supreme Court majority's decision to invalidate a West Virginia statute requiring public-school students to participate in flag-salute exercises:

> I am not justified in writing my private notions of policy into the Constitution, no matter how deeply I may cherish them or how mischievous I may deem their disregard . . . [O]ne's own opinion about the wisdom or evil of a law should be excluded altogether when one is doing one's duty on the bench. The only opinion of our own . . . that is material is our opinion whether legislators could in reason have enacted such a law.[5]

While in many ways judicial activism may be viewed as the opposite of judicial restraint, it is not best, or even most fairly, viewed in that way. Most important, judicial activism supports the use of judicial power to establish new law or policy where, in the court's judgment, it is needed in the best interests of society. Activists see the judges' role, particularly federal judges insulated from the usual politics and passions by their lifetime appointments, as responsible for insuring justice and fairness and keeping society on its proper course by considering not only the letter of the law, but its spirit as well. They have clear policy preferences, and they work to bring about the results they believe are necessary and required. Adopting a "broad construction" attitude toward interpreting statutes or the Constitution, these jurists believe that

> there is (or should be) a judicial remedy for social wrongs brought before the Court. The opinions of the great activist justices ring out with declarations of the judicial obligation to guard the Constitution, promote justice, abort evil, protect liberty,

guarantee equality, and so on. . . . The great activists tend to preach, to lecture
. . . about good and evil, right and wrong.⁶

Finally, activist judges generally bring a particular social philosophy to their legal judgments that operates in tandem with their legal views, bringing to their decisions a wider scope than would otherwise be applied.

The result is that, in contrast to restraintist jurists, activists are quicker to grant standing to sue and see issues as "riper" than their more restrained brethren. They are also less restrained about moving from the narrower confines of decisions based on a statute to the broader domain of the Constitution. They do not feel constrained about injecting morality, values, and opinions into legal controversies. Nor are they insecure regarding judgments about what might be proper or improper in school curriculum or practice. Consider, for example, the activist characteristics contained in the Supreme Court decision that invalidated a 1919 Nebraska statute forbidding teaching in a foreign language, or teaching a foreign language to students in eighth grade or below:

> While this court has not attempted to define with exactness the liberty thus guaranteed . . . the established doctrine is that this liberty may not be interfered with, under the guise of protecting the public interest. . . . Determination by the legislature of what constitutes proper exercise of police power is not final or conclusive but is subject to supervision by the courts. . . .
> Mere knowledge of the German language cannot reasonably be regarded as harmful. . . . It is well known that proficiency in a foreign language seldom comes to one not instructed at an early age, and experience shows that this is not injurious to the health, morals or understanding of the ordinary child.⁷

In this decision, the activist definitions of general terms such as "liberty" and "the public interest" are used to set aside the will of the Nebraska legislature. These judges believed that the Constitution requires, or at least allows, them to make judgments about the value of foreign-language study and the proper age for maximizing such study. We see here the evidence supporting the claim that activists always believe there is "a judicial remedy for social wrongs" and "tend to preach . . . about . . . right and wrong." Restraintist jurists would view such judgments, and such consideration of the value of foreign-language training or the proper age for it to take place, as clearly beyond the authority and competence of a court. The attitude of judicial restraint would be that a judge's "opinion about the wisdom or evil of a law should be excluded altogether." The only proper judicial judgment would be that which considers "whether legislators could in reason have enacted such a law."

The U.S. Supreme Court's 1954 decision in *Brown* v. *Board of Education of Topeka* marked a clear break with the restraintist position. In declaring racial segregation of public-school students to be in violation of the Constitution's equal protection clause, the Warren Court set its liberal and activist course. It showed its eagerness to accept the judgments of social scientists to support its liberal views, and overturned a half-century of practice in many states in order to impose its view of what was just and right in the field of education. The following passage from the *Brown* decision is instructive:

> To separate them [children in elementary and high schools] from others of similar age and qualifications solely because of their race generates a feeling of inferiority . . . that may affect their minds and hearts in a way unlikely to ever be undone. The effect of this separation on their educational opportunities was well stated by a finding in the Kansas case . . . "Segregation of white and colored children in public schools has a detrimental effect upon the colored children . . . [as it] is usually interpreted as denoting the inferiority of the Negro group. A sense of inferiority affects the motivation of a child to learn. Segregation with the sanction of law, therefore, has a tendency to [retard] the education and mental development of Negro children. . . . " This finding is amply supported by modern authority.
>
>   We conclude that in the field of public education the doctrine of "separate but equal" has no place. Separate educational facilities are inherently unequal.[8]

This famous decision illustrates many of the activist tendencies to which restraintists object. In *Brown*, it is the willingness of the Court to invalidate long-standing state laws, as well as a previous precedent established by the Supreme Court, on the basis of "modern authority" provided by psychologists and sociologists about "the hearts and minds" of students, and what condition "generates a feeling of inferiority." Yet this was a unanimous decision. Activist-restraintist differences among Court members had been set aside because of a more powerful force—the sense of what was right and wrong in American society. Restraintists saw this as more important than abstract notions about the role of the judiciary. The history of American courts reveals that activism and restraint are both used to mask imposition of personal philosophies. While it is true that in education cases, activism is most closely related to liberal causes and restraint most supportive of conservative positions, this linking is not a consistent historical thread. Consider the following analysis:

> Liberals who deplored the institutional power of the Courts in the 1930s and then defended that very same power in the 1950s and 1960s when it happened to advance policies with which they were personally sympathetic, assume a posture which is intellectually untenable, if not downright dishonest. Ditto for conservatives who managed precisely the opposite reversal of field.[9]

Judges do take restraintist or activist positions in accordance with how well either position suits their social and political philosophies. Most educationally liberal positions have required judicial activism for their expression, while conservative educational positions have been best served by the practice of judicial restraint. The great enlargement of civil-rights applications to education, a liberal philosophy, has required unprecedented court activism, just as the weakening of state and local school control, anathema to conservatives, has best been combatted by judicial restraint. The great educational controversies of recent decades have centered on expanding the rights of all kinds of weaker and minority groups, not entirely restricted to race, but including religion, sex, handicapped students, and other categories as well. These controversies have also focused on the general expansion of civil liberties within the educational arena. Therefore, with care and caution, activist judicial positions in education cases during the fifties, sixties, and the early seventies can be labeled liberal, while judicial restraint during that period may be associated with conservatism. This has occurred simply because of the issues and conditions associated with those years. As conservatives gained power in the late seventies, they began reversing liberal judicial gains. Then it was the conservatives who were the activists and the embattled liberals who practiced judicial restraint. Thus, Justice John Paul Stevens, in addressing the 1984 convention of the American Bar Association, criticized his conservative colleagues for casting aside judicial restraint in moving the law to the right through broad opinions reversing precedents set during the years of the Warren Court. He disparaged them for the activist practice of making law instead of just interpreting it.

Summary Principles

The elements to be considered in forming judgments about court attitudes underlying education decisions can now be summarized.

Liberal court decisions are those having one or more of the following implicit or explicit characteristics:

1. Belief in the limitless perfectibility of people through the use of their intelligence
2. Belief in the power of societal institutions to change people and society for the better, primarily in the secular and material spheres
3. Willingness for change to proceed at a rate of speed suggested by the need for it and the capacity of the changes to solve problems
4. Openness to change encompassing piecemeal to wholesale change
5. An orientation toward the present and future for guidance in decisions, rather than on the past
6. An educational philosophy oriented toward the development of individual uniqueness and reason, along with student choice and participation in educational policy
7. Support of libertarian, egalitarian causes in the secular tradition.

In contrast, the characteristics that influence and guide conservative judicial opinion are:

1. Reliance on the continuity of tradition and proven practice to guide current judgment
2. Wariness about Utopian solutions to issues that make seductive uses of reason
3. Advocacy of the most cautious, gradual, piecemeal change as best for the welfare of society
4. An orientation toward seeking guidance from the past and present

5. Equal concern for the spiritual and material aspects of living
6. An educational philosophy emphasizing meritocratic principles and strong adult control of student behavior, curriculum, and teaching methods so that youth can be molded to standards fashioned by adult authority
7. Support of reemerging "old-fashioned" virtues emphasizing religious values
8. Belief in the need to maintain or, when necessary, reassert the legitimate authority of adults over children.

   Judicial activism in education has these general characteristics:

1. Willingness to grant easy access to the courts through relatively loose standards for determining standing to sue
2. A tendency toward "loose" legal construction and judicial policy making
3. A veiw of the court's role as guardian of the rights and liberty of the people against tendencies by government to encroach on these rights and liberties as interpreted by the court
4. A willingness to develop new issues and legal interests when, in the judgment of jurists, the public welfare requires this
5. A view of the court's role as introducing and championing secular moral causes and social justice, and explaining where good or evil may lie, in controversies before the court.

   Contrasted with these activist principles are the following restraintist tendencies:

1. Interpretation of the role of judges as apolitical arbiters of the law, in which their opinion of right or wrong must defer to the clear letter of the law; that is, strict constructionism
2. Careful abstention from judicial policy-making
3. Deference to the will of state and national legislature (as well as local school boards) as the proper sources of law and judgment, only to be overruled when there is preponderant evidence of illegal action
4. Reluctance to grant standing when issues are unclear, not sufficiently "ripe," or not based on firm legal ground.

IMPLICATIONS OF COURT ATTITUDES
FOR EDUCATIONAL-POLICY FORMULATION

Investigations of the impact of the ground swell of educational litigation engulfing schools during recent decades have revealed confusion and uncertainty. On the one hand there are laments that the courts have substantially usurped the educational-policy-making functions of local school boards and state legislatures.[10] On the other hand, there is evidence that educators, the ones who in the last analysis must be relied upon to translate court judgments into policy and practice, have relatively incomplete awareness and understanding of court decisions affecting education.[11] In addition, there is also evidence that even when court decisions are known and understood, they are, at times, disregarded with impunity when local authorities disagree with them.[12]

As a result of this situation, educators responsible for policy analysis and policy formulation must balance a number of considerations in order to achieve adequate understanding of educational-policy issues with legal implications, and to contribute to the most useful policy and implementation practices that flow from it. The attitudes expressed by judicial opinion must be evaluated in relation to the attitudes of state and/or local education personnel, boards of education, and the publics served by affected public-school systems. This issue of attitudes can be most sharply focused and managed by the liberal-conservative analytical framework; for in most school-law decisions, identification of the prevailing liberal or conservative opinion will endow the decision with greater meaning, understanding, and direction for policy formulation and implementation than provided by the legal substance alone. In much the same way, the activist or restraintist tendency of a judge may shape an opinion.

A first order of business is to understand, as the expression goes, "where the judge is coming from." In this regard, the following passage is instructive: "[W]hether liberal or conservative . . . the court always reflects the personalities and attitudes of the men who are on the bench at a particular time. When the judges decide whether or not a law should stand, their own attitudes, philosophies and backgrounds shadow their legal decisions."[13]

Next, it is necessary for educators to evaluate the legal substance and judicial attitude expressed in terms of their own understanding, as colored by their own attitudes. For example, in considering the translation of court-ordered procedural due process requirements to be used in school suspension and expulsion cases (*Goss* v. *Lopez,* 1975), Kirp speculated: "If school authorities share the perception . . . that due process in the schools will undercut basic organizational patterns by radically altering administrators' and teachers' lives, the meaning of the concept is likely to be altered in a way that . . . strips due process of the very characteristics that imbue it with worth."[14]

The concepts and principles that apply to educational law will most likely be understood and well implemented into policy and procedure when educators have the advantage of viewing decisions from the liberal-conservative perspective. This perspective allows for evaluating the philosophical, political, and social values motivating the decision, which puts the strictly legal material in a more comprehensive framework, allowing for deeper, more thorough understanding by educators.

Educational policy analysts and formulators must also accept that their role is not that of passive receivers of judicial opinions. They also have the ability, and the responsibility, to influence courts. This is particularly true because the courts, following the lead in *Brown* v. *Board of Education,* have chosen to include social-science evidence and opinion into the process of judicial decision making. The inherently tentative and contradictory nature of much of social-science research has allowed liberal and conservative opinion to hold much more influential sway over court opinions than was true before *Brown*. The legal battleground is now open to the easy marshaling of any attitude on either side of the liberal-conservative pole, through supporting social-science data. This provides judges with the convenience of supporting their attitudes with ''scientific'' evidence. The responsibility for providing the theories and supporting research rests with educators. Wolf, in her account of the Detroit school desegregation case (*Bradley* v. *Milliken,* 1974) points out: ''The aim of a lawsuit is not to improve the judge's grasp of a subject but to propagandize and convince him. . . . There is no one at a trial whose only interest is to clarify and synthesize, in short, to teach.''[15] As educators accept this reality, they will become more effective in influencing the educational programs for which they are responsible.

While educators may be more concerned with judicial propagandizing and convincing than teaching, one of the most important historic roles of the judiciary has been the court's role as teacher. Primarily from the activist tradition, the courts have instructed government and the body politic about such concepts as the nature of a democratic society and relationships between individuals, and between individuals, groups, and the government. Even restraintists provide instruction, when they define the meaning of a law or a constitutional provision in terms of their understanding of the intent of those who fashioned the legislation. As school administrators and board members understand the general legal principles controlling a decision, and the manner in which these principles have been shaped and modified through time by shifting liberal and conservative influences, they will be better able to respond to court educational influences.

SOURCES OF LAW

Court attitudes of liberalism or conservatism, restraint or activism, are tempered and proscribed by the legal framework in which they operate. This system limits judicial discretion and power within orderly, prescribed boundaries. The courts are only one of several sources of law that affect educational policy. They interact with these other sources to form the policy context of American education.

Federal and State Constitutions

The highest law in the nation is the U.S. Constitution. This provides the framework in which government operates, the powers of the government and its branches, and the relationship of government to the people, including civil-rights protections found in various constitutional amendments. The Constitution provides a broad framework, which leaves considerable leeway for interpretation and flexibility to allow the courts to apply constitutional tenets to current issues not envisioned by the Founding Fathers.

The U.S. Constitution is silent regarding education, leaving that area to the states, by virtue of the Tenth Amendment. Therefore, the constitution of each state represents the basic source of education law for its jurisdiction, provided it does not conflict with the national Constitution. Each state has provided, with varying degrees of specificity, for a state system of public education. Courts, legislatures, or executive officials cannot tamper with this basic framework. The only way to change a constitutional provision is through amendment or replacement of the constitution with a new one, in the manner prescribed within it.

Statutes

State laws, or statutes, fill in the framework provided by the state constitution. These laws may not conflict with state constitutional provisions or the Constitution and laws of the United States. Rules and regulations of state and local public-education agencies are generally considered to have the effect of statutes on educational governance. State statutory provisions governing education policy vary from very detailed regulation and control by the state, to statutes allowing maximum flexibility and decision making at the local level. In general, state statutes at least specify the basis for financial support of public schools, the conditions under which local school districts may be established and operated, teacher-certification requirements, the minimum length of the school day and year, and the duties and responsibilities of state and local school officials.

It is these statutes, along with state board and local district rules and regulations, that form the basic legal environment in which schools operate. They provide the pattern of obligations and restraints that guide the activities of state education agencies, local boards of education, school administrators, and teachers. The broad guidelines provided by constitutional articles on education allow for statutes and regulations to reflect the liberal or conservatives attitudes of state legislators as well as local boards of education.

Through court-sanctioned authority provided primarily through the general welfare clause of the U.S. Constitution, federal statutes also influence education policy. These statutes, to be explained more fully in the next chapter, influence education policy through categorical funding programs and civil-rights prescriptions.

Common Law and Court Precedent

Undergirding the legal system of enacted law is a body of accepted practice on the part of government and in the legal relationship of persons to one another in our society, which has been inherited from England as far back as the Anglo-Saxon period. These customary relationships became the accepted standards of conduct, and were given the force of law (common law) through court acceptance of them in deciding controversies where legislation did not provide answers. The courts then adopted a policy of insuring consistency and predictability for the developing common law by following the principle of *stare decisis*, Latin for "let the decision stand." In doing so, the American judiciary obligated itself to follow the rule of precedent—the practice of observing the principles established in one controversy to future issues that are similar in their legal context. The rule of *stare decisis*, or precedent, obligates lower courts to follow the interpretation of a legal principle established by a higher court in its jurisdiction. While state supreme courts and the U.S. Supreme Court are not obliged to adhere to their own past interpretations, custom and tradition influence their adherence to the rule of precedent. Clearly, strict observance of precedent is indicative of judicial restraint, and breaking with precedent is an instance of judicial activism.

THE JUDICIAL SYSTEM

The American judicial system is organized into parallel sets of state and federal courts. Within each are three court levels. At the lowest level (federal district court or state circuit court), the parties to a controversy present their cases, and the trial takes place. Evidence is presented, witnesses are examined and cross-examined, and judges or juries make decisions by applying relevant legal principles to the facts in a particular controversy. The trial court is the only arena in which the full scope of legal proceedings occurs.

Following the trial, litigants losing at the district or circuit court level may appeal, in federal cases, to the U.S. Court of Appeals for their district or, in state cases, an intermediate court of appeals or, if no intermediate level is provided, the highest court, usually called the state supreme court. At the appellate level, the case is not retried. The appellate courts, both state and federal, restrict themselves to reviewing the written record established at the trial court, and reviewing the briefs prepared and oral arguments of the attorneys related to the appeal.

Following appeal at the intermediate level, there remains appeal to the U.S. Supreme Court and, in state cases, the state supreme court. The same procedures apply as at the intermediate appeal levels. However, these "courts of last resort" are generally free to accept for review only those cases they agree to hear, except as provided in the respective constitutions. There are no mandatory reviews required for education cases.

The U.S. Supreme Court is required to consider for review all decisions of three-judge appellate-court decisions. However, full Supreme Court review occurs only when four of the nine justices agree to grant a *writ of certiorari,* which gives leave for the appellant to bring a case forward. Approval is given when at least four justices consider that a substantial and ripe issue of federal constitutional or statutory law is at issue. When the U.S. Supreme Court decides an issue, it becomes *res judicata*; that is, a thing judged, and not subject to further dispute. Supreme Court precedent is binding on all lower federal courts[16] and on all state courts in matters encompassing national law. In the same way, the decisions of federal appellate courts are binding on federal district courts within a particular circuit, and on state courts within the jurisdiction.

The legal system allows for state courts to hear controversies involving federal law. The decisions rendered on such issues are appealable to federal courts. In order for a federal court to entertain a case involving state law, an issue of federal constitutional or statutory law must pertain. The interaction among and between state and federal courts is further promoted by the rules of precedent. Opinions of courts in one state, while not binding on courts in another state, are considered "persuasive," provided there is no contradiction in the legislation of the states. The same is true for the decisions in a particular federal circuit upon cases heard in another circuit.

In the operation of the judicial system, it is important to observe that a court cannot act on its own initiative. No matter how activist may be the inclinations of a particular judge, he or she must wait for parties to a real dispute, who have substantial injury to complain about, to file a suit. The person initiating the action, whether a private party or government representative, must come before the court, requesting redress. Only then can the judicial process be activated. If nobody wishes to complain about a breach of education law or court policy, the court must remain passive. In this way, many violations of court principles or even statutory law may persist on a continual basis in schools.

NOTES

1. Quoted from Edmund Burke, *Reflections on the Revolution in France*, in G. Max Wingo, *The Philosophy of American Education* (New York: D. C. Heath, 1965), p. 58.
2. Charles Frankel, *The Case for Modern Man* (Boston: Beacon Press, 1959), p. 36.
3. Barry Goldwater, *The Conscience of a Conservative* (New York: William Books, 1960), pp. 10–11.
4. Seymour M. Lipset, *Political Man: The Social Bases of Politics* (Garden City, N.Y.: Doubleday & Co., 1960), pp. 102–103.
5. West Virginia v. Barnette, 319 U.S. 624 (1943) at 647.
6. Marvin Schick, "Judicial Activism on the Supreme Court," in S. C. Halpern and C. M. Lamb, eds., *Supreme Court Activism and Restraint* (Lexington, Mass.: Lexington Books, 1982), p. 48.
7. Meyer v. Nebraska, 262 U.S. 390 (1923).
8. Brown v. Board of Education, 347 U.S. 483 (1954).
9. Stephen C. Halpern, "On the Imperial Judiciary and Comparative Institutional Development and Power in America," in S. C. Halpern and C. M. Lamb, eds., *Supreme Court Activism and Restraint* (Lexington, Mass.: Lexington Books, 1982), p. 239.
10. See, for example, William R. Hazard, "Courts in the Saddle: School Boards Out," *Phi Delta Kappan* (December 1974), pp. 259–261, and Gary L. McDowell, "A Modest Remedy for Judicial Activism," *The Public Interest* (Spring 1982), pp. 3–20.
11. See, for example, Perry A. Zirkel, "A Test on Supreme Court Decisions Affecting Education," *Phi Delta Kappan* (April 1978) pp. 521–555, and Julius Menacker and Ernest Pascarella, "How Aware Are Educators of Supreme Court Decisions that Affect Them?" *Phi Delta Kappan* (February 1983), pp. 424–426.
12. Dale Doak, "Do Court Decisions Give Minority Rule?" *Phi Delta Kappan* (October 1963), pp. 20–24.
13. Barbara Habenstreit, *Changing America and the Supreme Court* (New York: Julian Messner, 1970), p. 9.
14. David L. Kirp, "School Norms and Due Process," *Administrators Notebook*, XXVII (7), 1978–79, pp. 1–4.
15. Eleanor P. Wolf, *Trial and Error: The Detroit School Desegregation Case* (Detroit: Wayne State University Press, 1981), p. 261.
16. The United States is divided into eleven federal court circuits, each containing several states. In addition, there is a federal court for the District of Columbia, and various special-purpose federal courts.

TWO

Government Authority in Education

The earliest American governmental interest in public education is found in the Massachusetts Colony's legislation of 1642 and 1647, which together charged parents with responsibility for educating their children, required that established communities appoint teachers, and permitted taxation for school support. The acts had religious and social bases rather than a political motivation, and the approaches various colonies took to the issue of education varied with the attitudes of the dominant religious group. The shift to assigning political importance to education was signaled by Thomas Jefferson's 1779 Bill for the More General Diffusion of Knowledge, proposed in the midst of the American Revolution. Jefferson's bill called for the development of public education in Virginia, including portions to be offered at public expense for those not able to pay for it. This was to be primarily secular education, and for a purpose consistent with the democratic revolution in which the colonies were then engaged. In Jefferson's words:

> In every government on earth is some trace of human weakness, some germ of corruption and degeneracy, which cunning will discover and wickedness insensibly open, cultivate, and improve. Every government degenerates when trusted to the rulers of the people alone. The people themselves therefore are its only safe depositories. And to render even them safe, their minds must be improved to a certain degree.[1]

Recognition of the democratic political importance of education continued in varying degrees among the new states and the fledgling government under the Constitution. The Ordinance of 1787, which regulated the process of land sales in the Ohio territory, provided that: "Religion, morality, and knowledge being necessary to good government and the happiness of mankind, schools and the means of education shall forever be encouraged." Shortly thereafter, the first ten amendments to the Constitution, known collectively as the Bill of Rights, were passed. The Tenth Amendment stated: "The powers not delegated to the United States by the Constitution, nor prohibited by it to the State, are reserved to the States respectively or to the people." Since education or schooling is not mentioned in the Constitution, this function has been "reserved" for state control.

The language of the Tenth Amendment, as well as the Constitution as a whole, is sufficiently broad to allow a national role in education. A direct source for this is found in Article 1, section 8 of the Constitution, which empowers Congress to "provide for the common defense and general welfare of the United States." This has led to court approval of federal policies of influencing education by offering federal money to states and local school districts for engaging in specific programs and practices it wishes to encourage. States and local districts may decide not to participate, thus forgoing the federal funds offered. However, acceptance of federal grants requires the states and districts to follow the federal mandates imposed by the grants. Another direct entry into national school governance is found in the Commerce Clause, which gives Congress power to "regulate Commerce . . . among the several states. . . . " This has been interpreted by the Supreme Court to allow some federal authority over school safety, transportation, and labor policies.

Less direct, but equally effective as a route for federal intervention in education, has been national guardianship of the civil rights of the people, guaranteed in the Constitution against abuse by states, or its agents, such as public-school districts, by the Fourteenth Amendment. While the Bill of Rights addressed only the relationship between the national government and the people of the United States, the Fourteenth Amendment, passed in 1868, provided due-process and equal-protection rights for people in relation to state governments. Then, beginning with the Supreme Court's decisions in *Gitlow* v. *New York,* 268 U.S. 652 (1925) and *Cantwell* v. *Connecticut,* 310 U.S. 296 (1940), the Court began a process of "absorption" or "incorporation" of the earlier national civil rights into the relationship between people and their state governments, based on a broad, activist, liberal reading of the Fourteenth Amendment. As a result, constitutional civil-rights litigation has become a pervasive, active field of federal intervention into state- and local-education policy and practice.

Although there is a federal role in public education, by virtue of the Tenth Amendment, education is the ultimate province of the state. State government has plenary power over public education, which is defined through provisions of state constitutions and statutes, as well as rules and regulations promulgated by state executive agencies. The constitutional articles and statutes define the legal relationship between the state and the local school districts, which are fundamentally state agents.

Local school districts are creations of the state, formed to acquit state responsibilities for public education. The state may delegate a variety of powers and authority to these state "quasi-corporations," but ultimate responsibility and authority for public education remains with the state, which cannot delegate away the responsibility assigned to it by a state constitution. However, once the state grants specific authority or functions to local districts in a legal manner, it must abide by the relationship until such time as the law is changed by the legislature or declared unconstitutional by the courts. The authority conveyed to school districts is of two kinds: express authority and implied authority. Courts have little trouble in identifying express authority; that is, clearly defined, specified powers conferred by statute. However, these grants of authority often suggest additional responsibilities and powers related to those specified; for instance, authority to hire and discharge teachers implies authority to set employment standards and to evaluate teachers. Courts are occasionally called upon to judge the extent to which various implied powers may reasonably accrue to school districts. Generally, courts will limit implied powers to those clearly dictated by educational need.

While almost all states have established local school districts (Hawaii is one exception) to carry out general state-education policy, it is not mandatory that this be done unless the state constitution requires it. Local districts are organized under governance by a local Board of Education, composed of lay citizens who make policy that conforms with state law and rules, while responding to unique local needs and conditions. The policies that they formulate are carried out through an appointed superintendent and the staff recommended for hiring to the Board by the superintendent.

Board members and administrative officers are assigned certain ministerial or mandatory duties by higher authorities, which often must be accomplished in prescribed ways. The necessary authority accompanies the assignment of responsibility. Ministerial or mandatory functions typically include conducting school for a prescribed minimum number of days or implementing state health and safety regulations. While such matters may be delegatable to other officers within the school system, courts will require that they be carried out as prescribed, or hold the responsible personnel liable for misfeasance or nonfeasance. Boards and administrators also possess discretionary authority, provided to them for the necessary exercise of judgment in formulating policy related to mandatory authority and responsibility. Discretionary authority is not delegatable, and involves such matters as policies for hiring and firing teachers, setting teachers' salaries and assignments, student control, and student grading. Courts will judge challenges to the use of discretionary authority by evaluating the skill, reasonableness, and judgment of those responsible for the policy or decision.[2]

American education is a three-tiered enterprise, in which national, state, and local entities interact in a somewhat cloudy legal relationship to one another. Pervading these governmental relationships is the juxtaposition of the people to these levels of government. They may chafe at the actions of one level or another, and appeal for assistance or responsiveness to one level for redress against another one, manipulating relationships to their advantage as best they can. The three levels of government respond according to the political perceptions of those in power, for superimposed upon the governmental structure is a political structure that is often more influential in determining outcomes than the structure of governmental relationships would suggest.

In this process of political response to educational issues, all three branches of government play a role. The legislative branch passes statutes, the executive branch issues implementing regulations and interpretations of statutes, and the judiciary referees disputes, passing on the legality of statute and executive actions. Judges also decide the proper roles and spheres of authority germane to levels and branches of government.

In deciding the legality of government relations to one another and to the people served by the public schools, the activist or restraintist attitudes of jurists play an important role. Restraintist judges hesitate to substitute their judgment about educational policy for the judgment of a school board or legislature. Activist judges will be less reluctant to do so, particularly when they see their interposition as important to furthering social justice or other democratic ideals. This has given rise to complaints that jurists have set themselves up as "black-robed school boards" usurping the proper authority of local boards and state governments. The importance of this trend is seen in the frequent apologies made by activist judges for substituting their judgments for those of elected officials or professional educators, or making policy decisions for which they lack comprehensive knowledge. The delicate balance among the three branches of government may often be strained by activist court decisions, leading to calls for legislative restrictions on the areas of judicial intervention and closer control over the appointment and election of judges, to insure that not they, but state legislative and executive officials and local boards of education, govern public schools.

In addition to that issue, another that has emerged in governmental relationships is the extent to which national educational policy may be imposed upon state governments and their local school districts. Next in line is the issue of growing statism, the trend in which state governments seek to play an increasingly larger role in educational policy at the expense of local control of educational decision making. A final issue is that of establishing the proper balance between the responsibility of the state in insuring that all students are educated according to what the state sees as necessary to its interests, as opposed to the rights of parents to determine the direction and emphasis in the education of their children. Related to this issue are the narrower matters of the equivalency of nonpublic educational standards to those imposed by the state, and the role of compulsory education.

The liberal and conservative strains that have emerged in court adjudication of governmental relationships to each other, as well as the relationships of branches of government to one another and the relationship of educational government to the people, have roots in contrasting Hamiltonian and Jeffersonian political philosophy. Alexander Hamilton had less trust than Jefferson in the capacity of the people to govern themselves, and less fear of strong central governments. The conflicting views of these two Founding Fathers resulted in a series of constitutional compromises that through the years have created enough ambiguity in governmental relationships and government's relation to the people, to allow great latitude for judicial influence in education policy.

The liberal attitude has encouraged jurists to take an activist position in reading into the general-welfare and commerce clauses broad latitude for federal intervention into education, with a correspondingly limited interpretation of the restraints on national intervention imposed by the Tenth Amendment. The activist position generally adopted by liberals has been directed at allowing the national government to promote relatively quick change in education, directed at achieving federal goals oriented toward its perception of rapidly changing present and future needs. Coupled with this has been the liberal encouragement of federal intervention in public education to promote greater personal choice and freedom for students, parents, and teachers in the exercise of civil liberty. However, when the exercise of personal freedom is seen as an inhibition to rational-scientific progress based on traditional (especially religious) attitudes, the liberal position is reversed. Then, liberals take a strong position in supporting government educational objectives over the personal values of those they see as out of step with progress.

Conservatives are more inclined to limit national civil-rights intervention into the schools, as the relationship of public schools to the people is seen as more properly within the state purview. When they would intervene in disputes between the state and its people, the conservative tendency is to support traditional values, including fundamentalist religious values. Finally, conservative jurists are far less inclined to substitute their judgments for those of local school boards in matters of educational policy and practice.

Principles of Government-Authority Relationships in Education

1. The Tenth Amendment reserves plenary power over education to the states.
2. Article VI of the U.S. Constitution establishes the principle of federal supremacy when state and federal law conflict.
3. The Supreme Court has approved the constitutionality of several avenues of federal intervention in education, based on the Constitution's "general welfare" clause, commerce clause, and civil-rights amendments, as well as national civil-rights statutes of a general or educationally specific nature.

4. Most states have chosen to delegate broad authority for local school policy and administration to boards of education placed in charge of local school districts. Once these relationships are established, the state cannot exercise authority over school districts that contravenes these arrangements without duly constituted legal changes. State government cannot delegate to local districts basic responsibilities assigned to it by the state constitution.

5. The authority of local school districts, as well as state educational agencies, is circumscribed by powers expressly granted or reasonably implied by state statutes. Administrative agencies will be restrained by the courts from actions that are *ultra vires;* that is, beyond its power. Similarly, school-board members and officers are required to execute ministerial functions and may exercise reasonable discretionary authority where appropriate.

6. Government control over education is attended by a system of checks and balances among national, state, and local governments, as well as to each government's executive, legislative, and judicial branches.

7. The traditional approach to federal school influence has been one in which the schools are used to help accomplish noneducational national goals; for instance, eliminating poverty, strengthening national defense.

8. The authority of state or local district educational government over the people must be balanced by the inherent rights of parents to participate in decisions affecting the development of their children. In this relationship, the courts have established the principle of *parens patriae,* which is the right of the state to be "father or guardian" for all children regarding their development in ways that serve the interests of the state and all of its people. This principle has established the right of the state, among other things, to impose compulsory school-attendance laws.

9. Constitutional protection-of-liberty interests held by parents assures reasonable parental choice of educational options, provided that they do not conflict with overriding state interests to develop law-abiding, productive, loyal citizens.

10. A state may regulate private schools, but such regulations must be reasonable; that is, not overly restrictive or excessive.

11. The legality of parental decisions to provide home instruction as an alternative to compulsory school attendance depends on state statute and judicial interpretation. Where the law is silent, judicial interpretation prevails. Where home instruction is allowed by statute, it generally must be proven equivalent to the public-school program.

12. Federal civil-rights legislation and related laws protecting special groups in education (such as minorities, women, handicapped) have greatly increased federal influence and policy making in schools.

13. Whenever possible, courts will decide issues on the narrowest grounds possible. Thus, when a statute can provide the basis for a decision, it will be used in preference to a constitutional provision.

PARENTAL RIGHTS VERSUS STATE INTERESTS

Who has the final say in the kind of education a child will receive—the state or the parent? How far can the state go in imposing its educational will on parents through their children? Can the people be forced to support educational institutions they feel are unnecessary, or even destructive of their values? How far can parents go in providing nontraditional forms of education? Can the state require attendance only at a public school? At the other extreme, can parents opt to exclude their children entirely from any formal education?

While the doctrine of *parens patriae* had clearly established the authority of states to impose compulsory school-attendance laws by the latter decades of the nineteenth century, citizens of Kalamazoo, Michigan, challenged the right of the state, through the agency of its local school district, to require taxpayers to support a public high school. They considered this an unnecessary educational frill, meeting the needs and interests of only the higher classes of people, given such curricular elements as foreign languages and instruction in classical topics, which were of no practical value to the common people. This "higher learning" was deemed by plaintiffs to be a commodity properly paid for by those wishing it. The decision of the Michigan Supreme Court in *Stuart* v. *Kalamazoo* (1874) confirmed the authority of local school districts following processes established by statute, to expand the concept of the "common school" to include the high school, regardless of the objections lodged by some taxpayers to supporting it. In reviewing the state constitution and relevant statutes, the court concluded that there was "a general state policy . . . in which [free] education, and at their option the elements of classical education, might be brought within the reach of all the children of the state. . . ."[3] The principle of state/school-district authority to expand common-school education through the high school was viewed with approval by other states, and was followed by compulsory-high-school-attendence laws. Equally important, the authority of public education was strengthened.

A more direct issue joining the opposing interests of parents and the state was to be faced in 1923, in the landmark U.S. Supreme Court decision in *Meyer* v. *Nebraska*. At issue was a Nebraska law prohibiting both instruction in languages other than English and the teaching of foreign languages below the high-school level. The Nebraska Supreme Court approved these measures as consistent with the state's public-safety and general-welfare interests.

The reasoning of the legislature was that foreign influences could be transmitted through foreign languages, and these influences could be detrimental to the development of American attitudes and loyalty. Meyer, a parochial elementary teacher who instructed in German (the major language resented following World War I), challenged the constitutionality of the law on grounds that it violated the liberty guaranteed by the Fourteenth Amendment. In agreeing that it did, the Supreme Court addressed the liberty of parents to decide what was taught to their children, as well as who would teach them. A key passage addressing the roles of parents and the state in controlling the education of children, noted that Americans "have always regarded education and acquisition of knowledge as matters of supreme importance" and "it is the natural duty of the parent to give his children education suitable in life."[4] The Court went on to spell out parental rights as applied to the specific issue at hand by noting that "[m]ere knowledge of the German language cannot reasonably be regarded as harmful." Further, Meyer's "right thus to teach and the rights of parents to engage him so to instruct their children, we think, are within the liberty of the [Fourteenth] Amendment."[5]

Then, in order not to suggest that the balance between state and parental authority was weighted in favor of the parent, the court described the general range and limits of state authority as follows: "The authority of the state to compel attendance at some school and to make reasonable regulations for all schools . . . is not questioned. Nor has challenge been made of the state's power to prescribe a curriculum for institutions which it supports."[6] If the practice in question had constituted a clear emergency or threat for the states, the Court suggested that the issue might have been viewed differently. Since the Court could see no danger or threat from teaching German or any other foreign language, the Court viewed the liberty interests of Meyer to teach, and of parents to decide on this educational matter, more important than the interests of the state to promote its unique instructional and curricular views.

In *Meyer,* the Supreme Court held the state's authority to compel attendance at *some* school to be unquestioned. What if the state demanded attendance only in public schools? This was the issue framed before the Supreme Court two years later in *Pierce* v. *Society of Sisters* (1925). This decision provided the general answer to the questions undergirding the policy conflicts between parental- and state-authority relationships in education. At issue was an Oregon law requiring parents to enroll all children between ages eight and sixteen in a public school. The Society of Sisters challenged the law, based on the liberty and property interests guaranteed under the Fourteenth Amendment. The more important issue that emerged here, as it had in *Meyer,* was the extent to which the state could control the education of children over the objections of parents.

The U.S. Supreme Court could see in this legislation no important government interest justifying the destruction of private-school-property interests. As to the liberty interests of parents, the Court held:

> Under the doctrine of [*Meyer*] we think it entirely plain that the [Oregon] Act . . . unreasonably interferes with the liberty of parents and guardians to direct the upbringing and education of children under their control. . . . [R]ights guaranteed by the Constitution may not be abridged by legislation which has no reasonable relation to some purpose within the competency of the state. The fundamental theory of liberty under which all governments in this Union repose excludes any general power of the state to standardize its children by forcing them to accept instruction from public teachers only. The child is not the mere creature of the state; those who nurture him and direct his destiny have the right, coupled with the high duty, to recognize and prepare him for additional obligations.[7]

The *Pierce* decision has been referred to as "the *Pierce* Compromise,"[8] since it not only established the right of parental authority and decision making in educational choice, but also, in so doing, clearly supported the power of the state to compel and control education. This later consideration is specified in the following passage from *Pierce:*

> No question is raised concerning the power of the state reasonably to regulate all schools; to inspect, supervise, and examine them, their teachers, and pupils; to require that all children of proper age attend some school, that teachers shall be of good moral character and patriotic disposition; that certain studies plainly essential to good citizenship must be taught, and that nothing be taught which is manifestly inimical to the public welfare.[9]

Pierce provides an excellent example of judicial balance. A unanimous Supreme Court was activist enough to restrain the state from forcing its will on parents without sufficient cause, and restraintist enough to neither make new law nor diminish the state's plenary power over education in doing so. Liberal regard for parental liberties and conservative regard for state authority and traditional values were also well balanced.

The balance struck in *Pierce* between parental and state authority would be tested two years later in a case considering the extent of government control over private schools. As in *Meyer* and *Pierce*, the 1927 case of *Farrington* v. *Tokushige* revealed government motivations to control influences considered inimical to its efforts at "Americanizing" and developing loyal, productive citizens. The territory of Hawaii passed legislation tightly restricting, licensing, and supervising Japanese foreign-language academies, for the purpose of limiting the ability of these private schools to inhibit the Americanization of Japanese-Americans. The Supreme Court unanimously struck down the legislation as unnecessarily restrictive of parental rights:

> [T]he School Act . . . [goes] far beyond mere regulation of privately supported schools, where children obtain instruction deemed valuable by their parents and which is not obviously in conflict with any public interest. They give affirmative direction concerning the intimate and essential details of such schools, intrust their control to public officers, and deny both owners and patrons reasonable choice and discretion in respect of teachers, curriculum, and text-books. Enforcement of the act probably would destroy most, if not all, of them; and certainly, it would deprive parents of their opportunity to procure for their children instruction which they think important and we cannot say is harmful.[10]

In 1950, a decision of the Supreme Court of Pennsylvania indicated one of the limits of parental authority. Moslem parents withheld their child from public school each Friday for religious reasons. This violated the Pennsylvania compulsory-education requirement for "continuous attendance." Citing both *Meyer* and *Pierce* in its decision, the court found the parents in violation of the compulsory-education law. The state's interest in insuring continuous attendance overrode parental interests and authority in this case, as the parents did not choose a private educational option consistent with both their interests and those of the state. The decision in *Commonwealth* v. *Bey* reasoned that while *Pierce* held that the "fundamental theory of liberty excludes . . . any power of the state to standardize its children by forcing them to accept instruction from public teachers only, when parents elected to send their children to public schools, appellants are bound to perform all the requirements of the compulsory education provisions."[11]

Parents have options, but not the option of withholding a child from any educational program deemed appropriate by the state. How long must this education extend? What about an alternative, nonclassroom education that appears to meet the needs of a unique, self-contained community? These were among the concerns presented in *Wisconsin* v. *Yoder*, 406 U.S. 205 (1972). At issue was the desire of Amish parents to withhold their children from that part of the Wisconsin compulsory-attendance law requiring postelementary-school attendance (ages fourteen to sixteen). The reason was that this devout religious community believed that schooling beyond the elementary level encouraged values alienating their children from their religion and community. The sect rejects the competitive spirit, deemphasizes material success, and encourages isolation from the modern world and its trappings. The Amish believed that their system of apprenticing youth to productive community work was better preparation for their adult life than what the public high school could provide. For its part, the state believed its *parens patriae* role required that it provide the benefits of high-school education for all of its youth, which overrode the religious objections of the parents. The Wisconsin Supreme Court found for the Amish, and the state appealed to the U.S. Supreme Court. In a divided opinion, the Supreme Court found for the Amish. It required the state to prove that it not only had a rational basis for its position, but also, more difficult to prove, the compelling-interest standard. Given the historic evidence of religious commitment and productive, self-sufficient, law-abiding behavior of the Amish community, the state could not establish a compelling interest in requiring compulsory attendance to age sixteen for Amish children to the satisfaction of the Court's majority.

However, in providing this unusual partial-compulsory-attendance relief for the Amish, the Court was careful to rule narrowly and reemphasize the state's preeminent role in requiring school attendance. Even with these conservative, restraintist caveats, *Yoder* stands as an exemplar of the activist tendency to override state authority and make new (if severely limited) law.

In later cases, parental rights collided with liberal Court attitudes favoring desegregation. In *Runyon* v. *McCarey* (1976), the U.S. Supreme Court voided the practice of private schools denying admission to students on the basis of race, regardless of parental preferences. In this case, the Court reviewed "the Meyer-Pierce-Yoder" doctrine of parental rights and held that, while parents could choose private schools as an alternative means of meeting the state's education interests, the states could reasonably regulate alternatives to public education, and recalled that "the Court in *Pierce* expressly acknowledged the power of the state reasonably to regulate all schools, to inspect, supervise, and examine them, their teachers, and pupils."[12]

CONTROVERSY OVER CHRISTIAN FUNDAMENTALIST SCHOOLS

When a determined, committed minority decides to follow private-education practices severely different from established state minimum standards, how much accommodation must the state provide? What policies can balance the contending interests of state requirements and citizen desires for unique educational approaches?

In recent years, court decisions creating greater separation of church and state alienated fundamentalist Christian sects from public education, while decisions such as *Wisconsin v. Yoder* encouraged them to develop nontraditional, idiosyncratic alternatives. Conflicts have arisen between the rights of parents and the state's interest to insure the equivalency of these schools to state standards,· and the right of the state, as held by *Pierce* and other decisions, "reasonably to regulate all schools, to inspect, supervise, and examine them, their teachers, and pupils."

As fundamentalist schools grew to what was estimated as over a million students by the end of the 1970s,[13] their practices became increasingly disparate from those of public schools and their resistance to state regulation increased, making court challenges inevitable.

In 1979, the Kentucky Supreme Court relied on a provision of the state constitution that held, "nor shall any man be compelled to send his child to any schools to which he is conscientiously opposed," to decide that the state could not require the fundamentalist schools to meet state standards of teacher certification, textbooks, and similar criteria, especially since the standardized test results of the students exceeded average public-school scores (*Kentucky State Board v. Pridasill*, 589 S.W. 2d 877 [1979]). Fundamentalist parents were also successful in a court challenge in Ohio in which they were charged with violating compulsory-education laws because their school failed to conform to the minimum state standards (*State v. Whisner*, 351 N.E. 2d 750 [1976]). The Ohio court found that the state standards in question (curriculum content, teaching methods, physical facilities, and so on) were too excessive and restrictive in regard to the rights of parents to exercise educational direction for their children.

These decisions contrasted sharply with earlier decisions in Nebraska, where, in *Meyerkorth v. State*, 115 N.W. 2d 585 (1962), the state supreme court held that statutes requiring private-school students to be "substantially the same" as those in public schools did not violate parental or student religious freedom. Similarly, the North Dakota Court, in a ruling precisely opposite that of *Whisner*, upheld state authority over parents enrolling students in a highly nontraditional fundamentalist Christian academy. In *State v. Shaver* (1980), parents were found to be violating compulsory-education laws by sending their children to a school not approved by the state. The school lacked certified teachers and relied on a self-study curriculum based on Bible-oriented learning packets. Even though student learning outcomes compared favorably with public-school students', the court held that the state's regulations were reasonable, and did not constitute an unjustifiable burden on the parents and their religious interests. Further, the state had a "legitimate and compelling interest . . . in educating its people"[14] that put private-school regulation within the state's purview.

The next year, the Iowa Department of Education found a similar institution below standards for state teacher certification and curriculum. The Iowa Supreme Court found for the state, without considering the constitutional church-state issue (*State* v. *Moorhead*, 308 N.W. 2d 60 [1981]).

Nebraska was the scene for another 1981 case concerning regulation of a Christian fundamentalist school (*State* v. *Faith Baptist Church*, 301 N.W. 2d 571 [1981]). At issue was the school's refusal to submit its program to state review for religious reasons, refusal to furnish the state education board with student names and addresses, and the school's employment of noncertified teachers. The defendant school argued that the state had no authority over a religious school's operation. Its position was that the Bible required the integration of religion with teaching, and public-education authorities could not properly supervise this because they followed the antithetical philosophy of "secular humanism." The Nebraska Supreme Court found for the state, upholding its regulations and authority to withhold approval, preventing the operation of the school. An appeal to the U.S. Supreme Court was dismissed for lack of a substantial constitutional question. This was possible, since the case was argued on the issue of the legitimate interests of the state to obtain information rather than on the constitutional grounds of separation of church and state.

The issue languished during the early 1980s, with six church parents jailed for refusing to testify about the school, whose minister had fled to another state to avoid prosecution. They had continued to send their children to the school until they were jailed for contempt in 1984. The agreement under which they were released acknowledged the failure of the school to meet state-accreditation and teacher-certification standards, and included the parents' promise not to return their children to the school until it complied with state law or the law changes. The charges against the fugitive minister remained in force, until overturned by a 1985 appellate court order.

Fundamentalist church schools were more successful in the state of Maine in 1983. Ten schools, led by the Maine Association of Christian Schools, successfully challenged the constitutionality of state laws and regulations requiring private-school approval by the Maine State Board of Education. The Maine court held that while the church schools, as all private schools, were subject to health and safety requirements as well as obligations under truancy laws, private schools were not required to seek or obtain state approval or furnish information to the state in order to be free to operate (*Bangor Baptist Church* v. *State of Maine*, 576 F. Supp. 1299 [1983]).

Home Instruction

In addition to the Christian fundamentalist school movement, parents opposed to traditional public- and state-regulated private schools have also explored
the option of home instruction. In some states, statutes and courts do not interfere with this option. In other states, courts are reluctant to grant such an
option unless there is express statutory authority to do so. Where such statutes
exist, they generally require that home instruction be substantially equivalent to
school instruction. As a result, court decisions in this area pay close attention to
the specifics contained in relevant state statutes. For example, in *State* v. *Massa*
(1967), the New Jersey Superior Court considered the legality of the Massas educating their daughter at home. Neither parent had a teaching certificate, and
Mrs. Massa, who took primary instructional responsibility, had only a high-
school diploma. The state objected on the grounds that the statute required
"equivalent instruction" and this was not met by Mrs. Massa's lack of a teaching certificate and evidence that her daughter's social development was retarded.
For her part, Mrs. Massa was able to present standardized test scores showing
equivalency with public-school norms. Since the state statute was silent about
such matters as parent qualifications, the court focused on the meaning of
"equivalent" and decided it related solely to academic equivalency, not social
equivalency, which would appear to run counter to the idea of home instruction.
Since the student demonstrated equivalent academic outcomes, the court found
the home instruction permissible. In the words of the court: "The language of
the New Jersey statute . . . requires only a showing of academic equivalence.
. . . [T]o hold that the statute requires equivalent social contact and development
as well would emasculate this alternative. . . . "[15] Prior to the enactment of the
home-instruction proviso, the New Jersey court had ruled that home instruction
was not permissible precisely because it did not include, *inter alia,* interaction
with other students (*Stephens* v. *Bongart,* 189 A. 131 [1937]). It was the court's
reading of the exact meaning of the statute that lead to its contrary decision in
Massa. In California, the absence of statutory reference to home instruction resulted in court judgment that it did not qualify as a private-school alternative to
public education (*People* v. *Turner,* 263 P.2d 685 [1953]).

A Virginia case (*Grigg* v. *Commonwealth of Virginia,* 297 S.E. 2d 799, [1982])
centered on the statute's requirement that home instruction be "by a tutor or
teachers of qualifications prescribed by the State Board of Education." While
the court put the burden of proof on the state to show the parents (neither of
whom had teaching certificates or bachelor's degrees) were unqualified, the state
acquitted that burden to the court's satisfaction. In Illinois, which does not have
a home-instruction statute, the court put the burden of proof on the parents to
show that their instruction was equivalent to approved school programs, which
they were able to do merely by demonstrating that instruction was provided in
good faith and the prescribed courses were being covered (*People* v. *Levison,* 90
N.E. 2d [1950]).

In 1983, the Delcontes had received approval from their local New York school board to instruct their children at home. The parents continued this practice upon moving to North Carolina, using New York State and Wake Christian Academy materials. Even though the Delcontes children scored well on standardized tests, the North Carolina State Office of Nonpublic Education objected. The North Carolina Appellate Court held that the state's compulsory-attendance law only countenanced established nonpublic schools, and home instruction is not its equivalent. The state's interest in public education was held to outweigh the family interest in religiously motivated home instruction (*Delcontes* v. *State,* 308 S.E. 2d 898 [1983]).

Finally, even in the state of New York, which had allowed home instruction for the Delcontes children, that privilege was not unlimited. In order to evaluate the "equivalency" of home education within its district, the Cayuga-Onondaga Non-Public Schools Evaluation Committee requested an opportunity to review instruction provided in the home. The parents refused permission for on-site evaluation, holding it to be an unwarranted intrusion on their right of religion, privacy, and childrearing. New York Family Court disagreed, stating:

> If the frequency of visitation were such as to annoy or to discourage home instruction, that would present another case. . . .
>
> I cannot find that this infrequent, unobtrusive home visitation . . . violates any . . . constitutionally protected rights. . . . [Parents] have no absolute right to educate their children at home free from all state regulation or control: having chosen to utilize the statutory exemption to public education, they must observe the reasonable requirements imposed upon home schooling by those charged with responsibility for the children's proper home education.[16]

An earlier New York case had resulted in approval of home instruction when the children were found to be reading above grade level, and a surprise visit to the home found the children busy at a clear course of study (*In re Foster,* 330 N.Y.S. 2d 8 [1972]).

STATE VERSUS LOCAL CONTROL

Once the state has delegated to local school boards various policy-making functions, what is the nature of the plenary power retained by the state and state-level education agencies? Viewed from the opposite perspective, how much independence and power does a local district have? Does its independent authority extend to compelling the state to perform certain tasks and acquit particular obligations? If disputes arise between state and local government regarding educational authority, what standards do courts apply to resolve such controversies?

The state's authority over education is limited by provisions of the federal Constitution and state constitutions. Actions of state legislatures and state-level agencies are also limited by the requirements of state statute. Further, state legislative authority is limited to just that—legislative authority—with administration the province of executive agencies. The concept of checks and balances applied to relations between state legislative and executive authority also applies to state authority in relation to lawfully enacted local educational authority. Another aspect of the local-state relationship is that local board members are viewed by the courts as state officials rather than local officers in performing their duties of presiding over public education. In carrying out their functions, courts recognize that state statutes empower local boards with both express and implied authority. On the other hand, courts also recognize that local districts have no inherent power; they have only the authority granted in state law or reasonably implied by state grants of authority.

State courts referee these intergovernmental relationships. A Michigan court indicated the primacy of the state over education in this way: "The legislature has entire control over the schools of the state. . . . The division . . . into districts, the conduct of the school, the qualifications of teachers, the subjects to be taught therein, are all within its control. . . . "[17] Similarly, the Pennsylvania court held that a "School District is a creature or agency of the Legislature and has only the powers that are granted by statute."[18]

On the other hand, the New York Court of Appeals noted the wide discretion available to school boards through implied powers attending state legislation authorizing local school districts, in a case involving board assignment of students to particular schools:

> There can be no question that the Board of Education, by statute, has the power and responsibility to manage and administer the affairs of the school district, including the assignment of students to schools therein. The Education Law . . . specifically grants district school boards power to have in all respects the superintendence, management, and control of the educational affairs of the district and . . . all the powers reasonably necessary to exercise powers granted expressly or by implication. . . .[19]

While case law clearly recognizes the predominant authority of the state, local school boards are not totally subordinated to the will of state agencies. In *State* v. *Lally* (1963), state education officials sought to remove members of a local board of education for not revealing information to the local electorate that state officers believed it should have. The issue was the soil conditions on property where a school building was to be erected, subject to voter approval of a referendum for that purpose. Finding no basis in statutes for assuming board members had to provide voters with all details related to their policy decisions, the court found for the local board. In making its decision, the court spelled out the broad authority for local schools boards:

> [T]he activities of members of boards of education should be the exercise of their own discretion. . . . To accept the contention of the state would . . . relegate a board of education to the status of a group of fact gatherers, rather than the elected representatives of the school district."[20]

An Illinois case illustrates how courts may limit the authority of state agencies over local districts. An Illinois law required local boards to revise school attendance patterns in order to prevent segregation. To carry forth this legislation, the state board ordered districts to have in each school 15 percent of the district's minority population, and to report annually on this matter under penalty of probation and potential loss of funding. The Aurora East school district sued, claiming that this action was *ultra vires,* beyond the power of the state board. The high court agreed. It found that the state board's action exceeded the scope of express and implied power granted to it by the Illinois Constitution and state statutes. The state board had contended that such power was found in that (1) it was a constitutionally created agency, suggesting that its implied powers were strong and extensive; and (2) its rule-making power was authorized by constitutional and statutory provisions. The former states that "the Board, except as limited by law, may establish goals, determine policies, provide for planning and evaluating educational programs, and recommend financing." As to the latter, the state board relied on a school-code provision authorizing it "to make rules necessary to carry into efficient and uniform effect all laws for establishing and maintaining free school in the state." The Illinois Supreme Court's reading of these provisions led to a different conclusion. Its ruling went beyond limiting the excessiveness of the state board regulation, to holding that the board was "without any power whatsoever" to promulgate the rules in question. In commenting on the role of state administrative agencies, the court held that "inasmuch as an administrative agency is a creature of statutes, any power or authority claimed by it must find its source within the provisions of the statute by which it was created."[21] The high court established that administrative rules to facilitate desegregation were properly the province of the local board of education, not the state board (*Aurora East* v. *Cronin* [1982]).

FEDERAL CONTROL VERSUS STATE-LOCAL AUTHORITY

At what point do the indirect routes available to the national government for involvement with local schools constitute an infringement on state authority? How much federal control should follow grants of federal funds to schools? Does the small proportion of school budgets represented by federal funds justify the extensive control and litigation produced because of it? Does the interposition of court policy making in disputes related to federal education policy and civil-rights legislation constitute improper control of education?

While national government influence over education is indirect, it is nevertheless powerful. Complaints include criticisms of national executive, legislative, and judicial interference. Conservatives and restraintists object to the large federal role as violating the Jeffersonian concept of keeping government as close as possible to the people. Liberals and activists encourage the federal role as the surest source of social justice in education.

While the most active avenue for federal involvement has been expanded civil-rights laws and adjudication, related paths are also important, such as legislation directed at specific school populations and programs. The Civil Rights Act of 1964, Title IX of the Education Amendments of 1972, and the 1975 Education for All Handicapped Children Act are prime examples of the general nonconstitutional area of civil-rights legislation. It is also important to understand the broader arena in which the federal-control issue operates. The federal approach identifies various national goals, and often uses the schools as a vehicle contributing to their accomplishment, regardless of the direct impact on educational policy. For example, the National Defense Education Act of 1958 used the schools to improve national defense through strengthening science and mathematics programs. In 1965, Congress passed the Elementary and Secondary Education Act, in which schools were used as one of the vehicles for eliminating poverty, in line with President Johnson's "War on Poverty" program. Through such programs, the influence of the national government over education is expanded. However, in these statutes, Congress is careful to avoid legal vulnerability to charges of unconstitutional direct education control or usurpation of state authority. It keeps in mind such Supreme Court admonishments as the following, made in 1925:

> Congress cannot, under the pretext of executing delegated power, pass laws for the accomplishment of objectives not intrusted to the federal government. And we accept as established doctrine that any provision of an act of Congress ostensibly enacted under power granted by the Constitution, not naturally and reasonably adapted to the effective exercise of such power, but solely to the achievement of something plainly within power reserved to the states, is invalid and cannot be enforced.[22]

This restraintist Supreme Court position caused Congress to proceed with caution as it entered the period of expanded educational legislation of recent decades. Thus, statutes such as Title IX and the Education for All Handicapped Children Act have been couched in terms threatening to cut off federal funding to states or districts not conforming to the national goals implicit in the acts. Once funds are accepted, state and local districts are obligated to observe the myriad regulations attending the legislation, creating a powerful mechanism of federal control. This control emanates not only from the legislation itself, but from attending administrative regulations developed by executive agencies of the national government.

Noneducational legislation, of which the Civil Rights Act of 1964 is the best example, also exerts control over education. This equality-of-opportunity legislation has been used by the courts in a number of education cases in preference to considering the equal-protection clause of the Fourteenth Amendment, in conformance with the restraintist position of deciding issues on the narrowest possible legislative grounds.

Civil Rights Act of 1964

Title VI of the Civil Rights Act of 1964 bars discrimination based on "race, color, or national origin" in programs receiving federal financial assistance. The U.S. Supreme Court invoked this provision, avoiding the broader policy implications of the Constitution's equal protection clause, in *Lau* v. *Nichols* (1974). At issue was the failure of the San Francisco public-school system to offer remedial instruction in English to about eighteen hundred Chinese-speaking students. The Civil Rights Act authorized the development of federal executive agency (HEW) regulations to further its antidiscrimination goals. The then-existing Department of Health, Education, and Welfare developed a guideline requiring that when language handicap caused by lack of English-speaking ability impedes a student's education, the school must take affirmative measures.

Is this federal executive policy interference with state and local school policy? The Court did not specifically address that issue. Instead, it accepted that the receipt of federal funds by the San Francisco schools bound them to observe Title VI. It further determined that Title VI and the HEW implementing regulations superseded California law allowing the school district to decide proper bilingual-instruction policy. The Court then trod a delicate line between judicial policy making and restraint in substituting its judgment for that of educators. First it noted that "no specific remedy is urged upon us. Teaching English to the students . . . who do not speak the language is one choice. Giving instruction to this group in Chinese is another. There may be others." The court went on to claim: "Basic English skills are at the very core of what these public schools teach. Imposition of a requirement that, before a child can effectively participate in the educational program, he must already have acquired those basic skills, is to make a mockery of public education."[23] In a concurring opinion exhibiting some restraintist apprehension about this kind of Court policy making, Justice Blackmun wrote:

> I merely wish to make plain that when, in another case we are concerned with a very few youngsters, or with a single child [speaking] any language other than English, I would not regard today's decision . . . as conclusive upon the issue whether the statute or the guideline requires the funded school district to provide special instruction. For me, numbers are at the heart of this case, and my concurrence is to be understood accordingly.[24]

The applicability of the Civil Rights Act of 1964 was also an issue in a federal district court case decided in 1972. In *Adams* v. *Richardson,* federal-education and civil-rights officers were sued for nonenforcement of Title VI, in that they permitted federal funds to continue to districts not complying with its nondiscrimination mandate. The Court found against the federal offices of HEW and Civil Rights, holding:

> Where a substantial period of time has elapsed, during which period attempts toward voluntary compliance have been either not attempted, or have been unsuc-

cessful or been rejected, defendants' (HEW, OCR) limited discretion is ended and they have the duty to effectuate the provisions . . . that funds should be terminated. . . . In these cases, defendants cannot in their discretion permit further advances of federal assistance in violation of the statute, but have the duty of accomplishing the purposes of the statute through administrative enforcement proceedings or by other legal means.[25]

We see that the courts not only consider whether federal statutes apply to state and school districts in terms of allowing for federal control, but also may *require* federal administrators to enforce the intent of the Congress to help schools. In its administrative functions, the executive branch may be making new policy or contravening legislative policy intentions. The intergovernmental policy conflict between national legislative-executive branches, as well as between legislative and judicial branches, is epitomized in the adjudication surrounding Title IX of the Education Amendments of 1972.

Sex Equality in Education and Conflicts Over Title IX

Title IX was part of the historic civil-rights impetus pursued by the national government that began with the Supreme Court's *Brown* v. *Board of Education of Topeka* decision in 1954. It addressed the specific issue of sex discrimination in education programs. It was to encounter the vicissitudes of liberal and conservative changes to a remarkable degree. Title IX, similar to the Civil Rights Act of 1964, provides for withholding federal funds from schools violating its prohibition of sex discrimination. The first few years of its enactment was characterized by various lower-court cases dealing with participation of girls on boys' interscholastic athletic teams and vice versa, as well as questions of equality of athletic equipment, facilities, and programs. Issues of enrollment in courses, programs, and schools traditionally reserved for one·sex or the other also surfaced in the courts. The inevitable judicial policy making, primarily of a liberal nature, led to the first U.S. Supreme Court review of this statute in 1982, followed by another in 1984, in which Court interpretation of the intent of Congress and the conformance of executive actions to Congressional intent were at issue.

North Haven Board of Education v. *Bell* (1982) focused on whether or not Congress intended school employees to be covered by Title IX along with students, as federal administrators had assumed in promulgating implementing regulations. Lower courts disagreed on the issue, and the Supreme Court decided that Congress intended that employees be included. This expansion of federal control was tempered by the Court's decision that the statute was "program-specific;" that is, federal funds could only be withheld from the particular offending program rather than the school or district as a whole. The Court took a further restraintist position in declining to "undertake to define 'program' in this opinion."[26] The issue of defining "program" and the restrictiveness or breadth with which Title IX could be applied was joined in *Grove City College* v. *Bell* (1984), a case dealing with a college that received no direct federal aid, but whose students received federal financial assistance. Since students cover all programs, and the school's financial-aid office has a comprehensive function, what education-law interpretation would be most reasonable? It depends on one's liberal or conservative position. The Reagan administration, reversing the position of three previous administrations, took the conservative view of restricting Title IX application, while civil-rights groups argued for its broad applicability in this situation.

The U.S. Court of Appeals had ruled that the entire college was covered by Title IX, since the financial-aid program, even though indirect, covered the institution. This squared with *North Haven,* which held that Title IX must be given "a sweep as broad as its language."[27] However, in deciding the appeal, the U.S. Supreme Court took a restraintist position on how much "sweep" was permitted by the language of Title IX, which bars sex bias in "any education program or activity receiving federal financial assistance." Education programs were narrowly defined as specific departments or activities within an institution, not the institution itself. Further, the Supreme Court's six-to-three decision in *Grove City College* v. *Bell* showed conservative distaste for government intervention in private affairs by holding that a private college that eschews federal assistance cannot be forced to observe Title IX in all of its programs simply because some of its students receive federal financial assistance administered by the Financial Aid Office. The majority "found no persuasive evidence suggesting that Congress intended that . . . regulatory authority follows federally aided students from classroom to classroom, building to building, or activity to activity."[28] This cannot be what Congress intended, the majority reasoned, since then "an entire school would be subject to Title IX merely because one of its students received a small BEOG or one of its departments received an earmarked federal grant. This cannot be squared with Congress' intent."[29]

In his dissent to *Grove,* Justice Brennan, joined by Marshall, noted the clear legislative intent of Congress to pattern Title IX after Title VI of the Civil Rights Act of 1964, which had been afforded broad applicability to eliminate institutional discrimination. The liberal, activist dissent also reasoned:

> The absurdity of the Court's decision is further demonstrated by examining its practical effect. According to the Court, the "financial aid program at Grove City College may not discriminate on the basis of sex because it is covered by Title IX, but the College is not prohibited from discriminating in its admissions, its athletic programs, or even its various academic departments. The Court thus sanctions practices that Congress clearly could not have intended. . . . "[30]

Rights and Protections of Handicapped Students

The leadership exerted by the national government in promoting liberal conceptions of equality and fairness that produced the Civil Rights Act of 1964 and Title IX of the Education Amendments of 1972 was next directed at the needs of exceptional children, resulting in passage of PL 94–142, the Education for All Handicapped Children Act. This legislation combined features of both civil-rights legislation and categorical education funding legislation. Thus, once agreeing to accept federal handicapped-student funding, state and local districts were bound by civil-rights protections afforded to handicapped students as well as complex procedural and programmatic administrative details.

The policy impetus for PL 94–142 originated in the federal courts. The historic inadequacy of public-school service to students with varying degrees of physical, mental, and emotional handicaps became an issue in *Pennsylvania Association for Retarded Children (PARC)* v. *Commonwealth* (1971). In that case, a federal district court ruled that the traditional exclusion of various categories of children from the public schools violated (in addition to federal constitutional civil-rights provisions) the state constitutional guarantee of public education for *all* children. The court ruled that "having undertaken to provide a free public education to all its children, including its exceptional children, the Commonwealth of Pennsylvania may not deny any mentally retarded child access to a free public program of education and training."[31] A consent decree was issued providing for schooling appropriate to the handicapped student's capacity, with regular public-school class preferable to special class placement, and special public-school class placement preferable to placement in a special alternative type of institution. In the next year, *Mills* v. *Board of Education of the District of Columbia* was decided. Since the District is federal territory, only the U.S. Constitution and federal statutes were applicable. Plaintiffs claimed that the exclusion of handicapped students violated their civil rights. The school district replied that such an educational undertaking would create an excessive financial burden. The court found for the plaintiffs, declaring:

> If sufficient funds are not available to finance all the services and programs that are needed and desirable in the system then the available funds must be expended equitably in such a manner that no child is entirely excluded from a publicly supported education consistent with his needs and ability. . . . The inadequacy of the District . . . School System whether occasioned by insufficient funding or administrative inefficiency, certainly cannot be permitted to bear more heavily on the exceptional or handicapped child than on the normal child."[32]

The awareness of the issue of inadequate educational response to the handicapped highlighted by these decisions combined with Congressional receptivity to extend the civil-rights movement to this new area. The result was the Education for All Handicapped Children Act of 1975. It provided a minimum of funding for states to initiate programs for handicapped students with a maximum of accompanying regulations. Most prominent were requirements for individual education plans, parental involvement in placement decisions, careful due-process requirements in placement decisions, and the policy of education in the "least restrictive environment." The most pervasive feature of PL 94–142 was the assurance that all handicapped children were to have access to "a free appropriate public education and related services designed to meet their unique needs."

Early court tests of the legislation resulted in liberal, activist decisions requiring schools to be in session for more days for handicapped children, to exempt handicapped students from the usual disciplinary policy and procedures, and even to interpret PL 94–142 as requiring schools to provide in-school catheterization services for students suffering from spina bifida. The district court did not see catheterization (removal of fluid from the child's bladder) as part of "related services" it should provide as this was a medical service, and medical services were to be limited to diagnosis and evaluation. The appellate court disagreed *(Tatro* v. *Texas,* 625 F. 2d 557, [1980]), holding that this was required, since without it, the child could not attend her self-contained special-education class, as called for in the student's Individual Education Plan.

While *Tatro* was being appealed to the Supreme Court, the High Court issued its first PL 94–142 decision in the case of *Hudson* v. *Rowley* (1982). In this case, the Court majority decided that the Act did not require that a sign-language interpreter needed to be provided for a deaf student who already was receiving adequate compensatory services. By a six-to-three vote, the majority concluded that the Act did not require a state to maximize the potential of each handicapped child, but rather only "to enable the child to achieve passing marks and advance from grade to grade."[33] This interpretation favored local decision making and defined one limitation on the continually expanding scope of federal influence under PL 94–142. However, when *Tatro* was finally decided by the Supreme Court *(Irving* v. *Tatro,* Slip Opinion No. 83–558, [1984]), the court held that catheterization should be provided, as it fell under the "supportive services" provision of the Act and was not technically a "medical" service, which was limited to diagnosis and evaluation.

In this arena of the Education for All Handicapped Children Act, the Supreme Court has moved to strike a balance between federal influence and local decision making. While a school district is not required to maximize a student's educational opportunity, it must provide whatever services are necessary to afford a student a reasonable educational opportunity, provided the service falls within the school district's "supportive services" capacity.

POLICY CONSIDERATIONS

Almost all school policy issues, at one point or another, test and define the boundaries of government authority in education. Several elements form the critical mass that will determine the outcomes of struggles to define authority. These conflicts pit national authority against state authority, state against local district, one branch of government against another, and levels of government against the people. The critical mass is composed first of legislation that defines the relationships of one branch of government (executive, legislative, judicial) to the other, as well as the relationship of levels of government (local, state, national) to one another. Legislatures promulgate the defining legislation, executives develop implementing regulations and execute legislative policy, and courts referee interbranch and intergovernmental disputes, while also passing on the meaning and constitutionality of laws and reasonableness of executive actions. Interbranch and intergovernmental relations are mainly characterized by broad guidelines, allowing for latitude of interpretation and flexibility of implementation. There are few clear-cut answers as to where the authority of one level or branch of government ends and that of another begins. This makes the judgment and action of education-policy wielders and jurists a critical factor in determining the pattern of educational-authority relationships.

The other major element in the critical mass of government relations is the fact of the political system superimposed upon the governmental system. Political leaders in all branches and levels, including judges and school officials, sniff the political winds before deciding on particular positions on educational issues. Considerations about consolidating personal power, insuring reelection, and using the schools to promote various political and social ideologies are involved in government relations.

The "*Pierce* Compromise" illustrates the tenuous relationships surrounding the legal sharing of educational authority between parent and government. Parents have court-approved rights to direct the education of their children, but this is limited when parental direction conflicts with the state's interest as *parens patriae*. Courts will balance the interests of the state against the educational choices of parents and students. We know that the courts will not permit the state to require attendance only at public schools, or to restrict teaching of particular subjects at private schools without strong reasons to do so. Further, it has been established that with sufficient justification, the courts will excuse students from state compulsory-attendance laws.

On the other hand, parents are not free to depart from educational standards with impunity, or to ignore the interests the state has in developing productive, law-abiding, literate citizens. This position is in line with the political and social philosophers influencing our government who developed the view that citizens give up some of their natural liberty to the government so that a society devoted to the common good can be established.

The variety of state laws and court policy settlements in different states in regard to fundamentalist schools, home instruction, and the regulative rights of the states over the education of its citizens illustrates at least these two policy considerations. Regardless of educational nationalizing trends promoted by national judicial, executive, and legislative action, the states still retain much effective authority in determining the scope and variety of educational choice within their jurisdictions. Also, the political and social climate in each state will be a critical factor in the educational policy that decides a controversy. Decisions regarding fundamentalist academies in Kentucky, Ohio, and Maine minimized state regulation, as opposed to decisions on the same issues in North Dakota, Iowa, and Nebraska.

Even with such differences, it is clear that the Supreme Court has defined clear limits as to how far the states may go in limiting parental choice when rights guaranteed by the national Constitution are implicated. The ''Meyer-Pierce-Yoder'' doctrine requires that states acknowledge that their educational authority is matched by the authority of parents. In this shared-authority relationship, courts require states to justify limitations on parental choice as clearly required by state welfare interests.

The state does not bear a similar burden in relation to the school districts it has created. The state has plenary power in this area. However, state action is limited by statutes defining state-local relationships. A further policy consideration in the exercise of state authority over its local districts is the concept of local control, which remains a potent political force in an era of growing state and national influence over educational policy and practice. The Jeffersonian principle of keeping government as close to the people as possible has particular application to that most intimate government service of schooling. This political pressure counters state efforts toward growing statism, as it seeks continually to increase control over local school policy. Local administrators and boards may risk offending state authorities who can exert financial and administrative punishments, since the courts will hold the state accountable to its own laws and regulations restricting state authority and that of its administrative agencies. The state will be loath to use its ultimate weapon—that of abolishing local districts—because of the political repercussions of such an act.

State politicians would be further restrained from such an extreme act because it would deprive them of the protection afforded by being able to deflect education-related criticism on local districts. Thus, the plenary power of the state is balanced not only by state statutes empowering districts with particular areas of authority, but also by political realities favoring local districts. As a result, state-local governmental relations in education remain, for the policy formulator and those implementing policy, a relatively fluid area. States cannot dictate to local districts with impunity, nor can local districts ignore the plenary authority that the state imposes upon them.

The relationship of the federal government to public schools, just as with the other areas of government involvement, is responsive to the political climate. While government officials certainly are motivated by what they feel is right and good for the nation, their positions are also influenced by political expediency. It is doubtful that the *Grove College* v. *Bell* decision would have been rendered in the political climate of the early seventies, when Title IX was passed. By the same token, it is doubtful that the Education for All Handicapped Children Act could have become law in the early eighties. The political climate, as well as the political and social attitudes of politicians and jurists, determine the orientation and extent of federal educational influence in any period. The one certainty is that federal educational involvement is an important policy consideration. It is the rare school district that, even if it wished, can be free of federal influence. Grove City College did not participate in federal categorical-aid programs, but even there, its students received federal financial aid, placing it within the ambit of some federal control. The extent and tradition of various forms of categorical federal aid to education have made it an expected form of assistance that most schools depend upon in varying degrees. In this dependency, schools fall under both the regulations accompanying categorical funding, as well as broader civil-rights laws.

These conditions raise fears of federal control, especially given the extensive litigation in which courts have generally supported the expansion of the federal role. Especially vexing to conservative opponents of federal aid (and the influence and control accompanying it) is that the 6 to 10 percent of school budgets contributed by the national government appears to allow for influence disproportionate to that level of contribution. Congressmen, federal bureaucrats, and judges, far removed from the particular interests and conditions that have given rise to such controversies as alleged sex discrimination, unfair treatment of handicapped children, misuse of categorical funding, and race discrimination, decide them on grounds more germane to general national views than the needs or desires of local communities. In this way, a subtle but pervasive trend continues toward a national system of education, regardless of constitutional sanctions or the weight of American political tradition for keeping public education under the closest possible control of those affected by it.

The proponents of federal school aid are less concerned about local control than they are about promoting social justice through the educational system. In this quest, the national government is seen as the single most powerful and dependable ally. The historic record reveals that, while certainly not without blemish, the federal government has been far more sensitive and effective regarding the needs of the poor, the disadvantaged, and all of the weaker, less favored elements of society. Thus, the issue of federal intervention is not one of purely legal and constitutional abstractions centered on the Tenth Amendment or the federal-welfare clause. It is also a matter of imposing the national sense of justice upon the important function of public education.

Of course, the sense of right and wrong emanating from Washington changes from time to time depending on popular opinions, as do the views of those holding judicial power. Further, the federal government has no monopoly on goodness or superior moral standing, or a necessarily better method of arriving at social and moral correctness. Certainly the state and local authorities are closer to educational issues that must be addressed, but the federal government may have a more balanced perspective. Yet, this perspective changes, depending on who occupies the White House and controls Congress. For example, the federal stances toward education during the Johnson and Reagan administrations were quite different. The final interpreter of right or wrong and the proper authority to be exercised by government, or any particular government or branch of government, is the court.

The court may only apply its interpretation to deciding what a statute allows, forbids, or requires, and whether or not the statute itself conforms to or violates the higher law embodied in a state constitution or the national Constitution. The legislature, confronted with the way the court interprets a statute, is free to pass another designed to accomplish its will without interference from the court. Thus, after the *Grove* decision, legislators displeased with the limits *Grove* placed on Title IX sex-equality enforcement immediately set about designing a new civil-rights act. The new attempted legislation was designed to eliminate from Title IX and similar statutes (Title VI of the Civil Rights Act of 1964, Section 504 of the Rehabilitation Act of 1973, and so on) references to "program or activity" and substitute the term "recipient," so that an entire institution would be prohibited from behavior proscribed by Title IX-type legislation when any of its programs or component activities received federal funds. This is the process through which the legislature can invalidate the "final" policy decision of the courts and retain legislative-policy supremacy.

Another interbranch method of resisting court decisions is the approach used by the executive branch to reduce the effectiveness of the *Lau* decision. When the Reagan administration scrapped the Carter administration's implementing guidelines without replacing them, this national impetus was reduced. While those interested in the social-justice aspects of *Lau* might object to this, those in favor of local initiatives as the proper response to school-policy issues viewed this as the proper course of action.

Even with such devices, the courts clearly stand as the major guardian and referee of relationships among levels and within branches of government. In doing so, policy analysts are left to judge how well the courts subscribe to the admonition of Chief Justice Harlan F. Stone, who once remarked: "While unconstitutional exercise of power by the executive and legislative branches is subject to judicial restraint, the only check upon our [judicial] exercise of power is our own sense of self-restraint."[34]

Has court activism in educational policy issues created a "black-robed school board?" If so, will board lawyers become more influential determiners of local school policy than the local school board? Further, is national influence creating pressures that are leading to school conformity that amounts to a national school system? Equally important, how can it be determined if these trends are good or bad? Overriding these questions is the more basic one of deciding the proper roles and balance among levels and branches of government. The closeness of education to the people, and the importance attached to it, will continue to keep these relationships in flux, as the political system manipulates governmental relations in education.

Pierce v. Society of Sisters
268 U.S. 510 (1925)

These appeals are from decrees, based upon undenied allegations, which granted preliminary orders restraining appellants from threatening or attempting to enforce the Compulsory Education Act under the initiative provision of her Constitution by the voters of Oregon. . . .

The challenged Act requires every parent, guardian or other person having control or charge or custody of a child between eight and sixteen years to send him "to a public school for the period of time a public school shall be held during the current year" in the district where the child resides; and failure so to do is declared a misdemeanor. The manifest purpose is to compel general attendance at public schools by normal children, between eight and sixteen, who have not completed the eighth grade. And without doubt enforcement of the statute would seriously impair, perhaps destroy, the profitable features of appellees' business and greatly diminish the value of their property.

Appellee, the Society of Sisters, is an Oregon corporation, with power to care for orphans, educate and instruct the youth, establish and maintain academies or schools, and acquire necessary real and personal property. It has long devoted its property and effort to the secular and religious education and care of children, and has acquired the valuable good will of many parents and guardians. In its primary schools many children between those ages are taught the subjects usually pursued in Oregon public schools during the first eight years. Systematic religious instruction and moral training according to the tenets of the Roman Catholic Church are also regularly provided. All course of study, both temporal and religious, contemplate continuity of training under appellee's charge; the primary schools are essential to the system and the most profitable. It owns valuable buildings, especially constructed and equipped for school purposes. The business is remunerative—the annual income from primary schools exceeds thirty thousand dollars—and the successful conduct of this requires long time contracts with teachers and parents. The Compulsory Education Act of 1922 has already caused the withdrawal from its schools of children who would otherwise continue, and their income has steadily declined. The appellants, public officers, have proclaimed their purpose strictly to enforce the statute.

After setting out the above facts the Society's bill alleges that the enactment conflicts with the right of parents to choose schools where their children will receive appropriate mental and religious training, the right of the child to influence the parents' choice of a school, the right of schools and teachers therein to engage in a useful business or profession, and is accordingly repugnant to the Constitution and void. And, further, that unless enforcement of the measure is enjoined the corporation's business and property will suffer irreparable injury.

Appellee, Hill Military Academy, is a private corporation organized in 1908 under the laws of Oregon, engaged in owning, operating and conducting for profit an elementary, college preparatory and military training school for boys between the ages of five and twenty-one years. [T]he courses of study conform to the requirements of the State Board of Education. Military instruction and training are also given, under the supervision of an Army officer. It owns considerable real and personal property, some useful only for school purposes. The business and incident good will are very valuable. Appellants, law officers of the State and County, have publicly announced that the Act is valid and have declared their intention to enforce it. By reason of the statute and threat of enforcement appellee's business is being destroyed and its property depreciated.

The Academy's bill states the foregoing facts and then alleges that the challenged Act contravenes the corporation's rights guaranteed by the Fourteenth Amendment and that unless appellants are restrained from proclaiming its validity and threatening to enforce it irreparable injury will result. The prayer is for an appropriate injunction.

The court ruled that the Fourteenth Amendment guaranteed appellees against the deprivation of their property without due process of law consequent upon the unlawful interference by appellants with the free choice of patrons, present and prospective. It declared the right to conduct schools was property and that parents and guardians, as a part of their liberty, might direct the education of children by selecting reputable teachers and places. Also, that these schools were not unfit or harmful to the public, and that enforcement of the challenged statute would unlawfully deprive them of patronage and thereby destroy their owners' business and property. Finally, that the threats to enforce the Act would continue to cause irreparable injury; and the suits were not premature.

No question is raised concerning the power of the State reasonably to regulate all schools, to inspect, supervise and examine them, their teachers and pupils; to require that all children of proper age attend some school, that teachers should be of good moral character and patriotic disposition, that certain studies plainly essential to good citizenship must be taught, and that nothing be taught which is manifestly inimical to the public welfare.

The inevitable practical result of enforcing the Act under consideration would be destruction of appellees' primary schools, and perhaps all other private primary schools for normal children within the State of Oregon. These parties are engaged in a kind of undertaking not inherently harmful, but long regarded as useful and meritorious. Certainly there is nothing in the present records to indicate that they have failed to discharge their obligations to patrons, students or the State. And there are no peculiar circumstances or present emergencies which demand extraordinary measures relative to primary education.

Under the doctrine of *Meyer* v. *Nebraska* we think it entirely plain that the Act of 1922 unreasonably interferes with the liberty of parents and guardians to direct the upbringing and education of children under their control. As often heretofore pointed out, rights guaranteed by the Constitution may not be abridged by legislation which has no reasonable relation to some purpose within the competency of the State. The fundamental theory of liberty upon which all governments in the Union repose excludes any general power of the State to standardize its children by forcing them to accept instruction from public teachers only. The child is not the mere creature of the State; those who nurture him and direct his destiny have the right, coupled with the high duty, to recognize and prepare him for additional obligations.

Appellees are corporations and therefore, it is said, they cannot claim for themselves the liberty which the Fourteenth Amendment guarantees. Accepted in the proper sense, this is true. But they have business and property for which they claim protection. These are threatened with destruction through the unwarranted compulsion which appellants are exercising over present and prospective patrons of their schools. And this court has gone very far to protect against loss threatened by such action.

Generally it is entirely true, as urged by counsel, that no person in any business has such an interest in possible customers as to enable him to restrain exercise of proper power of the State upon the ground that he will be deprived of patronage. But the injunctions here sought are not against the exercise of any *proper* power. Plaintiffs asked protection against arbitrary, unreasonable and unlawful interference with their patrons and the consequent destruction of their business and property. Their interest is clear and immediate.

State v. Faith Baptist Church
301 N.W. 2d 571 (1981)

This was an action brought by the State of Nebraska against Faith Baptist Church of Louisville, Nebraska, and certain individuals being officers and employees of the principal defendant. It sought to enjoin the operation of an elementary and secondary school by the defendants because there had been no compliance with the school laws of the State of Nebraska. From a judgment granting such relief, the defendants have appealed to this court. Upon consideration de novo on the record, we affirm.

On August 29, 1977, the defendants began operating the Faith Christian School in Louisville, Nebraska. The curriculum employed by this school is that supplied by Accelerated Christian Education (A.C.E.), and consists of a series of booklets called Packet of Accelerated Christian Education (PACE), which contain instructional information and self-test questions in various subjects and at different instructional levels. Each student works at his or her own speed, and, after completing each PACE and attaining a grade of at least 80 percent on the self test and the PACE test given under the supervision of the supervisor, moves on to the next sequentially numbered PACE. The teachers as such are supervisors who administer the tests and are available for helping a particular student who may be having difficulty. Their function is not to teach, but to monitor or supervise. The instruction is Bible-oriented.

In spite of requests from the various local and state school officials, the defendants have refused to furnish "third-day reports" containing the names and addresses of all students enrolled in their school, as required by Neb.Rev.Stat. § 79-207. This is necessary so as to check parents' compliance with compulsory attendance laws. They have stated that they have not and will not request approval of their A.C.E. program, even though they have been told that it would be approved, and they have neglected and refused to employ accredited teachers and to seek approval from the State of Nebraska to operate their school. It is their position that the operation of the school is simply an extension of the ministry of the church, over which the State of Nebraska has no authority to approve or accredit.

According to the defendants, a Christian education is mandated by the Bible. Their belief is that teaching is a way of life and not simply a 5-hours-a-day, 5-days-a-week proposition. It is the defendents' belief that the public schools of today are overrun with an increase in crime, drug and alcohol addiction, teacher assaults, vandalism, and disrespect for authority and property. Additionally, and basically, secular humanism is the basic philosophy of the public educational system, which is in direct opposition to the defendants' belief in biblical Christianity. It is because of these beliefs that the Faith Christian School was organized. Defendants further maintain that, because their philosophy is

Christian and that of the State Department of Education is not, the latter is not capable of judging the philosophy of the defendants' school. Finally, because the state school laws require inspection of the schools by the county superintendent, the defendants cannot submit to such control because the State has no right to inspect God's property.

At first blush, it would appear that the case of *Meyerkorth* v. *State,* (1962), is squarely in point and dispositive of the case, to the prejudice of the defendants. There the issue involved was the constitutionality of various statutes of the State of Nebraska concerning compulsory school attendance, certification of teachers, and supervision of nonpublic schools, the forerunners of the statutes involved here. The plaintiffs there, seeking a declaration that those laws were unconstitutional as a violation of their first amendment rights, raised arguments similar to those with which we are here faced: "The plaintiffs argue that the certification of teachers . . . and the minimal school standards provided for . . . above set forth, and the regulations promulgated by the Nebraska Department of Education, have no relevance to the interests of the state in children not educated in public, tax-supported schools; that none of these . . . have any materiality to testing children educated in parochial schools to ascertain if they know the language of their country, understand its government, and are able to participate in the democratic process; and that the above-mentioned sections and regulations infringe upon the rights of the parent and the constitutional right guaranteed to the citizens of the State of Nebraska."

This court reviewed the holding of the U.S. Supreme Court in *Meyer* v. *Nebraska,* (1923), and cited the following language: " 'The power of the State to compel attendance at some school and to make reasonable regulations for all schools, including a requirement that they shall give instructions in English, is not questioned.' "

In *Meyerkorth,* we also cited *Pierce* v. *Society of Sisters* (1925), which struck down an Oregon law requiring all children to attend a public school. "No question is raised concerning the power of the State reasonably to regulate all schools, to inspect, supervise, and examine them, their teachers and pupils; to require that all children of proper age attend some school, that teachers shall be of good moral character and patriotic disposition, that certain studies plainly essential to good citizenship must be taught, and that nothing be taught which is manifestly inimical to the public welfare."

This court concluded by saying: "As we view the statutes here involved, there is nothing arbitrary, unreasonable, or unconstitutional relating to the qualifications of teachers to teach in the parochial, denominational, private, or public schools of this state or with the requirements of compulsory education and attendance at such schools."

However, it is the defendants' position that the test of reasonableness as declared in *Meyerkorth* must give way to one of compelling state interest, which, they allege, is the rule announced in *Wisconsin* v. *Yoder.*

The majority opinion in *Yoder,* then, although employing a "compelling interest" rule, nevertheless was greatly, if not completely, influenced by the process of balancing the specific interest of the state in 1 or 2 years of education beyond the eighth grade for students not expected to enter the mainstream of modern-day life against competing religious principles and practices nearly 3 centuries old. It is somewhat difficult to develop a generalized rule from the court's specific holding. The concurring opinion of Mr. Justice White is more illuminating of the rule in its general application. "This would be a very different case for me if respondents' claim were that their religion forbade their children from attending any school at any time *and from complying in any way with the educational standards set by the State.*"

Finally, defendants refer us to *Kentucky State Bd., Etc.* v. *Pudasill,* (Ky. 1979), in which the author of that opinion, testing school certification statutes against a constitutional provision which provided that "nor shall any man be compelled to send his child to any school to which he may be conscientiously opposed," wrote the following: "Certainly, the receipt of 'a bachelor's degree from a standard college or university' is an indicator of the level of achievement, but it is not a sine qua non the absence of which establishes that private and parochial school teachers are unable to teach their students to intelligently exercise the elective franchise."

We are not suggesting as an absolute that every person who has earned a baccalaureate degree in teaching is going to become a good teacher, any more than one who has obtained the appropriate training and education will become a good engineer, lawyer, beauty operator, welder, or pipefitter. However, we think it cannot fairly be disputed that such a requirement is neither arbitrary nor unreasonable; additionally, we believe it is also a reliable indicator of the probability of success in that particular field. We believe that it goes without saying that the State has a compelling interest in the quality and ability of those who are to teach its young people.

The cases we have cited should leave no doubt as to the critical interest which the State has in the quality of the education provided its youth. Although parents have a right to send their children to schools other than public institutions, they do not have the right to be completely unfettered by reasonable government regulations as to the quality of the education furnished. Defendants insist that this can be accomplished by annual comparative tests. The problem with testing is that it sometimes comes too late. If the deficiency of the education being afforded is not discovered until the end of the year, the child has wasted that year. The requirements as to curriculum as imposed by the state board appear to be very minimal in nature. All that is required is that certain subjects be taught. There is no effort to dictate in what manner that knowledge shall be imparted. As a matter of fact, the defendants have complained, in part, because no course of study has been prescribed by the State. The defendants concede, and the State confirms, that the curriculum utilized by the defendants, the A.C.E. program, is acceptable and approved and being used by other schools within the state. The refusal of the defendants to comply with the compulsory education laws of the State of Nebraska as applied in this case is an arbitrary and unreasonable attempt to thwart the legitimate, reasonable, and compelling interests of the State is carrying out its educational obligations, under a claim of religious freedom.

The judgment of the District Court is affirmed.

Affirmed.

KRIVOSHA, Chief Justice, concurring in part, and in part dissenting.

I find that I must in part concur with, and in part dissent from, the majority opinion in this case.

I concur in that portion of the majority opinion which holds that the State, having a high responsibility for the education of its citizens, has the power to impose *"reasonable regulations"* for the control and duration of basic education. I believe that principle applies even though the reasonable regulations may, in some manner, affect what an individual or group maintains is their religious belief.

However, based upon the record in this case, I must respectfully dissent from that portion of the majority opinion which in effect upholds the State's requirement that all elementary and secondary teachers, public or private, hold a baccalaureate degree before a student's attendance at such school may satisfy the State's compulsory attendance laws. I do not believe either logic or experience, or current law, justifies such a conclusion.

Just as no group may obtain a first amendment exemption from all State regulations by merely asserting that the regulated activity has some basis in a religious belief, neither can the State regulate or control all action of a group under the bald assertion that such regulation is necessary to preserve and maintain the health, safety, or welfare of such group. We have traditionally attempted to balance those concepts and have diligently sought to find a reasonable middle ground.

In this case, I believe that we have failed to bring about the necessary balance and have unnecessarily opted in favor of the State when such result is neither required nor justified.

While I recognize that we do not require attendance in a public school, but will certify a private school if its teachers all hold baccalaureate degrees, I find nothing either in our statutes or in logic which compels a conclusion that one may not teach in a private school without a baccalaureate degree if the children are to be properly educated. Under one holding today, Eric Hoffer could not teach philosophy in a grade school, public or private, and Thomas Edison could not teach the theories of electricity. While neither of them could teach in the primary or secondary grades, both of them coud teach in college. I have some difficulty with a law which results in requiring that those who teach must have a baccalaureate degree, but those who teach those who teach need not. The logic of it escapes me. The experience of time has failed to establish that requiring all teachers to earn a baccalaureate degree from anywhere results in providing children with a better education.

While it may be appropriate for a state to set such requirements in a public school where state funds are expended and, in effect, the state is the employer, I find no basis in law or fact for imposing a similar requirement in a private school. The failure of the private school to have as adequate and as trained teachers as the public school may be a factor which parents will take into account in deciding whether their children should be enrolled in that private school. I do not believe, however, that it should disqualify children from satisfying the compulsory attendance laws. I could accept a regulation which required instructors in such schools to satisfy the state that they were adequately trained to perform the functions they were hired to perform. I believe, however, that such functions may be adequately performed absent a baccalaureate degree.

The record in this case clearly establishes that the failure of all instructors in appellants' school to hold a baccalaureate degree has not in any manner detracted from the quality of the education being given its students. No evidence was offered that, absent a baccalaureate degree, one is not qualified to teach. Likewise, the State conceded at oral argument before this court that the program of instruction offered by appellant school was, indeed, satisfactory, and if submitted to the State for approval, would undoubtedly be approved. Yet that approval would not result in the school's being certified or in the students' status being such as to satisfy the compulsory attendance law. That defect could not be cured unless and until all instructors held a baccalaureate degree, as if the earning of such a degree somehow magically bestowed upon the recipient that knowledge which one without such a degree could not otherwise obtain.

It may be argued, as the State does, that any other requirements would impose a severe burden upon the State, in that it would then be required to conduct various tests of students in these schools in order to determine whether, in fact, they are receiving an adequate education. No one, however, has ever suggested that the mere fact that action required to be performed by the government may be difficult justifies the government's refusal to perform the required act.

The majority points out that to wait until after a period of time has expired before we test the students may be too late. If the holding of a baccalaureate degree by a teacher in and of itself ensured that students would thereby be educated and able to pass the test, that argument might wash. Experience, however, discloses that students taught by teachers holding baccalaureate degrees do not necessarily receive an adequate education in each and every instance. The record in this case supports that view. Witnesses who qualified as experts in the field of education ventured the opinion that the mere fact that a person held a baccalaureate degree did not mean that he or she would be a good teacher.

In my view, attempting to strike a balance between the various interests of the parties herein does not justify requiring that all persons teaching in appellants' school can qualify as a teacher only by holding a baccalaureate degree. I believe there are other reasonable regulations which can be adopted for private schools that would permit these schools to continue, thereby striking the necessary balance between the two competing interests. I would have so held.

Aurora East Public School District v. Cronin
442 N.E. 2d 511 (1982)

This case involves the plaintiff school districts' challenge to the validity of the Rules Establishing Requirements and Procedures for the Elimination and Prevention of Racial Segregation in Schools (Rules). The Rules were promulgated by the defendant Joseph Cronin, the State Superintendent of Education (Superintendent), and adopted by the defendant State Board of Education (Board).

The defendants filed a countercomplaint alleging that Aurora failed to comply with the Armstrong Act. This act provides, in part:

"As soon as practicable, and from time to time thereafter, the [local] board shall change or revise existing [attendance centers] or create new [attendance centers] in a manner which will take into consideration the prevention of segregation and the elimination of separation of children in public schools because of color, race or nationality."

The circuit court declared the Rules void, and permanently enjoined their enforcement. It further determined that Aurora's practices regarding segregation did not violate the Armstrong Act. A majority of the appellate court affirmed on the grounds that the Rules were unreasonable and arbitrary, and that the circuit court's ruling with respect to the countercomplaint was not contrary to the manifest weight of the evidence.

The following questions are raised on appeal: (1) Does the Board have authority to promulgate and enforce rules designed to prevent racial segregation? (2) If so, are these particular rules valid? (3) Has Aurora failed to comply with the requirements of the Armstrong Act? Because of the results reached in this case, it is necessary to address only the first and third issues.

The Rules were originally promulgated in 1971 for the purpose of enforcing the Armstrong Act. Subsequently, in 1973, the legislature enacted the Moore Amendment, which provides:

"Nothing herein shall be construed to permit or empower the State Superintendent of Public Instruction* to order, mandate or require busing or other transportation of pupils for the purpose of achieving racial balance in any school." [*In 1975, the duties of the Superintendent of Public Instruction were delegated to the Board.]

Although not raised by defendants as an issue, they refer to two footnotes to article X, section 2(a), of the 1970 Illinois Constitution. This provision states in part:

"The Board, *except as limited by law,* may establish goals, determine policies, provide for planning and evaluating education programs and recommend financing. The Board shall have such other duties and powers as provided by law."

Even assuming that this section would ordinarily authorize the Board to promulgate the Rules, that authority has been limited by the General Assembly. The Moore Amendment, enacted subsequent to our 1970 constitution, places a clear limit on the Board's power regarding segregation and busing. As later discussed, prior to the enactment of the Moore Amendment, section 10–22.5 authorized *local boards* "[t]o assign pupils to the several schools in the district; to admit non-resident pupils when it can be done without prejudice to the rights of resident pupils and provide them with any services of the school including transportation; to fix the rates of tuition in accordance with Section 10–20.12a, and to collect and pay the same to the treasurer for the use of the district; *but no pupil shall be excluded from or segregated in any such school on account of his color, race, sex or nationality.''* This provision placed the duty to prevent segregation squarely in the hands of the local boards. In passing the Moore Amendment, the legislature emphasized that methods of achieving desegregation are policy decisions to be made by the school districts.

For this reason, we do not believe that the constitutional provision, standing alone, grants to defendants the extensive authority now sought. The question therefore centers on whether any statutory provisions empower the Board to promulgate the Rules.

Defendants contend that the School Code authorizes the promulgation of rules to enforce the Armstrong Act. This section provides that the Board shall have the power:

> "To determine for all types of schools conducted under this Act efficient and adequate standards for the physical plant, heating, lighting, ventilation, sanitation, safety, equipment and supplies, instruction and teaching, curriculum, library, operation, maintenance, administration and supervision, and to grant certificates of recognition to schools meeting such standards by attendance centers or school districts; to determine and establish efficient and adequate standards for approval of credit for courses given and conducted by schools outside of the regular school term."

In the instant case, the defendants seek to promulgate rules relative to desegration. Nowhere in section 2–3.25 is the Board granted express authority to determine standards for racial desegregation. And the fact that the Board may set standards for the "operation, maintenance, administration and supervision" of schools does not imply the authority now sought. If we were to hold otherwise, it would be difficult to conceive of any regulation which could not be justified under section 2–3.25.

"This court has consistently held that, inasmuch as an administrative agency is a creature of statute, any power or authority claimed by it must find its source within the provisions of the statute by which it is created." The duties and powers of the Board are set forth in article 2 of the School Code. We have carefully reviewed the provisions therein, and are unable to find any which delegate to the Board the authority it now seeks. The most that can be said is that the legislature has granted the Board general rulemaking power and the authority to supervise public schools. We do not agree that these general provisions authorize defendants to promulgate and adopt rules relative to the Armstrong Act.

As plaintiffs point out, when the legislature intended to delegate authority to the Board, it did so expressly and specifically.

That the legislature did not intend to delegate to the Board the power which it seeks is apparent for another reason. There are no standards or guidelines governing the Board's discretion to enforce the Armstrong Act. "[T]he absence from the statute of any standards, criteria or procedure for [promulgating the Rules] confirms that no power to [do so] was intended by the legislature to be given the Board."

Significantly, however, the legislature *did* establish a procedure by which the Board could combat segregation. [T]he School Code provides, in part:

"Upon the filing of a complaint with the Superintendent of Public Instruction * * * alleging that any pupil has been excluded from or segregated in any school on account of his color, race, nationality, religion or religious affiliation * * * by or on behalf of the school board of such district, the Superintendent of Public Instruction shall fix a date * * * for a hearing upon the allegations [in the complaint]. He may also fix a date for a hearing whenever he has reason to believe that such discrimination may exist in any school district. * * *

If he determines that a violation exists, he shall request the Attorney General to apply to the appropriate circuit court for such injunctive or other relief as may be necessary to rectify the practice complained of."

We agree with the plaintiffs that this comprehensive provision limits, rather than expands, the Board's authority to regulate desegregation. Section 22–19 clearly recites the powers which the legislature intended the Board to have. Nowhere does the section authorize the Board to promulgate its own rules and sanctions for enforcing the Armstrong Act.

Similarly, section 22–19 authorizes the defendant to investigate districts suspected of maintaining segregation, and to refer complaints to the Attorney General for prosecution. The Board has completely ignored this provision and instead has adopted rules incorporating its own methods for dealing with perceived segregation.

Further, if defendants were dissatisfied with the current law, they could have requested a modification thereof. Section 1A–4 C of the School Code provides, in part:

"The Board shall analyze the present and future aims, needs, and requirements of education in the State of Illinois and recommend to the General Assembly the powers which should be exercised by the Board. The Board shall recommend the passage and the legislation necessary to determine the appropriate relationship between the Board and local boards of education and the various State agencies and shall recommend desirable modifications in the laws which affect schools."

The Board has apparently disregarded this alternative in favor of pursuing its own policies without first securing legislative approval.

There is yet another reason which counsels against the defendants' authority to enforce the Armstrong Act. This provision is located in article 10 of the School Code. This article relates to the powers and responsibilities of the *local* school boards, not the Board. It is thus clear that the legislature has charged the local districts with the responsibility of enforcing the Armstrong Act. Consequently, promulgating rules relative thereto should be the duty of the local school boards.

Defendants argue, however, that the legislature impliedly approved the Board's authority to adopt the Rules. They assert that, by enacting the Moore Amendment, the legislature recognized the Board's power to promulgate guidelines and merely limited that power to exclude mandatory busing. We do not agree that the express disapproval of a particular rule impliedly approves defendant's authority to promulgate and adopt the other rules.

Thus, the pupose of the Moore Amendment was to clarify that methods of preventing segregation are the obligation of the local boards, as implied in section 10–22.5. In performing this duty, the districts could not be required to bus students. There is no indication that, in enacting the amendment, the legislature thereby approved of any other Rules, or the defendants' authority to adopt them. The other Rules were simply not in question during the passage of the Moore Amendment and consequently the board's authority to adopt them was not addressed.

As previously indicated, section 22–19 of the School Code establishes the procedure by which defendants may combat segregation. In particular, if defendants investigate and determine that discrimination exists, they may request the Attorney General to file suit for appropriate relief. This procedure insures that the Board will not assume the role of prosecutor, judge, and enforcer of its own sanctions. Consequently, the proper course is for defendants to conduct a hearing and refer to the Attorney General any findings of discrimination. This is the extent of the Board's obligation. It is for the Attorney General, as representative of the People, to file suit when a district engages in discriminatory practices.

It is for the reasons stated herein that we affirm the judgments of the appellate court in the consolidated cases before us.

Judgments affirmed.

Hendrick Hudson Dist. Board of Education v. Rowley
458 U.S. 176 (1982)

JUSTICE REHNQUIST delivered the opinion of the Court.

This case presents a question of statutory interpretation. Petitioners contend that the Court of Appeals and the District Court misconstrued the requirements imposed by Congress upon States which receive federal funds under the Education of the Handicapped Act. We agree and reverse the judgment of the Court of Appeals.

II

This case arose in connection with the education of Amy Rowley, a deaf student in the Hendrick Hudson Central School District, Peekskill, N. Y. Amy has minimal residual hearing and is an excellent lipreader. During the year before she began attending Furnace Woods, a meeting between her parents and school administrators resulted in a decision to place her in a regular kindergarten class in order to determine what supplemental services would be necessary to her education. Several members of the school administration prepared for Amy's arrival by attending a course in sign-language interpretation, and a teletype machine was installed in the principal's office to facilitate communication with her parents who are also deaf. At the end of the trial period it was determined that Amy should remain in the kindergarten class, but that she should be provided with an FM hearing aid which would amplify words spoken into a wireless receiver by the teacher or fellow students during certain classroom activities. Amy successfully completed her kindergarten year.

As required by the Act, an IEP was prepared for Amy during the fall of her first-grade year. The IEP provided that Amy should be educated in a regular classroom at Furnace Woods, should continue to use the FM hearing aid, and should receive instruction from a tutor for the deaf for one hour each day and from a speech therapist for three hours each week. The Rowleys agreed with parts of the IEP but insisted that Amy also be provided a qualified sign-language interpreter in all her academic classes in lieu of the assistance proposed in other parts of the IEP. Such an interpreter had been placed in Amy's kindergarten class for a 2-week experimental period, but the interpreter had reported that Amy did not need his services at that time. The school administrators likewise concluded that Amy did not need such an interpreter in her first-grade classroom. They reached this conclusion after consulting the school district's Committee on the Handicapped, which had received expert evidence from Amy's parents on the importance of a sign-language interpreter, received testimony from Amy's teacher and other persons familiar with her academic and social progress, and visited a class for the deaf.

When their request for an interpreter was denied, the Rowleys demanded and received a hearing before an independent examiner. After receiving evidence from both sides, the examiner agreed with the administrators' determination that an interpreter was not necessary because "Amy was achieving educationally, academically, and socially" without such assistance. The examiner's decision was affirmed on appeal by the New York Commissioner of Education on the basis of substantial evidence in the record. Pursuant to the Act's provision for judicial review, the Rowleys then brought an action in the United States District Court claiming that the administrators' denial of the sign-language interpreter constituted a denial of the "free appropriate public education" guaranteed by the Act.

The District Court found that Amy "is a remarkably well-adjusted child" who interacts and communicates well with her classmates and has "developed an extraordinary rapport" with her teachers. It also found that "she performs better than the average child in her class and is advancing easily from grade to grade," but "that she understands considerably less of what goes on in class than she could if she were not deaf" and thus "is not learning as much, or performing as well academically, as she would without her handicap." This disparity between Amy's achievement and her potential led the court to decide that she was not receiving a "free appropriate public education," which the court defined as "an opportunity to achieve [her] full potential commensurate with the opportunity provided to other children." According to the District Court, such a standard "requires that the potential of the handicapped child be measured and compared to his or her performance, and that the resulting differential or 'shortfall' be compared to the shortfall experienced by nonhandicapped children." The District Court's definition arose from its assumption that the responsibility for "giv[ing] content to the requirement of an 'appropriate education' " had "been left entirely to the [federal] courts and the hearing officers."

A divided panel of the United States Court of Appeals affirmed.

We granted certiorari to review the lower courts' interpretation of the Act. Such review requires us to consider two questions: What is meant by the Act's requirement of a "free appropriate public education"? And what is the role of state and federal courts in exercising the review granted by 20 U. S. C. § 1415? We consider these questions separately.

III

This is the first case in which this Court has been called upon to interpret any provision of the Act. As noted previously, the District Court and the Court of Appeals concluded that "[t]he Act itself does not define 'appropriate education,' " but leaves "to the courts and the hearing officers" the responsibility of "giv[ing] content to the requirement of an 'appropriate education.' " Petitioners contend that the definition of the phrase "free appropriate public education" used by the courts below overlooks the definition of that phrase actually found in the Act. Respondents agree that the Act defines "free appropriate public education," but contend that the statutory definition is not "functional" and thus "offers judges no guidance in their consideration of controversies involving 'the identification, evaluation, or educational placement of the child or the provision of a free appropriate public education.' "

Like many statutory definitions, this one tends toward the cryptic rather than the comprehensive, but that is scarcely a reason for abandoning the quest for legislative intent. Whether or not the definition is a "functional" one, as respondents contend it is not, it is the principal tool which Congress has given us for parsing the critical phrase of the Act. We think more must be made of it than either respondents or the United States seems willing to admit.

According to the definitions contained in the Act, a "free appropriate public education" consists of educational instruction specially designed to meet the unique needs of the handicapped child, supported by such services as are necessary to permit the child "to benefit" from the instruction. Almost as a checklist for adequacy under the Act, the definition also requires that such instruction and services be provided at public expense and under public supervision, meet the State's educational standards, approximate the grade levels used in the State's regular education, and comport with the child's IEP. Thus, if personalized instruction is being provided with sufficient supportive services to permit the child to benefit from the instruction, and the other items on the definitional checklist are satisfied, the child is receiving a "free appropriate public education" as defined by the Act.

Noticeably absent from the language of the statute is any substantive standard prescribing the level of education to be accorded handicapped children. Certainly the language of the statute contains no requirement like the one imposed by the lower courts—that States maximize the potential of handicapped children "commensurate with the opportunity provided to other children." That standard was expounded by the District Court without reference to the statutory definitions or even to the legislative history of the Act.

When the language of the Act and its legislative history are considered together, the requirements imposed by Congress become tolerably clear. Insofar as a State is required to provide a handicapped child with a "free appropriate public education," we hold that it satisfies this requirement by providing personalized instruction with sufficient support services to permit the child to benefit educationally from the instruction. Such instruction and services must be provided at public expense, must meet the State's educational standards, must approximate the grade levels used in the State's regular education, and must comport with the child's IEP. In addition, the IEP, and therefore the personalized instruction, should be formulated in accordance with the requirements of the Act and, if the child is being educated in the regular classrooms of the public education system, should be reasonably calculated to enable the child to achieve passing marks and advance from grade to grade.

IV

In assuring that the requirements of the Act have been met, courts must be careful to avoid imposing their view of preferable educational methods upon the States. The primary responsibility for formulating the education to be accorded a handicapped child, and for choosing the educational method most suitable to the child's needs, was left by the Act to state and local educational agencies in cooperation with the parents or guardian of the child. The Act expressly charges States with the responsibility of "acquiring and disseminating to teachers and administrators of programs for handicapped children significant information derived from educational research, demonstration, and similar projects, and [of] adopting, where appropriate, promising educational practices and materials." In the face of such a clear statutory directive, it seems highly unlikely that Congress intended courts to overturn a State's choice of appropriate educational theories in a proceeding conducted pursuant to § 1415(e)(2).

We previously have cautioned that courts lack the "specialized knowledge and experience" necessary to resolve "persistent and difficult questions of educational policy." We think that Congress shared that view when it passed the Act. As already demonstrated, Congress' intention was not that the Act displace the primacy of States in the field of education, but that States receive funds to assist them in extending their educational systems to the handicapped. Therefore, once a court determines that the requirements of the Act have been met, questions of methodology are for resolution by the States.

V

Entrusting a child's education to state and local agencies does not leave the child without protection. Congress sought to protect individual children by providing for parental involvement in the development of state plans and policies, and in the formulation of the child's individual educational program. As this very case demonstrates, parents and guardians will not lack ardor in seeking to ensure that handicapped children receive all of the benefits to which they are entitled by the Act.

VI

Applying these principles to the facts of this case, we conclude that the Court of Appeals erred in affirming the decision of the District Court. Neither the District Court nor the Court of Appeals found that petitioners had failed to comply with the procedures of the Act, and the findings of neither court would support a conclusion that Amy's educational program failed to comply with the substantive requirements of the Act. On the contrary, the District Court found that the ''evidence firmly establishes that Amy is receiving an 'adequate' education, since she performs better than the average child in her class and is advancing easily from grade to grade.'' In light of this finding, and of the fact that Amy was receiving personalized instruction and related services calculated by the school administrators to meet her educational needs, the lower courts should not have concluded that the Act requires the provision of a sign-language interpreter. Accordingly, the decision of the Court of Appeals is reversed, and the case is remanded for further proceedings consistent with this opinion.

NOTES

1. Thomas Jefferson, *Notes on the State of Virginia* (Richmond: J.W. Randolph, 1853), p. 160.
2. E. Gordon Gee and David J. Sperry, *Education Law and the Public Schools: A Compendium* (Boston: Allyn and Bacon, 1978), pp. D-31–D-33.
3. Stuart v. School District No. 1 of the Village of Kalamazoo, 30 Michigan 69 (1874) at 84.
4. Meyer v. Nebraska, 262 U.S. 390 (1923) at 627.
5. Id.
6. Id. at 402.
7. Pierce v. Society of Sisters of the Holy Names of Jesus and Mary, 268 U.S. 510 (1925) at 534–35.
8. David L. Kirp and Mark G. Yudof, *Education Policy and the Law* (Berkeley: McCutchan Publishing Corp., 1974), 3.
9. Pierce at 534.
10. Farrington v. Tokushige, 273 U.S. 284 (1927) at 298.
11. Commonwealth v. Bey, 166 Pa. Super. 136 (1950).
12. Runyon v. McCarey, 427 U.S. 160 (1976) at 178.
13. *Education Commission of the States, Law and Education Center,* Footnotes, (October 1981), p. 8.
14. State v. Shaver, 294 N.W. 2d 883 (1980) at 899.
15. State v. Massa, 231 A. 2d 252 (1967) at 257.
16. Matter of Kilroy, 467 N.Y.S. 2d 318 (1983) at 321.
17. Child Welfare Society of Flint v. Kennedy School District, 189 N.W. 1002 (1922) at 1004.
18. Barth v. Philadelphia School District, 143 A. 2d 909 (1958) at 911.
19. Older v. Board of Education of Union Free School District No. 1, Town of Mamaroneck, 266 N.E. 2d 812 (1971) at 813.
20. State v. Lally 194 A. 2d 252 (1963) at 258.
21. Aurora East Public School District No. 131 v. Cronin, 442 N.E. 2d 511 (1982) at 517.
22. Linder v. United States, 268 U.S. 5 (1925) at 17 (cited with approval in United States v. Butler, 297 U.S. 1 [1936] at 69).
23. Lau v. Nichols, 414 U.S. 563 (1974) at 566.
24. Id. at 572.
25. Adams v. Richardson, 351 F. Supp. 636 (1972) at 641.
26. North Haven Board of Education v. Bell, 102 S. Ct. 1912 (1982) at 1927.
27. Id. at 1918.
28. Grove City College v. Bell, 104 S. Ct. 1211 (1984) at 1222.
29. Id. at 1221.
30. Id. at 1236.
31. Pennsylvania Association for Retarded Children (PARC) v. Commonwealth, 334 F. Supp. 1257 (1971) at 1259.
32. Mills v. Board of Education of the District of Columbia, 348 F. Supp. 866 (1972) at 876.
33. Board of Education of Hendrick Hudson Central School Dist. v. Rowley, 458 U.S. 176 (1982) at 204.
34. United States v. Butler, 297 U.S. 1 (1936) at 79.

THREE

Religious Controversies in Public-School Policy

It is significant that our Founding Fathers, in acquitting their commitment to amend the new Constitution with provisions protecting citizens against the potential for abuse of the newly strengthened national power, first attended to the matter of religious freedom. The importance of how religion would be accommodated within the new political structure was related to several issues. Many Americans had come to the New World to escape the religious persecution and intolerance of Europe, where church and state were often united or shared control. Also, over half of the colonies had official religions that would render free movement of Americans throughout the United States less hospitable to them than would otherwise be the case. Americans represented a variety of religions and sects, and developing an American consciousness required removing such deeply felt allegiances as religion from the political arena. The history of European religious domination in politics revealed trends of intolerance for differences, persecution based on religious rivalry, and a generally undemocratic religious attitude on the part of government and the body politic. Even in the American colonies, the prominence of religion in political life had produced, for example, the following events:

> The Maryland Toleration Act of 1649 guaranteed religious liberty to Trinitarian Christians but not to other Christians or non-Christians.

A New York law of 1700 provided that Roman Catholic priests performing religious rites or teaching Catholic doctrine be imprisoned for life.

A Maryland law of 1704 prohibited the baptism of children by Roman Catholic priests.

A Virginia policy (1768–1774) allowed for sentencing persons discovered to be Baptists to be whipped, jailed, and fined.

In Virginia of 1776 (the year it joined other colonies in the Declaration of Independence, holding "all men are created equal"), that colony subjected those denying the Trinity to a three-year term of imprisonment and deprived Unitarians and freethinkers of the custody of their children.[1]

While the attitudes of religious intolerance were being transplanted in the New World, the Protestant tradition of salvation through personal reading of the Bible and understanding of scripture was also established. Thus, from its very beginnings in America, education was intertwined with religious purpose. The first public law to establish schools in America, promulgated by the Massachusetts colony in 1647, was justified by the express purpose of the necessity for promoting literacy and scriptural knowledge in order to resist the "old deluder, Satan."

There were also countercurrents of religious freedom and separation of church and state evident in colonial America. In 1647 the Rhode Island charter guaranteed separation of church and state, and in 1786 Virginia passed Jefferson's Act for Establishing Religious Freedom, disestablishing the Anglican Church as that state's official religion, to name just two instances. As the new nation was established under the Constitution, the attempts to work out the proper accommodation between church and state continued. The liberal and conservative strains are seen in the conservative desire to maintain religious prominence and protection in the new nation as a traditional value to be preserved. The liberal view is represented by the desire to free people of arbitrary restraints and inhibitions to their personal views of how self-development can best occur. The liberals trusted in unfettered human reason to guide moral development, while conservatives placed their reliance on the established conventions of the ages, which had served to enhance human progress in spiritually and morally rich directions.

The result was the first part of the First Amendment to the Constitution. The fact that religion was the first issue dealt with in the Bill of Rights demonstrates the importance of the issue to the new American nation. The Amendment contains these words: "Congress shall make no law respecting an establishment of religion, or prohibiting the free exercise thereof." The meanings behind the "establishment" and "free exercise" clauses have been matters of spirited, deep-felt contention by religious and educational liberals and conservatives throughout its history. While President Jefferson privately declared in 1802 that "religion is a matter which lies solely between man and God," best protected by "building a wall of separation between church and state,"[2] as late as 1848 Horace Mann, the architect of the free, universal public school, declared that public schools should not be "irreligious, an anti-Christian, or an un-Christian system." Rather, it was seen as "a system which invokes a religious spirit . . . that . . . welcomes the Bible."[3]

It was left to courts of the twentieth century, particularly the U.S. Supreme Court, to define the relationships of church and state in public education and even in private education, which continues through the present day. The religion clauses of the First Amendment leave wide interpretive latitude into which liberal and conservative opinion may be placed. In general, the conservative judicial position places a restraintist emphasis on the religion clauses, when states have acted to introduce elements of religion into the schools or provide public support to parochial-school functions. The conservative willingness to defer to state interpretations of definitions of separation of church and state that aid religious institutions is born of its support for traditional religious virtues and concern for the spiritual needs of mankind. Conservative opposition to state restrictions of parochial-school policies is similarly based. As one Supreme Court decision noted: "We are a religious people whose institutions presuppose a Supreme Being."[4] This view has led conservatives to support an interpretation of the establishment clause in which its meaning is limited to prohibiting the federal government from establishing an official national religion. Particularly distressing to them is the liberal judicial elevation of Jefferson's privately articulated metaphor suggesting the need for "a wall of separation between church and state" to the status of a constitutional principle.

Liberals have taken an activist judicial stance by interpreting the religion clauses to mean a good deal more, in terms of restrictions, than they say. They have used Jefferson's concept of a "wall of separation between church and state" to erect a variety of barriers between church and state, when the Supreme Court used the Fourteenth Amendment to extend the Bill of Rights to the relationship between states and their residents. They see religious intermingling with education as an obstruction to the use of secular reason and human intelligence in perfecting societal institutions. Further, liberals read history in ways that see destruction and backwardness resulting to government and religion from their commingling. As one Supreme Court opinion noted, "a union of government and religion tends to destroy government and to degrade religion."[5]

Thus have the philosophical lines been drawn between liberals and conservatives regarding the legal interpretations of the establishment and free-exercise clauses. In order for educational policy to negotiate this area of adjudication, which has been labeled one of "consistent inconsistency,"[6] it is necessary to understand the principles that guide the decisions of jurists, regardless of their liberal or conservative leanings. This will still leave considerable room for ambiguity, but it will at least provide some parameters to the church-state litigation arena, based on established precedent.

Principles of Church-State Educational Relations

1. American government is secular. This position is the result of the belief of our Founding Fathers that governmental connection with religion would have a divisive effect on the diverse, heterogeneous population of the United States.

2. The First Amendment requires states (by virtue of the Fourteenth Amendment) to be neutral in relation to religion. Specifically, the establishment clause means that a state (or public school) may not pass laws or regulations that favor one or even all religions. The free-exercise clause means that a state (or public school) may not inhibit the free choice or practice of religion.

3. The establishment and free-exercise clauses may at times collide with each other. School efforts at keeping its program completely secular may inhibit one's right to practice religion as dictated by conscience and religious principles.

4. In adjudicating the role of religion in government areas, the U.S. Supreme Court balances the accepted values of religion to the nation against the recognized evils of sectarian persecution, intimidation, and governmental favoritism.

5. Some conservatives believe the establishment clause only means that Congress cannot establish an official national religion. Others see it more broadly, as forbidding national or state governments from favoring one religion over another, as well as prohibiting an official religion. Liberals believe that religion should be strictly separated from all government, including public schools.

6. The Supreme Court has developed a three-part test in applying the establishment clause to church-state education issues. Based on the concept of state neutrality, the three tests are: (1) the statute must have a secular purpose; (2) its principal or primary effect must be one that neither advances nor inhibits religion; and (3) the statute must be free of excessive government entanglement with religion.

7. The conservative position on the free-exercise clause is that government may not in any way inhibit religious preference or practice in the schools. The opposite liberal position is difficult to define. It mirrors the Supreme Court's comment that the clause "embraces two concepts—freedom to believe, and freedom to act. The first is absolute, but in the nature of things, the second cannot be."[7]

8. A state or public school may no more adopt a "religion" of secularism that is hostile to religion than it may adopt a preference for conventional religion.

9. Religious freedom, as with any other constitutionally protected civil liberty, is not unlimited. The interests of the state in conducting public education may at times override religious freedom. In other instances, education considerations may be required to give way to religious freedom.

THE FINANCIAL-AID ISSUE

Can public funds be used in support of parochial schools? If not, does this arbitrarily exclude citizens choosing private schools from not only the benefits, but also the goals, of public policy? If some forms of public support are possible, what guidelines obtain? At what point would Jefferson's "wall of separation" be breached? Does allowing tax benefits for parochial-school parents represent a breach in the wall? What about public funds for parochial-school texts, transportation, secular instructional services, or materials? How are public-policy goals advanced or frustrated by public financial aid accruing to, or being withheld from, parochial schools?

The first occasion on which the Supreme Court considered financial support to parochial education predated the Court's absorption of the First Amendment's application to the states under the Fourteenth Amendment. In 1930, *Cochran* v. *Louisiana* posed the question of whether the Fourteenth Amendment's prohibition against using public funds for a private purpose was violated by a Louisiana law authorizing public loans of textbooks to parochial-school students. A unanimous Supreme Court held that no such violation existed, as the public funds benefited the children in question, not the church operating the school. The Court reasoned: "It was for their benefit and the resulting benefit to the state, that the appropriations were made. . . . The [parochial] schools, however, are not the beneficiaries of these appropriations. They obtain nothing from them. . . . The school children and the state alone are the beneficiaries."[8]

This gave birth to the child-benefit theory, allowing public aid to parochial education, provided the aid benefited the student directly, for a reasonable public purpose, and did not constitute aid to the religious institution. The issue was reconsidered in *Everson* v. *Board of Education* (1947) in regard to the establishment clause, which had by then become applicable to the states under the Fourteenth Amendment. While the Court approved the New Jersey statute allowing local boards to reimburse parents (including parochial-school parents) for school-transportation expenses, it was only done with the bare five-to-four voting split. The majority recognized a collision here between the establishment and free-exercise clauses, within a restraintist attitude that "we must not strike that state statute down if it is within the State's constitutional power even though it approaches the verge of that power."[9] It held that while the establishment clause forbids spending tax funds to support institutions teaching a religious faith, neither could it hamper the free exercise of religion or exclude them from receiving the benefits of public-welfare legislation. The majority opinion concluded:

> Measured by these standards, we cannot say that the First Amendment prohibits . . . spending tax-raised funds to pay the bus fares of parochial school students as part of a general program. . . . [The First] Amendment requires the state to be neutral in its relations with groups of religious believers and non-believers; it does not require the state to be their adversary.[10]

While the five members of the majority thus rejected the First Amendment challenge to the child-benefit theory, it was accompanied by four vigorous dissents in which liberal views supported an interpretation of the establishment clause as demanding total denial of state support to parochial schools and students. One dissent directly attacked the child-benefit theory by pointing out:

> It is of no importance in this situation whether the beneficiary . . . is primarily the parochial school or incidentally the student, or whether the aid is directly bestowed on the pupil with indirect benefits to the school. The State cannot maintain a Church and it can no more tax its citizens to furnish free carriage to those who attend a Church. The prohibition against establishment of religion cannot be circumvented by . . . reimbursement of expenses to individuals for receiving religious instruction and indoctrination. . . .[11]
>
> Another dissenting justice believed: "Not simply an established church, but any law respecting an establishment of religion is forbidden. . . . . The prohibition broadly forbids state support . . . of religion in any guise, form, or degree. It outlaws all use of public funds for religious purposes."[12]

Justice Rutledge, who authored this dissent, predicted that with the application of the "child benefit" distinction to the prohibition of "establishment of religion," the Jeffersonian wall would continue to be breached. He was right. In the 1968 case of *Board of Education* v. *Allen,* the Supreme Court approved a New York law that widened the policy set in *Cochran* for public-textbook loans by *requiring* public-school boards to furnish to parochial schools any texts approved by their boards. Cautioning against loaning books to be used for religious instruction, the Court majority held that since public boards could distinguish between religious and secular books, the statute met the test of the establishment clause.

Among the three dissents to this decision was that of Justice Black, who had voted with the majority in *Everson.* He distinguished his positions in the two cases by writing that:

> . . . upholding a state's power to pay bus or streetcar fares for school children cannot provide support for . . . using tax-raised funds to buy school books for a religious school. The First Amendment's bar to establishment of religion must preclude a state from using funds levied from all of its citizens to purchase books for use by sectarian schools.[13]

Black saw the distinction between the majority opinion in *Everson,* which he authored, and the decision in *Allen* to rest on the critical educational function of textbooks, as opposed to the relatively removed function of transportation. As Rutledge had said of the *Everson* decision, so did Black say that *Allen* would further breach the "wall of separation" demanded between church and state. However, as the nation entered the 1970s, the Supreme Court demonstrated the limits of public aid to parochial education allowable under the establishment clause.

In 1971, *Lemon* v. *Kurtzman* (*Lemon I*) raised questions about Pennsylvania and Rhode Island statutes designed to improve secular education in nonpublic schools by supplementing the salaries of teachers of secular subjects in such schools. This decision led to a clear statement of Supreme Court standards governing the application of the establishment clause to church-school relations. In order to be valid under the establishment clause, a statute must (1) have a secular legislative purpose, (2) have a neutral principal effect; that is, it must neither advance nor inhibit religion, and (3) it must not foster "an excessive government entanglement with religion."[14]

The three-part test whose full development had extended from *Everson* through *Lemon I* provided a bulwark against further breaches of the wall between church and state attempted in 1973, when a variety of approaches to "parochaid" were struck down. In *Committee* v. *Nyquist,* 413 U.S. 756 (1973), a state provision of funds for repair and maintenance of qualifying nonpublic schools in New York was declared unconstitutional, along with tuition reimbursements at state expense and state income-tax credits for tuition-paying parochial-school parents. A seven-to-two Supreme Court majority found the repair-and-maintenance provision to unconstitutionally advance religion, and the reimbursement and state-tax-credit provisions to have the defects of both advancing religion and fostering excessive entanglement. In *Sloan* v. *Lemon,* 413 U.S. 472 (1973), a Pennsylvania provision for reimbursing parents of nonpublic-school students for a portion of tuition expenses was designed to avoid the "excessive entanglement" criticism of the earlier provision for paying parochial-school teachers of secular subjects struck down in *Lemon I*. Still, the Supreme Court found the new law to fail, because it had a primary effect that advanced religion.

In the same year, and again in 1975 and 1977, a variety of other "parochaid" approaches were struck down. These included *Levitt* v. *Commission,* 413 U.S. 472 (1973), in which a New York statute allowing reimbursement to parochial schools for performing various services (such as testing) required by the state was rejected because it fostered excessive entanglement, and *Meek* v. *Pittinger,* 421 U.S. 349 (1975), in which state aid to nonpublic schools for auxiliary services, textbooks, and instructional material provided free to public-school students was invalidated for the same reason.

In *Wolman* v. *Walters,* 433 U.S. 229 (1977), the supporters of parochaid achieved their first victory since *Allen*. Here, the Court considered an Ohio law authorizing state aid to parochial schools for a variety of functions (secular texts, standardized testing and scoring, diagnostic services, therapeutic services, and remedial services administered by public-school personnel at religiously neutral sites, secular instructional material and equipment, and field-trip transportation). The Court distinguished among these areas, finding the loan of instructional material to private schools, rather than students, and support of field trips to be unconstitutional advancements of religion. This latter service also was considered to foster excessive entanglement. However, the other publicly supported services were deemed constitutional, thus adding testing and diagnostic services, as well as publicly administered therapeutic and remedial services at neutral locations, into state-church practices approved under the establishment clause.

As the 1980s opened, the Court further widened the breach in the "wall of separation." After the *Levitt* decision had struck down the New York attempt to reimburse nonpublic schools for performing such required state functions as testing, that state passed a new law providing reimbursement to nonpublic schools for actual costs incurred in supplying state enrollment/attendance data and administering state-prepared and -mandated examinations. The Supreme Court, in *Committee* v. *Regan,* 444 U.S. 464 (1980), upheld the statute by a five-to-four vote, since the statute provided safeguards against excessive reimbursement and since the tests were prepared by the state, insuring against use for religious purposes.

In 1985, the Supreme Court returned to the issue of public-school instructional services to parochial schools in two cases decided on the same day—July 1, 1985. Both cases, *Grand Rapids* v. *Ball,* No. 83–990, and *Aguilar* v. *Felton,* No. 84–237, concerned the respective Michigan and New York practices of sending public-school teachers into parochial schools to provide Title I, ESEA remedial instruction. In *Grand Rapids* v. *Ball* the Court also considered the Grand Rapids policy of providing public funding for parochial-school teachers to provide secular "community education" courses for children and adults after school hours in the parochial schools.

Addressing the more complex *Grand Rapids* case first, a five-to-four majority declared the practice in violation of the establishment clause. The majority applied the three-part *Lemon* test to the challenged programs and found that the "effects" test was violated, as the programs created "the symbolic union of government and religion in one sectarian enterprise."[15] The basic reasoning behind the decision was stated as follows:

> The state-paid instructors, influenced by the pervasively sectarian nature of the religious schools in which they work, may subtly or overtly indoctrinate the students in particular religious tenets at public expense. The symbolic union of church and state inherent in the provision of secular, state-provided instruction in the religious school buildings threatens to convey a message of state support for religion. Finally, the programs in effect subsidize the religious functions of the parochial schools by taking over a substantial portion of their responsibility for secular subjects.[16]

Turning next to *Aguilar* v. *Felton,* the same bare five-to-four majority found the New York Title I practice of sending public-school teachers into parochial schools to provide remedial instruction similarly violative of the establishment clause, even though New York provided a monitoring system to insure against the introduction of religious content. Given the weaker grounds of disallowing this program on the "effects" test, *Aguilar* went on to impale the New York program on the "excessive entanglement" prong of the "*Lemon* test," because of the way church and state must interact in the administration of the public funds supportive of the program.

Even with this liberal strengthening of the "wall of separation," the conservative view had found a new avenue for strengthening public support for religious education just two years before the *Grand Rapids* and *Aguilar* decisions. In *Mueller* v. *Allen,* 103 S. Ct. 3062 (1983), a divided Court reversed a history of rejections of state-sponsored tax benefits for the parents of parochial students, by approving a Minnesota statute that did so. The statute met the three-part test for constitutionality under the establishment clause because it provided both public- and private-school parents with tax-deduction benefits for tuition and related education expenses, and excluded religious textbooks. The fact that tuition-paying parochial-school parents had an inordinate tax advantage over public school parents did not trouble the Court majority, nor did the possible entanglement potentially generated by state determination of which textbooks would be excluded as religious. More important to the majority was its view of the beneficial public-policy effects of a law promoting a well-educated citizenry while relieving the burden on public education. The Court's application of the three-part test concluded that the statute had a secular purpose of promoting well-educated citizens; a primary effect that did not advance religion because public- and private-school parents benefited; and only minor, incidental entanglement of church and state.

PUBLIC-SCHOOL INVOLVEMENT WITH RELIGIOUS PURPOSE

How much cooperation can public schools provide to religious activities? Are certain stances of government neutrality actually inhibitions of religious freedom? Do they unnecessarily limit a well-rounded education? Do certain stances constitute support of what is tantamount to a religion of secular humanism? How is the basic religious (or antireligious) nature of a particular school practice or policy to be defined? Can moral development pursued by the public schools be completely separated from religious concepts? Can appreciation for America's and Western civilization's cultural heritage be properly conveyed without some attention to and recognition of the contributions of religious values, rituals, literature, and symbols?

Public-School Cooperation with Religion

Court adjudication of religious ritual in public schools began with the relatively low emotional context of public-school–church cooperation regarding student released time for religious instruction. The customary practice in which public schools set aside part of one school day for clergy to come into the building to provide religious instruction to members of their faith was challenged in *McCullom* v. *Board of Education* (1948). Students wishing to participate were released from regular class activities, while nonparticipants continued their secular studies. The U.S. Supreme Court invalidated this practice as a violation of the establishment clause because it aided religion by providing an assembled audience, added the school's influence to the program, and supported the program through attendance procedures. Further, public facilities should not be used to further religious doctrines, whether one or many. In the words of the eight-to-one Court majority:

> Here not only are the state's tax-supported public school buildings used for the dissemination of religious doctrines. The State also affords sectarian groups an invaluable aid in that it helps to provide pupils for their religious classes through use of the state's compulsory public school machinery. This is not separation of church and state.[17]

This Illinois case prompted education-policy formulators in New York City to develop a plan in which students were released from public school during the school day to attend, on a voluntary basis, religious services at their church or synagogue for one hour per week. Would this change (primarily one of locating religious instruction outside the school building, but still during the school day) satisfy the Supreme Court? The answer was yes. In *Zorach* v. *Clauson* (1952), the six-member majority distinguished it from *McCullum* in that here, neither public facilities nor public funds were involved. The Court concluded:

> The present record indeed tells us that the school authorities are neutral . . . and do no more than release students whose parents so request. If in fact coercion were used, if it were established that any one or more teachers were using their office to persuade or force students to take religious instruction, a wholly different case would be presented. Hence we put aside that claim of coercion both as respects the "free exercise" of religion and "an establishment of religion" within the meaning of the First Amendment. . . .
>
> We are a religious people whose institutions presuppose a Supreme Being. . . . When the state encourages religious instruction or cooperates with religious authorities by adjusting the schedule of public events to sectarian needs, it follows the best of our traditions.[18]

The Court felt that to do otherwise than accommodate such a policy would be adopting a "philosophy of hostility to religion."[19] Clearly, whether prohibiting released time from the regularly prescribed secular curriculum constituted "hostility to religion" depends on one's liberal or conservative leanings regarding the interpretation of the constitutional separation of church and state.

The hair-splitting over released-time programs indicates the difficulty courts have in determining how far public schools may go in supporting religious instruction. In 1981, a tenth circuit federal court adjudicated the issue of whether a released-time program allowing public-school students to take religion courses at parochial schools was permissible, along with receiving public-school credit for such courses. The court ruled that while released time to take such courses was permissible, allowing public-school credit for them was not. The latter accommodation constituted excessive entanglement (*Lanner* v. *Wimmer,* 662 F. 2d 1349 [1981]).

The Issue of Religious Ritual in Public Schools

The released-time issue focused on how much cooperation there could be between public school and church in promoting religious instruction. During the next decade, the issue of public-school promotion of religion was joined in a much more deeply felt emotional context. In 1962, the liberal Warren Court introduced what has become one of the most persistently controversial Supreme Court areas of decision making in public education. The New York State Board of Regents had composed and recommended for public school use a nondenominational prayer, as follows: "Almighty God, we acknowledge our dependence on Thee, and we beg Thy blessings upon us, our parents, teachers, and our Country." Upon adoption by local school districts, the practice of this prayer ritual was challenged as a violation of the establishment clause. While the New York court sustained the practice, since no student was compelled to participate in the prayer, the U.S. Supreme Court struck it down as violative of the establishment clause. The Court, by a six-to-one vote, held:

> [G]overnment in this country, be it state or federal, is without power to prescribe by law any particular form of prayer . . . in carrying on any program of governmentally sponsored religious activity. . . .
>
> Neither the fact that the prayer may be denominationally neutral, nor the fact that its observance . . . is voluntary, can serve to free it from the limitations of the Establishment Clause . . . [which] unlike the Free Exercise Clause, does not depend on any showing of direct governmental compulsion and is violated by the enactment of laws which establish an official religion. . . . [A] union of government and religion tends to destroy government and degrade religion.[20]

Particularly in this last sentence, the activist nature of the decision is made evident. Here we see the Supreme Court going beyond the Constitution in deciding not merely the constraints and latitude allowed by the First Amendment, but also what, in its opinion, is the effect of government-religion interaction. The Court majority reaffirmed and extended its position the following year in the companion cases of *School District of Abington Township* v. *Schempp* and *Murray* v. *Curlett* (1963). These cases challenged Pennsylvania and Maryland statutes allowing prayer and Bible-reading rituals in public schools. In Abington, Pennsylvania, the challenged rule was that "at least ten verses of the Holy Bible shall be read, without comment, at the opening of each public school on each school day." Children were excused from attending the reading upon parental request. In Maryland, the issue was reading from the Bible and/or the Lord's Prayer.

Clearly, both practices were sectarian religious rituals. The Court declared the Pennsylvania and Maryland practices violative of the establishment clause by a vote of eight to one. Again, excusing students objecting to being parties to these rituals was not considered an adequate remedy, given the moral authority of the school and the social pressure of peers. The wall that should separate church and state did not require completely ignoring the Bible and its contributions to civilization; only that the Bible could not be used as an element of religious ritual in public schools. The majority agreed that:

> . . . one's education is not complete without a study of comparative religion or the history of religion and its relationship to the advancement of civilization. It certainly may be said that the Bible is worthy of study for its literary and historic qualities. Nothing we have said here indicates that such study of the Bible or of religion, when presented objectively as part of a secular program of education, may not be effected consistent with the First Amendment. But the exercises here do not fall into those categories. They are religious exercises, required by the States in violation of the command of the First Amendment that the Government maintain strict neutrality, neither aiding nor opposing religion.[21]

This liberal decision allowed the "escape hatch" of introducing religious content as study for its "literary and historic qualities . . . when presented objectively as part of a secular program of education. . . ." Exactly what did this allow? One answer was supplied by the Supreme Court in *Stone* v. *Graham* (1980). In this case, the Court struck down a Kentucky statute requiring the posting of the Ten Commandments in all public-school classrooms. Cognizant of the Supreme Court's demand for state neutrality in religion, and the requirement that such a statute have a secular purpose and be free of excessive state-church entanglement, the posters were privately financed (but the state treasurer served as collector), and the posters noted, in small print: "The secular application of the Ten Commandments is clearly seen in its adoption as the fundamental legal code of Western Civilization and Common Law of the United States."[22] In its finding that this statute violated the establishment clause, the Court compared the Kentucky practice to the standard established in *Abington* and the three-part test completed in *Lemon,* and found it wanting. The Court majority noted that the Ten Commandments, taken as a whole, constituted "a sacred text in the Jewish and Christian faith" that included such nonsecular matters as banning idolatry, observing the sabbath, and not taking the Lord's name in vain. Further, it fell outside the *Abington* guidelines because it was not integrated into a secular study of history, civilization, or comparative religion. Nor was the fact that the message was posted rather than recited of any consequence.

If this relatively innocuous introduction of religion into the classroom was unconstitutional, what might be allowed? An answer was provided in *Florey* v. *Sioux Falls School District* (1980), a case decided by a federal appellate-court panel in the same year the Supreme Court decided *Stone*. Parental objection to the religious content of elementary-school holiday programs resulted in the appointment of a citizens review committee, which approved guidelines allowing "unbiased, objective, prudent" uses of religious symbols, art, music, and literature in observation of holidays with "religious and secular bases." Not satisfied, parent Florey sued, producing a two-to-one decision favoring the Sioux Falls policy, holding that the permissive nature of the program mitigated the free-exercise problem, and the establishment clause was satisfied by the policy's primary secular purpose of advancing student knowledge of "culture and religious heritage, as well as . . . an opportunity . . . to perform a full range of music, poetry, and drama."[23] The dissenting judge believed that school sponsorship of Christmas assemblies with religious music endorsed the beliefs of one religion. "The school district has placed its power, prestige, and financial support of the government behind the Christmas holiday." Further, the dissenter believed the desired knowledge could as easily be advanced by nonreligious means, through the regular curriculum. He concluded: "In any case, the observance of religious holidays as a means of accomplishing this secular goal of knowledge and tolerance discriminates against non-belief."[24] The Supreme Court placed its approval on the *Florey* decision in its mandatory review of all three-judge appellate-court decisions. It refused a full review over the unusually strong objections of liberal justices Brennan and Marshall.

Meanwhile, conservative legislatures were pursuing another tack for accommodating some aspect of religious tradition and values in public-school affairs through legislation that variously authorized silent prayer, meditation, or, more simply, "a moment of silence" as part of the public-school day. State and federal courts had generally upheld such statutes when they were voluntary and restricted to "meditation" or "silence," but had generally struck down those that seemed motivated as a subterfuge for advocating public prayer. Such statutes enacted by New Mexico (*Duffy* v. *Los Cruces Public School,* 557 F. Supp. 103 [1983]) and Tennessee (*Beck* v. *McElrath,* 548 F. Supp. 1161 [1982]) had been invalidated as violating the establishment clause. Even when a New Jersey statute omitted the word "prayer" from its "moment of silence" statute, a federal court declared it unconstitutional, as this was seen as a "cosmetic" change that did not alter the basic religious purpose of the statute (*May* v. *Cooperman,* 572 F. Supp. 1561 [1983]). In contrast, a federal court upheld a Massachusetts statute authorizing one minute "for meditation or prayer." This court reasoned that the option to either pray or meditate cured the law of any constitutional defect (*Gaines* v. *Anderson,* 421 F. Supp. 337 [1976]).

The Supreme Court was to enter this aspect of the public-school religious-ritual controversy because of the decisions made by Judge Hand of the federal district court in Alabama during the early 1980s. Judge Hand delivered three opinions (*Jaffree* v. *James,* 544 F. Supp. 727 [1982], *Jaffree* v. *Board of Mobile County,* 544 F. Supp. 1104 [1983], and *Jaffree* v. *James,* 554 F. Supp. 1130 [1983]) concerning the constitutionality of three Alabama statutes. The first (16-1-120) authorized a minute of silent meditation in public schools, the second authorized a minute for meditation or silent prayer (16-1-120.1), and the third authorized teachers to lead willing students in a prescribed prayer (16-1-120.2). Judge Hand found nothing wrong with the silent meditation authorized by 16-1-120, but found both 16-1-120.1 and 16-1-120.2 invalid under Supreme Court precedents interpreting the establishment clause. Having done so, he proceeded to "overrule" the Supreme Court by declaring the latter two statutes constitutional because he interpreted the establishment clause as not even inhibiting the State of Alabama from establishing a state religion if it chose to do so. In his view, the clause only prohibited Congress from establishing a national religion. In making this point, Judge Hand provided a carefully researched and reasoned conservative, restraintist opinion.

The appellate court (*Jaffree* v. *Wallace,* 705 F.2d 1526 [1983]) subsequently held those latter two statutes unconstitutional, while the validation of the "silent meditation" statute was not challenged. The invalidation of 16–1–120.1 (meditation or silent prayer) was appealed and the Supreme Court considered this challenge in the companion case of *Wallace* v. *Jaffree* (1985) and *Smith* v. *Jaffree,* Slip Opinion No. 83–929 (1985). The six-to-three majority applied the three-part *Lemon* test to the meditation or silent-prayer statute and struck it down because its legislative history showed it to be completely devoid of secular purpose. They saw it as clearly intended to promote public-school prayer through state endorsement and encouragement of prayer as the favored practice over meditation. The opinion stated: "Such an endorsement is not consistent with the established principle that the government must pursue a course of complete neutrality toward religion,"[25] thus impaling the statute on the second prong of the *Lemon* test.

Even so, the decision cannot be viewed as a clear victory for the liberal forces opposing religious practice in public schools. All the members of the Court agreed that states could allow time in public schools for voluntary silent prayer along with meditation, provided that prayer is not presented as the preferred position or otherwise promoted by the state. In her concurring opinion, Justice O'Connor noted that "moment of silence laws in many states pass Establishment Clause scrutiny because they do not favor the child who chooses to pray during a moment of silence over the child who chooses to meditate or reflect."[26] Thus, prayer is permissible during moments of silence, provided it is not encouraged over meditation.

Justice Rehnquist's dissent took the trail blazed by Judge Hand. He not only argued the wrongness of allowing Jefferson's private metaphor about "the wall of separation between church and state" to influence judicial policy; he also argued that the First Amendment's framers never intended such separation, but only wanted to insure against the establishment of an official national religion. Equally important, he criticized the *Lemon* test as unworkably inconsistent and counterproductive.

Wallace v. *Jaffree* brought some clarification to the policy question of religious ritual as related to prayer/meditation statutes. The Supreme Court confirmed the general lower-court judgments of approving laws authorizing moments of silence for meditation in public schools and inquiring into the intent of statutes coupling prayer with a moment of silence or meditation. If the law appears to favor prayer over meditation, was primarily intended to strengthen prayer, or was otherwise motivated by religious goals, it falls afoul of the establishment clause.

The issue remains cloudy as it continues to be fought in state and national legislatures as well as the courts. An example of the variety of strategies employed in this continuing school-policy arena was found in the higher-education case of *Widmar* v. *Vincent,* 454 U.S. 263 (1981). In that case, the U.S. Supreme Court upheld the right of student prayer groups to the same rights to meet as an extracurricular activity as secular-interest groups. The decision was based on the right to free speech at a public university, which was held as an open forum, giving religious groups the same access rights as secular groups. The free-speech–open-forum strategy for bringing prayer into the school in this modified form, approved by the Supreme Court in *Widmar,* soon found legislative expression in the national Equal Access Act of 1984. The Act provides that when public secondary schools allow time during noninstructional periods for student-initiated meetings to pursue topics not covered in the curriculum, the "limited open forum" thus created requires that equal access be permitted to student-initiated religious groups for such purposes as prayer. This approach is narrow, and based on free speech, not religious freedom. It combines with efforts at posing a constitutional amendment permitting school prayer and a relentless series of state statutes, court tests, and executive manipulations to ensure the continued prominence of public-school accomodation of religious ritual as a school-law policy issue.

CONTROVERSY OVER TEACHING RELIGIOUS CONCEPTS OF CREATION

Should devout Christians be protected against what they consider to be anti-Christian attitudes in the public school? If they cannot prohibit the teachings of theories they consider hostile, such as evolution, should they not be permitted to present their counter-theories? On what basis can rival theories of creation be judged constitutionally permissible or impermissible for inclusion in the school curriculum? Does allowing the teaching of evolution theory while forbidding the teaching of religious-creation theory violate the "free exercise" clause?

In 1968 an Arkansas statute that prohibited public schools from teaching the Darwinian theory of the evolution of man was considered by the Supreme Court. In *Epperson* v. *Arkansas* (1968), the Court's six-to-three vote invalidated the statute because it judged the purpose of the law to be elimination of any and all subjects from the curriculum that fundamentalists considered to be antagonistic to their particular interpretation of the Bible. Therefore, the statute did not observe neutrality and was violative of the establishment clause. In making its decision, however, the Court issued a statement of restraintist philosophy, which, while perhaps at odds with the decision, invited state and local educational authorities to consider policy alternatives to aims blocked by this decision:

Judicial interposition in the operation of the public school . . . raises problems requiring care and restraint. Our courts, however, have not failed to apply the First Amendment's mandate . . . where essential to safeguard the fundamental values of . . . belief. . . . Courts do not and cannot intervene in the resolution of conflicts which arise in the daily operation of school systems and which do not directly and sharply implicate basic constitutional values.[27]

What policy could respond to the concern of conservatives that teaching evolution would erode the traditional beliefs of the religious view of creation and human development? The answer was to develop statutes requiring equal time to be given to both Biblical and evolutionist theories in the curriculum. In 1981, the Arkansas law requiring such a balance was enacted. To counteract the obvious attack on Biblical theory as religious dogma, it was labeled "creation science," or, more popularly, "scientific creationism." The liberal legal challenge came quickly. In *McLean* v. *Arkansas* (1982), the state argued that: (1) the literal Genesis view of creation does not, per se, mean that creation science is religious; (2) the statute's reference to creation from nothing does not necessarily imply the nature of the creator; and (3) merely teaching about a creator concept is not a religious exercise.

The federal district court disagreed, finding: (1) the creator concept a conception of God; (2) the sudden-creation-from-nothing concept inherently religious; and (3) the reliance on Genesis left no doubt that the law was designed to advance religious beliefs. The judge then laid down principles under which "science" could be defined:

(1) it is guided by natural law; (2) it has to be explanatory by reference to natural law; (3) it is testable against the empirical world; (4) its conclusions are tentative, i.e., are not necessarily the final work; and (5) it is falsifiable. Under this definition, creation-science is not a science, but, instead is a religious doctrine which was, in this case, imposed on the youth by state law.[28]

This decision supported those of other federal courts, which had taken *Epperson* to prohibit, in the words of the decision, "that teaching and learning must be tailored to the principles or prohibitions of any religious sect or dogma."[29] When religious plaintiffs complained that their free exercise of religion was being restrained and they were forced to be subjected to the religion of "secular humanism," the courts rejected the contention (*Daniel* v. *Waters,* 515 F. 2d 458 [1975]; *Steele* v. *Waters,* 527 S.W. 2d [1975]). A notable exception to this predominant trend in court reasoning is found in Judge Hand's opinion in *Jaffree* v. *James* (1982), in which he stated:

It is apparent from a reading of the decision law that the courts acknowledge that Christianity is the religion to be proscribed. . . . The religions of atheism, materialism, agnosticism, communism and socialism have escaped the scrutiny of the courts. . . . It can clearly be argued that as to Christianity [the word "Goddamn"] . . . is blasphemy and is the establishment of an advancement of humanism, secularism or agnosticism. If the state cannot teach or advance Christianity, how can it teach or advance the Antichrist?[30]

Judge Hand's view was rejected. However, his point has been entered into court literature as fundamentalist groups continue to search for an equal-time formula that will meet with general court approval.

POLICY CONSIDERATIONS

Formulating and executing public-school policy involving religious attitudes involves the potential for highly charged emotional controversy. There is hardly a topic that inspires as widespread and deep personal feelings among the people involved. The issues attending church-state educational relations have led to a national movement to overturn the Supreme Court ban on public-school prayer and Bible reading through constitutional amendment. During the early spring of 1984, there was hardly a newspaper or television station in America that did not report on the activities in Congress on this issue. The *Jaffree* v. *Board of Mobile County* (1983) defiance of the Supreme Court's judgment on this issue, by "overruling" it and lecturing it on the "proper" interpretation of constitutional history and reasoning, heightened tension. Quixotic as that was, the assertion of conservative principles was cheered in many quarters, and encouraged continued resistance to liberal interpretations of church-state relations in education. The three dissenters to *Wallace* v. *Jaffree* and Justice Rehnquist's careful, strong dissent in that case add more traditional support to the conservative case.

Some of the fruits of *Jaffree* v. *Mobile County* may be seen in the Supreme Court's decision in *Mueller* v. *Allen,* in which a more conservative attitude is experienced than previously in allowing tax benefits for private-school parents. But this was soon countered by the liberal decisions in *Grand Rapids* v. *Ball* and *Aguilar* v. *Fenton.* Thus, the "consistent inconsistency" of Supreme Court policy on what is and what is not constitutionally permissible public aid or cooperation with parochial education remains a policy-analysis and -application quagmire, supporting Justice Rehnquist's criticism of the *Lemon* criteria as an adequate base for judicial policy making. Public schools may release students to attend off-campus religious instruction, but may not allow such instruction within the school. Secular textbooks may be lent to parochial schools, but public funding for purchase of materials or field trips is forbidden. Public reimbursement for private-school administration of state prepared and required tests is permissible, but reimbursement for teacher-prepared tests is forbidden. Provision of auxiliary services to parochial schools is permissible off school premises, but not within the school. Similarly, providing public funding of secular instruction in the parochial school is unconstitutional, while allowing these services outside the parochial school for the same students is not. The Ten Commandments may not be posted in public-school classrooms, but public schools may have Christmas programs that include explicitly Christian symbols and music.

Adding to the controversy and confusion is the question of when silent-meditation-and prayer statutes fall within or outside of the First Amendment.

When official intention to favor prayer is discerned, the statute is unconstitutional, but if the option to pray or meditate seems offered in a balanced, noncoercive way, the law would be valid. Clearly, the matter of proving legislative intention would be difficult. Then there is the issue of evolution theory versus "creation science." The Supreme Court held in *Epperson* that the state or school board cannot exclude the teaching of evolution theory under the establishment clause, but courts will not allow equal time in the curriculum for the Biblical theory of creation by virtue of that same clause, including when this is presented as "scientific creationism."

Persons charged with responsibility for formulating or executing school policies touching on church-state relationships have to consider several matters. The public school is generally regarded to have a moral, character-building mission along with its cognitive one. Also, it is recognized that we are a religious nation, and religion is considered as important and positive to our society. The courts recognize these tenets. However, America had as a founding principle that religion was to be separated from government, and religious freedom—to practice it, abstain from it, and be free from its various sectarian pressures—is the birthright of all Americans. The First Amendment's free-exercise and establishment clauses were promulgated to insure these conditions. Or were they?

The general principles established by the Supreme Court, and added to by lower courts, provide the broad guidelines to inform policy. The school should neither support nor oppose religion, but need not ignore important American traditions that have religious elements in exercising this neutrality. Religious values may not be ignored; neither may they be imposed on the unwilling. When secular purposes are at stake, religious schools can be assisted by government in attaining these goals, but only in carefully prescribed ways.

The questions that the school official must ask, in deciding issues variously dealing with the establishment and free-exercise clauses, include the following:

1. Does the statute, regulation, or practice put the weight and prestige of the government, as personified by the public school, behind a specific religion, all religions, or against religion? If so, it is most likely not constitutionally permissible. This does not include advocacy of the moral virtues inherent in religion (or secular humanism), but rather the tenets, faith, and rituals of the religion or opposing atheist position. The former is in most cases permissible, while the latter is not. In this sense, school-sponsored recognition of the religious importance and sanctity of Christmas might be unconstitutional under the establishment clause. Similarly, holding school on Christmas Day would probably be considered unconstitutional under the free-exercise clause. However, recognizing the moral and cultural values of Christianity to our nation would be permissible, but prohibition of pagan rites or devil worship (to use an extreme example to make the point clear) would most likely not be upheld by any court as violating the free-exercise rights of pagans or devil worshipers. The courts recognize religious traditions as important elements of our heritage and culture, but there are limits to how far this recognition will extend. The Supreme Court has agreed that we are a religious nation. At the same time, government (and public schools as its agent) must avoid involvement, whether supporting or opposing, in religious affairs, at least to a reasonable degree.

2. Is the statute, regulation, or act primarily motivated by religious doctrine or by concepts of good moral and character development? This is particularly hard to decide, since moral and character development are so closely interwoven with the precepts of the major religions. The question can be best answered by looking for signs of religious intent or preference wrapped up in the policy. This is the approach the Supreme Court has taken in the silent-prayer/meditation controversy. Silent prayer is as permissible as meditation. What is forbidden is government support and encouragement of prayer as the preferred activity.

3. Does the school policy *unnecessarily* restrain the student from practicing his or her religion? If so, the free-exercise clause has been violated. Remember, the key word is *unnecessarily*. Civil liberties, including freedom of religion, are not unlimited. However, when government, through its schools, restricts freedom of religion, it must have an important purpose in doing so. The Supreme Court found that not allowing release time for students to attend off-site religious instruction would be tantamount to hostility to religion, and hence an unnecessary restraint. Similarly, a statute forbidding silent prayer during a meditation period would violate the free-exercise clause. How about requiring students to salute the flag or participate in dance instruction or wear certain gym uniforms against their religious beliefs? In all these examples, the courts have held the requirements to be unnecessary restraints to the exercise of accepted religious practice of seriously religious students, as, for example, Jehovah's Witnesses. What about religious objections to disease inoculations? There, courts have held that religious principle must give way to the greater importance of general public safety.

4. How far can the public school go in using the Bible and other religious literature in the curriculum? Good judgment is the key to this policy matter. The school official must insure that the emphasis is on the use of these materials for understanding the cultural and moral heritage, not to promote religious positions. Thus, attaching reverential procedures in the use of such literature might constitute "an establishment of religion," or subjecting them to severe criticism or attack would violate free exercise. Religious literature is best treated as would be any secular great literature—as important sources to inform and educate students.

5. How much assistance, and in what forms, is permissible in public assistance to parochial schools? This is the area in which the courts have provided the most confusing, hair-splitting guidelines. What is certain is that policies clearly benefiting students, but neutral toward the sponsoring church, are permissible. Also, aid that contributes to important public purposes is permissible, as improving educational outcomes, health, and service to remedial or handicapped students. However, great care is necessary here to avoid excessive entanglement. This involves questions of where services are offered and who is providing them. Finally, how can it be decided whether any benefit derives to the sponsoring church? These are difficult matters to decide. Certainly, supplying religious textbooks and paraphernalia to parochial schools at public expense would be out of bounds, and transportation services and secular texts within bounds. In the variety of gray areas in between these extremes, the school officials can do no better than recite the three-part test established by the Supreme Court, at least until it is modified or abandoned. Does the statute have a secular purpose? Is its primary effect one that neither advances nor inhibits religion? Is the statute free of excessive church-state entanglement?

6. Is there a curricular imbalance that works against the student's belief in and appreciation for his or her own religious heritage? If so, what can be done about it? The first question was raised by and answered affirmatively by fundamentalist Christians responding to the Supreme Court's *Epperson* decision. Their answer to

the second question is to provide equal time through the study of creation science. The courts have disallowed this policy approach on the grounds that creation science is not science, but religion. School officials may well encounter similar attempts to balance what is perceived as antireligious, secular humanist curricular positions. When such attempts introduce religious rebuttals under the guise of science, they cannot be allowed. However, what of secular arguments disputing evolution on purely scientific grounds? Certainly, they would be permissible. Even if the counter-evidence had religious motivations at its base, it would be difficult to exclude strictly scientific alternatives to evolution theory from the curriculum. None have yet appeared, but it is possible that they will be developed. When such a theory is presented, school officials should be careful to determine that they are based on the theory and canons of science rather than of religion.

Perhaps the broadest and most basic question to consider is whether religious fervor is destructive to the unity and purpose of public education for a diverse citizenry. Or, to look at the general issue from the opposite perspective, can American public education be a truly authentic representation of the American ethos if it denies the religious nature of its students?

Wolman v. Walter
433 U.S. 229 (1977)

MR. JUSTICE BLACKMUN delivered the opinion of the Court.

This is still another case presenting the recurrent issue of the limitations imposed by the Establishment Clause of the First Amendment, made applicable to the States by the Fourteenth Amendment, on state aid to pupils in church-related elementary and secondary schools.

I

In broad outline, the statute authorizes the State to provide nonpublic school pupils with books, instructional materials and equipment, standardized testing and scoring, diagnostic services, therapeutic services, and field trip transportation.

Funds so appropriated are paid to the State's public school districts and are then expended by them. All disbursements made with respect to nonpublic schools have their equivalents in disbursements for public schools, and the amount expended per pupil in nonpublic schools may not exceed the amount expended per pupil in the public schools.

The parties stipulated that during the 1974–1975 school year there were 720 chartered nonpublic schools in Ohio. Of these, all but 29 were sectarian. More than 96% of the nonpublic enrollment attended sectarian schools, and more than 92% attended Catholic schools. It was also stipulated that, if they were called, officials of representative Catholic schools would testify that such schools operate under the general supervision of the bishop of their diocese; that most principals are members of a religious order within the Catholic Church; that a little less than one-third of the teachers are members of such religious orders; that "in all probability a majority of the teachers are members of the Catholic faith"; and that many of the rooms and hallways in these schools are decorated with a Christian symbol. All such schools teach the secular subjects required to meet the State's minimum standards. The state-mandated five-hour day is expanded to include, usually, one-half hour of religious instruction. Pupils who are not members of the Catholic faith are not required to attend religion classes or to participate in religious exercises or activities, and no teacher is required to teach religious doctrine as a part of the secular courses taught in the schools.

II

The mode of analysis for Establishment Clause questions is defined by the three-part test that has emerged from the Court's decisions. In order to pass muster, a statute must have a secular legislative purpose, must have a principal or primary effect that neither advances nor inhibits religion, and must not foster an excessive government entanglement with religion.

In the present case we have no difficulty with the first prong of this three-part test. We are satisfied that the challenged statute reflects Ohio's legitimate interest in protecting the health of its youth and in providing a fertile educational environment for all the schoolchildren of the State. As is usual in our cases, the analytical difficulty has to do with the effect and entanglement criteria.

We have acknowledged before, and we do so again here, that the wall of separation that must be maintained between church and state "is a blurred, indistinct, and variable barrier depending on all the circumstances of a particular relationship." Nonetheless, the Court's numerous precedents "have become firmly rooted," and now provide substantial guidance. We therefore turn to the task of applying the rules derived from our decisions to the respective provisions of the statute at issue.

III   Textbooks

Section 3317.06 authorizes the expenditure of funds:

"(A) To purchase such secular textbooks as have been approved by the superintendent of public instruction for use in public schools in the state and to loan such textbooks to pupils attending nonpublic schools within the district or to their parents. Such loans shall be based upon individual requests submitted by such nonpublic school pupils or parents. Such requests shall be submitted to the local public school district in which the nonpublic school is located. Such individual requests for the loan of textbooks shall, for administrative convenience, be submitted by the nonpublic school pupil or his parent to the nonpublic school which shall prepare and submit collective summaries of the individual requests to the local public school district."

[W]e conclude that § 3317.06 (A) is constitutional.

IV   Testing and Scoring

Section 3317.06 authorizes expenditure of funds:

"(J) To supply for use by pupils attending nonpublic schools within the district such standardized tests and scoring services as are in use in the public schools of the state."

These tests "are used to measure the progress of students in secular subjects." Nonpublic school personnel are not involved in either the drafting or scoring of the tests. The statute does not authorize any payment to nonpublic school personnel for the costs of administering the tests.

There is no question that the State has a substantial and legitimate interest in insuring that its youth receive an adequate secular education. The State may require that schools that are utilized to fulfill the State's compulsory-education requirement meet certain standards of instruction, and may examine both teachers and pupils to ensure that the State's legitimate interest is being fulfilled. Under the section at issue, the State provides both the schools and the school district with the means of ensuring that the minimum standards are met. The nonpublic school does not control the content of the test or its result. This serves to prevent the use of the test as a part of religious teaching. Similarly, the inability of the school to control the test eliminates the need for the supervision that gives rise to excessive entanglement. We therefore agree with the District Court's conclusion that § 3317.06 (J) is constitutional.

V   Diagnostic Services

Section 3317.06 authorizes expenditures of funds:

"(D) To provide speech and hearing diagnostic services to pupils attending nonpublic schools within the district. Such service shall be provided in the nonpublic school attended by the pupil receiving the service."
"(F) To provide diagnostic psychological services to pupils attending nonpublic schools within the district. Such services shall be provided in the school attended by the pupil receiving the service."

It will be observed that these speech and hearing and psychological diagnostic services are to be provided within the nonpublic school.

Appellants assert that the funding of these services is constitutionally impermissible. They argue that the speech and hearing staff might engage in unrestricted conversation with the pupil and, on occasion, might fail to separate religious instruction from secular responsibilities. They further assert that the communication between the psychological diagnostician and the pupil will provide an impermissible opportunity for the intrusion of religious influence.

The District Court found these dangers so insubstantial as not to render the statute unconstitutional. We agree. This Court's decisions contain a common thread to the effect that the provision of health services to all schoolchildren—public and nonpublic—does not have the primary effect of aiding religion.

We conclude that providing diagnostic services on the nonpublic school premises will not create an impermissible risk of the fostering of ideological views. It follows that there is no need for excessive surveillance, and there will not be impermissible entanglement. We therefore hold that §§ 3317.06 (D) and (F) are constitutional.

VI   Therapeutic Services

Sections 3317.06 (G), (H), (I), and (K) authorize expenditures of funds for certain therapeutic, guidance, and remedial services for students who have been identified as having a need for specialized attention. Personnel providing the services must be employees of the local board of education or under contract with the State Department of Health. The services are to be performed only in public schools, in public centers, or in mobile units located off the nonpublic school premises.

[W]e hold that providing therapeutic and remedial services at a neutral site off the premises of the nonpublic schools will not have the impermissible effect of advancing religion. Neither will there be any excessive entanglement arising from supervision of public employees to insure that they maintain a neutral stance. It can hardly be said that the supervision of public employees performing public functions on public property creates an excessive entanglement between church and state. Sections 3317.06 (G), (H), (I), and (K) are constitutional.

VII
Instructional Materials and Equipment

Sections 3317.06 (B) and (C) authorize expenditures of funds for the purchase and loan to pupils or their parents upon individual request of instructional materials and instructional equipment of the kind in use in the public schools within the district and which is "incapable of diversion to religious use." Section 3317.06 also provides that the materials and equipment may be stored on the premises of a nonpublic school and that publicly hired personnel who administer the lending program may perform their services upon the nonpublic school premises when necessary "for efficient implementation of the lending program."

Although the exact nature of the material and equipment is not clearly revealed, the parties have stipulated: "It is expected that materials and equipment loaned to pupils or parents under the new law will be similar to such former materials and equipment except that to the extent that the law requires that materials and equipment capable of diversion to religious issues will not be supplied." Equipment provided under the predecessor statute, invalidated, included projectors, tape recorders, record players, maps and globes, science kits, weather forecasting charts, and the like. The District Court found the new statute, as now limited, constitutional because the court could not distinguish the loan of material and equipment from the textbook provisions.

In *Meek,* however, the Court considered the constitutional validity of a direct loan to nonpublic schools of instructional material and equipment, and, despite the apparent secular nature of the goods, held the loan impermissible. Mr. Justice Stewart, in writing for the Court, stated:

> "The very purpose of many of those schools is to provide an integrated secular and religious education; the teaching process is, to a large extent, devoted to the inculcation of religious values and belief. Substantial aid to

the educational function of such schools, accordingly, necessarily results in aid to the sectarian school enterprise as a whole. '[T]he secular education those schools provide goes hand in hand with the religious mission that is the only reason for the schools' existence. Within the institution, the two are inextricably intertwined.'''

Thus, even though the loan ostensibly was limited to neutral and secular instructional material and equipment, it inescapably had the primary effect of providing a direct and substantial advancement of the sectarian enterprise.

Appellees seek to avoid *Meek* by emphasizing that it involved a program of direct loans to nonpublic schools. In contrast, the material and equipment at issue under the Ohio statute are loaned to the pupil or his parent. In our view, however, it would exalt form over substance if this distinction were found to justify a result different from that in *Meek*. Despite the technical change, the program in substance is the same as before: The equipment is substantially the same; it will receive the same use by the students; and it may still be stored and distributed on the nonpublic school premises. In view of the impossibility of separating the secular education function from the sectarian, the state aid inevitably flows in part in support of the religious role of the schools.

Accordingly, we hold §§ 3317.06 (B) and (C) to be unconstitutional.

VIII   Field Trips

Section 3317.06 also authorizes expenditures of funds:

"(L) To provide such field trip transportation and services to nonpublic school students as are provided to public school students in the district. School districts may contract with commercial transportation companies for such transportation service if school district busses are unavailable."

There is no restriction on the timing of field trips; the only restriction on number lies in the parallel the statute draws to field trips provided to public school students in the district. The parties have stipulated that the trips "would consist of visits to governmental, industrial, cultural, and scientific centers designed to enrich the secular studies of students." The choice of destination, however, will be made by the nonpublic school teacher from a wide range of locations.

The District Court held this feature to be constitutionally indistinguishable from that with which the Court was concerned in *Everson* v. *Board of Education*. We do not agree. In *Everson* the Court approved a system under which a New Jersey board of education reimbursed parents for the cost of sending their children to and from school, public or parochial, by public carrier. The Court analogized the reimbursement to situations where a municipal common carrier is ordered to carry all schoolchildren at a reduced rate, or where the police force is ordered to protect all children on their way to and from school. The critical factors in these examples, as in the *Everson* reimbursement system, are that the school has no control over the expenditure of the funds and the effect of the expenditure is unrelated to the content of the education provided. Thus, the bus fare program in *Everson* passed constitutional muster because the school did not determine how often the pupil traveled between home and school—every child must make one round trip every day—and because the travel was unrelated to any aspect of the curriculum.

The Ohio situation is in sharp contrast. First, the nonpublic school controls the timing of the trips and, within a certain range, their frequency and destinations. Thus, the schools, rather than the children, truly are the recipients of the service and, as this Court has recognized, this fact alone may be sufficient to invalidate the program as impermissible direct aid. Second, although a trip may be to a location that would be of interest to those in public schools, it is the individual teacher who makes the field trip meaningful. The experience begins with the study and discussion of the place to be visited; it continues on location with the teacher pointing out items of interest and stimulating the imagination; and it ends with a discussion of the experience. The field trips are an integral part of the educational experience, and where the teacher works within and for a sectarian institution, an unacceptable risk of fostering of religion is an inevitable byproduct.

Moreover, the public school authorities will be unable adequately to insure secular use of the field trip funds without close supervision of the nonpublic teachers. This would create excessive entanglement.

We hold § 3317.06 (L) to be unconstitutional.

IX

In summary, we hold constitutional those portions of the Ohio statute authorizing the State to provide nonpublic school pupils with books, standardized testing and scoring, diagnostic services, and therapeutic and remedial services. We hold unconstitutional those portions relating to instructional materials and equipment and field trip services.

The judgment of the District Court is therefore affirmed in part and reversed in part.

Mueller v. Allen
103 S. Ct. 3062 (1983)

JUSTICE REHNQUIST delivered the opinion of the Court.

Minnesota permits state taxpayers to claim a deduction from gross income for certain expenses incurred in educating their children. The deduction is limited to actual expenses incurred for the "tuition, textbooks and transportation" of dependents attending elementary or secondary schools.

Petitioners—certain Minnesota taxpayers—sued in the United States District Court claiming that § 290.09(22) violated the Establishment Clause by providing financial assistance to sectarian institutions. The District Court granted respondent's motion for summary judgment, holding that the statute was "neutral on its face and in its application and does not have a primary effect of either advancing or inhibiting religion." On appeal, the Court of Appeals affirmed, concluding that the Minnesota statute substantially benefited a "broad class of Minnesota citizens."

One fixed principle in this field is our consistent rejection of the argument that "any program which in some manner aids an institution with a religious affiliation" violates the Establishment Clause. For example, it is now well-established that a state may reimburse parents for expenses incurred in transporting their children to school, and that it may loan secular textbooks to all schoolchildren within the state.

Notwithstanding the repeated approval given programs such as those in *Allen* and *Everson,* our decisions also have struck down arrangements resembling, in many respects, these forms of assistance. In this case we are asked to decide whether Minnesota's tax deduction bears greater resemblance to those types of assistance to parochial schools we have approved, or to those we have struck down.

The general nature of our inquiry in this area has been guided, since the decision in *Lemon* v. *Kurtzman,* by the "three-part" test laid down in that case:

> "First, the statute must have a secular legislative purpose; second, its principle or primary effect must be one that neither advances nor inhibits religion . . . ; finally, the statute must not foster 'an excessive government entanglement with religion.' "

While this principle is well settled, our cases have also emphasized that it provides "no more than [a] helpful signpost" in dealing with Establishment Clause challenges. With this *caveat* in mind, we turn to the specific challenges raised under the *Lemon* framework.

Little time need be spent on the question of whether the Minnesota tax deduction has a secular purpose. Under our prior decisions, governmental assistance programs have consistently survived this inquiry even when they have run afoul of other aspects of the *Lemon* framework. This reflects, at least in part, our reluctance to attribute unconstitutional motives to the states, particularly when a plausible secular purpose for the state's program may be discerned from the face of the statute.

A state's decision to defray the cost of educational expenses incurred by parents—regardless of the type of schools their children attend—evidences a purpose that is both secular and understandable. An educated populace is essential to the political and economic health of any community, and a state's efforts to assist parents in meeting the rising cost of educational expenses plainly serves this secular purpose of ensuring that the state's citizenry is well-educated. Similarly, Minnesota, like other states, could conclude that there is a strong public interest in assuring the continued financial health of private schools, both sectarian and non-sectarian. By educating a substantial number of students such schools relieve public schools of a correspondingly great burden—to the benefit of all taxpayers.

We turn therefore to the more difficult but related question whether the Minnesota statute has "the primary effect of advancing the sectarian aims of the nonpublic schools." Under our prior decisions, the Minnesota legislature's judgment that a deduction for educational expenses fairly equalizes the tax burden of its citizens and encourages desirable expenditures for educational purposes is entitled to substantial deference.

Other characteristics of § 290.09(22) argue equally strongly for the provision's constitutionality. Most importantly, the deduction is available for educational expenses incurred by *all* parents, including those whose children attend public schools and those whose children attend non-sectarian private schools or sectarian private schools.

We also agree with the Court of Appeals that, by channeling whatever assistance it may provide to parochial schools through individual parents, Minnesota has reduced the Establishment Clause objections to which its action is subject. It is true, of course, that financial assistance provided to parents ultimately has an economic effect comparable to that of aid given directly to the schools attended by their children. It is also true, however, that under Minnesota's arrangement public funds become available only as a result of numerous, private choices of individual parents of school-age children. It is noteworthy that all but one of our recent cases invalidating state aid to parochial schools have involved the direct transmission of assistance from the state to the schools themselves. Where, as here, aid to parochial schools is available only as a result of decisions of individual parents no "imprimatur of State approval," can be deemed to have been conferred on any particular religion, or on religion generally.

The Establishment Clause of course extends beyond prohibition of a state church or payment of state funds to one or more churches. We do not think, however, that its prohibition extends to the type of tax deduction established by Minnesota. The historic purposes of the clause simply do not encompass the sort of attenuated financial benefit, ultimately controlled by the private choices of individual parents, that eventually flows to parochial schools from the neutrally available tax benefit at issue in this case.

Petitioners argue that, notwithstanding the facial neutrality of § 290.09(22), in application the statute primarily benefits religious institutions. Petitioners rely, as they did below, on a statistical analysis of the type of persons claiming the tax deduction. They contend that most parents of public school children incur no tuition expenses, and that other expenses deductible under § 290.09(22) are negligible in value; moreover, they claim that 96% of the children in private schools in 1978–1979 attended religiously-affiliated institutions. Because of all this, they reason, the bulk of deductions taken under § 290.09(22) will be claimed by parents of children in sectarian schools. Respondents reply that petitioners have failed to consider the impact of deductions for items such as transportation, summer school tuition, tuition paid by parents whose children attended schools outside the school districts in which they resided, rental or purchase costs for a variety of equipment, and tuition for certain types of instruction not ordinarily provided in public schools.

We need not consider these contentions in detail. We would be loath to adopt a rule grounding the constitutionality of a facially neutral law on annual reports reciting the extent to which various classes of private citizens claimed benefits under the law. Such an approach would scarcely provide the certainty that this field stands in need of, nor can we perceive principled standards by which such statistical evidence might be evaluated. Moreover, the fact that private persons fail in a particular year to claim the tax relief to which they are entitled—under a facially neutral statute—should be of little importance in determining the constitutionality of the statute permitting such relief.

Finally, private educational institutions, and parents paying for their children to attend these schools, make special contributions to the areas in which they operate. "Parochial schools, quite apart from their sectarian purpose, have provided an educational alternative for millions of young Americans; they often afford wholesome competition with our public schools; and in some States they relieve substantially the tax burden incident to the operation of public schools." If parents of children in private schools choose to take especial advantage of the relief provided by § 290.09(22), it is no doubt due to the fact that they bear a particularly great financial burden in educating their children. More fundamentally, whatever unequal effect may be attributed to the statutory classification can fairly be regarded as a rough return for the benefits, discussed above, provided to the state and all taxpayers by parents sending their children to parochial schools. In the light of all this, we believe it wiser to decline to engage in the type of empirical inquiry into those persons benefited by state law which petitioners urge.

Thus, we hold that the Minnesota tax deduction for educational expenses satisfies the primary effect inquiry of our Establishment Clause cases.

Turning to the third part of the *Lemon* inquiry, we have no difficulty in concluding that the Minnesota statute does not "excessively entangle" the state in religion. The only plausible source of the "comprehensive, discriminating, and continuing state surveillance" necessary to run afoul of this standard would lie in the fact that state officials must determine whether particular textbooks qualify for a deduction. In making this decision, state officials must disallow deductions taken from "instructional books and materials used in the teaching of religious tenets, doctrines or worship, the purpose of which is to inculcate such tenets, doctrines or worship." Making decisions such as this does not differ substantially from making the types of decisions approved in earlier opinions of this Court.

For the foregoing reasons, the judgment of the Court of Appeals is

Affirmed.

JUSTICE MARSHALL, with whom JUSTICE BRENNAN, JUSTICE BLACKMUN and JUSTICE STEVENS join, dissenting.

The Establishment Clause of the First Amendment prohibits a State from subsidizing religious education, whether it does so directly or indirectly. In my view, this principle of neutrality forbids any tax benefit, including the tax deduction at issue here, which subsidizes tuition payments to sectarian schools. I also believe that the Establishment Clause prohibits the tax deductions that Minnesota authorizes for the cost of books and other instructional materials used for sectarian purposes.

That the Minnesota statute makes some small benefit available to all parents cannot alter the fact that the most substantial benefit provided by the statute is available only to those parents who send their children to schools that charge tuition. It is simply undeniable that the single largest expense that may be deducted under the Minnesota statute is tuition. The statute is little more than a subsidy of tuition masquerading as a subsidy of general educational expenses.

Contrary to the majority's suggestion, the bulk of the tax benefits afforded by the Minnesota scheme are enjoyed by parents of parochial school children not because parents of school children fail to claim deductions to which they are entitled, but because the latter are simply *unable* to claim the largest tax deduction that Minnesota authorizes.

That this deduction has a primary effect of promoting religion can easily be determined without any resort to the type of "statistical evidence" that the majority fears would lead to constitutional uncertainty. The only factual inquiry necessary is whether the deduction permitted for tuition expenses primarily benefits those who send their children to religious schools. [T]he Minnesota tuition tax deduction is not available to *all* parents, but only to parents whose children attend schools that charge tuition, which are comprised almost entirely of sectarian schools. More importantly, the assistance that flows to parochial schools as a result of the tax benefit is not restricted, and cannot be restricted, to the secular functions of those schools.

In my view, Minnesota's tax deduction for the cost of textbooks and other instructional materials is also constitutionally infirm. The majority is simply mistaken in concluding that a tax deduction, unlike a tax credit or a direct grant to parents, promotes religious education in a manner that is only "attenuated." A tax deduction has a primary effect that advances religion if it is provided to offset expenditures which are not restricted to the secular activities of parochial schools.

There can be little doubt that the State of Minnesota intended to provide, and has provided, "[s]ubstantial aid to the educational function of [church-related] schools," and that the tax deduction for tuition and other educational expenses "necessarily results in aid to the sectarian school enterprise as a whole." It is beside the point that the State may have legitimate secular reasons for providing such aid. In focusing upon the contributions made by church-related schools, the majority has lost sight of the issue before us in this case.

For the first time, the Court has upheld financial support for religious schools without any reason at all to assume that the support will be restricted to the secular functions of those schools and will not be used to support religious instruction. This result is flatly at odds with the fundamental principle that a State may provide no financial support whatsoever to promote religion. As the Court stated in *Everson,* and has often repeated,

"No tax in any amount, large or small, can be levied to support any religious activities or institutions, whatever they may be called, or whatever form they may adopt to teach or practice religion."

I dissent.

Abington School Dist. v. Schempp
374 U.S. 203 (1963)

MR. JUSTICE CLARK delivered the opinion of the Court.

Once again we are called upon to consider the scope of the provision of the First Amendment to the United States Constitution which declares that "Congress shall make no law respecting an establishment of religion, or prohibiting the free exercise thereof. . . . " These companion cases present the issues in the context of state action requiring that schools begin each day with readings from the Bible. While raising the basic questions under slightly different factual situations, the cases permit of joint treatment. In light of the history of the First Amendment and of our cases interpreting and applying its requirements, we hold that the practices at issue and the laws requiring them are unconstitutional under the Establishment Clause, as applied to the States through the Fourteenth Amendment.

I

The Facts in Each Case: No. 142. The Commonwealth of Pennsylvania by law requires that "At least ten verses from the Holy Bible shall be read, without comment, at the opening of each public school on each school day. Any child shall be excused from such Bible reading, or attending such Bible reading, upon the written request of his parent or guardian." The Schempp family, husband and wife and two of their three children, brought suit to enjoin enforcement of the statute, contending that their rights under the Fourteenth Amendment to the Constitution of the United States are, have been, and will continue to be violated unless this statute be declared unconstitutional as violative of these provisions of the First Amendment.

No. 119. In 1905 the Board of School Commissioners of Baltimore City adopted a rule pursuant to the Annotated Code of Maryland. The rule provided for the holding of opening exercises in the schools of the city, consisting primarily of the "reading, without comment, of a chapter in the Holy Bible and/or the use of the Lord's Prayer." The petitioners, Mrs. Madalyn Murray and her son, William J. Murray III, are both professed atheists. Following unsuccessful attempts to have the respondent school board rescind the rule, this suit was filed for mandamus to compel its rescission and cancellation.

V

The wholesome "neutrality" of which this Court's cases speak thus stems from a recognition of the teachings of history that powerful sects or strong groups might bring about a fusion of governmental and religious functions or a concert or dependency of one upon the other to the end that official support of the State or Federal Government would be placed behind the tenets of one or of all orthodoxies. This the Establishment Clause prohibits. And a further reason for neutrality is found in the Free Exercise Clause, which recognizes the value of religious training, teaching and observance and, more particularly, the right of every person to freely choose his own course with reference thereto, free of any compulsion from the state. This the Free Exercise Clause guarantees. Thus, as we have seen, the two clauses may overlap. As we have indicated, the Establishment Clause has been directly considered by this Court eight times in the past score of years and, with only one Justice dissenting on the point, it has consistently held that the clause withdrew all legislative power respecting religious belief or the expression thereof. The test may be stated as follows: what are the purpose and the primary effect of the enactment? If either is the advancement or inhibition of religion then the enactment exceeds the scope of legislative power as circumscribed by the Constitution. That is to say that to withstand the strictures of the Establishment Clause there must be a secular legislative purpose and a primary effect that neither advances nor inhibits religion. The Free Exercise Clause, likewise considered many times here, withdraws from legislative power, state and federal, the exertion of any restraint on the free exercise of religion. Its purpose is to secure religious liberty in the individual by prohibiting any invasions thereof by civil authority. Hence it is necessary in a free exercise case for one to show the coercive effect of the enactment as it operates against him in the practice of his religion. The distinction between the two clauses is apparent—a violation of the Free Exercise Clause is predicated on coercion while the Establishment Clause violation need not be so attended.

Applying the Establishment Clause principles to the cases at bar we find that the States are requiring the selection and reading at the opening of the school day of verses from the Holy Bible and the recitation of the Lord's Prayer by the students in unison. These exercises are prescribed as part of the curricular activities of students who are required by law to attend school. They are held in the school buildings under the supervision and with the participation of teachers employed in those schools. The trial court in No. 142 has found that such an opening exercise is a religious ceremony and was intended by the State to be so. We agree with the trial court's finding as to the religious character of the exercises. Given that finding, the exercises and the law requiring them are in violation of the Establishment Clause.

There is no such specific finding as to the religious character of the exercises in No. 119, and the State contends (as does the State in No. 142) that the program is an effort to extend its benefits to all public school children without regard to their religious belief. Included within its secular purposes, it says, are the promotion of moral values, the contradiction to the materialistic trends of our times, the perpetuation of our institutions and the teaching of literature. But even if its purpose is not strictly religious, it is sought to be accomplished through readings, without comment, from the Bible. Surely the place of the Bible as an instrument of religion cannot be gainsaid, and the State's recognition of the pervading religious character of the ceremony is evident from the rule's specific permission of the alternative use of the Catholic Douay version as well as the recent amendment permitting nonattendance at the exercises. None of these factors is consistent with the contention that the Bible is here used either as an instrument for nonreligious moral inspiration or as a reference for the teaching of secular subjects.

The conclusion follows that in both cases the laws require religious exercises and such exercises are being conducted in direct violation of the rights of the appellees and petitioners. Nor are these required exercises mitigated by the fact that individual students may absent themselves upon parental request, for that fact furnishes no defense to a claim of unconstitutionality under the Establishment Clause. Further, it is no defense to urge that the religious practices here may be relatively minor encroachments on the First Amendment. The breach of neutrality that is today a trickling stream may all too soon become a raging torrent and, in the words of Madison, "it is proper to take alarm at the first experiment on our liberties."

It is insisted that unless these religious exercises are permitted a "religion of secularism" is established in the schools. We agree of course that the State may not establish a "religion of secularism" in the sense of affirmatively opposing or showing hostility to religion, thus "preferring those who believe in no religion over those who do believe." We do not agree, however, that this decision in any sense has that effect. In addition, it might well be said that one's education is not complete without a study of comparative religion or the history of religion and its relationship to the advancement of civilization. It certainly may be said that the Bible is worthy of study for its literary and historic qualities. Nothing we have said here indicates that such study of the Bible or of religion, when presented objectively as part of a secular program of education, may not be effected consistently with the First Amendment. But the exercises here do not fall into those categories. They are religious exercises, required by the States in violation of the command of the First Amendment that the Government maintain strict neutrality, neither aiding nor opposing religion.

Finally, we cannot accept that the concept of neutrality, which does not permit a State to require a religious exercise even with the consent of the majority of those affected, collides with the majority's right to free exercise of religion. While the Free Exercise Clause clearly prohibits the use of state action to deny the rights of free exercise to *anyone,* it has never meant that a majority could use the machinery of the State to practice its beliefs.

The place of religion in our society is an exalted one, achieved through a long tradition of reliance on the home, the church and the inviolable citadel of the individual heart and mind. We have come to recognize through bitter experience that it is not within the power of government to invade that citadel, whether its purpose or effect be to aid or oppose, to advance or retard. In the relationship between man and religion, the State is firmly committed to a position of neutrality. Though the application of that rule requires interpretation of a delicate sort, the rule itself is clearly and concisely stated in the words of the First Amendment. Applying that rule to the facts of these cases, we affirm the judgment in No. 142. In No. 119, the judgment is reversed and the cause remanded to the Maryland Court of Appeals for further proceedings consistent with this opinion.

Florey v. Sioux Falls School Dist. 49–5
619 F. 2d 1311 (1980)

I

In response to complaints that public school Christmas assemblies in 1977 and prior years constituted religious exercises, the School Board of Sioux Falls, South Dakota, set up a citizens' committee to study the relationship between church and state as applied to school functions. The committee's deliberations, which lasted for several months, culminated in the formulation of a policy statement and set of rules outlining the bounds of permissible school activity. After a public hearing, the School Board adopted the policy statement and rules recommended by the committee.

The appellants brought suit for declaratory and injunctive relief, alleging that the policy statement and the rules adopted by the School Board violate the Establishment and Free Exercise Clauses of the First Amendment to the United States Constitution. The district court reviewed the practices of the Sioux Falls School District and found that the 1977 Christmas program that was the subject of the initial complaints "exceeded the boundaries of what is constitutionally permissible under the Establishment Clause." The court also found, however, that programs similar to the 1977 Christmas program would not be permitted under the new School Board guidelines and concluded that the new rules, if properly administered and narrowly construed, would not run afoul of the First Amendment.

II

The close relationship between religion and American history and culture has frequently been recognized by the Supreme Court of the United States. Nevertheless, the First Amendment to the Constitution explicitly prescribes the relationship between religion and government: "Congress shall make no law respecting an establishment of religion, or prohibiting the free exercise thereof * * *." This apparently straightforward prohibition can rarely be applied to a given situation with ease, however. As the Supreme Court has noted, "total separation [between church and state] is not possible in an absolute sense." As a result, the Court has developed a three-part test for determining when certain governmental activity falls within the constitutional boundaries:

"First, the [activity] must have a secular * * * purpose; second, its principal or primary effect must be one that neither advances nor inhibits religion, * * * finally, the [activity] must not foster "an excessive governmental entanglement with religion."

A. Purpose

The appellants' contention that the School Board's adoption of the policy and rules was motivated by religious considerations is unsupportable. The record shows that the citizens' committee was formed and the rules drawn up in response to complaints that Christmas observances in some of the schools in the district contained religious exercises. The motivation behind the rules, therefore, was simply to ensure that no religious exercise was a part of officially sanctioned school activities. This conclusion is supported by the opening words of the policy statement: "It is accepted that no religious belief or non-belief should be promoted by the school district or its employees, and none should be disparaged." The statement goes on to affirmatively declare the purpose behind the rules:

> The Sioux Falls School District recognizes that one of its educational goals is to advance the students' knowledge and appreciation of the role that our religious heritage has played in the social, cultural and historical development of civilization.

The express language of the rules also leads to the conclusion that they were not promulgated with the intent to serve a religious purpose.

Thus, although the rules permit the schools to observe holidays that have both a secular and a religious basis, we need not conclude that the School Board acted with unconstitutional motives. To the contrary, we agree with the district court's finding that the School Board did not adopt the policy statement and rules for the purpose of advancing or inhibiting religion.

B. Effect

The appellants contend that, notwithstanding the actual intent of the School Board, the "principal or primary effect" of the rules is to either advance or inhibit religion. We cannot agree. The First Amendment does not forbid all mention of religion in public schools; it is the *advancement* or *inhibition* of religion that is prohibited. Hence, the *study* of religion is not forbidden "when presented objectively as part of a secular program of education." We view the term "study" to include more than mere classroom instruction; public performance may be a legitimate part of secular study. This does not mean, of course, that religious ceremonies can be performed in the public schools under the guise of "study." It does mean, however, that when the primary purpose served by a given school activity is secular, that activity is not made unconstitutional by the inclusion of some religious content. As the district court noted in its discussion of Rule 3, "[t]o allow students *only* to study and *not* to perform [religious art, literature and music when] such works * * * have developed an independent secular and artistic significance would give students a truncated view of our culture."

To determine whether religion is advanced or inhibited by the rules, then, we must look to see if a genuine "secular program of education" is furthered by the rules. It is unquestioned that public school students may be taught about the customs and cultural heritage of the United States and other countries. This is the principal effect of the rules. They allow the presentation of material that, although of religious origin, has taken on an independent meaning.

The district court expressly found that much of the art, literature and music associated with traditional holidays, particularly Christmas, has "acquired a significance which is no longer confined to the religious sphere of life. It has become integrated into our national culture and heritage." Furthermore, the rules guarantee that all material used has secular or cultural significance: Only holidays with both religious and secular bases may be observed; music, art, literature and drama may be included in the curriculum only if presented in a prudent and objective manner and only as a part of the cultural and religious heritage of the holiday; and religious symbols may be used only as a teaching aid or resource and only if they are displayed as a part of the cultural and religious heritage of the holiday and are temporary in nature. Since all programs and materials authorized by the rules must deal with the secular or cultural basis or heritage of the holidays and since the materials must be presented in a prudent and objective manner and symbols used as a teaching aid, the advancement of a "secular program of education," and not of religion, is the primary effect of the rules.

C. Entanglement

The appellants contend that the new guidelines in Sioux Falls unconstitutionally "foster 'an excessive government entanglement with religion.' " All the Supreme Court cases cited by the appellants in support of the "entanglement" test deal with governmental aid to sectarian institutions, not with the permissible scope of activity in the public schools. In the present case, by contrast, the school district is called upon to determine whether a given activity is religious. This type of decision inheres in every curriculum choice and would be faced by school administrators and teachers even if the rules did not exist. Indeed, the rules are guidelines designed to aid in the decisionmaking process. Rather than entangling the schools in religion, the rules provide the means to ensure that the district steers clear of religious exercises. We think the district court was correct in finding that the new rules do not unconstitutionally entangle the Sioux Falls school district in religion or religious institutions.

III

The appellants also contend that implementation of the policy and rules of the Sioux Falls School Board should be enjoined because the rules violate the Free Exercise Clause of the First Amendment. This contention does not withstand scrutiny.

The public schools are not required to delete from the curriculum all materials that may offend any religious sensibility.

These inevitable conflicts with the individual beliefs of some students or their parents, in the absence of an Establishment Clause violation, do not necessarily require the prohibition of a school activity. On the other hand, forcing any person to participate in an activity that offends his religious or nonreligious beliefs will generally contravene the Free Exercise Clause, even without an Establishment Clause violation. In this case, however, the Sioux Falls School Board recognized that problem and expressly provided that students may be excused from activities authorized by the rules if they so choose.

IV

We recognize that this opinion affirming the district court will not resolve for all times, places or circumstances the question of when Christmas carols, or other music or drama having religious themes, can be sung or performed by students in elementary and secondary public schools without offending the First Amendment. The constitutionality of any particular school activity conducted pursuant to the rules, in association with any particular holiday, cannot be determined unless and until there is a specific challenge, supported by evidence, to the school district's implementation of the rules. We simply hold, on the basis of the record before us, that the policy and rules adopted by the Sioux Falls Board of Education are not violative of the First Amendment.

For the foregoing reasons, the judgment of the district court is affirmed.

McMILLIAN, Circuit Judge, dissenting.

First, I am not totally persuaded that the policy and rules reflect a clearly secular legislative purpose. It cannot be overlooked that complaints about the religious content of several Christmas assemblies prompted the formation of the citizens' advisory committee and the adoption of the policy and rules by the school board. Against this background I am inclined to view the school board's rejection of the proposed "secular aspects only" amendment as indicative of a purpose to permit more than the study (including performance when appropriate) of religion, subjects with religious content or significance and religious traditions. In addition, the rules refer exclusively to "religious holidays." No doubt this singular orientation reflects the non-existence of agnostic or atheistic occasions. The rules do not address the observance of *non-religious* holidays. To the extent the policy and rules focus only on religious holidays, I would find the policy and rules unconstitutionally operate as a preference of religion.

Like the majority, I too accept "the thrust of these rules to be the advancement of the students' knowledge of society's cultural and religious heritage." I do not deny that knowledge of society's cultural and religious heritage and the encouragement of tolerance (religious and other kinds) and mutual understanding are admirable secular goals. However, I find several problems in the relationship between the rules and these secular goals. First, I do not understand how the *observance* of religious holidays promotes these secular goals. Moreover, I do not understand how the observance of particular religious holidays (*i. e.* Christian and Jewish holidays) but not others encourages student knowledge and appreciation of religious and cultural diversity. For example, the observance of the holidays of religions less familiar to most American public school children than either Christian or Jewish holidays would seem more likely to increase student knowledge and promote religious tolerance.

Second, even assuming the observance of religious holidays does advance these secular goals, those secular goals can be achieved in public education without the "observance" of religious holidays.

Here the school district seeks to accomplish secular goals by religious means, the observance of religious holidays. Surely the school district can advance student knowledge and tolerance of religious diversity as effectively by *non* religious means, that is, through the study of comparative religions or as part of the history or social studies curriculum. In any case, the observance of religious holidays as a means of accomplishing the secular goals of knowledge and tolerance clearly discriminates against non-belief.

Second, do the rules, particularly to the extent they permit the preparation and presentation of Christmas assemblies, have a principal or primary effect which either advances or inhibits religion? Unlike the majority, I think they do. Christmas assemblies have a substantial impact, both in favor of one religion and against other religions and nonbelief, on the school district employees, the students, the parents and relatives of the students and the community.

Third, I think the rules necessarily foster an excessive entanglement of the school district with religion. As noted by the majority, the rules call upon the school district to determine whether a given activity is religious.

As in the case of financial aid to parochial schools, proponents in favor of religious holiday observances, opponents against religious holiday observances and advocates for specific religious (or non-religious) holidays will engage in considerable political activity either to elect school board members whose views are compatible with their own views or to influence the school board.

It would be unrealistic to ignore the fact that many people confronted with issues of this kind will find their votes aligned with their faith.

Ordinarily political debate and division, however vigorous or even partisan, are normal and healthy manifestations of our democratic system of government, but political division along religious lines was one of the principal evils against which the First Amendment was intended to protect. The potential divisiveness of such conflict is a threat to the normal political process.

Of course, "every vestige, however slight, of cooperation or accommodation between religion and government" is *not* unconstitutional. There is nothing unconstitutional about the use of religious subjects or materials in public schools *as long as it is presented as part of a secular program of education.* However, to the extent the policy and rules adopted by the Sioux Falls School District authorizes the observance of religious holidays, particularly Christmas assemblies, in a manner other than as part of a secular program of education, I would hold the policy and rules violate the Establishment Clause.

It is implicit in the history and character of American public education that the public schools serve a uniquely *public* function: the training of American citizens in an atmosphere free of parochial, divisive, or separatist influences of any sort—an atmosphere in which children may assimilate a heritage common to all American groups and religions. This is a heritage neither theistic nor atheistic, but simply civic and patriotic.

I would reverse the judgment of the district court.

Wallace v. Jaffree
83–812
1985

JUSTICE STEVENS delivered the opinion of the Court.

At an early stage of this litigation, the constitutionality of three Alabama statutes was questioned: (1) § 16-1-20, enacted in 1978, which authorized a one-minute period of silence in all public schools "for meditation"; (2) § 16-1-20.1, enacted in 1981, which authorized a period of silence "for meditation or voluntary prayer"; and (3) § 16-1-20.2, enacted in 1982, which authorized teachers to lead "willing students" in a prescribed prayer to "Almighty God . . . the Creator and Supreme Judge of the world."

At the preliminary-injunction stage of this case, the District Court distinguished § 16-1-20 from the other two statutes. It then held that there was "nothing wrong" with § 16-1-20, but that § 16-1-20.1 and § 16-1-20.2 were both invalid because the sole purpose of both was "an effort on the part of the State of Alabama to encourage a religious activity." After the trial on the merits, the District Court did not change its interpretation of these two statutes, but held that they were constitutional because, in its opinion, Alabama has the power to establish a state religion if it chooses to do so.

The Court of Appeals agreed with the District Court's initial interpretation of the purpose of both § § 16-1-20.1 and 16-1-20.2, and held them both unconstitutional. We have already affirmed the Court of Appeals' holding with respect to § 16-1-20.2. Moreover, appellees have not questioned the holding that § 16-1-20 is valid. Thus, the narrow question for decision is whether § 16-1-20.1, which authorizes a period of silence for "meditation or voluntary prayer," is a law respecting the establishment of religion within the meaning of the First Amendment.

I

In its lengthy conclusions of law, the District Court reviewed a number of opinions of this Court interpreting the Establishment Clause of the First Amendment, and then embarked on a fresh examination of the question whether the First Amendment imposes any barrier to the establishment of an official religion by the State of Alabama. After reviewing at length what it perceived to be newly discovered historical evidence, the District Court concluded that "the establishment clause of the first amendment to the United States Constitution does not prohibit the state from establishing a religion." In a separate opinion, the District Court dismissed appellees' challenge to the three Alabama statutes because of a failure to state any claim for which relief could be granted. The court's dismissal of this challenge was also based on its conclusion that the Establishment Clause did not bar the States from establishing a religion.

The Court of Appeals consolidated the two cases; not surprisingly, it reversed. The Court of Appeals noted that this Court had considered and had rejected the historical arguments that the District Court found persuasive, and that the District Court had misapplied the doctrine of *stare decisis*. The Court of Appeals then held that the teachers' religious activities violated the Establishment Clause of the First Amendment. With respect to § 16-1-20.1 and § 16-1-20.2, the Court of Appeals stated that "both statutes advance and encourage religious activities." The Court of Appeals then quoted with approval the District Court's finding that § 16-1-20.1, and § 16-1-20.2, were efforts "to encourage a religious activity. Even though these statutes are permissive in form, it is nevertheless state involvement respecting an establishment of religion."

II

Our unanimous affirmance of the Court of Appeals' judgment concerning § 16-1-20.2 makes it unnecessary to comment at length on the District Court's remarkable conclusion that the Federal Constitution imposes no obstacle to Alabama's establishment of a state religion. Before analyzing the precise issue that is presented to us, it is nevertheless appropriate to recall how firmly embedded in our constitutional jurisprudence is the proposition that the several States have no greater power to restrain the individual freedoms protected by the First Amendment than does the Congress of the United States.

As is plain from its text, the First Amendment was adopted to curtail the power of Congress to interfere with the individual's freedom to believe, to worship, and to express himself in accordance with the dictates of his own conscience. Until the Fourteenth Amendment was added to the Constitution, the First Amendment's restraints on the exercise of federal power simply did not apply to the States. But when the Constitution was amended to prohibit any State from depriving any person of liberty without due process of law, that

Amendment imposed the same substantive limitations on the States' power to legislate that the First Amendment had always imposed on the Congress' power. This Court has confirmed and endorsed this elementary proposition of law time and time again.

III

When the Court has been called upon to construe the breadth of the Establishment Clause, it has examined the criteria developed over a period of many years. Thus, in *Lemon* v. *Kurtzman* (1971), we wrote:

> "Every analysis in this area must begin with consideration of the cumulative criteria developed by the Court over many years. Three such tests may be gleaned from our cases. First, the statute must have a secular legislative purpose; second, its principal or primary effect must be one that neither advances nor inhibits religion; finally, the statute must not foster 'an excessive government entanglement with religion.'"

It is the first of these three criteria that is most plainly implicated by this case. As the District Court correctly recognized, no consideration of the second or third criteria is necessary if a statute does not have a clearly secular purpose. For even though a statute that is motivated in part by a religious purpose may satisfy the first criterion, the First Amendment requires that a statute must be invalidated if it is entirely motivated by a purpose to advance religion.

In applying the purpose test, it is appropriate to ask "whether government's actual purpose is to endorse or disapprove of religion." In this case, the answer to that question is dispositive. For the record not only provides us with an unambiguous affirmative answer, but it also reveals that the enactment of § 16-1-20.1 was not motivated by any clearly secular purpose—indeed, the statute had *no* secular purpose.

IV

The sponsor of the bill that became § 16-1-20.1, Senator Donald Holmes, inserted into the legislative record—apparently without dissent—a statement indicating that the legislation was an "effort to return voluntary prayer" to the public schools. Later Senator Holmes confirmed this purpose before the District Court. In response to the question whether he had any purpose for the legislation other than returning voluntary prayer to public schools, he stated, "No, I did not have no other purpose in mind." The State did not present evidence of *any* secular purpose.

The unrebutted evidence of legislative intent contained in the legislative record and in the testimony of the sponsor of § 16-1-20.1 is confirmed by a consideration of the relationship between this statute and the two other measures that were considered in this case. The District Court found that the 1981 statute and its 1982 sequel had a common, nonsecular purpose. The wholly religious character of the later enactment is plainly evident from its text. When the differences between § 16-1-20.1 and its 1978 predecessor, § 16-1-20, are examined, it is equally clear that the 1981 statute has the same wholly religious character.

The legislative intent to return prayer to the public schools is, of course, quite different from merely protecting every student's right to engage in voluntary prayer during an appropriate moment of silence during the school day. The 1978 statute already protected that right, containing nothing that prevented any student from engaging in voluntary prayer during a silent minute of meditation. Appellants have not identified any secular purpose that was not fully served by § 16-1-20 before the enactment of § 16-1-20.1. Thus, only two conclusions are consistent with the text of § 16-1-20.1: (1) the statute was enacted to convey a message of State endorsement and promotion of prayer; or (2) the statute was enacted for no purpose. No one suggests that the statute was nothing but a meaningless or irrational act.

We must, therefore, conclude that the Alabama Legislature intended to change existing law and that it was motivated by the sole purpose of expressing the State's endorsement of prayer activities for one minute at the beginning of each school day. The addition of "or voluntary prayer" indicates that the State intended to characterize prayer as a favored practice. Such an endorsement is not consistent with the established principle that the Government must pursue a course of complete neutrality toward religion.

The importance of that principle does not permit us to treat this as an inconsequential case involving nothing more than a few words of symbolic speech on behalf of the political majority. For whenever the State itself speaks on a religious subject, one of the questions that we must ask is "whether the Government intends to convey a message of endorsement or disapproval of religion." The well-supported concurrent findings of the District Court and the Court of Appeals—that § 16-1-20.1 was intended to convey a message of State-approval of prayer activities in the public schools—make it unnecessary, and indeed inappropriate, to evaluate the practical significance of the addition of the words "or voluntary prayer" to the statute. Keeping in mind, as we must, "both the fundamental place held by the Establishment Clause in our constitutional scheme and the myriad, subtle ways in which Establishment Clause values can be eroded," we conclude that § 16-1-20.1 violates the First Amendment.

The judgment of the Court of Appeals is affirmed.

JUSTICE REHNQUIST, dissenting.

*   *   *   *   *   *

It would seem from this evidence that the Establishment Clause of the First Amendment had acquired a well-accepted meaning: it forbade establishment of a national religion, and forbade preference among religious sects or denominations. The Establishment Clause did not require government neutrality between religion and irreligion nor did it prohibit the federal government from providing non-discriminatory aid to religion. There is simply no historical foundation for the proposition that the Framers intended to build the "wall of separation" that was constitutionalized in *Everson.*

Notwithstanding the absence of an historical basis for this theory of rigid separation, the wall idea might well have served as a useful albeit misguided analytical concept, had it led this court to unified and principled results in Establishment Clause cases. The opposite, unfortunately, has been true; in the 38 years since *Everson* our Establishment Clause cases have been neither principled nor unified. Our recent opinions, many of them hopelessly divided pluralities, have with embarrassing candor conceded that the "wall of separation" is merely a "blurred, indistinct, and variable barrier," which "is not wholly accurate" and can only be "dimly perceived."

But the greatest injury of the "wall" notion is its mischievous diversion of judges from the actual intentions of the drafters of the Bill of Rights. The "wall of separation between church and State" is a metaphor based on bad history, a metaphor which has proved useless as a guide to judging. It should be frankly and explicitly abandoned.

The Court has more recently attempted to add some mortar to *Everson's* wall through the three-part test of *Lemon* v. *Kurtzman,* which served at first to offer a more useful test for purposes of the Establishment Clause than did the "wall" metaphor. Generally stated, the *Lemon* test proscribes state action that has a sectarian purpose or effect, or causes an impermissible governmental entanglement with religion.

[T]he *Lemon* test has no more grounding in the history of the First Amendment than does the wall theory upon which it rests. The three-part test represents a determined effort to craft a workable rule from an historically faulty doctrine; but the rule can only be as sound as the doctrine it attempts to service. The three-part test has simply not provided adequate standards for deciding Establishment Clause cases, as this Court has slowly come to realize. Even worse, the *Lemon* test has caused this Court to fracture into unworkable plurality opinions, depending upon how each of the three factors applies to a certain state action. The results from our school services cases show the difficulty we have encountered in making the *Lemon* test yield principled results.

For example, a State may lend to parochial school children geography textbooks that contain maps of the United States, but the State may not lend maps of the United States for use in geography class. A State may lend textbooks on American colonial history, but it may not lend a film on George Washington, or a film projector to show it in history class. A State may lend classroom workbooks, but may not lend workbooks in which the parochial school children write, thus rendering them nonreusable. A State may pay for bus transportation to religious schools but may not pay for bus transportation from the parochial school to the public zoo or natural history museum for a field trip. A State may pay for diagnostic services conducted in the parochial school but therapeutic services must be given in a different building; speech and hearing "services" conducted by the State inside the sectarian school are forbidden, but the State may conduct speech and hearing diagnostic testing inside the sectarian school. Exceptional parochial school students may receive outside counseling, but it must take place outside of the parochial school, such as in a trailer parked down the street. A State may give cash to a parochial school to pay for the administration of State-written tests and state-ordered reporting services, but it may not provide funds for teacher-prepared tests on secular subjects. Religious instruction may not be given in public school, but the public school may release students during the day for religion classes elsewhere, and may enforce attendance at those classes with its truancy laws.

These results violate the historically sound principle "that the Establishment Clause does not forbid governments . . . to [provide] general welfare under which benefits are distributed to private individuals, even though many of those individuals may elect to use those benefits in ways that 'aid' religious instruction or worship." It is not surprising in the light of this record that our most recent opinions have expressed doubt on the usefulness of the *Lemon* test.

If a constitutional theory has no basis in the history of the amendment it seeks to interpret, is difficult to apply and yields unprincipled results, I see little use in it. The "crucible of litigation" has produced only consistent unpredictability, and today's effort is just a continuation of "the sisyphean task of trying to patch together the 'blurred, indistinct and variable barrier' described in *Lemon v. Kurtzman.*" We have done much straining since 1947, but still we admit that we can only "dimly perceive" the *Everson* wall. Our perception has been clouded not by the Constitution but by the mists of an unnecessary metaphor.

The true meaning of the Establishment Clause can only be seen in its history. As drafters of our Bill of Rights, the Framers inscribed the principles that control today. Any deviation from their intentions frustrates the permanence of that Charter and will only lead to the type of unprincipled decisionmaking that has plagued our Establishment Clause cases since *Everson.*

The Framers intended the Establishment Clause to prohibit the designation of any church as a "national" one. The Clause was also designed to stop the Federal Government from asserting a preference for one religious denomination or sect over others. Given the "incorporation" of the Establishment Clause as against the States via the Fourteenth Amendment in *Everson,* States are prohibited as well from establishing a religion or discriminating between sects. As its history abundantly shows, however, nothing in the Establishment Clause requires government to be strictly neutral between religion and irreligion, nor does that Clause prohibit Congress or the States from pursuing legitimate secular ends through nondiscriminatory sectarian means.

The Court strikes down the Alabama statute in *Wallace v. Jaffree,* because the State wished to "endorse prayer as a favored practice." It would come as much of a shock to those who drafted the Bill of Rights as it will to a large number of thoughtful Americans today to learn that the Constitution, as construed by the majority, prohibits the Alabama Legislature from "endorsing" prayer. George Washington himself, at the request of the very Congress which passed the Bill of Rights, proclaimed a day of "public thanksgiving and prayer, to be observed by acknowledging with grateful hearts the many and signal favors of Almighty God." History must judge whether it was the father of his country in 1789, or a majority of the Court today, which has strayed from the meaning of the Establishment Clause.

The State surely has a secular interest in regulating the manner in which public schools are conducted. Nothing in the Establishment Clause of the First Amendment, properly understood, prohibits any such generalized "endorsement" of prayer. I would therefore reverse the judgment of the Court of Appeals in *Wallace v. Jaffree.*

NOTES

1. Sam Drucker, *The Public Schools and Religion* (New York: Harper and Row, 1966), pp. 15–16.
2. Lawrence Byrnes, *Religion and Public Education* (New York: Harper and Row, 1975), p. 54.
3. Id., pp. 50–51.

4. Zorach v. Clauson, 343 U.S. 306 (1952) at 313–14.
5. Engle v. Vitale, 370 U.S. 421 (1962) at 431.
6. Christiane Hyde Citron, "Consistent Inconsistency: Supreme Court Decisions on Public Aid to Private Education," *ECS Law and Education Center Footnotes,* no. 8 (October 1981), 9–10.
7. Cantwell v. Connecticut, 310 U.S. 296 (1940) at 303–304.
8. Cochran v. Louisiana Board of Education, 281 U.S. 370 (1930) at 374–75.
9. Everson v. Board of Education, 330 U.S. 1 (1947) at 15–16.
10. Id. at 17–18.
11. Id. at 24.
12. Id. at 31 and 33.
13. Board of Education v. Allen, 392 U.S. 236 (1968) at 252.
14. Lemon v. Kurtzman, 403 U.S. 602 (1971) at 612.
15. Grand Rapids v. Ball, Slip Opinion No. 83–237 (1985) at 19.
16. Id. at 23–34.
17. People of State of Ill. ex rel. McCullom v. Board of Education of School District No. 71, Champaign County, 333 U.S. 203 (1948) at 212.
18. Zorach v. Clauson at 311–14.
19. Id. at 315.
20. *Engle* at 430–31.
21. School District of Abington Township v. Schempp and Murray v. Curlett, 374 U.S. 203 (1963) at 225.
22. Stone v. Graham, 449 U.S. 39 (1980) at 39–40.
23. Florey et al. v. Sioux Falls Schools Dist. No. 49-5, 619 F. 2d 1311 (1980) at 1316 and 1314.
24. Id. at 1326 and 1324.
25. Wallace v. Jaffree, Slip Opinion No. 83–812 (1985) at 21.
26. Id., O'Connor concurrence at 11.
27. Epperson v. Arkansas, 393 U.S. 97 (1968) at 104.
28. McLean v. Arkansas Board of Education, 529 F. Supp. 1255 (1982) at 1267.
29. Epperson at 106.
30. Jaffree v. James, 544 F. Supp. 727 (1982) at 732.

FOUR

Defining the Limits of First Amendment Rights of Expression

Following the religion clauses, the First Amendment goes on to forbid Congress from ''abridging the freedom of speech, or of the press; or the right of the people to peaceably assemble; or to petition the Government for a redress of grievances.'' Court doctrine governing freedom of speech and press prohibits both prior censorship and subsequent punishment for words disapproved by government authorities, absent libel, slander, or legal obscenity. Prior censorship is viewed more strictly than subsequent punishment, but both types of action must be defended by compelling reasons, rather than just a rational relationship to government objectives.

The Supreme Court has endowed the First Amendment with powerful efficacy. Justice Brandeis explained it like this in 1927:

> Fear of serious injury alone cannot justify suppression of free speech and assembly. Men feared witches and burned women. It is the function of speech to free men from the bondage of irrational fears. To justify suppression of free speech, there must be reasonable grounds to fear that serious evil will result if free speech is practiced. There must be reasonable grounds to believe that the evil to be prevented is a serious one. . . .
>
> If there be time to expose through discussion the falsehoods and fallacies, to avert the evil by the process of education, the remedy to be applied is more speech, not enforced silence.[1]

A few years earlier, Justice Holmes illustrated the limits of free speech by holding that "free speech would not protect a man in falsely shouting fire in a theatre and causing a panic." He went on to explain: "The question in every case is whether the words used are used in such circumstances and are of such a nature as to create a clear and present danger."[2]

While freedom of speech, the press, and association had been staunchly protected as vital to the informed, intelligent governance of a democratic society, only in recent decades has this attitude been applied to school affairs. Prior to that, the courts took a conservative, restraintist view of application of First Amendment rights to the public school. Policy governing the expression of personal views by teachers and students was considered the province of school board and administrator discretion. Attending a school, as well as holding a teaching position, was considered a privilege. This "privilege doctrine" allowed administrators and boards of education to exert enormous control over the personal and professional life of teachers. When teachers challenged the unreasonable restraint on them occasioned by regulations requiring abstinence from smoking, dancing, dating, or marriage, they were told they had a right to personal choice and expression, but no right to be a teacher. That was a privilege.

The attitude toward students was even more restrictive. Buttressed by the common-law principle of *in loco parentis,* teachers and administrators assumed virtually unrestricted control over students. Courts supported such restrictions on expression as speaking against school policy at a student-body meeting, joining a social fraternity, and requiring students to inform on others who wrote "dirty" words on a school wall.[3] Since public schooling was viewed as a "privilege," and the legal status of minors was weak at best, the courts would not seriously entertain student complaints about restrictions of their rights of expression.

The privilege doctrine was grounded in conservative theory, as well as court restraint. Such control was related to traditionally approved practice, and influenced by conservative educational philosophy, which viewed children's conduct as requiring strong control. It also supported the restraintist view of deference to the will of duly constituted authorities to decide what was right or wrong, proper or improper, in the conduct of public education.

This changed with the ascendancy of the Warren Court and the civil-rights revolution of the fifties and sixties, which were interactive influences on one another. The area of freedom of expression is illustrative of how the rights of teachers and students are intertwined. Just as the attitude pervading the courts and schools causes constraints on one group to reinforce constraints on the other, conference of rights to one group expands protections for the other.

Proceeding from issues of pure speech and press to those of symbolic speech and related concerns of association, dress, and grooming, teachers' academic freedom within and outside the classroom, and the censorship of school books, First Amendment rights have become a major school-law battleground. The opening round occurred in the forties. Two cases were decided by the Supreme Court in that decade involving the right of students to express themselves by withholding speech. Taken together, they exemplify the range of liberal-conservative and activist-restraintist attitudes, and the effect that the times and concerns of the larger society have on court judgments concerning educational policy.

In the first case (*Minersville* v. *Gobitis,* 1940), the Supreme Court considered the question of whether the state could compel students who were Jehovah's Witnesses to participate in the flag-salute exercise, which conflicted with their religious principles. In making its decision, the Court used the analytical model of the balancing test, in which the speech and religion rights of the Jehovah's Witnesses children were weighed against the legitimate interests of the state to promote and develop loyalty and patriotism. The fact that 1940 was a year of nationalist fervor preceding American entry into the Second World War certainly was an influence on the attitudes of the Supreme Court. The eight-to-one Court majority left no question about its restraintist approach to the conflict, holding:

> The wisdom of training children in patriotic impulses by those compulsions which necessarily pervade so much of the educational process is not for our independent judgment. . . . The courtroom is not the arena for debating issues of educational policy. It is not our province to choose among competing considerations in the subtle process of securing effective loyalty. . . . So to hold would in effect make us the school board for the country. That authority has not been given to this court, nor should we assume it.[4]

The restraintist philosophy was returned to later in the opinion:

> Judicial review, itself a limitation on popular government, is a fundamental part of our constitutional scheme. But to the legislature, no less than the courts, is committed the guardianship of deeply-cherished liberties. Where all the effective means of inducing political changes are left free from interference, education in the abandonment of foolish legislation is itself a training in liberty. To fight out the wise use of legislative authority in the forum of public opinion and before legislative assemblies rather than to transfer such a contest to the judicial arena, serves to vindicate the self-confidence of a free people.[5]

Operating on these principles, the Court decided that the national interests overrode the appeal for exemption based on First Amendment considerations of religion and speech. The lone dissent argued that the compulsory expression of collective loyalty was a poor reason to override individual constitutional freedoms of speech and religion.

Just three years later, the Supreme Court addressed the very same issue again, in *West Virginia* v. *Barnette* (1943). In this case, the Court broke with its own recent precedent and reversed itself, lifting the reasoning of the *Minersville* v. *Gobitis* dissent to the majority opinion. In an opinion replete with liberal, activist sentiment, the Court decided the application of First Amendment rights such as speech (and withholding speech) was at least as important in the school as it was elsewhere in society. The school was not insulated from the Constitution. Speaking for the majority, Justice Jackson issued a ringing statement of liberal belief in freeing people from arbitrary restraints on their reason and intelligence:

> If there is any fixed star in our constitutional constellation, it is that no official, higher or petty, can prescribe what shall be orthodox in politics, nationalism, religion, or other matters of opinion, or force citizens to confess by word or act their faith therein. If there are any circumstances which permit an exception, they do not now occur to us.[6]

As to the now-activist predilection of the Court, Jackson defended the Court in overruling the judgment of West Virginia legislators and education officials as follows:

> Nor does our duty to apply the Bill of Rights to assertions of official authority depend upon our possession of marked competence in the field where the invasion of rights occurs. . . . We cannot, because of modest estimates of our competence in such specialties as public education, withhold the judgment that history authenticates as the function of this court when liberty is infringed.[7]

First Amendment speech was clearly placed in the purview of liberties specially protected as fundamental within the scope of the Fourteenth Amendment responsibilities of state governments to their people. This required a state not only to show that its restriction was reasonable, but that the restriction involved a compelling state need or interest. Applying the compelling-interest test to the balance between the state's interest in developing patriotism and the students' preferred liberties of speech and religious freedom, the Court found compulsion to salute the flag *reasonable,* but not *compelling.* There were other ways to promote patriotism. Further, the liberally rational, activist position included a piece of liberal educational philosophy in holding:

> The Fourteenth Amendment, as now applied to the states, protects the citizen against the state itself and all of its creatures—Boards of Education not excepted. That they are educating the young for citizenship is reason for scrupulous protection of Constitutional freedoms of the individual, if we are not to strangle the free mind at its source and teach youth to discount important principles of government as mere platitudes.[8]

Years later, state and federal courts would apply the principles laid down in *Barnette* to issues of free expression for teachers that were not complicated by the religious issue. The action of a school board in dismissing regularly scheduled classes to allow student and teacher attendance at an antiwar rally was invalidated by a New York court, as such action compelled teachers and students to display their positions on the issue (*Nistad* v. *Board of Educ.,* 304 N.Y.S. 971 [1969]). Then, exactly thirty years after *Barnette,* the Supreme Court refused to review a decision in which a federal appellate court upheld a teacher's right to stand silently while another teacher conducted the flag ceremony. The court held that this action was a personal matter of conscience and "we ought not impugn the loyalty of a citizen . . . merely for refusing to pledge allegiance any more than we ought necessarily to praise the loyalty of a citizen who without conviction or meaning, and with mental reservation, recites the pledge by rote each morning."[9] Further, the court reasoned in *Russo* v. *Central School Dist.* (1972) that "the right to remain silent in face of an illegitimate demand for speech is as much a part of First Amendment protections as the right to speak out in the face of an illegitimate demand for silence."[10]

This liberal trend does not extend to extremes of complete license. Contrasting with *Russo* was *Palmer* v. *Board of Education of the City of Chicago,* 603 F. 2d 1271 (1979), cert. denied 444 U.S. 1026 (1980). A teacher refused to teach the pledge of allegiance, observe patriotic events, and celebrate holidays. The court acknowledged her right to personal belief, but not her right to impose those beliefs on the teaching program, in opposition to the prescribed curriculum. In much the same way, students' rights to say or not say what they please have been subjected to reasonable restraint. For example, boycotting classes, noisy protests disturbing a school, or walking out of school during the conduct of the regular programs, as an expression of the right not to tacitly support school activities to which they object, have not been upheld by the courts (*Hobson* v. *Bailey,* 309 F. Supp. 1393 [1970]; *Grayned* v. *Rockford,* 408 U.S. 104 [1972]; *Rhyne* v. *Childs,* 359 F. Supp. 1085 [1973]).

However, with the advent of the Warren Court, freedom-of-expression rights for teachers and students underwent great expansion, attended by greater definition of the political position of schools and their major actors. Administrators and board members were removed from their positions of almost unquestioned authority to one where they were forced to defend and explain their policies in regulating student and teacher behavior to extents that made their work perhaps more sensitive to constitutional theory, but much more difficult and complex. For example, school boards and administrators must now be cautious about the manner in which they expunge books from school libraries. Judgment about what books are to be excluded has become an educational liberal-conservative battleground refereed by the courts. The controversy turns on the fundamental issue of censorship.

The manner in which pure use of speech and press in the school has been viewed by the courts (as opposed to speech outside the school) provides a clear view of the ebb and flow of liberal-conservative, activist-restraintist sentiment. The same is true for those uses of expression that are removed from pure speech and press, as dress and grooming, other forms of symbolic expression, and personal-association rights. What are the permissible limits if we are to have orderly schools supportive of the goals of the community and nation, but that do not "strangle the free mind at its source and teach youth to discount important principles of government as mere platitudes?" Finally, there is the issue of academic freedom. How can we have an orderly, dependable teaching force that transmits knowledge consistent with the goals of government and the community if teachers are free to pursue educational goals according to their own preferences? On the other hand, can we expect rigorous pursuit of truth and knowledge if teachers are fearful that methods of inquiry or findings will displease authorities and lead to their disgrace and dismissal?

Principles Governing First Amendment Rights of Expression in Education

1. Freedom of speech and press is grounded in the American conviction that a free, democratic society cannot be maintained without full and free exchange of ideas, so that all views may be weighed in arriving at the best one.
2. Freedom of speech has been expanded by the Supreme Court to include symbolic expression.
3. Freedom of speech and press is not unlimited. Disruption of the educational process and jeopardizing health and safety are reasons for limiting it.
4. First Amendment rights are considered "fundamental" interests. Therefore, restrictions upon them require a showing of a *compelling* reason to do so, rather than just showing a rational basis for the action.
5. The "privilege" doctrine allowing almost complete authority over teacher and student expression has been replaced by the judicial "balancing of interests" test, in which the court weighs the needs of the state (school) in restricting expression against the rights of the individual to practice it.
6. Academic freedom invests teachers with rights of personal and professional expression of broad latitude, to prevent casting a "pall of orthodoxy" over the classroom, or removing from educational debate a most informed, interested group. However, academic freedom does not protect expression unrelated to the subject taught or inappropriate regarding student sex or age. Nor does it protect against disruption of education or serious damage to principal-teacher or school-community relations.
7. Rules restricting First Amendment rights must be characterized by clear, reasonable guidelines. Requirements for absolute, unrestrained prior censorship is an example of a rule falling afoul of the First Amendment. Rules based on intuition about possible disruption, rather than factual evidence, would similarly fail to meet First Amendment standards.
8. While school authorities, empowered by statute, may regulate the type of book allowed into the curriculum or library and books to be expunged from the curriculum, removing books from a library is more restricted. Libraries have "special characteristics" that require a showing of reasoned, unbiased deliberation about the educational unsuitability of books to be expunged.

SPEECH AND PRESS RIGHTS OF TEACHERS AND STUDENTS

Does involvement with public schooling, either as a teacher or student, place special constraints on freedom of speech or press, or should it provide special protection and privilege? How can freedom of speech and press be reconciled with the need for orderly control in schools and a unified pursuit of educational goals? At what point does the exercise of speech and press rights transcend the authority of school boards and administrators to set policy and maintain school order and control? How do the courts distinguish between "pure" speech and related concepts of "symbolic expression" and opinion even further removed from pure speech?

There were two major cases settled by the U.S. Supreme Court that provide many of the answers to these questions. Both were activist, liberal decisions. One dealt with the right of students to symbolic expression, seen as an attribute of free speech. The other dealt with teachers' rights to freedom of the press. Both were products of the changing times of the sixties, when liberalism and court activism were at high tide. In 1968, the Supreme Court decided *Pickering* v. *Board.* At issue was whether a school board was justified in firing a teacher for writing a letter published in a local newspaper criticizing his superintendent and school board for their spending decisions and for not informing the district citizens about their decisions. The Court applied the "balance of interests" test and decided that, since Pickering's letter had not disrupted the educational process, his right to freedom of speech outweighed any interest the board had in punishing him for exercising his freedom of the press. Thus died the "privilege doctrine," in which teachers were expected to relinquish their First Amendment rights at the pleasure of the school board and administrators. *Pickering* established that, henceforth, exercise of the civil right of expression for teachers would be balanced against the needs of the school to restrict such rights for the good of the public school and its mission. The teacher's right to speech and press was not absolute. If it seriously damaged relationships between superior and subordinate, was deliberately false and reckless, or impeded the conduct of education, the exercise of speech or press could be cause for dismissal. However, the burden of justification rested with the school authorities, who had to sustain not only a rational reason for the dismissal, but a compelling interest as well.

The second case involved student-speech rights, and occurred the year after *Pickering* was decided. In 1969, the Supreme Court delivered its opinion in *Tinker* v. *Des Moines.* The case considered whether students had the right to wear black armbands in school as a silent protest against the Vietnam War, even though the school administration had forbidden it. In its precedent-setting decision, the Court majority held that students had the right to engage in "symbolic speech" as an extension of pure speech. Students were persons protected by the Constitution, and school authorities may not restrict their civil rights without a compelling reason to do so. Such reason must be more than "undifferentiated fear or apprehension of disturbance." Rather, it must be based on evidence showing that the forbidden activity would "materially and substantially" interfere with school discipline and operation. Not only was the abandonment of the "privilege doctrine" applied to student rights, but the court bound the rights of students and teachers together as participants in the education process by announcing: "It can hardly be argued that either students or teachers shed their constitutional right to freedom of speech or expression at the schoolhouse gate."[11]

This divided decision brought a powerful dissent from the politically liberal Justice Black, who exhibited his conservative educational philosophy emphasizing adult authority over teaching methods, curriculum, and student behavior. In one of the sharp, incisive passages of his dissent, Black opined that the decision "subjects all the public schools of the country to the whims and caprices of their loudest-mouthed, but maybe not their brightest students."[12]

The progeny of *Pickering* and *Tinker* greatly expanded the "pure" speech and press rights of students and teachers, as well as related expression rights. However, as the liberal period of the Vietnam War and Civil Rights era waned, a conservative balance would be introduced.

Teachers' Speech and Press Rights

The freedom-of-press rights of teachers received a variety of elaborations. For example, in 1970, a federal district court considered the constitutionality of a school board's action in responding to a particular, limited problem that attended the general distribution of literature by banning all distribution of literature not strictly related to the curriculum. In *Friedman* v. *Union Free School Dist.*, 314 F. Supp. 223 (1970), the court held that this type of broad restriction to cope with a specific issue violates the freedom-of-press rights of teachers. In the related area of petition, a Vermont court held that a teacher could not be disciplined for promoting a petition within the school for a controversial political symposium, however poor the teacher's judgment may have been, since no material disruption resulted (*Petition of Davenport,* 283 A. 2d 452 [1971]).

The growth of teachers' unions in the years following *Pickering* occasioned another Supreme Court decision regarding teachers' press freedom in 1983 that involved a teachers' organization rather than an individual teacher. The *Perry* v. *Perry* decision introduced an element of conservative leavening into the area of teachers' press rights. The Perry School District allowed access to the internal mail system of the District to the approved teachers' collective-bargaining unit, as well as such groups as the Cub Scouts and YMCA. A rival teachers' union claimed denial of First Amendment rights because it was not permitted access to the mail system. In a five-to-four decision, the Court held that the restriction was permissible, since the District's mail system did not constitute an "open public forum," but rather was a "limited public forum" allowing for the exercise of the District's reasonable discretion as to which groups may be permitted access. Therefore, school authorities could bar access to a rival teachers' association as "a means of insuring labor peace within the schools. The policy serves to prevent the District's schools from becoming a battleground for inter-union squabbles."[13] The four-member dissenting minority focused on the issue of equal access rather than whether the District constituted an open or limited forum. They saw the crucial issue as being that, since the mail system had been opened for one teachers' union, rival unions should be given equal access to it.

Once access to a school's mail system is granted, what limitations does press freedom permit in regulating the use of that access? That was the question adjudicated in *Ysleta Fed. of Teachers* v. *Ysleta Indep. School Dist.*, 720 F. 2d 1429 (1983). The district granted union access to its internal mail system, but authorized the Superintendent to decide which mail would be permitted access, with authority to suspend the privilege if material was not submitted for clearance. The ruling was that while the district was not obliged to open its system to the union, once it did so it could not exercise unbridled discretion as to its use, since the mail system must then be viewed as a "public forum" for the union.

Two 1973 cases illustrate the manner in which *Pickering* and *Tinker* stimulated expanded free-speech protection for teachers. In *James* v. *Board of Educ. of Central Dist. No. 1,* 461 F. 2d 566 (1973), a federal appellate court upheld the right of a teacher to silently protest the Vietnam War by wearing a black armband, as had the Supreme Court supported the same right for students. In *Lusk* v. *Estes* (1973), a federal district court considered whether a teacher's firing for publicly criticizing Dallas schools and staff violated his speech rights. The criticisms received wide attention from the media and school parents, and were repeated in person to the school board and city council. The board fired Lusk for "public breach of ethics." In disallowing the dismissal, the court held that Lusk's opinions were germane to important public concerns. Therefore, in applying the balance-of-interests test, the judge decided that "society's interest in information concerning the operation of the schools far outweighs any strain on the teacher-principal relationship."[14]

What if such criticism were expressed in private? The Supreme Court considered that question in *Givhan* v. *Western Line Consolidated School Dist.*, 439 U.S. 410 (1979). A unanimous Court held that a teacher's private (even if overly rigorous) criticism of the principal and school policies, expressed in the privacy of the principal's office, cannot serve as the primary reason for firing the teacher. The teacher's right to free speech protected her from that, provided there were not other legitimate reasons for dismissal.

This latter point had been made clear in a 1977 Supreme Court decision that put some conservative balance into the context of teachers' First Amendment rights. In *Mt. Healthy* v. *Doyle,* 429 U.S. 274 (1977), the Court considered a teacher's claim that his firing was retaliation for criticizing the schools in a telephone call aired on a radio station. The Court noted that Doyle's dismissal was predicated upon a variety of actions, including altercations with students and teachers, making an obscene gesture to a female student, *and* the call to the radio station. The Court held that a teacher cannot find safety from dismissal for a constitutionally protected act, if there were additional infractions not so protected that justified the dismissal.

In 1983, a federal appellate court took the liberal view in a case in which two assistant football coaches were involuntarily transferred for publicly criticizing the head coach's disciplining of students, and offering the concerned parents the opinion that the head coach should be fired for his action. The court held that involuntary transfers had the same "chilling effect" on free speech as discharge, and in applying the balance of interests test to the issue, the court decided: "In our mind, the public's need to know whether children are being mistreated in school outweighs the other legitimate concerns of the [government]."[15]

Focus on the issue of public concern produced a decision favoring the school board the next year. In *Renfroe* v. *Kirkpatrick,* 722 F. 2d 714 (1984), Renfroe, a nontenured teacher, refused to split a job with another nontenured teacher, leading to the filing of a grievance and the subsequent offer of the position to the other teacher. Renfroe claimed a violation of First Amendment rights, in that she was not rehired because she filed a grievance. The school board's action was upheld, since the First Amendment claim was invalidated because there was no issue of public concern present. Renfroe's action was a matter of personal concern without sufficient implication to make her "speech" interest a public issue of importance.

Students' Speech and Press Rights

In his dissent to *Tinker,* Justice Black interpreted the decision as transferring control of pupils from elected officials of the schools to the courts, presaging a flood of litigation on First Amendment issues. He was right. Among the press cases were *Scoville* v. *Board* (1970), in which the federal appellate court used *Tinker* as its authority in deciding that a school's expulsion by students who distributed in school an off-campus publication critical of school policies and authorities, was unconstitutional. According to the court:

> The *Tinker* rule narrows the question before us to whether the writing of "Grass High" and its sale in school . . . could "reasonably have led [the Board] to forecast substantial disruption of or material interference with school activities . . . or intru[sion] into the school affairs or the lives of others . . . [W]here rules infringe upon freedom of expression, the school officials have the burden of showing justification."[16]

Similarly, in 1972, another federal appellate court considered whether a school board was justified in suspending students for violating a school rule regarding the requirement of administrative review prior to the distribution of student publications. The students peacefully distributed their "underground newspaper" before and after class outside the school. The court found for the students, noting the absence of disruption or its reasonable forecast. Further, the prior-review policy was found too vague and without standards to guide its application or resolve dispute. The judge spiced his decision with clear statements of liberal educational philosophy, such as: "Perhaps newer educational theories have become in vogue since our day, but our recollection of the learning process is that the purpose of education is to spread, not to stifle, ideas and views. Ideas must be freed from despotic dispensation by all men, be they robed as academicians or judges or citizen members of a board of education."[17]

Continuing this philosophical position, the decision concluded that "Tinker's dam to school absolutism does not leave dry the fields of school discipline . . . [but] it would be well if those entrusted to administer the teaching of American history and government . . . began . . . practicing the document on which that history and government are based."[18] This reinforced a federal appellate court decision in the previous year, in which a school-board policy requiring prior administrative approval of student publications was struck down because it was not sufficiently specific. It provided no guidelines indicating the rules for submission and related concerns, and hence violated students' press rights (*Eisner* v. *Stamford Board of Educ.*, 440 F. 2d 803 [1971]).

An indication of the limits of students' press freedom was found in *Trachtman* v. *Anker* (1977), in which the federal court approved administrative refusal to a student newspaper editor to distribute a sex-information questionnaire to students on the grounds that it might cause psychological harm to students. This "forecast" was supported by the testimony of psychologists and psychiatrists. In expressing the restraintist, conservative view, the judge remarked:

> We believe that the school authorities are sufficiently experienced and knowledgeable concerning these matters, which have been entrusted to them by the community; a federal court ought not impose its own views in such matters where there is a rational basis for the decisions and actions of the school authorities. . . . The First Amendment right to express one's views does not include the right to importune others to respond to questions . . . that . . . may result in harmful consequences.[19]

The area of student speech rights experienced post-*Tinker* expansion that includes many symbolic-speech issues related to pure speech. For example, student symbolic-speech rights were upheld in *Banks* v. *Muncie Community Schools,* 433 F. 2d 292 (1970). An Indiana school voted to adopt symbols related to the Confederacy, which upset black students, who constituted 13 percent of the school's enrollment. Finding no evidence of disruption or racial-bias motivation, the federal appellate court, while commenting on the "offensive" and "unwise" choice of symbols, upheld the right of the student majority to make its choice. In doing so, the court expressed disappointment that the school administration had not intervened to prevent the extant circumstances. The court observed principles of judicial restraint in making its decision. It resisted the temptation to act as it believed the school authorities should have.

Even so, courts distinguished between the fuller expression rights of teachers, as adults, and those of students, whose character and intellect are still being formed, and must necessarily be subjected to limitations of expression for purposes of school order and acquitting of curricular goals. Thus, in applying the balancing-of-interests test in *Guzick* v. *Drebus,* 431 F. 2d 594 (1970), the federal court ruled for the school board, in its regulation barring students from all wearing of buttons, badges, and other symbols in order to prevent disruption. Since past disruptive evidence was presented, and the rule was of long standing and applied equally to all, the First Amendment rights of students wanting to wear various insignia in school had to give way to the overriding need of the school to maintain order. Similarly, a student's suspension for wearing a Confederate symbol on his jacket was upheld by an appellate court because of evidence of past disruption that justified the administration's forecast of disruption if the student's symbolic expression was not curtailed (*Melton* v. *Young,* 465 F. 2d 1332 [1972]).

Limiting student speech when it constitutes "fighting words" has also been confirmed by the courts. In *Fenton* v. *Stear,* 423 F. Supp. 767 (1967), a student's vulgarity directed at a teacher outside of school led to the imposition of disciplinary penalties. Fenton's claim that this infringed on his right to free speech was rejected, as speech of this nature falls outside the protection intended by the First Amendment. In similar decisions, courts continue to show the limits allowed by *Tinker*. For example, in upholding the school's suspension of a student refusing to take off a badge containing a vulgar word in its antidraft message, the California Court of Appeals declared in 1981 that, while students did not "shed their rights to freedom of speech or expression at the schoolhouse gate," the school is entitled to exercise greater control over their behavior than can be generally imposed on adults. Students have no right to "unlimited expression" within the school (*Hinze* v. *Marin County,* 174 Cal. Rgstr. 403 [1981]). Where student expression is permissible or unpermissible is a question of judgment about its effect on the school's responsibilities and upon other students.

How Far May Speech and Press Rights Be Extended from Pure Speech?

The majority of state and federal courts considering the application of constitutionally protected expression to such areas as hairstyle and other aspects of grooming, as well as dress codes, have generally found such matters beyond the sweep of the First Amendment. The U.S. Supreme Court has never accepted a case that addressed any of these extended applications of First Amendment rights. Thus, the highest case law emanates from state high courts and federal appellate courts. The positions taken by these federal courts have been at variance with one another. For example, five circuits (the first, third, fourth, seventh, and eighth) have conferred constitutional protection for student choice of hairstyle, while four others (the fifth, sixth, ninth, and tenth) have not.[20] Even in those circuits that have elevated hairstyle to a constitutionally protected interest, the First Amendment has rarely served as the basis for it. While one district court ruled that long hair was protected when used as symbolic speech protesting the Vietnam War (*Church* v. *Board of Educ.*, 339 F. Supp. 538 [1972]), the position articulated in *Karr* v. *Schmidt* (1972) is more typical. The court concluded that "it is doubtful that the wearing of long hair has sufficient communicative content to entitle it to the protection of the First Amendment."[21]

The same general position has been taken regarding teachers' rights to First Amendment protection that strays substantially from pure speech, as the right to wear a beard, or to not wear a tie, or for female teachers to wear slacks. The view presented by the seventh circuit appellate court is typical. "If a school board should correctly conclude that a teacher's style of dress or plumage has an adverse impact on the educational process, and if that conclusion conflicts with the teacher's interest in selecting his own life style, we have no doubt that the interest of the teacher is subordinate to the public interest."[22]

In applying this balancing test, the court rarely concludes that personal dress or grooming outweighs the interests of the school, provided that the school authorities can show that their regulations are not too broad or vague and are related to legitimate educational interests, which are due-process issues that generally combine with the free-speech issue being considered.

While First Amendment claims relatively far removed from pure speech have been generally put to rest, they do resurface in various forms from time to time. In *Seyfried* v. *Walton* (1981), the third circuit court of appeals considered the claim of students that their First Amendment rights were violated when school authorities canceled production of a school play. After a few rehearsals, a parent complained that the play mocked religion. Upon review, the school superintendent decided that, while the play did not mock religion, it did contain sexual material inappropriate for high-school students, and the play was canceled on that ground. The appellate court affirmed the lower court's distinguishing of this form of expression from constitutionally protected forms of student opinion. Even while cautioning schools against excessive restraint of teacher and student expression within school-sponsored activities, the court held that the school was justified in its action, as the play was integral to the school's educational program, which distinguished it from the principles laid down in *Tinker*. Further, "no student was prohibited from reading the script . . . and no one was punished or reprimanded for any expression of ideas. In light of these facts, the court could find no reasonable threat of a chilling effect on the free exchange of ideas within the school community."[23] In balancing the interests at hand, the court therefore found it must favor the school's right "to decide how its limited resources can be best used to achieve the goals of educating and socializing its students."[24]

While extensions of freedom of expression appear limited, it is well to note that the restraintist, conservative approach applied to this area is not without its liberal, activist dissenters. The contending attitudes are well represented by the attitudes expressed by Supreme Court Justices Douglas and Black during the liberal period of the late sixties and early seventies. In supporting a petition for Supreme Court review of a case (*Ferrell* v. *Dallas* [1968]) restraining a student from wearing long hair, in which he was the lone supporter for granting certiorari, Douglas wrote:

> I suppose that a nation bent on turning out robots might insist that every male have a crew cut and every female wear pigtails. But the ideas of "life, liberty, and the pursuit of happiness" expressed in the Declaration of Independence, later found specific definition in the Constitution itself, including, of course, freedom of expression and a wide zone of privacy. I had supposed those guarantees permitted idiosyncracies to flourish, especially when they concern the image of one's personality and his philosophy toward government and his fellow men.[25]

In contrast to this liberal, activist view is Black's opinion, written three years later, in denying a motion to him arising out of *Karr* v. *Schmidt* (1971):

> The words used . . . are calculated to leave the impression that this case over the length of hair has created or is about to create a great national "crisis." . . . The only thing about it that borders on the serious to me is the idea that anyone should think the Federal Constitution imposes on the United State's courts the burden of supervising the length of hair that public school students should wear.

> . . . Surely the federal judiciary can perform no greater service to the nation than to leave the states unhampered in the performance of their purely local affairs. Surely, few policies can be thought of that the states are more capable of deciding than the length of the hair of school boys. . . . [I]t would be difficult to prove by reason, logic, or common sense [that] the federal judiciary is more competent to deal with hair length than are the local school authorities and state legislatures of all our 50 states.[26]

The Black view is currently in vogue, but it cannot be assumed that it will always remain so. The heirs to the Douglas view may become the majority, given the facilitating national climate and conditions.

THE SPECIAL FIRST AMENDMENT STATUS OF ACADEMIC FREEDOM

Does the status of teachers as conveyors of knowledge allow them to present material and opinions, or use methods, deemed unseemly by school authorities and/or parents? If so, how far does such license extend? Under what conditions may school authorities limit the professional exercise of judgment by teachers in assigning materials, introducing controversial topics, and using controversial teaching methods? What about teacher expression outside the classroom? Can a teacher be a Communist or subscribe to other views condemned by the school authorities?

The concept of academic freedom originated as a protection for university scholars seeking truth to be free of restraints imposed upon them by popular opinion or political regimes. While elementary- and high-school teachers dispense academic information and skills, rather than conduct research to extend knowledge that they subsequently present to their students, courts have established that the First Amendment provides common-school teachers with some of the special protection of academic freedom. While this protection may not be as strong for common-school teachers as for those in higher education, it nevertheless has served as a formidable attribute in judicial balancing tests that seek to establish how far boards may go in dictating what materials, methods, and related instructional activities teachers may use. In this type of balancing test, teachers' academic freedom is weighed against the state's interest in presenting particular views, insuring teachers' neutrality on controversial issues, and using teachers to deliver its conception of the curriculum.

The *Pickering* and *Epperson* (see Chapter 3) cases, previously discussed, provided ill-defined but supportive precedents for teachers' academic freedom. They established that in the balancing test between teachers' free speech and state control of education, the school authorities must show that the limits imposed on teachers' professional activities related to academic expression are required for *overriding, compelling* reasons.

Academic Freedom within the Classroom

The liberal, activist expansion of teachers' academic freedom was highlighted by such cases as *Keefe* v. *Geanakos* (1969), *Mailloux* v. *Kiley* (1971), and *Parducci* v. *Rutland* (1974). In *Keefe,* a high-school English teacher distributed to his class an article from the *Atlantic* containing vulgar language and attitudes supporting radical views including protest and revolt. Students were advised that if the article offended them, they could opt for an alternative one. While there was no evidence of negative student reaction, outraged parents prevailed upon the school board to stop Keefe from such activity. Keefe refused, and was threatened with dismissal, whereupon he sued, contending his First Amendment right to academic freedom was being violated. The federal appellate court found for Keefe. The court found the article "scholarly, thoughtful, and thought provoking" and the "dirty" word was used for educational purposes. Further, the dirty word must be viewed in its context, which was appropriate, and students were well aware of the word. More important to educational policy, the court concluded that parents cannot be allowed to be the sole judges of what is educationally proper. While some regulation of classroom speech is certainly permissible, the court believed that its use in this case "demeans any proper concept of education."[27]

Another English teacher, Mailloux, was seeking in his class to develop an understanding of taboo words by writing one on the board and encouraging discussion of it in relation to taboos on the use of such words. Parental complaints led to his dismissal, for which he sued on First Amendment grounds. In rescinding Mailloux's dismissal, the court noted that school authorities had provided no guidelines advising Mailloux that this "lesson" was a proscribed activity, nor had it shown that the approach used was without academic merit.

Therefore, the vital interest represented by the First Amendment had been violated. Teachers should not have to guess about what approach or remark might cost them their job (*Mailloux* v. *Kiley,* 448 F. 2d 1242 [1971]).

Similarly, in *Parducci* v. *Rutland,* a teacher's use of a controversial reading was upheld by a federal appellate court, even though she was dismissed after the principal had requested her to discontinue use of the Kurt Vonnegut, Jr., satire, *Welcome to the Monkey House.* The school board failed to show that the assignment was bad for the students, that it disrupted the educational process, or that there was a regulation showing the assigned book was forbidden. The court took pains to clarify the concept of academic freedom:

> Although academic freedom is not among the enumerated rights of the First Amendment, the Supreme Court has on numerous occasions emphasized that the right to teach, to inquire, to evaluate, and to study is fundamental to a democratic society. . . .

> The right to academic freedom, however . . . is not absolute, and must be balanced against the competing interests of society. . . . [I]n order for the state to restrict the First Amendment . . . it must first demonstrate that "the forbidden conduct would *materially* and *substantially* interfere with . . . the operation of the school. . . .

> When a teacher is forced to speculate as to what conduct is proscribed, he is apt to be overly cautious and reserved in the classroom. Such a reluctance on the part of the teacher to investigate and experiment with new and different ideas is anathema to the entire concept of academic freedom.[28]

The limits of academic freedom were indicated in subsequent years. In *Brubaker* v. *Board* (1974) a federal appellate court found that dismissal of teachers for distributing controversial material in their classroom that had no relationship to their subjects, fell outside of the constitutional protection afforded by academic freedom. Three eighth-grade teachers of French, language arts, and industrial arts distributed "Woodstock" brochures showing and condoning the use of drugs and sexual promiscuity, replete with an abundance of vulgar language. In answering the teachers' petition for First Amendment protection for their behavior, the court combined an activist tendency to make school policy with a conservative attitude, agreeing with the school board's decision.

> As a message to the minds of eighth graders, the brochure's poetry . . . must be fairly read as an alluring invitation and a beckoning for them to throw off the dull discipline imposed on them by the moral environment . . . and in exchange a new world of love and freedom—freedom to use acid and grass, freedom to take their clothes off and to get an early start in the use of such vulgarities as "shit," "fucking," and their companions.

> . . . Is it only a forlorn hope, however, that most of our young ladies will never employ that kind of speech? . . .

. . . Appellants say that the Board was wrong because it reached its conclusion as to the poetry's impropriety "[w]ithout the benefit of any supporting expert testimony in the fields of literature, obscenity, or drugs." Experts should not be needed to support a conclusion that is obvious. . . . [W]e consider that these teachers should have known better than to hand to their young students something that invited the use of the described drugs. . . .

The validity of our conclusion that the District Court properly found no violation of appellants' First Amendment or Civil Rights emerges so clearly that we decline to add . . . to the abundant literature. . . . [29]

Brubaker also defined the limits of academic freedom. It does not extend to offensive conduct unnecessary to accomplishing educational objectives, and was further limited by balancing teachers' academic decisions against students' age and sophistication, as well as the educational purpose and context and manner of presentation.

In the same year, the Louisiana Court of Appeals upheld the dismissal of an experienced (fifteen years of tenure) teacher for comments about interracial sexual relations to his world-history class. His comments included remarks about white males' sexual exploitation of black females and the characterization of white women as superior lovers. While there was no disruption of the educational process, the court ruled that his statements were "irrelevant" and in order for his action to be protected by First Amendment academic freedom there must be some serious educational purpose underlying the use of a phrase or a word. Since the court determined that the remarks were not clearly relevant to educational objectives, they were not entitled to First Amendment protection (*Simon* v. *Davis Parish School Board,* 289 So. 2d 511 [1974]).

Then, in 1978, a New York Court of Appeals showed the limits of the *Keefe-Mailloux-Parducci* academic freedom theory for use of methods and materials. In *Harris* v. *Mechanicville Central School Dist.,* 408 N.Y.S. 2d 384 (1978), teacher Harris had agreed to stop using *Catcher in the Rye* after parental complaints had precipitated school authorities to request that he do so. A year later, he began using *Catcher in the Rye* again, without warning, in disregard of the written understanding that he would not. As a result, he was dismissed for insubordination. The court approved his dismissal because he had entered into a voluntary agreement not to use the book, and then violated it. Academic freedom does not, according to the New York court, protect teachers in such conduct.

The conservative view was further strengthened by state court decisions in 1982. The New York Appellate Court upheld the dismissal of a photography teacher for showing his class a film considered pornographic (*Shurgin* v. *Ambach,* 451 N.Y.S. 2d 722 [1982]). In the same year, a North Dakota court upheld the dismissal of a biology teacher for devoting too much time to "scientific creationism" (*Dale* v. *Board of Educ., Lemmon Indep. School Dist. 52-2,* 316 N.W. 2d 108 [1982]).

Teachers' Rights to Independence in Political Views and Associations

The First Amendment provides for freedom of association under its assembly and petition clauses. The issue of the extent to which this applies to teachers is a matter of interpreting the limits of academic freedom. This is an area that clearly shows how court attitudes can change to reflect the temper of the moment. During the fifties and sixties, the Supreme Court demonstrated how its legal reasoning becomes sensitive to national political pressure.

In *Adler* v. *Board* (1952), the Supreme Court upheld the New York "Feinberg Law," which authorized the dismissal of teachers belonging to organizations considered subversive. In rationalizing this conservative, restraintist position, the Court reasoned:

> A teacher works in a sensitive area in the classroom. There he shapes the attitude of young minds towards the society in which they live. In this, the state has a vital concern. It must preserve the integrity of the schools. That the school authorities have the right and duty to screen . . . employees as to their fitness to maintain the integrity of the schools . . . cannot be doubted. One's associates, past and present, as well as one's conduct, may properly be considered in determining fitness and loyalty.[30]

As to claims of First Amendment protection for teachers to hold to private unpopular views, the Court asserted the then-current privilege doctrine, holding that public-school teaching is not a right, but a privilege, conditioned on reasonable state requirements. A teacher had the right to subscribe to unpopular political views, but not the right to do that and hold a teaching position. Teachers "have no right to work for the . . . school system on their own terms. . . . They may work . . . upon the reasonable terms laid down by . . . New York. If they do not choose to work on such terms, they are at liberty to retain their beliefs and associations and go elsewhere."[31]

This conservative attitude stimulated by the McCarthy Era of political repression was reinforced by the Supreme Court's decision in *Beilan* v. *Board* (1958). Here, a suspected communist Philadelphia teacher refused to answer questions about his political affiliations posed by his superintendent, leading to his being fired for incompetency. The Court, in rejecting Beilan's claim of First Amendment protection of speech, association, and belief, held: "By engaging in teaching in the public schools, petitioner did not give up his right to freedom of belief, speech, or association. He did, however, undertake obligations of . . . answering inquiries . . . into his fitness . . . as a public school teacher."[32]

As the liberal period of the sixties emerged, the Supreme Court majority threw off the last vestiges of the McCarthy Era by reconsidering the Feinberg Law and this time finding it unconstitutional. It did so on the due-process grounds of being overly vague. In the process, its decision in *Keyishian* v. *Board*

(1967) reaffirmed the state's interest in protecting its integrity, as stated in *Adler,* but went on to highlight the vital importance of protecting academic freedom:

> Our nation is deeply committed to safeguarding academic freedom, which is of transcendent value to all of us and not merely to the teachers concerned. That freedom is therefore a special concern of the First Amendment, which does not tolerate laws that cast a pall of orthodoxy over the classroom.

> "The vigilant protection of constitutional freedoms is nowhere more vital than in the community of American schools." The classroom is peculiarly the "marketplace of ideas."[33]

Thus can court attitude change from conservative to liberal in conformance with changing attitudes in the larger political and social structure. While *Keyishian* was a higher-education case, its message for the common schools, while different in degree, was the same in kind. Guilt by association and leaping to conclusions based on people's thoughts, rather than their actions, was impermissible.

CENSORSHIP OF SCHOOL BOOKS

Are there any limits to the authority of school boards to decide which books may be allowed into the school and which may not? Does that authority change when applied to the library, as opposed to the classroom? If there are First Amendment limits to book control, what guidelines apply? Is a decision not to allow a book into a school library as constitutionally strong as one to expunge a book from it?

The importance the courts have given to the concept of the First Amendment's protection of diverse opinion for an informed, enlightened democracy has provided strong protections against book censorship. However, the application of book censorship to schools creates complexities for the court. It must balance school-board responsibility for decisions about curriculum and materials against board manipulation and control of ideas as represented in books. There are two sides to this issue—conflict over selection of library and textbooks, and their removal from the library or curriculum. Conflict occurs when school boards forbid adoption of particular books or act to expunge books already adopted. The courts support the right of school boards to decide adoptions, provided no malevolent intent is shown. However, the First Amendment looms larger when boards decide to expunge books from the school.

The traditionally restraintist-conservative view of courts in supporting boards' adoption authority is exemplified in *Rosenberg* v. *Board of Education* (1949). Parents objected to the adoption of *The Merchant of Venice* and *Oliver Twist,* claiming they encouraged anti-Semitism. In upholding the school board's authority to retain the books, the New York court took this position:

Educational institutions are concerned with free inquiry and learning. The administrative officers must be free to guide teachers and pupils toward that goal. Their discretion must not be interfered with in the absence of proof of malevolent intent. Interference by the court will result in suppression of the intended purpose of aiding those seeking education.[34]

This decision of 1949 was reaffirmed in *President's Council* v. *Board* (1972), in which a federal appellate court saw no First Amendment violation in a school board's "constant process of selection and winnowing" of library books. It held that policy over what books would and would not be housed in the school library rested with the school board, and courts could not properly impose themselves to decide "either the wisdom or the efficacy of the determination of the board."[35] However, another federal appellate court separated the issue of board authority to decide which books to purchase, from the matter of removing books already in the library. In *Minarcini* v. *Strongsville* (1976), the court agreed that the school board could refuse to purchase books recommended by the English faculty because of objections by a citizens' committee. However, the school board also followed the committee's recommendation to remove two books (Kurt Vonnegut's *God Bless You, Mr. Rosewater* and Joseph Heller's *Catch-22*) from the library. Here, the court found that the First Amendment had been violated, because: "A library is a storehouse of knowledge . . . not subject to being withdrawn by succeeding school boards whose members might desire to 'winnow' the library for books . . . which occasioned their displeasure or disapproval."[36]

The question of how far the First Amendment extended to protect against school-board censorship of books, once they have gained admittance to "the marketplace of ideas," gathered in momentum and intensity in the late seventies and initial years of the eighties, because of the assaults against various types of books by increasingly militant and single-minded pressure groups. These included religious fundamentalists opposed to atheistic, sacrilegious literature; "League of Decency" types wishing to root out "filth" from the schools; anticommunists; minority-rights groups opposed to books denigrating blacks and other minorities; and more. Eventually, the U.S. Supreme Court accepted a case dealing with the First Amendment issue of a school board's decision to remove books from its school libraries, motivated by recommendations received at a meeting of a group called People of New York United. Two board members returned from the meeting to find copies of books on the removal list in the school libraries, which led to the Board's ordering the principal to remove the books.

The school superintendent objected, taking the position that board policy required a broadly based committee to consider book complaints, and one book ordered removed had previously received board approval. Nevertheless, the books were removed, precipitating the Supreme Court's review of *Island Trees District* v. *Pico* (1982). The Court's divided opinion avoided the broader question of board authority to remove books from the curriculum; the majority confined its attention to only the issues of: (1) whether the First Amendment imposed *any* limitations on the discretion of school boards to remove books from high school libraries; and (2) if the answer to (1) is affirmative, is there a possibility that the board might have exceeded those limitations?

The Court answered the first question affirmatively, as "the special characteristics" of the school library make that environment especially appropriate for the recognition of the First Amendment rights of students."[37] The second question also was answered affirmatively, leading to the case being remanded to the trial court for reconsideration consistent with the Supreme Court opinion. However, in the interim the school board voted to return the books to the libraries. Even though this prevented a final delineation of the extent to which boards are constrained from removing library books, the Supreme Court made two points of educational policy clear.

1. There must be an overriding, compelling reason for the "suppression of ideas" that accompanies removal of books from a library.
2. Review procedures should be established for book removal based on considerations of "educational suitability," and the procedures should be free from personal bias or procedural unfairness.

POLICY CONSIDERATIONS

It is commonly accepted that a free, democratic society cannot remain so without freedom of speech and press. Together with freedom of association and petition, and the symbolic-speech and academic-freedom extensions, this constitutional battleground has become a minefield for beleaguered school administrators and board members. Stripped of their former almost absolute power over teachers and students, school authorities must now rely on actions and policies that agree with shifting court concepts of how the First Amendment applies to schools. In this way, the schools, which are an important training ground for citizenship, reinforce the goals of American democratic society. However, there are costs associated with this—less order and control, distractions from the objectives set by school authorities, teachers raising their voices against principals and school boards, and, worse, students protesting the orders and regulations of teachers, principals, and other school authorities under the banner of the First Amendment.

Is the price of imbuing students and teachers with the constitutional protections of expression found in the general society too high a price to pay? No, answer school-policy analysts who agree with Justice Jackson that, since school authorities "are educating the young for citizenship, [this] is reason for scrupulous protection of Constitutional freedoms of the individual if we are not to strangle the free mind at its source and teach youth to discount important principles of government as mere platitudes" (*W. Virginia* v. *Barnette*). To such educators, the proof of democracy is in its practice, inefficient and clumsy as it may at times render the control and administration of the public schools.

For the more conservative educator, the words of Justice Black, in his dissent to the *Tinker* decision, that the idea of students and teachers carrying full rights of freedom of expression into the schools renders them prey to the havoc to be wreaked by the "loudest-mouthed but maybe not their brightest students" (*Tinker* v. *Des Moines*), seems an appropriate criticism. To these educators, schools do students a disservice when they allow the young and, by definition, not fully educated, to be distracted from the educative path led by those empowered to direct them by weight of government authority and professional competence. As for teachers, this conservative view suggests that they should leave their personal views behind when practicing their profession. They should take their direction from board and administrator and not consider the classroom a platform for personal positions. In a sense, this position is a variant of a famous phrase about war and generals. In this case, "education is too important to be left to teachers."

The challenge to administrators and board members, regardless of where they stand on the liberal-conservative continuum, is to devise governance policies and practices that allow for order and control within the First Amendment expression framework of liberties imposed by the judiciary. This means several things. First and foremost, boards and administrators should resist the temptation to restrain teacher or student expression for no better reason than that it clashes with their subjective, idiosyncratic notions of right and wrong. Limitations on expression should be grounded in the clear need to prevent disruption of the educational process, insure the safety of students and teachers, or protect the expression and privacy rights of others. This does not necessarily force educators to maintain order with one hand tied behind their backs. It does require the expenditure of more time and effort in developing constitutionally sound approaches to orderly discourse within the school that tolerate dissent and opposing views, provided the expression of those views does not injure others or the educational process.

In regard to students' press rights, this means staying away from prior censorship based on undefined, broadly based review powers. Instead, clear, rational guidelines should be developed, which provide teachers and students with both knowledge of what is proscribed and why. Distribution of literature may likewise be reasonably regulated as to time and place. As for speech and symbolic expression, "fighting words," irrelevant, vulgar, disruptive, impertinent pure or symbolic speech need not be tolerated, except before the most excessively liberal jurist. We would do well to consider that the more generally important the topic and serious the reputation of the speaker or purveyor of expression, the more leeway he or she should be provided.

While the Supreme Court had cloaked the public schools in such First Amendment phrases as "a marketplace of ideas" that must be free of the "pall of orthodoxy," and allowed teachers to harshly criticize administrators, it had also allowed teacher firing even where constitutionally protected speech was implicated, and approved school-board denial of free access to the district mail system by a union rivaling the approved one. The position sketched out by lower federal and state courts shows even greater diversity regarding First Amendment application to the schools.

This suggests that in the subsidiary areas of academic freedom for teachers, censorship of school books, and teachers' association rights, as well as the "purer" forms of speech and press, those in authority should develop and rehearse their own objective balancing tests in anticipation of their application by a court, considering whether the action falls within or outside of the judicial standards developed for the First Amendment's application to the schools.

Consider the possible ramifications of a school policy that requires teachers to "present and support the American political and economic systems as the best developed by any society in human history." If a teacher objected to the policy on the grounds of academic freedom, or sought that concept's protection when threatened with dismissal for violating the policy, would most courts be likely to support the school authorities or the teacher? What elements would be likely to sway the court in one or the other direction? Clear opposition to and denigration of the American systems would probably be found to be too extreme to find comfort in courts restraining authorities from casting a "pall of orthodoxy" over teaching. On the other hand, merely suggesting that how one views the merits of one political or economic system over another depends on circumstance, history, and culture might be approved as appropriate to the school's role as a "marketplace of ideas." Certainly the age of the students would be germane to the decision, as would the qualifications of the teacher. Considering the policy itself, does it represent an affront to academic freedom? Cannot a state, through its schools, assert what should be inculcated as societal values? Yet the Supreme Court contends that "no official, high or petty, can prescribe what shall be orthodox in politics . . . or other matters of opinion" (*W. Virginia* v. *Barnette*). Still, the courts, including the Supreme Court, have clearly supported the authority of school boards and state agencies to establish and enforce curricular and academic standards. Finally, in making this decision, school authorities might consider whether this policy is justified by *compelling* reasons or is merely rationally related to educational objectives. While the former justification is more difficult to prove, it will establish the strongest case.

What if the school board wishes to dismiss a teacher found to be a member of the John Birch society or the Black Panthers, or whatever group offends the board? Can it do this within the confines of the First Amendment? Probably not, unless the *overriding, compelling* interest to do so for adequate educational reasons or for the peace and safety of the school community can be established. Keep in mind that *Tinker* held that "undifferentiated fear or apprehension of disturbance is not enough to overcome the right to freedom of expression."[38] Therefore, dismissing a teacher based on what that person did rather than what he or she may think, and based on something more than guilt by association, will be needed.

What if the library of a school populated by Jewish children of survivors of Nazi concentration camps contained a copy of Hitler's *Mein Kampf*, or if a teacher assigned the book to a class? We know that *Minarcini* established that the school board has strong control over what goes into the library, but *Pico* held that expunging a book from the library may collide with the First Amendment. Thus, *Mein Kampf* could be more easily kept out of the library than removed from it. Removal would have to be occasioned by broad-based group deliberation free from substantive or procedural bias. The decision should be based on compelling reasons of educational unsuitability sufficient to override the "special characteristics" of the library and the charge of "suppression of ideas." Even given the emotional justification of parents and students, whether removal of *Mein Kampf* would be approved is problematic.

The teacher's assignment of *Mein Kampf* would involve such questions as the pupils' ages, whether there was a clear policy to guide the teacher, and whether or not the assignment disrupted the classroom educational process or created school-community conflict. If the students were at the elementary level, and the answers to the other three foregoing points are yes, suppression of the assignment or teacher dismissal would probably be upheld. If the answers were no, and the students were high-school seniors, the teacher's action would probably be sustained in the balancing of interests between state authority to control the curriculum and the teacher's academic freedoms.

The balancing of interests between pure speech and press use by students or teachers allows for stricter, clearer (but still rather unclear) standards emanating from the First Amendment because of the *Pickering* and *Tinker* decisions. Neither "students or teachers shed their constitutional rights to freedom of speech or expression at the schoolhouse gate" (*Tinker* v. *Des Moines*). Further, *Pickering* found: "Free and open debate is vital. . . . Teachers are, as a class . . . most likely to have informed and definite opinions . . . [on] the operation of the schools. . . . [I]t is essential that they be able to speak out freely on such questions without fear of retaliatory dismissal."[39] Thus, restrictions on students' or teachers' speech and press must be shown to be justified by compelling reasons related to educational effectiveness, safety, and order.

Pickering v. Board of Education
391 U.S. 563 (1968)

MR. JUSTICE MARSHALL delivered the opinion of the Court.

Appellant Marvin L. Pickering was dismissed from his position by the appellee Board of Education for sending a letter to a local newspaper in connection with a recently proposed tax increase that was critical of the way in which the Board and the district superintendent of schools had handled past proposals to raise new revenue for the schools. Appellant's dismissal resulted from a determination by the Board, after a full hearing, that the publication of the letter was "detrimental to the efficient operation and administration of the schools of the district" and hence, under the relevant Illinois statute, that "interests of the school require[d] [his dismissal]."

Appellant's claim that his writing of the letter was protected by the First and Fourteenth Amendments was rejected. For the reasons detailed below we agree that appellant's rights to freedom of speech were violated and we reverse.

I

The letter constituted, basically, an attack on the School Board's handling of the 1961 bond issue proposals and its subsequent allocation of financial resources between the schools' educational and athletic programs. It also charged the superintendent of schools with attempting to prevent teachers in the district from opposing or criticizing the proposed bond issue.

The Board dismissed Pickering for writing and publishing the letter. Pursuant to Illinois law, the Board was then required to hold a hearing on the dismissal. At the hearing the Board charged that numerous statements in the letter were false and that the publication of the statements unjustifiably impugned the "motives, honesty, integrity, truthfulness, responsibility and competence" of both the Board and the school administration. The Board also charged that the false statements damaged the professional reputations of its members and of the school administrators, would be disruptive of faculty discipline, and would tend to foment "controversy, conflict and dissension" among teachers, administrators, the Board of Education, and the residents of the district. Testimony was introduced from a variety of witnesses on the truth or falsity of the particular statements in the letter with which the Board took issue. The Board found the statements to be false as charged. No evidence was introduced at any point in the proceedings as to the effect of the publication of the letter on the community as a whole or on the administration of the school system in particular, and no specific findings along these lines were made.

The Illinois courts reviewed the proceedings solely to determine whether the Board's findings were supported by substantial evidence and whether, on the facts as found, the Board could reasonably conclude that appellant's publication of the letter was "detrimental to the best interests of the schools." Pickering's claim that his letter was protected by the First Amendment was rejected on the ground that his acceptance of a teaching position in the public schools obliged him to refrain from making statements about the operation of the schools "which in the absence of such position he would have an undoubted right to engage in."

II

To the extent that the Illinois Supreme Court's opinion may be read to suggest that teachers may constitutionally be compelled to relinquish the First Amendment rights they would otherwise enjoy as citizens to comment on matters of public interest in connection with the operation of the public schools in which they work, it proceeds on a premise that has been unequivocally rejected in numerous prior decisions of this Court. At the same time it cannot be gainsaid that the State has interests as an employer in regulating the speech of its employees that differ significantly from those it possesses in connection with regulation of the speech of the citizenry in general. The problem in any case is to arrive at a balance between the interests of the teacher, as a citizen, in commenting upon matters of public concern and the interest of the State, as an employer, in promoting the efficiency of the public services it performs through its employees.

III

An examination of the statements in appellant's letter objected to by the Board reveals that they, like the letter as a whole, consist essentially of criticism of the Board's allocation of school funds between educational and athletic programs, and of both the Board's and the superintendent's methods of informing, or preventing the informing of, the district's taxpayers of the real reasons why additional tax revenues were being sought for the schools. The statements are in no way directed towards any person with whom appellant would normally be in contact in the course of his daily work as a teacher. Thus no question of maintaining either discipline by immediate superiors or harmony among co-workers is presented here. Appellant's employment relationships with the Board and, to a somewhat lesser extent, with the superintendent are not the kind of close working relationships for which it can persuasively be claimed that personal loyalty and confidence are necessary to their proper functioning. Accordingly, to the extent that the Board's position here can be taken to suggest that even comments on matters of public concern that are substantially correct may furnish grounds for dismissal if they are sufficiently critical in tone, we unequivocally reject it.

We next consider the statements in appellant's letter which we agree to be false. The Board's original charges included allegations that the publication of the letter damaged the professional reputations of the Board and the superintendent and would foment controversy and conflict among the Board, teachers, administrators, and the residents of the district. However, no evidence to support these allegations was introduced at the hearing. So far as the record reveals, Pickering's letter was greeted by everyone but its main target, the Board, with massive apathy and total disbelief.

In addition, the fact that particular illustrations of the Board's claimed undesirable emphasis on athletic programs are false would not normally have any necessary impact on the actual operation of the schools, beyond its tendency to anger the Board. For example, Pickering's letter was written after the defeat at the polls of the second proposed tax increase. It could, therefore, have had no effect on the ability of the school district to raise necessary revenue, since there was no showing that there was any proposal to increase taxes pending when the letter was written.

More importantly, the question whether a school system requires additional funds is a matter of legitimate public concern on which the judgment of the school administration, including the School Board, cannot, in a society that leaves such questions to popular vote, be taken as conclusive. On such a question free and open debate is vital to informed decision-making by the electorate. Teachers are, as a class, the members of a community most likely to have informed and definite opinions as to how funds allotted to the operation of the schools should be spent. Accordingly, it is essential that they be able to speak out freely on such questions without fear of retaliatory dismissal.

In addition, the amounts expended on athletics which Pickering reported erroneously were matters of public record on which his position as a teacher in the district did not qualify him to speak with any greater authority than any other taxpayer. The Board could easily have rebutted appellant's errors by publishing the accurate figures itself, either via a letter to the same newspaper or otherwise. We are thus not presented with a situation in which a teacher has carelessly made false statements about matters so closely related to the day-to-day operations of the schools that any harmful impact on the public would be difficult to counter because of the teacher's presumed greater access to the real facts.

What we do have before us is a case in which a teacher has made erroneous public statements upon issues then currently the subject of public attention, which are critical of his ultimate employer but which are neither shown nor can be presumed to have in any way either impeded the teacher's proper performance of his daily duties in the classroom or to have interfered with the regular operation of the schools generally. In these circumstances we conclude that the interest of the school administration in limiting teachers' opportunities to contribute to public debate is not significantly greater than its interest in limiting a similar contribution by any member of the general public.

IV

In sum, we hold that, in a case such as this, absent proof of false statements knowingly or recklessly made by him, a teacher's exercise of his right to speak on issues of public importance may not furnish the basis for his dismissal from public employment. Since no such showing has been made in this case regarding appellant's letter, his dismissal for writing it cannot be upheld.

Tinker v. Des Moines School Dist.
393 U.S. 503 (1969)

MR. JUSTICE FORTAS delivered the opinion of the Court.

In December 1965, a group of adults and students in Des Moines held a meeting at the Eckhardt home. The group determined to publicize their objections to the hostilities in Vietnam and their support for a truce by wearing black armbands during the holiday season and by fasting on December 16 and New Year's Eve. Petitioners and their parents had previously engaged in similar activities, and they decided to participate in the program.

The principals of the Des Moines schools became aware of the plan to wear armbands. On December 14, 1965, they met and adopted a policy that any student wearing an armband to school would be asked to remove it, and if he refused he would be suspended until he returned without the armband. Petitioners were aware of the regulation that the school authorities adopted.

On December 16, Mary Beth and Christopher wore black armbands to their schools. John Tinker wore his armband the next day. They were all sent home and suspended from school until they would come back without their armbands. They did not return to school until after the planned period for wearing armbands had expired—that is, until after New Year's Day.

I

The District Court recognized that the wearing of an armband for the purpose of expressing certain views is the type of symbolic act that is within the Free Speech Clause of the First Amendment. As we shall discuss, the wearing of armbands in the circumstances of this case was entirely divorced from actually or potentially disruptive conduct by those participating in it. It was closely akin to "pure speech" which, we have repeatedly held, is entitled to comprehensive protection under the First Amendment.

First Amendment rights, applied in light of the special characteristics of the school environment, are available to teachers and students. It can hardly be argued that either students or teachers shed their constitutional rights to freedom of speech or expression at the schoolhouse gate. This has been the unmistakable holding of this Court for almost 50 years. On the other hand, the Court has repeatedly emphasized the need for affirming the comprehensive authority of the States and of school officials, consistent with fundamental constitutional safeguards, to prescribe and control conduct in the schools. Our problem lies in the area where students in the exercise of First Amendment rights collide with the rules of the school authorities.

II

The problem posed by the present case does not concern aggressive, disruptive action or even group demonstrations. Our problem involves direct, primary First Amendment rights akin to "pure speech."

The school officials banned and sought to punish petitioners for a silent, passive expression of opinion, unaccompanied by any disorder or disturbance on the part of petitioners. There is here no evidence whatever of petitioners' interference, actual or nascent, with the schools' work or of collision with the rights of other students to be secure and to be let alone. Accordingly, this case does not concern speech or action that intrudes upon the work of the schools or the rights of other students.

The District Court concluded that the action of the school authorities was reasonable because it was based upon their fear of a disturbance from the wearing of the armbands. But, in our system, undifferentiated fear or apprehension of disturbance is not enough to overcome the right to freedom of expression. Any departure from absolute regimentation may cause trouble. Any variation from the majority's opinion may inspire fear. Any word spoken, in class, in the lunchroom, or on the campus, that deviates from the views of another person may start an argument or cause a disturbance. But our Constitution says we must take this risk, and our history says that it is this sort of hazardous freedom—this kind of openness—that is the basis of our national strength and of the independence and vigor of Americans who grow up and live in this relatively permissive, often disputatious, society.

In order for the State in the person of school officials to justify prohibition of a particular expression of opinion it must be able to show that its action was caused by something more than a mere desire to avoid the discomfort and unpleasantness that always accompany an unpopular viewpoint. Certainly where there is no finding and no showing that engaging in the forbidden conduct would "materially and substantially interfere with the requirements of appropriate discipline in the operation of the school," the prohibition cannot be sustained.

In the present case, the District Court made no such finding, and our independent examination of the record fails to yield evidence that the school authorities had reason to anticipate that the wearing of the armbands would substantially interfere with the work of the school or impinge upon the rights of other students.

In our system, state-operated schools may not be enclaves of totalitarianism. School officials do not possess absolute authority over their students. Students in school as well as out of school are "persons" under our Constitution. They are possessed of fundamental rights which the State must respect, just as they themselves must respect their obligations to the State. In our system, students may not be regarded as closed-circuit recipients of only that which the State chooses to communicate. They may not be confined to the expression of those sentiments that are officially approved. In the absence of a specific showing of constitutionally valid reasons to regulate their speech, students are entitled to freedom of expression of their views.

Under our Constitution, free speech is not a right that is given only to be so circumscribed that it exists in principle but not in fact. Freedom of expression would not truly exist if the right could be exercised only in an area that a benevolent government has provided as a safe haven for crackpots. The Constitution says that Congress (and the States) may not abridge the right to free speech. This provision means what it says. We properly read it to permit reasonable regulation of speech-connected activities in carefully restricted circumstances. But we do not confine the permissible exercise of First Amendment rights to a telephone booth or the four corners of a pamphlet, or to supervised and ordained discussion in a school classroom.

As we have discussed, the record does not demonstrate any facts which might reasonably have led school authorities to forecast substantial disruption of or material interference with school activities, and no disturbances or disorders on the school premises in fact occurred. These petitioners merely went about their ordained rounds in school. Their deviation consisted only in wearing on their sleeve a band of black cloth, not more than two inches wide. They wore it to exhibit their disapproval of the Vietnam hostilities and their advocacy of a truce, to make their views known, and, by their example, to influence others to adopt them. They neither interrupted school activities nor sought to intrude in the school affairs or the lives of others. They caused discussion outside of the classrooms, but no interference with work and no disorder. In the circumstances, our Constitution does not permit officials of the State to deny their form of expression.

MR. JUSTICE BLACK, dissenting.

The Court's holding in this case ushers in what I deem to be an entirely new era in which the power to control pupils by the elected "officials of state supported public schools . . . " in the United States is in ultimate effect transferred to the Supreme Court.

As I read the Court's opinion it relies upon the following grounds for holding unconstitutional the judgment of the Des Moines school officials and the two courts below. First, the Court concludes that the wearing of armbands is "symbolic speech'' which is ''akin to 'pure speech' '' and therefore protected by the First and Fourteenth Amendments. Secondly, the Court decides that the public schools are an appropriate place to exercise ''symbolic speech'' as long as normal school functions are not ''unreasonably'' disrupted. Finally, the Court arrogates to itself, rather than to the State's elected officials charged with running the schools, the decision as to which school disciplinary regulations are ''reasonable.''

Assuming that the Court is correct in holding that the conduct of wearing armbands for the purpose of conveying political ideas is protected by the First Amendment, the crucial remaining questions are whether students and teachers may use the schools at their whim as a platform for the exercise of free speech—''symbolic'' or ''pure''—and whether the courts will allocate to themselves the function of deciding how the pupils' school day will be spent. While I have always believed that under the First and Fourteenth Amendments neither the State nor the Federal Government has any authority to regulate or censor the content of speech, I have never believed that any person has a right to give speeches or engage in demonstrations where he pleases and when he pleases.

Even a casual reading of the record shows that this armband did divert students' minds from their regular lessons, and that talk, comments, etc., made John Tinker ''self-conscious'' in attending school with his armband. I think the record overwhelmingly shows that the armbands did exactly what the elected school officials and principals foresaw they would, that is, took the students' minds off their classwork and diverted them to thoughts about the highly emotional subject of the Vietnam war. And I repeat that if the time has come when pupils of state-supported schools, kindergartens, grammar schools, or high schools, can defy and flout orders of school officials to keep their minds on their own schoolwork, it is the beginning of a new revolutionary era of permissiveness in this country fostered by the judiciary.

I deny, therefore, that it has been the ''unmistakable holding of this Court for almost 50 years'' that ''students'' and ''teachers'' take with them into the ''schoolhouse gate'' constitutional rights to ''freedom of speech or expression.'' The truth is that a teacher of kindergarten, grammar school, or high school pupils no more carries into a school with him a complete right to freedom of speech and expression than an anti-Catholic or anti-Semite carries with him a complete freedom of speech and religion into a Catholic church or Jewish synagogue. Nor does a person carry with him into the United States Senate or House, or into the Supreme Court, or any other court, a complete constitutional right to go into those places contrary to their rules and speak his mind on any subject he pleases. It is a myth to say that any person has a constitutional right to say what he pleases, where he pleases, and when he pleases.

In my view, teachers in state-controlled public schools are hired to teach there. [C]ertainly a teacher is not paid to go into school and teach subjects the State does not hire him to teach as a part of its selected curriculum. Nor are public school students sent to the schools at public expense to broadcast political or any other views to educate and inform the public. The original idea of schools, which I do not believe is yet abandoned as worthless or out of date, was that children had not yet reached the point of experience and wisdom which enabled them to teach all of their elders. It may be that the Nation has outworn the old-fashioned slogan that "children are to be seen not heard," but one may, I hope, be permitted to harbor the thought that taxpayers send children to school on the premise that at their age they need to learn, not teach.

Change has been said to be truly the law of life but sometimes the old and the tried and true are worth holding. The schools of this Nation have undoubtedly contributed to giving us tranquility and to making us a more law-abiding people. Uncontrolled and uncontrollable liberty is an enemy to domestic peace. We cannot close our eyes to the fact that some of the country's greatest problems are crimes committed by the youth, too many of school age. School discipline, like parental discipline, is an integral and important part of training our children to be good citizens—to be better citizens. Here a very small number of students have crisply and summarily refused to obey a school order designed to give pupils who want to learn the opportunity to do so. One does not need to be a prophet or the son of a prophet to know that after the Court's holding today some students in Iowa schools and indeed in all schools will be ready, able, and willing to defy their teachers on practically all orders. This is the more unfortunate for the schools since groups of students all over the land are already running loose, conducting break-ins, sit-ins, lie-ins, and smash-ins. Students engaged in such activities are apparently confident that they know far more about how to operate public school systems than do their parents, teachers, and elected school officials. It is no answer to say that the particular students here have not yet reached such high points in their demands to attend classes in order to exercise their political pressures. Turned loose with lawsuits for damages and injunctions against their teachers as they are here, it is nothing but wishful thinking to imagine that young, immature students will not soon believe it is their right to control the schools rather than the right of the States that collect the taxes to hire the teachers for the benefit of the pupils. This case, therefore, wholly without constitutional reasons in my judgment, subjects all the public schools in the country to the whims and caprices of their loudest-mouthed, but maybe not their brightest, students. I, for one, am not fully persuaded that school pupils are wise enough, even with the Court's expert help from Washington, to run the 23,390 public school systems in our 50 States. I wish, therefore, wholly to disclaim any purpose on my part to hold that the Federal Constitution compels the teachers, parents, and elected school officials to surrender control of the American public school system to public school students. I dissent.

Mt. Healthy City Board of Education v. Doyle
429 U.S. 274 (1977)

MR. JUSTICE REHNQUIST delivered the opinion of the Court.

Respondent Doyle sued petitioner Mt. Healthy Board of Education in the United States District Court for the Southern District of Ohio. Doyle claimed that the Board's refusal to renew his contract in 1971 violated his rights under the First and Fourteenth Amendments to the United States Constitution. After a bench trial the District Court held that Doyle was entitled to reinstatement with backpay. The Court of Appeals for the Sixth Circuit affirmed the judgment, and we granted the Board's petition for certiorari.

Doyle was first employed by the Board in 1966. He worked under one-year contracts for the first three years, and under a two-year contract from 1969 to 1971. In 1969 he was elected president of the Teachers' Association, in which position he worked to expand the subjects of direct negotiation between the Association and the Board of Education. During Doyle's one-year term as president of the Association, and during the succeeding year when he served on its executive committee, there was apparently some tension in relations between the Board and the Association.

Beginning early in 1970, Doyle was involved in several incidents not directly connected with his role in the Teachers' Association. In one instance, he engaged in an argument with another teacher which culminated in the other teacher's slapping him. Doyle subsequently refused to accept an apology and insisted upon some punishment for the other teacher. His persistence in the matter resulted in the suspension of both teachers for one day, which was followed by a walkout by a number of other teachers, which in turn resulted in the lifting of the suspensions.

On other occasions, Doyle got into an argument with employees of the school cafeteria over the amount of spaghetti which had been served him; referred to students, in connection with a disciplinary complaint, as "sons of bitches"; and made an obscene gesture to two girls in connection with their failure to obey commands made in his capacity as cafeteria supervisor. Chronologically the last in the series of incidents which respondent was involved in during his employment by the Board was a telephone call by him to a local radio station. It was the Board's consideration of this incident which the court below found to be a violation of the First and Fourteenth Amendments.

In February 1971, the principal circulated to various teachers a memorandum relating to teacher dress and appearance, which was apparently prompted by the view of some in the administration that there was a relationship between teacher appearance and public support for bond issues. Doyle's response to the receipt of the memorandum—on a subject which he apparently understood was to be settled by joint teacher-administration action—was to convey the substance of the memorandum to a disc jockey at WSAI, a Cincinnati radio station, who promptly announced the adoption of the dress code as a news item. Doyle subsequently apologized to the principal, conceding that he should have made some prior communication of his criticism to the school administration.

Approximately one month later the superintendent made his customary annual recommendations to the Board as to the rehiring of nontenured teachers. He recommended that Doyle not be rehired. [T]he recommendation was adopted by the Board. Shortly after being notified of this decision, respondent requested a statement of reasons for the Board's actions. He received a statement citing "a notable lack of tact in handling professional matters which leaves much doubt as to your sincerity in establishing good school relationships." That general statement was followed by references to the radio station incident and to the obscene-gesture incident.

The District Court found that all of these incidents had in fact occurred. It concluded that respondent Doyle's telephone call to the radio station was "clearly protected by the First Amendment," and that because it had played a "substantial part" in the decision of the Board not to renew Doyle's employment, he was entitled to reinstatement with backpay. The Court of Appeals affirmed in a brief *per curiam* opinion.

Doyle's claims under the First and Fourteenth Amendments are not defeated by the fact that he did not have tenure. Even though he could have been discharged for no reason whatever, and had no constitutional right to a hearing prior to the decision not to rehire him, he may nonetheless establish a claim to reinstatement if the decision not to rehire him was made by reason of his exercise of constitutionally protected First Amendment freedoms.

That question of whether speech of a government employee is constitutionally protected expression necessarily entails striking "a balance between the interests of the teacher, as a citizen, in commenting upon matters of public concern and the interest of the State, as an employer, in promoting the efficiency of the public services it performs through its employees." There is no suggestion by the Board that Doyle violated any established policy, or that its reaction to his communication to the radio station was anything more than an ad hoc response to Doyle's action in making the memorandum public. We therefore accept the District Court's finding that the communication was protected by the First and Fourteenth Amendments. We are not, however, entirely in agreement with that court's manner of reasoning from this finding to the conclusion that Doyle is entitled to reinstatement with backpay.

The District Court made the following "conclusions" on this aspect of the case:

"1) If a non-permissible reason, e.g., exercise of First Amendment rights, played a substantial part in the decision not to renew—even in the face of other permissible grounds—the decision may not stand.

"2) A non-permissible reason did play a substantial part. That is clear from the letter of the Superintendent immediately following the Board's decision, which stated two reasons—the one, the conversation with the radio station clearly protected by the First Amendment."

At the same time, though, it stated that

"[i]n fact, as this Court sees it and finds, both the Board and the Superintendent were faced with a situation in which there did exist in fact reason . . . independent of any First Amendment rights or exercise thereof, to not extend tenure."

Since respondent Doyle had no tenure, and there was therefore not even a state-law requirement of "cause" or "reason" before a decision could be made not to renew his employment, it is not clear what the District Court meant by this latter statement. Clearly the Board legally *could* have dismissed respondent had the radio station incident never come to its attention. One plausible meaning of the court's statement is that the Board and the Superintendent not only could, but in fact *would* have reached that decision had not the constitutionally protected incident of the telephone call to the radio station occurred. We are thus brought to the issue whether, even if that were the case, the fact that the protected conduct played a "substantial part" in the actual decision not to renew would necessarily amount to a constitutional violation justifying remedial action. We think that it would not.

A rule of causation which focuses solely on whether protected conduct played a part, "substantial" or otherwise, in a decision not to rehire, could place an employee in a better position as a result of the exercise of constitutionally protected conduct than he would have occupied had he done nothing. The difficulty with the rule enunciated by the District Court is that it would require reinstatement in cases where a dramatic and perhaps abrasive incident is inevitably on the minds of those responsible for the decision to rehire, and does indeed play a part in that decision—even if the same decision would have been reached had the incident not occurred. The constitutional principle at stake is sufficiently vindicated if such an employee is placed in no worse a position than if he had not engaged in the conduct. A borderline or marginal candidate should not have the employment question resolved against him because of constitutionally protected conduct. But that same candidate ought not to be able, by engaging in such conduct, to prevent his employer from assessing his performance record and reaching a decision not to rehire on the basis of that record, simply because the protected conduct makes the employer more certain of the correctness of its decision.

This is especially true where, as the District Court observed was the case here, the current decision to rehire will accord "tenure." The long-term consequences of an award of tenure are of great moment both to the employee and to the employer. They are too significant for us to hold that the Board in this case would be precluded, because it considered constitutionally protected conduct in deciding not to rehire Doyle, from attempting to prove to a trier of fact that quite apart from such conduct Doyle's record was such that he would not have been rehired in any event.

Initially, in this case, the burden was properly placed upon respondent to show that his conduct was constitutionally protected, and that this conduct was a "substantial factor"—or, to put it in other words, that it was a "motivating factor" in the Board's decision not to rehire him. Respondent having carried that burden, however, the District Court should have gone on to determine whether the Board had shown by a preponderance of the evidence that it would have reached the same decision as to respondent's reemployment even in the absence of the protected conduct.

We cannot tell from the District Court opinion and conclusions, nor from the opinion of the Court of Appeals affirming the judgment of the District Court, what conclusion those courts would have reached had they applied this test. The judgment of the Court of Appeals is therefore vacated, and the case remanded for further proceedings consistent with this opinion.

Guzick v. Drebus
431 F. 2d 594 (1970)

The complaint charged that Thomas Guzick, Jr., a seventeen year old, eleventh grade student at Shaw High School, had been denied the right of free speech guaranteed to him by the United States Constitution's First Amendment. He asserted that this right had been denied him when he was suspended for refusing to remove, while in the classrooms and the school premises, a button which solicited participation in an anti-war demonstration that was to take place in Chicago.

On March 11, 1969, young Guzick appeared at the office of defendant Drebus, principal of the high school, bringing a supply of pamphlets which advocated attendance at the same planned Chicago anti-war demonstration as was identified by the button. The boys were denied permission to distribute the pamphlets, and were also told to remove the buttons which both were then wearing. Guzick said that his lawyer, counsel for him in this litigation, told him that a United States Supreme Court decision entitled him to wear the button in school. Principal Drebus directed that he remove it and desist from wearing it in the school. Being told by Guzick that he would not obey, the principal suspended him and advised that such suspension would continue until Guzick obeyed.

The District Judge denied plaintiff's application for a preliminary injunction, and after a plenary evidentiary hearing, the complaint was dismissed.

Plaintiff insists that the facts of this case bring it within the rule of *Tinker* v. *Des Moines Independent Community School District* (1969). We are at once aware that unless *Tinker* can be distinguished, reversal is required. We consider that the facts of this case clearly provide such distinction.

The rule applied to appellant Guzick was of long standing—forbidding all wearing of buttons, badges, scarves and other means whereby the wearers identify themselves as supporters of a cause or bearing messages unrelated to their education. Such things as support the high school athletic teams or advertise a school play are not forbidden. The rule had its genesis in the days when fraternities were competing for the favor of the students and it has been uniformly enforced. The rule has continued as one of universal application and usefulness. While controversial buttons appeared from time to time, they were required to be removed as soon as the school authorities could get to them.

From the total evidence, including that of educators, school administrators and others having special relevant qualifications, the District Judge concluded that abrogation of the rule would inevitably result in collisions and disruptions which would seriously subvert Shaw High School as a place of education for its students, black and white.

1. The Rule of *Tinker*

Contrasting with the admitted long standing and uniform enforcement of Shaw's no symbol rule, the majority opinion in *Tinker* was careful to point out,

> "It is also relevant that the school authorities [in *Tinker*] did not purport to prohibit the wearing of all symbols of political or controversial significance. The record shows that students in some of the schools wore buttons relating to national political campaigns, and some even wore the Iron Cross, traditionally a symbol of Nazism. *The order prohibiting the wearing of armbands did not extend to these.* Instead, a particular symbol—black armbands worn to exhibit opposition to this Nation's involvement in Vietnam—was singled out for prohibition."

Further distinguishing *Tinker* from our case are their respective settings. No potential racial collisions were background to *Tinker,* whereas here the changing racial composition of Shaw High from all white to 70% black, made the no symbol rule of even greater good than had characterized its original adoption. In our view, school authorities should not be faulted for adhering to a relatively non-oppressive rule that will indeed serve our ultimate goal of meaningful integration of our public schools.

2. Shaw High School's Need for its Rule

In *Tinker* the Court concluded that a regulation forbidding expressions opposing the Vietnam conflict anywhere on school property would violate the students' constitutional rights,

> "at least *if it could not be justified* by a showing that the students' activities would materially and substantially disrupt the work and discipline of the school."

But in the case at bar, the District Judge, upon a valid appraisal of the evidence, did find that "if all buttons are permitted or if any buttons are permitted, a serious discipline problem will result, racial tensions will be exacerbated, and the educational process will be significantly and substantially disrupted." Again, in *Tinker,* the majority said,

> "But, in our system, undifferentiated fear or apprehension of disturbance is not enough to overcome the right of freedom of expression."

Here, the District Court, conscious of the commands of *Tinker,* said,

> "Furthermore, there is in the present case *much more than an 'undifferentiated fear of apprehension'* of disturbances likely to result from the wearing of buttons at Shaw High School. The wearing of buttons and other emblems and insignia has occasioned substantial disruptive conduct in the past at Shaw High. It is likely to occasion such conduct if permitted henceforth. The wearing of buttons and other insignia will serve to exacerbate an already tense situation, to promote divisions and disputes, including physical violence among the students, and to disrupt and interfere with the normal operation of the school and with appropriate discipline by the school authorities."

In our view, the potentiality and the imminence of the admitted rebelliousness in the Shaw students support the wisdom of the no-symbol rule. Surely those charged with providing a place and atmosphere for educating young Americans should not have to fashion their disciplinary rules only after good order has been at least once demolished.

3. Conclusion

We will not attempt extensive review of the many great decisions which have forbidden abridgment of free speech. We have been thrilled by their beautiful and impassioned language. They are part of our American heritage. None of these masterpieces, however, were composed or uttered to support the wearing of buttons in high school classrooms. We are not persuaded that enforcement of such a rule as Shaw High School's no-symbol proscription would have excited like judicial classics. Denying Shaw High School the right to enforce this small disciplinary rule could, and most likely would, impair the rights of its students to an education and the rights of its teachers to fulfill their responsibilities.

We must be aware in these contentious times that America's classrooms and their environs will lose their usefulness as places in which to educate our young people if pupils come to school wearing the badges of their respective disagreements, and provoke confrontations with their fellows and their teachers. The buttons are claimed to be a form of free speech. Unless they have some relevance to what is being considered or taught, a school classroom is no place for the untrammeled exercise of such right.

Judgment Affirmed.

Mailloux v. Kiley
323 F. Supp. 1387 (1971)

This case involves an action by a public high school teacher against the City of Lawrence, the members of its school committee, the superintendent of its schools, and the principal of its high school. Plaintiff claims that in discharging him for his classroom conduct in connection with a taboo word the school committee deprived him of his rights under the First and Fourteenth Amendments to the United States Constitution, and that, therefore, he has a cause of action under 42 U.S.C. § 1983.

These are the facts as found by this court after a full hearing.

Defendant principal assigned plaintiff to teach basic English to a class of about 25 students, boys and girls 16 and 17 years of age, all in the junior class or 11th grade.

Plaintiff assigned to the class for outside reading chapters in a novel, The Thread That Runs So True, by Jesse Stuart. Nowhere in the novel is there the word "fuck."

October 1, 1970, during a discussion of the book in class, [h]e then introduced the subject of society and its ways, as illustrated by taboo words. He wrote the word "goo" on the board and asked the class for a definition. No one being able to define it, plaintiff said that this word did not exist in English but in another culture it might be a taboo word. He then wrote on the blackboard the word "fuck," and, in accordance with his customary teaching methods of calling for volunteers to respond to a question, asked the class in general for a definition. After a couple of minutes a boy volunteered that the word meant "sexual intercourse." Plaintiff, without using the word orally, said: "we have two words, sexual intercourse, and this word on the board * * * one * * * is acceptable by society * * * the other is not accepted. It is a taboo word." After a few minutes of discussion of other aspects of taboos, plaintiff went on to other matters.

At all times in the discussion plaintiff was in good faith pursuing what he regarded as an educational goal. He was not attempting to probe the private feelings, or attitudes, or experiences of his students, or to embarrass them.

October 2, 1970, the parent of a girl in the class, being erroneously informed that plaintiff had called upon a particular girl in the class to define the taboo word, complained to the principal. He asked Miss Horner the head of the English department to investigate the incident. Plaintiff did admit that he had written on the board the taboo word. He also said he had "probably" called upon a specific girl to define the word. But this court is persuaded by all the testimony that he did not in fact call on any girl individually and that his statement to Miss Horner, repeated later to the union, of what he "probably" did is not an accurate statement of what he actually did. At his meeting with Miss Horner, plaintiff did not refer to the novel which the class had been discussing.

After plaintiff had been interviewed by Miss Horner, defendant superintendent on October 13, 1970 suspended him for seven days with pay.

The committee gave plaintiff and his counsel a hearing on October 20, 1970.

October 21, 1970 the committee dismissed plaintiff on the general charge of "conduct unbecoming a teacher." It made no finding as to any specific particular.

Following his discharge, plaintiff brought this action seeking temporary and permanent relief. After a two day hearing this court issued a temporary injunction ordering the defendant members of the school committee to restore plaintiff to his employment.

Defendants appealed and asked for a stay pending appeal. [T]he Court of Appeals denied the stay and dismissed the appeal. This court thereafter conducted a further hearing. Upon the basis of both hearings this court makes the following additional findings.

1. The topic of taboo words had a limited relevance to the Stuart novel which plaintiff's class was discussing, but it had a high degree of relevance to the proper teaching of eleventh grade basic English even to students not expecting to go to college and therefore placed in a "low track."

2. The word "fuck" is relevant to a discussion of taboo words. Its impact effectively illustrates how taboo words function.

3. Boys and girls in an eleventh grade have a sophistication sufficient to treat the word from a serious educational viewpoint. While at first they may be surprised and self-conscious to have the word discussed, they are not likely to be embarrassed or offended.

4. Plaintiff's writing the word did not have a disturbing effect. A class might be less disturbed by having the word written than if it had been spoken. Most students had seen the word even if they had not used it.

5. Plaintiff's calling upon the class for a volunteer to define the word was a technique that was reasonable and was in accordance with customs in plaintiff's class. It avoided implicating anyone who did not wish to participate.

6. The word "fuck" is in books in the school library.

7. In the opinion of experts of significant standing, such as members of the faculties of the Harvard University School of Education and of Massachusetts Institute of Technology, the discussion of taboo words in the eleventh grade, the way plaintiff used the word "fuck," his writing of it on the blackboard, and the inquiry he addressed to the class, were appropriate and reasonable under the circumstances and served a serious educational purpose. In the opinion of other qualified persons plaintiff's use of the word was not under the circumstances reasonable, or appropriate, or conducive to a serious educational purpose. It has

not been shown what is the preponderant opinion in the teaching profession, or in that part of the profession which teaches English.

The parties have not relied upon any express regulation of the Lawrence School Committee or the Lawrence High School. The regulations set forth in an attachment to the complaint have no general or specific provisions relevant to this case.

We now turn to questions of ultimate fact and of law.

Defendant members of the school committee acted for the state when they discharged plaintiff and were therefore subject to the Fourteenth Amendment's command.

[1] The Fourteenth Amendment recognizes that a public school teacher has not only a civic right to freedom of speech both outside and inside the schoolhouse, but also some measure of academic freedom as to his in-classroom teaching.

Here we have the use of teaching methods which divide professional opinion. There is substantial support from expert witnesses of undoubted competence that the discussion of taboo words was relevant to an assigned book, and, whether or not so relevant, was at least relevant to the subject of eleventh grade English, that "fuck" was an appropriate choice of an illustrative taboo word, and that writing it on the board and calling upon the class to define it were appropriate techniques. Yet there was also substantial evidence, chiefly from persons with experience as principals but also from the head of the English department at plaintiff's school, that it was inappropriate to use the particular word under the circumstances of this case. The weight of the testimony offered leads this court to make an ultimate finding that plaintiff's methods served an educational purpose, in the sense that they were relevant and had professional endorsement from experts of significant standing. But this court has not implied that the weight of opinion in the teaching profession as a whole, or the weight of opinion among English teachers as a whole, would be that plaintiff's methods were within limits that, even if they would not themselves use them, they would regard as permissible for others. To make a finding on that point would have required a more thorough sampling, especially of younger teachers, than the record offers.

When a male teacher asks a class of adolescent boys and girls to define a taboo sexual word the question must not go beyond asking for verbal knowledge and become a titillating probe of privacy. Here, it should be stated unequivocally, there is no evidence that this plaintiff transcended legitimate professional purposes. Indeed, the court has specifically found he acted in good faith. But the risk of abuse involved in the technique of questioning students precludes this court from concluding that the method was *plainly* permissible. Too much depends on the context and the teacher's good faith.

[2] Where, as here, a secondary school teacher chooses a teaching method that is not necessary for the proper instruction of his class, that is not shown to be regarded by the weight of opinion in his profession as permissible, that is not so transparently proper that a court can without expert testimony evaluate it as proper, but that is relevant to his subject and students and, in the opinion of experts of significant standing, serves a serious educational purpose, it is a heretofore undecided question whether the Constitution gives him any right to use the method or leaves the issue to the school authorities.

In support of a qualified right of a teacher, even at the secondary level, to use a teaching method which is relevant and in the opinion of experts of significant standing has a serious educational purpose is the central rationale of academic freedom. The Constitution recognizes that freedom in order to foster open minds, creative imaginations, and adventurous spirits. Our national belief is that the heterodox as well as the orthodox are a source of individual and of social growth. We do not confine academic freedom to conventional teachers or to those who can get a majority vote from their colleagues. Our faith is that the teacher's freedom to choose among options for which there is any substantial support will increase his intellectual vitality and his moral strength. The teacher whose responsibility has been nourished by independence, enterprise, and free choice becomes for his student a better model of the democratic citizen. His examples of applying and adapting the values of the old order to the demands and opportunities of a constantly changing world are among the most important lessons he gives to youth.

The secondary school more clearly than the college or university acts *in loco parentis* with respect to minors. It is closely governed by a school board selected by a local community. The faculty does not have the independent traditions, the broad discretion as to teaching methods, nor usually the intellectual qualifications, of university professors. Most parents, students, school boards, and members of the community usually expect the secondary school to concentrate on transmitting basic information, teaching "the best that is known and thought in the world," training by established techniques, and, to some extent at least, indoctrinating in the *mores* of the surrounding society. Moreover, it cannot be accepted as a premise that the student is voluntarily in the classroom and willing to be exposed to a teaching method which, though reasonable, is not approved by the school authorities or by the weight of professional opinion.

Bearing in mind these competing considerations, this court rules that when a secondary school teacher uses a teaching method which he does not prove has the support of the preponderant opinion of the teaching profession or of the part of it to which he belongs, but which he merely proves is relevant to his subject and students, is regarded by experts of significant standing as serving a serious educational purpose, and was used by him in good faith the state may suspend or discharge a teacher for using that method but it may not resort to such drastic sanctions unless the state proves he was put on notice either by a regulation or otherwise that he should not use that method. This exclusively procedural protection is afforded to a teacher not because he is a state employee, or because he is a citizen, but because in his teaching capacity he is engaged in the exercise of what may plausibly be considered "vital First Amendment rights." In his teaching capacity he is not required to "guess what conduct or utterance may lose him his position." If he did not have the right to be warned before he was discharged, he might be more timid than it is in the public interest that he should be, and he might steer away from reasonable methods with which it is in the public interest to experiment.

In the instant case it is not claimed that any regulation warned plaintiff not to follow the methods he chose. Nor can it be said that plaintiff should have known that his teaching methods were not permitted. There is no substantial evidence that his methods were contrary to an informal rule, to an understanding among school teachers of his school or teachers generally, to a body of disciplinary precedents, to precise canons of ethics, or to specific opinions expressed in professional journals or other publications. This was not the kind of unforeseeable outrageous conduct which all men of good will would, once their attention is called to it, immediately perceive to be forbidden.

Finally, in the face of the record of judicial uncertainty in this case it cannot be held that it was self-evident that a teacher should not have used the methods followed by plaintiff. We can hardly say that plaintiff should have known what was not evident to judges after taking evidence, hearing argument, and reflecting in chambers.

Nothing herein suggests that school authorities are not free after they have learned that the teacher is using a teaching method of which they disapprove, and which is not appropriate to the proper teaching of the subject, to suspend him until he agrees to cease using the method.

Board of Education, Island Trees Union Free School Dist. No. 26 v. Pico
102 S. Ct. 2799 (1982)

JUSTICE BRENNAN announced the judgment of the Court.

The principal question presented is whether the First Amendment imposes limitations upon the exercise by a local school board of its discretion to remove library books from high school and junior high school libraries.

I

In September 1975, petitioners attended a conference sponsored by Parents of New York United (PONYU), a politically conservative organization of parents concerned about education legislation in the State of New York. At the conference these petitioners obtained lists of books described as "objectionable," and "improper fare for school students." It was later determined that the High School library contained nine of the listed books, and that another listed book was in the Junior High School library. [T]he Board gave an "unofficial direction" that the listed books be removed from the library shelves and delivered to the Board's offices, so that Board members could read them. When this directive was carried out, it became publicized, and the Board issued a press release justifying its action. It characterized the removed books as "anti-American, anti-Christian, anti-Semitic, and just plain filthy," and concluded that "It is our duty, our moral obligation, to protect the children in our schools from this moral danger as surely as from physical and medical dangers."

A short time later, the Board appointed a "Book Review Committee" to read the listed books and to recommend to the Board whether the books should be retained, taking into account the books' "educational suitability," "good taste," "relevance," and "appropriateness to age and grade level." In July, the Committee made its final report to the Board, recommending that five of the listed books be retained. The Board substantially rejected the Committee's report, deciding that only one book should be returned to the High School library without restriction, that another should be made available subject to parental approval, but that the remaining nine books should "be removed from elementary and secondary libraries and [from] use in the curriculum." The Board gave no reasons for rejecting the recommendations of the Committee that it had appointed.

Respondents claimed that the Board's actions denied them their rights under the First Amendment. They asked the court for a declaration that the Board's actions were unconstitutional, and for ordering the Board to return the nine books to the school libraries and to refrain from interfering with the use of those books in the schools' curricula.

The District Court granted summary judgment in favor of petitioners. With this factual premise as its background, the court rejected respondents' contention that their First Amendment rights had been infringed by the Board's actions. Noting that statute, history, and precedent had vested local school boards with a broad discretion to formulate educational policy, the court concluded that it should not intervene in " 'the daily operations of school systems' " unless " 'basic constitutional values' " were " 'sharply implicate[d],' " and determined that the conditions for such intervention did not exist in the present case.

A three judge panel of the United States Court of Appeals reversed the judgment of the District Court, and remanded the action for a trial on respondents' allegations. Judge Sifton treated the case as involving "an unusual and irregular intervention in the school libraries' operations by persons not routinely concerned with such matters," and concluded that petitioners were obliged to demonstrate a reasonable basis for interfering with respondents' First Amendment rights.

II

We emphasize at the outset the limited nature of the substantive question presented by the case before us. For as this case is presented to us, it does not involve textbooks, or indeed any books that Island Trees students would be required to read. Respondents do not seek in this Court to impose limitations upon their school board's discretion to prescribe the curricula of the Island Trees schools. On the contrary, the only books at issue in this case are *library* books, books that by their nature are optional rather than required reading. [T]he only action challenged in this case is the *removal* from school libraries of books originally placed there by the school authorities, or without objection from them.

In sum, the issue before us may best be restated as two distinct questions. First, does the First Amendment impose *any* limitations upon the discretion of petitioners to remove library books from the Island Trees High School and Junior High School? Second, if so, do the affidavits and other evidentiary materials before the District Court, construed most favorably to respondents, raise a genuine issue of fact whether petitioners might have exceeded those limitations? If we answer either of these questions in the negative, then we must reverse the judgment of the Court of Appeals and reinstate the District Court's summary judgment for petitioners. If we answer both questions in the affirmative, then we must affirm the judgment below. We examine these questions in turn.

A

The Court has long recognized that local school boards have broad discretion in the management of school affairs. We are therefore in full agreement with petitioners that local school boards must be permitted "to establish and apply their curriculum in such a way as to transmit community values," and that "there is a legitimate and substantial community interest in promoting respect for authority and traditional values be they social, moral, or political."

At the same time, however, we have necessarily recognized that the discretion of the States and local school boards in matters of education must be exercised in a manner that comports with the transcendent imperatives of the First Amendment.

Of course, courts should not "intervene in the resolution of conflicts which arise in the daily operations of school systems" unless "basic constitutional values" are "directly and sharply implicate[d]" in those conflicts. But we think that the First Amendment rights of students may be directly and sharply implicated by the removal of books from the shelves of a school library. [W]e have recognized that "the State may not, consistently with the spirit of the First Amendment, contract the spectrum of available knowledge." In keeping with this principle, we have held that in a variety of contexts "the Constitution protects the right to receive information and ideas." First, the right to receive ideas follows ineluctably from the *sender's* First Amendment right to send them: "The right of freedom of speech and press . . . embraces the right to distribute literature, . . . and necessarily protects the right to receive it." "The dissemination of ideas can accomplish nothing if otherwise willing addressees are not free to receive and consider them. It would be a barren marketplace of ideas that had only sellers and no buyers."

More importantly, the right to receive ideas is a necessary predicate to the *recipient's* meaningful exercise of his own rights of speech, press, and political freedom. In sum, just as access to ideas makes it possible for citizens generally to exercise their rights of free speech and press in a meaningful manner, such access prepares students for active and effective participation in the pluralistic, often contentious society in which they will soon be adult members. Of course all First Amendment rights accorded to students must be construed "in light of the special characteristics of the school environment." But the special characteristics of the school *library* make that environment especially appropriate for the recognition of the First Amendment rights of students.

Petitioners emphasize the inculcative function of secondary education, and argue that they must be allowed *unfettered* discretion to "transmit community values" through the Island Trees schools. But that sweeping claim overlooks the unique role of the school library. It appears from the record that use of the Island Trees school libraries is completely voluntary on the part of students. Their selection of books from these libraries is entirely a matter of free choice; the libraries afford them an opportunity at self-education and individual enrichment that is wholly optional. Petitioners might well defend their claim of absolute discretion in matters of *curriculum* by reliance upon their duty to inculcate community values. But we think that petitioners' reliance upon that duty is misplaced where, as here, they attempt to extend their claim of absolute discretion beyond the compulsory environment of the classroom, into the school library and the regime of voluntary inquiry that there holds sway.

In rejecting petitioners' claim of absolute discretion to remove books from their school libraries, we do not deny that local school boards have a substantial legitimate role to play in the determination of school library content. We thus must turn to the question of the extent to which the First Amendment places limitations upon the discretion of petitioners to remove books from their libraries.

Petitioners rightly possess significant discretion to determine the content of their school libraries. But that discretion may not be exercised in a narrowly partisan or political manner. Our Constitution does not permit the official suppression of *ideas*. Thus whether petitioners' removal of books from their school libraries denied respondents their First Amendment rights depends upon the motivation behind petitioners' actions. If petitioners *intended* by their removal decision to deny respondents access to ideas with which petitioners disagreed, and if this intent was the decisive factor in petitioners' decision, then petitioners have exercised their discretion in violation of the Constitution. On the other hand, respondents implicitly concede that an unconstitutional motivation would *not* be demonstrated if it were shown that petitioners had decided to remove the books at issue because those books were pervasively vulgar. And again, respondents concede that if it were demonstrated that the removal decision was based solely upon the "educational suitability" of the books in question, then their removal would be "perfectly permissible." In other words, in respondents' view such motivations, if decisive of petitioners' actions, would not carry the danger of an official suppression of ideas, and thus would not violate respondents' First Amendment rights.

As noted earlier, nothing in our decision today affects in any way the discretion of a local school board to choose books to *add* to the libraries of their schools. Because we are concerned in this case with the suppression of ideas, our holding today affects only the discretion to *remove* books. In brief, we hold that local school boards may not remove books from school library shelves simply because they dislike the ideas contained in those books and seek by their removal to "prescribe what shall be orthodox in politics, nationalism, religion, or other matters of opinion."

We now turn to the remaining question presented by this case: Do the evidentiary materials raise a genuine issue of material fact whether petitioners exceeded constitutional limitations in exercising their discretion to remove the books from the school libraries? We conclude that the materials do raise such a question, which forecloses summary judgment in favor of petitioners.

Before the District Court, respondents claimed that petitioners' decision to remove the books "was based upon [their] personal values, morals and tastes." Respondents also claimed that petitioners objected to the books in part because excerpts from them were "anti-American." [T]he record developed in the District Court shows that when petitioners offered their first public explanation for the removal of the books, they relied in part on the assertion that the removed books were "anti-American," and "offensive to . . . Americans in general." Furthermore, while the Book Review Committee appointed by petitioners was instructed to make its recommendations based upon criteria that appear on their face to be permissible—the books' "educational suitability," "good taste," "relevance," and "appropriateness to age and grade level"—the Committee's recommendations that five of the books be retained and that only two be removed were essentially rejected by petitioners, without any statement of reasons for doing so. Finally, while petitioners originally defended their removal decision with the explanation that "these books contain obscenities, blasphemies, and perversion beyond description," one of the books, *A Reader for Writers,* was removed even though it contained no such language.

Standing alone, this evidence respecting the substantive motivations behind petitioners' removal decision would not be decisive. This would be a very different case if the record demonstrated that petitioners had employed established, regular, and facially unbiased procedures for the review of controversial materials. But the actual record in the case before us suggests the exact opposite. Respondents alleged that in making their removal decision petitioners ignored "the advice of literary experts," the views of "librarians and teachers within the Island Trees School system," the advice of the superintendent of schools, and the guidance of "publications that rate books for junior and senior high school students." Respondents also claimed that petitioners' decision was based solely on the fact that the books were named on the PONYU list received by petitioners and that petitioners "did not undertake an independent review of other books in the [school] libraries." The record shows that immediately after petitioners first ordered the books removed from the library shelves, the superintendent of schools reminded them that "we already have a policy . . . designed expressly to handle such problems," and recommended that the removal decision be approached through this established channel. But the Board disregarded the superintendent's advice, and instead resorted to the extraordinary procedure of appointing a Book Review Committee—the advice of which was later rejected without explanation. In sum, respondents' allegations and some of the evidentiary materials presented below do not rule out the possibility that petitioners' removal procedures were highly irregular and ad hoc—the antithesis of those procedures that might tend to allay suspicions regarding petitioners' motivations.

The evidence plainly does not foreclose the possibility that petitioners' decision to remove the books rested decisively upon disagreement with constitutionally protected ideas in those books, or upon a desire on petitioners' part to impose upon the students of the Island Trees High School and Junior High School a political orthodoxy to which petitioners and their constituents adhered. Of course, some of the evidence before the District Court might lead a finder of fact to accept petitioners' claim that their removal decision was based upon constitutionally valid concerns. But that evidence at most creates a genuine issue of material fact on the critical question of the credibility of petitioners' justifications for their decision: On that issue, it simply cannot be said that there is no genuine issue as to any material fact.

Affirmed.

JUSTICE POWELL, dissenting.

The plurality opinion today rejects a basic concept of public school education in our country: that the States and locally elected school boards should have the responsibility for determining the educational policy of the public schools. After today's decision any junior high school student, by instituting a suit against a school board or teacher, may invite a judge to overrule an educational decision by the official body designated by the people to operate the schools.

School boards are uniquely local and democratic institutions. Unlike the governing bodies of cities and counties, school boards have only one responsibility: the education of the youth of our country during their most formative and impressionable years. Apart from health, no subject is closer to the hearts of parents than their children's education during those years. For these reasons, the governance of elementary and secondary education traditionally has been placed in the hands of a local board, responsible locally to the parents and citizens of school districts. It is fair to say that no single agency of government at any level is closer to the people whom it serves than the typical school board.

I therefore view today's decision with genuine dismay. Whatever the final outcome of this suit and suits like it, the resolution of educational policy decisions through litigation, and the exposure of school board members to liability for such decisions, can be expected to corrode the school board's authority and effectiveness. As is evident from the generality of the plurality's "standard" for judicial review, the decision as to the educational worth of a book is a highly subjective one. Judges rarely are as competent as school authorities to make this decision; nor are judges responsive to the parents and people of the school district.

The plurality's reasoning is marked by contradiction. It purports to acknowledge the traditional role of school boards and parents in deciding what should be taught in the schools. It states the truism that the schools are vehicles for " 'inculcating fundamental values necessary to the maintenance of a democratic political system.' " Yet when a school board, as in this case, takes its responsibilities seriously and seeks to decide what the fundamental values are that should be imparted, the plurality finds a constitutional violation.

A school board's attempt to instill in its students the ideas and values on which a democratic system depends is viewed as an impermissible suppression of other ideas and values on which other systems of government and other societies thrive. Books may not be removed because they are indecent; extoll violence, intolerance and racism; or degrade the dignity of the individual. Although I would leave this educational decision to the duly constituted board, I certainly would not *require* a school board to promote ideas and values repugnant to a democratic society or to teach such values to *children*.

In different contexts and in different times, the destruction of written materials has been the symbol of despotism and intolerance. But the removal of nine vulgar or racist books from a high school library by a concerned local school board does not raise this specter. For me, today's decision symbolizes a debilitating encroachment upon the institutions of a free people.

NOTES

1. Whitney v. California, 274 U.S. 357 (1927) at 376–77.
2. Schenck v. United States, 249 U.S. 47 (1919) at 52.
3. Louis Fischer and David Schimmel, *The Rights of Students and Teachers* (New York: Harper and Row, 1982), p. 9.
4. Minersville School District v. Gobitis, 310 U.S. 586 (1940) at 598.
5. Id. at 600.
6. West Virginia State Board of Educ. v. Barnette, 319 U.S. 624 (1943) at 642.
7. Id. at 640.
8. Id. at 637.
9. Russo v. Central School District No 1, 469 F. 2d 623 (1972), cert. denied 411 U.S. 932 (1973).
10. Id. at 634.
11. Tinker v. Des Moines Commun. School Dist., 393 U.S. 503 (1969) at 506.
12. Id. at 526.
13. Perry Education Assn. v. Perry Local Educator's Assn., 103 S. Ct. 948 (1983) at 959.
14. Lusk v. Estes, 361 F. Supp. 653 (1973) at 663.
15. Bowman v. Pulaski Special School Dist., 723 F. 2d 640 (1983) at 45.
16. Scoville v. Board of Educ. of Joliet Township H.S. Dist. 204, 425 F. 2d 10 (1970) at 13.
17. Shanley v. Northeast Independent School Dist., 462 F. 2d 960 (1972) at 972.
18. Id. at 978.
19. Trachtman v. Anker, 563 F. 2d 512 (1977) at 519–520.
20. Kern Alexander and M. David Alexander, *The Law of Schools, Students and Teachers* (St. Paul, Minn.: West Publishing Co., 1984), p. 85.
21. Karr v. Schmidt, 460 F. 2d 609 (1972) at 667.
22. Miller v. School Dist. 167, Cook Co., Ill., 495 F. 2d 658 (1974) at 667.
23. Seyfried v. Walton, 668 F. 2d 214 (1981) at 216.
24. Id. at 217.
25. Ferrell v. Dallas, 393 U.S. 856 (1968) at 856.
26. Karr v. Schmidt, 401 U.S. 1201 (1971) at 1202–1203.
27. Keefe v. Geanakos, 418 F. 2d 359 (1969) at 362.
28. Parducci v. Rutland, 316 F. Supp. 352 (1970) at 355 and 357.
29. Brubaker v. Board of Educ., School Dist. 149, Cook County, Ill., 502 F. 2d 973 (1974) at 976–85.
30. Adler v. Board of Education, 342 U.S. 485 (1952) at 493.
31. Id. at 492.
32. Beilan v. Board of Public Educ. of Philadelphia, 357 U.S. 399 (1958) at 404.
33. Keyishian v. Board of Regents of Univ. of State of N.Y., 385 U.S. 589 (1967) at 602.
34. Rosenberg v. Board of Education, 92 N.Y.S. 2d 344 (1949) at 346.
35. President's Council, Dist. 25 v. Community School Board 25, 457 F. 2d 289 (1972), cert. denied, 409 U.S. 998 (1972) at 291.
36. Minarcini v. Strongsville City School Dist., 541 F. 2d 577 (1976) at 58.
37. Board of Educ., Island Trees Union Free School Dist. No. 26 v. Pico, 102 S. Ct. 2799 (1982) at 2809.
38. Tinker at 508.
39. Pickering v. Board of Educ., Lockport, Ill., 391 U.S. 563 (1968) at 572.

FIVE

The Concept
of Due Process:
Fairness in Educational
Administration

The idea of due process extends back to the English Magna Carta of 1215. Originally aimed at preventing the king from interrupting the liberty of freemen except "by the law of the land," it was expanded and developed to require that proper legal procedure must be followed when government attempts to deprive an individual of life, liberty, or property. The concept was written into the Fifth Amendment to the U.S. Constitution as follows: " . . . nor [shall any person] be deprived of life, liberty, or property, without due process of law. . . . " This protected the people against arbitrary procedures of the national government. Then, the Fourteenth Amendment was added in 1868, expressly granting people protection against due process violations by the states: " . . . nor shall any State deprive any person of life, liberty, or property, without due process of law. . . . "

From its English beginnings, the concept has been vague and difficult to define. Originally a guarantee for fair procedures—as the right to receive prompt and clear notice of charges and the opportunity to respond to them fully before an impartial tribunal—due process was gradually broadened to include further procedural protections, as the right to counsel when serious charges were leveled, and then to encompass broader, nonprocedural issues of fairness based on a generalized sense of right and wrong. This gave rise to a second legal arena for judging fairness, called substantive due process. Here the emphasis is on the

147

substance of a law, rule, or action. Actions or regulations judged to be arbitrary, capricious, or otherwise unreasonable, as presenting an irrefutable presumption, violate substantive due process. This is also true for rules that are so vague or broad that they defy clear understanding or reasonable limits, as well as unreasonable invasions of individual privacy. The defenses of government against charges that it deprived a person of life, liberty, or property without due process are either to show that due process was provided in sufficient proportion to the deprivation involved, or to show that its action had a rational relationship to a legitimate interest or purpose of government that overrode individual interests.

The heart of both due process concepts is fairness. Thus, while the two streams have distinctions, they are more properly viewed as part of the same whole. The extent of due process protection to be afforded an individual depends on the severity of the intended penalty. Thus, a threat of expulsion from school requires more procedural protection than a threat of suspension. In like manner, intended deprivations of teachers' liberty or property would carry a burden of due process procedures related to the weight of the consequences of official action. Also, the Supreme Court has applied strict scrutiny to due process violations involving rights the Court has identified as "fundamental," such as speech or religion. When strict scrutiny is applied, the official action must be justified as a compelling interest rather than just showing that the action bore a rational relationship to a legitimate purpose.

One of the best attempts to define the essence of this elusive but vitally important concept was made by Justice Frankfurter in 1951:

> "[D]ue process," unlike some legal rules, is not a technical conception with a fixed content unrelated to time, place, and circumstances. Expressing as it does . . . that feeling of just treatment through centuries . . . "due process" cannot be imprisoned within the treacherous limits of any formula. Representing a profound attitude of fairness between . . . the individual and government, "due process" is compounded of history, reason, the past course of decisions, and stout confidence in the strength of the democratic faith which we profess. Due process is not a mechanical instrument. It is not a yardstick. It is a process. It is a delicate process of adjustment inescapably involving the exercise of judgment. . . . [1]

The breadth and generality of the due process concept renders it amenable to strong, pervasive application to education by judicial activists or very slight application by judicial restraintists. Liberals are more likely to take the activist stance regarding due process, and easily grant standing to sue on due process grounds by seeing a "justicable" issue involving a teacher's or student's deprivation of liberty or property in the educational arena. For them, almost all due process issues are sufficiently "ripe" for action and involve substantial issues. Here is an area that is most conducive to liberal, activist lecturing on concepts of right and wrong. Further, liberal belief (in the educational and political wisdom of freeing students from those elements of authority they see as unnecessary and inhibiting of each person's unique development) finds comfort in the imposition of due process limitations on the exercise of power, as does support of teachers' independence and security.

Restraintists, of course, are wary of using this broad concept to make new law or substitute their personal judgment for that of legally constituted state and school-district officials. Due process restraintists are most likely to take conservative positions on educational philosophy that values strong adult control over the behavior of students and board-administrator control over teachers' behavior. Conservatives are less likely than liberals to recognize the required liberty or property interest in a suit that must be established to render a Fourteenth Amendment claim valid.

The first instance in which the Supreme Court allowed claims of liberty and property interests to be sufficient for it to adjudicate an education case was *Meyer* v. *Nebraska* (1923), in which the state's restriction preventing Meyer from teaching German in an elementary school was held to restrict Meyer's Fourteenth Amendment liberty. Although the decision was narrowly construed, it did restrain the state from interfering with the liberty guaranteed to Meyer against state action considered by the Court to be violative of substantive due process, in that the law was "arbitrary and without reasonable relation to any end within the competency of the state."[2]

Except for this instance of due process application to schools, and the *Pierce* case soon afterward, its use was relatively quiescent until the liberally activist sixties and seventies. The expansion of due process applications to education began with the federal appellate court decision in *Dixon* v. *Alabama State Board of Education* (1961), in which due process was applied to the liberty and property interests of students in their education. Some black students at a state college were expelled or placed on probation for Civil Rights demonstrations, including a lunch-counter sit-in. The court found that the misconduct for which disciplinary action was taken was never clearly specified, nor was it clear that all the expelled students participated in all the generalized charges made against them. Further, they were accorded neither notice nor a hearing before the disciplinary measures were taken. The court decided: "Whenever a governmental body acts so as to injure an individual, the Constitution requires that the act be consonant with due process of law. The minimum procedural requirements necessary to satisfy due process depend upon the circumstances and the interests of the parties involved."[3]

As to the importance of liberty and property interests in an education, the court was not reluctant to express its opinion:

> The precise nature of the private interest involved in this case is the right to remain at a public institution of higher learning in which the plaintiffs were students in good standing. It requires no argument to demonstrate that . . . [w]ithout sufficient education the plaintiffs would not be able to earn an adequate livelihood, to enjoy life to its fullest, or to fulfill as completely as possible the duties and responsibilities of good citizens.[4]

The court further held that education was a valuable commodity that must be protected against unlimited and arbitrary power exercised by a state. It set down standards of procedural due process that included a statement of specific charges that, if proven, would justify expulsion under existing Board rules; an opportunity for students to defend against the charges; their right to confront and examine adverse witnesses and present favorable witnesses, along with oral or written testimony; and to receive a full report of results and findings.

Dixon established that students could have sufficiently strong liberty and property interests in their education to require due process protections against state action. But these were college students, not minors who go to elementary and high school. Then, in 1967, the U.S. Supreme Court, in the landmark decision of *In re Gault,* extended due process protections to minors. The case did not involve school matters. Rather, it concerned the constitutionality of the trial of a fifteen-year-old boy that resulted in his being sentenced to six years in a state school for juvenile delinquents. His offense was using lewd language in an anonymous phone call to a woman. Gault had not been accorded any of the standard due process protections in his trial, as the then-prevailing theory was that juveniles had no need for such protection since the minor needed custody more than liberty and adults generally acted to protect the interests of minors. The severity of Gault's sentence led to its reversal by the Supreme Court, which held: "Due process of law is the primary and indispensible foundation of individual freedom. It is the basic essential term in the social compact which defines the right of individuals and delimits the powers which the state may exercise. . . . Under our Constitution, the condition of being a boy does not justify a kangaroo court."[5]

Dixon maintained that college students could establish sufficiently strong liberty and property interests in their education to require school authorities to provide them with careful procedural due process. Then *Gault* brought children of common-school age under the due process umbrella. Combined with the earlier *Meyer* decision, the stage was set for a large-scale liberal-activist judicial assault on school authority during the seventies. Boards of education, school administrators, and teachers would have their attention diverted from the business of education in order to provide formal notice and hearings, and a hesitancy would creep into what should be a firm and direct control of school discipline and other aspects of educational management. Expanded liberal application of due process to teachers and administrators would further sap the power of the state, operating through public districts, to exert its will in organizing and conducting the process of education according to the wishes of the legally constituted authorities.

At least that is the way conservatives viewed the expansion of due process into educational affairs. For their part, liberals saw it as essential to the democratization of education, enabling students and teachers to take greater advantage of the general, and specifically educational, benefits of a democratized school environment. In this view, it is reason, not authority, that should decide controversies in which educational liberty and property interests are implicated. From the perspective of liberal educational philosophy, learning is a profoundly voluntary activity. It cannot be compelled or demanded; hence the need for rational discourse, persuasion, and consensus in educational government, rather than authoritarian control. Due process was a concept that could greatly contribute to this liberal view.

The expansiveness and imprecision of the due process concept has allowed it to be introjected in education far beyond differences in educational philosophy and how the schools should be controlled and governed. Due process concepts brought into the educational arena fundamental questions of right and wrong regarding the roles and relationships of all the major groups that interacted within public schools. In particular, it carved out a much more influential role for courts in determining educational policy. Not only would courts determine if due process applied to a situation, but if the answer was in the affirmative, courts would also determine ''what process is due.'' Here the restraintist concept of not substituting its judgment for that of school authorities was abandoned in favor of activist court intervention in determining school policy. It would take a decade to stem this tide.

Given the broad scope and depth of due process as a concept, it was applied to a vast array of policies and behaviors. The trigger to due process proceedings is the question of when and to what extent personal liberty and property interests required due process protection against state laws or the actions of officials. In its broadest context, due process was related to the general behavior of educators and students in a host of personal situations—dress and grooming, sexual behavior, and various other forms of choices in human conduct that raised questions about fairness and the right to privacy; as part of the individual's liberty protected by the Fourteenth Amendment. A more specific, but still broad, area of concern was the question of due process required in student suspension/expulsion and teacher-dismissal proceedings. Narrower examples of due process issues are the use of tests to decide such matters as student placement and graduation, as well as teacher hiring, promotion, and retention.

In all these issues, the basic concern for the courts was to decide when it was appropriate to become involved, and, if they did insert themselves into a controversy, to determine a standard for fairness. This involves drawing on Anglo-American common law and applying it to the context and issues of modern schools. In doing this, the power relationships in education were juggled and confused, as liberals and conservatives, restraintists and activists, combined to strike a new balance in educational administration.

Principles of Due Process Applied to Education

1. The U.S. Supreme Court has determined that educators and students have, under certain circumstances, valid claims to liberty and property interests that entitle them to due process protections under the Fourteenth Amendment.
2. Due process, as a concept, requires fairness in the treatment of individ-

uals by government authorities. This fairness includes both fairness of procedures used to make decisions and substantive fairness; that is, rules and actions that are related to educational objectives in clearly understandable, unbiased, reasonable ways.

3. The basic attributes of procedural due process include the right to quick, clear information about charges and their basis, and the right to an impartial hearing on the charges in which the accused is given an opportunity to defend against the charges. As the severity of the potential penalty increases, so does the extent of due process procedural protections.

4. The basic attributes of substantive due process may be best understood by those features showing its absence. A rule, law, regulation, policy, or action violates substantive due process when it is overly broad or unnecessarily vague, is arbitrary or capricious, invades the protected zone of personal privacy, is unrelated to a valid educational objective, or does not use reasonable means to achieve the objective.

5. Procedural and substantive elements of due process are often interrelated. At times the distinction serves a useful purpose, but at other times it is more appropriate to view due process as a unitary concept.

6. In determining "what process is due," when courts determine that due process applies, a balancing-of-interests test is used to weigh the interests of society, as represented by the public school, against the rights of the individual. This form of balancing test is relatively free of complex technical rules. In their place is theory about what is fair and just, allowing for a considerable exercise of judicial judgment.

7. Due process claims become valid upon the court's acceptance that the plaintiff has established a sufficiently clear liberty or property interest that has been adversely affected by state action. The interpretation of what may be considered a liberty interest is particularly amenable to broad interpretation, allowing for a wide variety of protected conduct.

8. When liberty is restrained in areas of "fundamental" interest, as religion, speech, and press, school authorities must justify restraint by showing not just a rational purpose to their action, but that the restraint imposed was justified by a compelling interest.

9. Due process requires that dismissal of a teacher or student or other limitations of property or liberty be justified through showing a rational nexus between the proscribed activity and preventing a serious impairment of the educational process.

DEFINING THE APPLICABILITY AND EXTENT OF DUE PROCESS RIGHTS OF EDUCATORS

At what point should due process be applicable to teachers? How are liberty or property interests established for nontenured teachers, or for teachers seeking employment? What principles are used by the courts to balance the due process interests of teachers against the authority of school boards and educational interests of the state? Do school administrators qualify for due process protection? If so, are their liberty and property interests different from those held by teachers? Once it is determined that due process applies, what standards determine how much process is due?

The introduction of due process as a protection for teachers begun in *Meyer* was directly applied to teachers' employment rights in the Supreme Court's decision in *Weimann* v. *Updegraff* (1952), which invalidated an Oklahoma teacher-loyalty oath. The majority held: "We need not pause to consider whether an abstract right to public employment exists. . . . [C]onstitutional protection does extend to the public servant whose exclusion pursuant to a statute is potently arbitrary and discriminatory."[6] Twenty years later, the High Court "paused" long enough to specify the way due process liberty and property interests applied to both tenured and nontenured teachers' employment rights. While the cases concerned higher education, they have been subsequently applied to elementary- and high-school teachers. In *Board of Regents of State Colleges* v. *Roth* (1972), a university teacher hired on a one-year contract was not rehired. State law provided for tenure after four years, along with due process in termination proceedings against tenured teachers. Roth had not received a notice of reasons for nonretention, or a hearing, and sued, claiming deprivation of due process. The Supreme Court found Roth to be without sufficient liberty or property interests to warrant due process. If Roth had been dismissed during his contract year, a property interest would obtain, but being hired for one year had not established the expectation of continued employment that would trigger a property interest. As to his liberty interest, it would have been valid if he could show that nonretention damaged his standing and reputation so that he was limited in future employment possibilities. Since his nonretention carried no negative personal assessments, the Court could find no such liberty interest. Thus, the Court established that, when teachers' liberty or property interests were implicated in nonretention or dismissal, they were entitled to due process. However, they must first establish that such liberty and/or property interests are present.

A liberty interest was validated by charges that could "seriously damage his standing and associations. . . . [T]o be deprived not only of present employment but of future employment is no small injury."[7] As for property interests, they were defined as follows: "To have a property interest in a benefit, a person clearly must have more than an abstract need or desire for it. He must have more than a unilateral expectation of it. He must, instead, have a legitimate claim of entitlement to it."[8]

On the same day, the Supreme Court issued another decision indicating when procedural due process was required for a teacher without formal tenure who was rehired on continuing contracts. The *Perry* v. *Sindermann* (1972) decision illustrated that liberty and property interests might be secured without the acquisition of formal tenure. Sindermann had taught in a Texas community college for four years under one-year contracts. When his contract was not renewed without reasons or a hearing, he sued, claiming his procedural due process rights were violated. In his defense, he cited the college rule that while the school had no tenure system, it "wishes the faculty member to feel that he has permanent tenure as long as his teaching services are satisfactory and as long as he displays a cooperative attitude toward his co-workers and his superiors, and as long as he is happy in his work."[9] The policy created an "expectancy of reemployment," as distinguished from Roth's "abstract desire" for reemployment. Therefore, Sindermann was judged to have established a property interest in his position that required the protections of procedural due process if the employer wished to terminate him.

It is well established that teachers who have acquired formal tenure are entitled to procedural due process in decisions affecting their employment. *Regents* v. *Roth* and *Perry* v. *Sindermann* generally defined the due process rights of nontenured teachers. What rights obtain for prospective teachers? While states and local districts have the legal right to establish requirements for teaching positions, the principle of substantive due process requires that such regulations be "reasonable"; that is, there should be a valid relationship among the required qualifications, the anticipated professional tasks, and the legitimate objectives of the school. Due process has become a consideration here since court rejection of the privilege doctrine applied to teaching positions. While no one has a "right" to a teaching position, applicants do have a right to fair, reasonable treatment. The issue that is then litigated is whether particular qualifications are rational. Activists are more prone to impose their judgments about what is a reasonable requirement, while restraintists demur to the judgment of school authorities. Thus, the U.S. Supreme Court (*Ambach* v. *Norwick* [1978]) upheld a New York statute denying permanent certification to noncitizens not intending to apply for citizenship. The Court saw the regulation's rational relationship thus:

> Within the public school system, teachers play a critical part in developing students' attitudes toward government and understanding of the role of citizens in our society. . . . Further, a teacher serves as a role model for his students, exerting a subtle but important influence over their perceptions and values . . . toward government, the political process, and a citizens' social responsibilities. This influence is critical to continued good health of a democracy.[10]

Similarly, a federal court of appeals upheld a rule of the Cincinnati schools that teachers must reside within the district. The court reasoned that this would lead to greater commitment to and involvement within the district. This was seen as bearing a rational relationship to a legitimate objective of the school (*Werdwell* v. *Board of Education of Cincinnati*, 529 F. 2d 625 [1976]).

On the other hand, a federal district court struck down a Chicago-community-college regulation barring teachers from full-time outside employment because of the sporadic, inconsistent manner in which it was enforced. Clear standards were never developed or seriously communicated to the faculty. Violations would at one time be overlooked and at another time be enforced.

Therefore, the court concluded that the rule had been enforced in an arbitrary and capricious manner, violating the substantive due process rights of the teachers affected (*Kaufman* v. *Board of Trustees, Comm. College Dist. 508,* 552 F. Supp. 1143 [1982]).

Due Process Rights for Administrators

Regents v. *Roth* and *Perry* v. *Sindermann* provide general guidance about the due process boundaries for employed teachers. *Ambach* v. *Norwick* suggests guidelines for due process rights of applicants to teaching positions. What about the corresponding rights and protections accorded school administrators? The tenure rights of principals and superintendents are determined by state statutes that vary in their provisions. For example, principals in Virginia may acquire administrative tenure, but in Ohio, Tennessee, Illinois, and California, tenure cannot be acquired in administrative positions, although it may be gotten by administrators for teaching positions in the district.[11] Even where administrators have no recourse to protection in tenure rights, all administrators, whether tenured or not, are protected by the Fourteenth Amendment, provided that they can establish property or liberty interests. The unique position of a superintendent of schools puts that person in the legal position of a board officer rather than just a board employee. Superintendents rarely may acquire administrative tenure. Yet, even as board officers, they too can find protection in due process. In *Anderson* v. *Westwood Community School District,* 212 N.W. 2d 232 (1973), a Michigan superintendent protested his dismissal because he was denied a hearing. The trial court agreed, and a hearing was held, again resulting in his dismissal. He again sued, claiming he had received a biased hearing. Again the court agreed that due process was violated, holding that not only a hearing, but a fair, unbiased one, was required. An administrator is no less protected by the Fourteenth Amendment than are teachers or students.

Two state cases illustrate the manner in which property interests of administrators may or may not trigger property interests requiring due process. An Illinois principal was informed that he would be demoted to the position of teacher the following year. The principal sued, claiming an unconstitutional deprivation of property, even though in Illinois, tenure may be acquired as a teacher, but not as an administrator. The Illinois Appellate Court ruled for the district, holding that since a principal "does not acquire tenure as *principal* . . . but does acquire tenure as *certified employee* . . . [a] principal may be reassigned without notice and hearing to a teaching position at reduced salary, based upon some reasonable classification, provided that action is bona fide and not in the nature of chicanery or subterfuge. . . . "[12] This was legal since the principal had not established, to the court's satisfaction, that he had acquired a property interest in the principal's position.

In an Ohio case, a superintendent disputed his dismissal by the school board as violating substantive due process, as it was based on vague, unsubstantiated, biased charges. The court of common pleas agreed, finding evidence that three board members acted vindictively, and the charges were so vague as to lack any substantive basis (*Sorin* v. *Board of Education*, 315 N.E. 2d 848 [1974]). Due process requires that charges be clear and specific, and that those hearing the charges act in an unbiased, impartial manner.

The question of substantive due process was raised in a case involving a teacher's right to a position as principal, for which he was qualified. Webster had received a Chicago principal's certificate, but at about that time had been indicted for a felony, for which he was temporarily suspended from his teaching position. He was reinstated when the charges against him were dismissed due to a faulty police search warrant. He then met with a local school advisory group, which recommended him for the school-principal's position. At an executive session, other school administrators supported the recommendation to the board, despite the dismissed indictment. Some board members objected, since the indictment had been dismissed on a "technicality." The board voted against Webster's promotion, and continued to do so as he was recommended by local school advisory councils for other principalships. Neither Webster nor the local advisory councils were informed of the reasons why he was not approved by the board. The federal district court decided that Webster, as a teacher holding a valid principal's certificate, had both a liberty and a property interest in the position that he sought. His liberty was injured by the board's action, as were his property interests by this "arbitrary state action" (*Webster* v. *Redmond,* 443 F. Supp. 670 [1977]).

Determining the Extent of Procedural Due Process for Teachers

Not only do the courts decide when due process applies, but they also consider the extent to which procedural due process applies to any particular set of circumstances. The weight of the potential penalty and the burden placed on state educational functions are considered in making these judgments. The U.S. Supreme Court explained this consideration as involving:

> First, the private interests that will be affected by the official action; second, the risk of an erroneous deprivation of such interests through the procedures used, and the probable value, if any, of additional or substitute procedural safeguards; and finally, the Government's interest, including the function involved and the fiscal and administrative burdens that the additional or substitute procedural requirements would entail.[13]

Thus, the failure to provide sufficient notice invalidated a teacher's dismissal that otherwise probably would have been sustained (*Korstetter* v. *Evans,* 350 F. Supp. 209 [1971]). Similarly, notice that was unreasonably close to the date set for a hearing led a Texas federal district court to invalidate a teacher's dismissal (*Bates* v. *Hinds,* 324 F. Supp. 528 [1971]). Also, a New Hampshire federal court invalidated a teacher's dismissal based on the vote of an absent board member who later voted negatively to break a tie vote (*McDonough* v. *Kelly*, 329 F. Supp. 144 [1971]). Courts have also held procedural due process to have been violated in dismissal proceedings against a teacher when a board refused to subpoena a witness requested by the teacher (*Doran* v. *Board of Education*, 285 N.E. 825 [1972]), and in another case when the board refused to make information important to the termination decision available to the teacher and to the defending lawyer (*Springfield School Dist.* v. *Shellem*, 328 A. 2d 535 [1974]).

The U.S. Supreme Court decision in *Hortonville* v. *Hortonville* (1976) considered two basic due process interests (bias of the hearing tribunal and hearings afforded) in a case resulting from the board's firing of eighty-six teachers striking in violation of Wisconsin law. The teachers claimed that their due process rights were violated on two counts. The board was unwilling to provide a group hearing for all teachers, as they had requested, but offered only individual hearings. Second, the teachers claimed that the strike had been provoked by the board, and its role in the dispute disqualified it as an impartial tribunal sitting in judgment on the teachers with whom it had been locked in a bitter dispute. The Court majority found that the procedures for individual rather than the group hearing preferred by teachers met their due process requirements, and the role played by the board did not render it unconstitutionally biased to sit in judgment on the teachers. In the words of the opinion:

> Mere familiarity with the facts gained by an agency in the performance of its statutory role does not . . . disqualify a decision maker. Nor is a decision maker disqualified simply because he has taken a position . . . on a policy issue related to the dispute, in the absence of a showing that he is not capable of judging a particular controversy fairly on the basis of its own circumstances.[14]

The six-member majority balanced the interests of the state in managing its labor affairs against the amount of due process that should fairly be afforded to the teachers, and found that it was weighted in favor of the state.

> The state legislature has given to the Board the power to employ and dismiss teachers, as a part of the balance it has struck. . . . [A]ltering those statutory powers as a matter of federal due process clearly changes the balance. Permitting the Board to make the decision at issue here preserves its control over school district affairs, leaves the balance of power in labor relations where the state legislature struck it. . . .[15]

Similarly, in considering the due process right of a teacher suspended for mental illness, a federal appellate court ruled that the teacher was not entitled to a hearing prior to suspension. In weighing the teacher's rights to procedural due process against the risk of harm possible if a mentally ill teacher were permitted to continue teaching during due process procedures, the court found the balance weighted against the teacher (*Newman* v. *Board of Educ., City School Dist. of New York*, 494, F. 2d 299 [1979]). Finally, there is the case of the teacher who requested the rescheduling of a hearing regarding his nonretention, which was granted. His second request for rescheduling the hearing was not granted. In fact, he was told no further extensions would be allowed at the time that the board agreed to the first delay. The hearing was held without the presence of the teacher. The federal appellate court decided that the board had been fair enough in permitting one rescheduling, and even if the teacher was not present at the hearing, due process had been served in the balance between the state's interests and the teacher's rights (*White* v. *South Park Indep. School Dist.*, 693 F. 2d 1163 [1982]).

Determining the Extent of Substantive Due Process for Teachers

In 1934, the U.S. Supreme Court, in a noneducation case (*Snyder* v. *Commonwealth of Massachusetts*, 54 S. Ct. 330) showed how vague were the liberty and property interests possible under due process by opining that they were determined by examining our "collective conscience." Thus, the scope of teachers' behavior protected by substantive due process is determined by court opinion and precedent. Among the questions the court must consider is the degree to which the teacher's behavior involves a fundamental interest protected by the Constitution, as expression or religious freedom, and the effect of the conduct on the legitimate interests of the school. Viewed from the perspective of the school board's conduct, the questions become whether the board's regulations were reasonable, and whether they were too vague or general, or contained characteristics that are arbitrary and capricious.

What of a physical-education teacher dismissed because of obesity? The board justified its action on the basis of the teacher's being a poor physical role model and her limited capacity to perform certain physical-education activities. The teacher contended the action was arbitrary, as her teaching performance was not affected by her obesity. The court saw a valid due process claim, and the board bore the burden of proving the rational relationship of its decision to school interests. It could not do so to the court's satisfaction, as there was no evidence of unsatisfactory performance and the court considered it unreasonable for any teacher to embody all the virtues desired in any hypothetical role model (*Parosoli* v. *Board of Examiners of City of New York*, 285 N.Y.S. 2d 936 [1967]).

To take an entirely different area, what restrictions can be placed on a teacher's breast-feeding of her baby in school? The teacher had initially done so during her lunch period, in private. The principal asked her to discontinue this, based on school policy prohibiting teachers from bringing their children to school because of the possible disruptive effects and to avoid litigation if the child were injured. She assented, but the child soon developed an allergy to bottled milk, necessitating the teacher to take unpaid leave. She sued, and a U.S. appellate court held that she had a due process claim related to parental liberty in child-rearing. This protected liberty interest was not absolute. The board also had interests in preserving an orderly school that must be considered. Therefore, the appeals court referred the case back to the trial court to determine ''[w]hether these or other interests are strong enough to justify the school board's regulations, and whether the regulations are sufficiently narrowly drawn. . . . ''[16]

Substantive due process was the issue in the case of a teacher's dismissal for excessive absence. The dismissal was voided because of vague rules and rules unfairly applied. State and board policy allowed for teacher dismissal for ''excessive or unreasonable absences.'' However, these terms were not defined. A teacher absent 124 days over a four-year period was dismissed even though the board allowed 180 days' absence and salary deductions for absences thereafter. Since such periods of absence were considered by the board, dismissal based solely on the amount of absence was deemed unreasonable, especially since what was ''excessive'' had never been defined (*Steward* v. *Board of Educ. of Ritenaur,* 574 S.W. 2d 471 [1979]).

Another area of dispute involves the liberty interest teachers have in deciding how they will dress and groom themselves, as opposed to the interests of school authorities in expecting teachers to model and support accepted community standards of dress and grooming. A California teacher was disciplined for refusing to shave off his beard. He sued, and was supported by the California appellate court, which concluded that since there was no evidence that the beard impaired the teacher's effectiveness, this restriction on his liberty was not justified by educational interests and could not be supported (*Finot* v. *Pasadena City Board of Educ.,* 58 Cal. Rptr. 520 [1967]). A few years later, a federal appellate court reached a different conclusion. In *Miller* v. *School Dist. 167, Cook Co., Ill.,* 495 F. 2d 658 (1974), the court weighed the liberty interest involved in a teacher's wish to wear a beard against the board's need for freedom in making choices in such areas of school policy, and found the teacher's interest in wearing a beard too insubstantial when compared with the beard's policy needs. Soon after the *Miller* decision, a federal appellate panel ruled in favor of a teacher's right to violate the school dress code calling for him to wear a tie, because there was no support for the board's view that such a regulation was important to the professional image of teachers and to student respect and discipline. However, the rare step was taken in which all the judges of the circuit reheard the case *en banc.* They decided that court intervention in such matters trivialized the Constitution unless such restriction could be shown to be arbitrary or capricious. Such was not the case here, in the view of the second circuit's majority of judges (*East Hartford Educ. Assn.* v. *Board,* 562 F. 2d 828 [1977]).

The overbreadth and vagueness of rules were the cause for the U.S. Supreme Court's invalidation of a Florida statute requiring public employees to swear in writing that they had never provided ''aid, support, advice, counsel, or influence to the Communist Party.'' The act was challenged as unconstitutionally vague. The court majority agreed that the law was so vague that it was difficult for a teacher to determine what conduct is covered and what is not

(*Cramp* v. *Board of Public Instruction,* 368 U.S. 278 [1961]). Similarly "void-for-vagueness" were two statutes from the State of Washington. One required teachers to swear to "by precept and example . . . promote respect for the flag and the institutions of the United States." The other required all state employees to swear that they were not "subversive" persons. The Supreme Court held both statutes to violate due process because of their excessive vagueness and over-breadth (*Baggett* v. *Bullitt,* 377 U.S. 360 [1964]).

The U.S. Supreme Court decision in the companion cases of *Cleveland* v. *LaFleur, Cohen* v. *Chesterfield* (1974) showed another aspect of substantive due process in deciding whether it was violated by board rules governing when pregnant teachers (presumably married) must stop teaching and when they may return to their duties following the delivery of the child. The teachers argued that the rules were arbitrary restrictions on their privacy and freedom of personal choice in family matters, as the rules presumed all pregnant teachers or new mothers were unfit to teach. For their part, the school boards justified their rules as necessitated to insure continuity of instruction for students and to protect the health of the teacher and unborn or newborn child. The Court majority sustained the substantive due process rights of the teachers in this case: "This Court has long recognized that freedom of personal choice in matters of marriage and family life is one of the liberties protected by the Due Process Clause. . . . "[17] The majority examined the reasons for the limitations placed on the female teachers and concluded they did not constitute compelling reasons for limiting this fundamental liberty interest. Instead, they saw the restriction limiting pregnant teachers as "arbitrary cutoff dates . . . [which] have no rational relationship to the valid state interest of preserving continuity of instruction."[18] As for the concern for teachers' health, they were violative of substantive due process, since they amounted to "a conclusive presumption that every pregnant teacher who reaches the fifth or sixth month of pregnancy is physically incapable of continuing." Such rules amounted to "an irrebuttable presumption of physical incompetency . . . even when the medical evidence as to an individual woman's physical status might be wholly to the contrary."[19]

In dissent, Justice Rehnquist argued for the reasonableness of allowing legally constituted local officials to use their judgment in establishing relatively uniform rules to conduct the affairs of government. Setting them aside as "irrebuttable assumptions" applied to individuals, attacked the very foundations of the legal system.

However, three years later, the federal appellate court would apply the irrebuttable-presumption concept of substantive due process to a case in which a school board refused to hire a blind teacher, even though she met formal qualifications, including passing a required district examination. The court saw the school board creating the irrebuttable presumption that a blind person is automatically incapable of being a competent teacher. Since the board could not defend its position to the court's satisfaction, it found for the teacher (*Gurmankin* v. *Costanzo,* 556 F. 2d 184 [1977]).

DEFINING THE APPLICABILITY AND EXTENT OF DUE PROCESS RIGHTS FOR STUDENTS

Do students have liberty and property interests in their education? If so, how far do they extend, and how much process is due? How do courts balance their rights against the interests and authority of the state, operating through its public schools? What differences are there between procedural and substantive due process rights for students?

Dixon v. *Alabama,* while persuasive on other districts, set precedent only for one federal circuit. Further, it dealt with higher education and had overtones of race controversy in the South. The *Gault* decision of the Supreme Court did not involve the authority of the school directly. Even so, these two cases, combined with such decisions as *Tinker* v. *Des Moines,* paved the way for expanded and strengthened student due process rights. As the seventies opened, lower courts were divided about when the liberty and property interests of students in their schooling triggered due process. A federal appellate court (*Linwood* v. *Board,* 1972) held that "measures such as after-school detention, restriction to classrooms during free periods, reprimand, or admonition do not per se involve matters rising to the dignity of constitutional magnitude."[20] Likewise, another appellate court believed due process was not required for a student who wanted to be represented at a guidance conference. The student's request to be represented by an attorney was denied under the reasoning that the supervision of such disciplinary matters was not tantamount to criminal adversary proceedings, nor was a substantial stake in liberty or property involved in the potential results of a guidance conference (*Madera* v. *Board of Educ. of City of New York,* 386 F. 2d 778 [1967]).

On the other hand, when a school rule empowering the principal to "make such rules and regulations that may be necessary . . . in promoting its best interests . . . [and] enforce obedience to any reasonable and lawful command" was used as the only basis for expelling students for an activity (publishing an underground newspaper) not otherwise proscribed, it was struck down by a federal district court (*Sullivan* v. *Houston* [1969]). The court's reasoning was based on substantive due process:

> School rules probably do not need to be as narrow as criminal statutes, but if school officials contemplate severe punishment, they must do so on the basis of a rule which is drawn so as to reasonably inform the student what specific conduct is proscribed. Basic notions of justice and fair play require that no person shall be made to suffer for a breach unless standards of behavior have first been announced, for who is to decide what has been breached?[21]

> . . . Little can be said of a standard so grossly overbroad as "in the best interests of the school." . . . It cannot be contended that it supplies objective standards.[22]

In 1975, the Supreme Court undertook to provide specificity about when and how much procedural due process was required in school penalties of suspension and expulsion, as the relationship of such measures to liberty and property interests of students in their education was clear. *Goss* v. *Lopez* established that when a state makes a public-school education available to all children, those students obtain a property interest in their education. It was also established that the recording of suspensions in students' permanent files could create a stigma impairing the liberty interests of students in their "good name, reputation, honor, or integrity."

The case involved ten-day suspensions of students, imposed without any due process. School authorities held that such a penalty should not implicate due process protection. In a five-to-four decision, the Supreme Court held that not only was such a deprivation and penalty substantial enough to require procedural due process, but that even in shorter suspensions, some minimal procedural due process was required. Considering the inherent flexibility and importance of the due process concept, the Court provided the general policy guideline that: "At the very minimum . . . students facing suspension and the consequent interference with a protected property interest must be given some kind of notice and afforded some kind of hearing."[23] When the potential penalty increases, so must the due process protections, which could include the right to be represented by counsel and other courtroom trappings. The majority opinion noted that while a hearing should occur *before* suspension, in cases where students posed an immediate threat, they could be immediately removed, with the hearing delayed until it was practical.

The four dissenting justices saw ten-day suspensions as "a routine disciplinary measure that does not rise to constitutional significance." Expressing their restraintist attitude, they held that the decision substituted "[t]he discretion and judgment of federal courts . . . for that of the 50 state legislatures, the 14,000 school boards, and the 2,000,000 teachers who heretofore have been responsible for the administration of the American school system."[24] Conservative philosophy was also introduced into the dissent, holding that school disciplinary authority was undermined by the decision, which injured the development of proper character and morals, when school authorities were not hampered in delivering it to students. Finally, the dissenters saw no property or liberty interest implicated in this case. "[A] deprivation of not more than 10 days suspension from school, imposed as a routine disciplinary measure, does not assume constitutional dimensions . . . Due Process . . . comes into play only when the state subjects a student to a 'severe detriment or grievous loss.' "[25]

Goss v. *Lopez* represented the liberal high point in procedural due process applied to school policy. It was quickly applied to corporal punishment of students by a federal district court in the same year *Goss* was decided. In *Baker* v. *Owen*, 395 F. Supp. 294 (1975), a three-judge panel in North Carolina, relying on *Goss* v. *Lopez*, ruled that minimal due process procedures were required prior to imposing corporal punishment. This contradicted traditional judicial reasoning (for instance, *Sims* v. *Board of Educ. of Indep. School Dist.*, 307 F. Supp. 1328 [1969]; *Ware* v. *Estes*, 328 F. Supp. 657 [1971]) which saw due process as unnecessary and impractical in this area of school discipline. The Supreme Court undertook to settle this policy question in the 1977 case of *Ingraham* v. *Wright*. Two Florida students had been severely beaten for slowness in responding to their teacher's instructions, without benefit of notice or a hearing of any kind. By a five-to-four vote, the Supreme Court departed from the liberal view it had expressed in *Goss* v. *Lopez,* and took a conservative view of due process applied to corporal punishment, as distinguished from suspension. Favoring the need to support established, proven tradition, the Court majority found that, while corporal punishment clearly triggered the students' liberty interest in freedom from bodily restraint and punishment, due process still did not apply here. The reason was that its cumbersome, slow nature would reduce the punishment's value and unnecessarily impede school administration. "Hearings—even informal hearings—require time, personnel, and a diversion of attention from normal school pursuits."[26] Due process was constitutionally unnecessary since there were adequate alternative legal remedies available in civil damage suits and criminal proceedings against illegal physical violence. Further, the "openness of the school" protected students from unchecked violence on the part of their teachers. Thus, there were enough protections against corporal-punishment abuses without adding the administrative burden of procedural due process to the schools.

The four dissenters, of course, saw the issue differently. For one thing, the tort and criminal proceedings could only be instituted *after* the damage was done, and procedural due process was meant to protect against the infliction of harm. "Generally, adequate notice and a fair opportunity to be heard in advance of any deprivation of a constitutionally protected interest are essential."[27]

Ingraham v. *Wright* also invoked the claim that the students' Eighth Amendment protection against "cruel and unusual punishment" had been violated, but the majority disallowed that claim on their reading of that Amendment's history, which led them to conclude that it was intended to apply exclusively to criminal matters.

This decision appeared to foreclose the application of due process to the area of corporal punishment, even though the Court had acknowledged that student liberty interests were implicated under the Fourteenth Amendment. However, the case of *Hall* v. *Tawney* (1980) was brought before the federal appellate court on the specific basis of substantive due process, as distinct from procedural due process. This course had been left open by a footnote in *Ingraham*. A girl had been beaten severely by a teacher for a relatively minor infraction, causing ten days of hospitalization. The plaintiff made no claim to procedural due process protection, but asserted the liberty interests of students to be free from bodily punishment was protected under the Fourteenth Amendment. Therefore, the argument focused on the violation of the student's substantive due process rights. In finding for the student, the court held:

[S]ubstantive due process is concerned with violations of personal rights of privacy and bodily security. . . . [T]he substantive due process inquiry in school corporal punishment cases must be whether the force applied caused injury so severe, was so disproportionate to the need presented, and was so inspired by malice and sadism . . . that it amounted to a brutal and inhuman abuse of official power literally shocking to the conscience.[28]

This 1980 federal appellate court case was followed by a federal district court case in 1983, involving a student who had been disciplined by her teacher's piercing her arm with a pin. Relying on the *Hall* v. *Tawney* decision's test of whether the action was "literally shocking to the conscience," this judge decided his conscience was not sufficiently shocked to elevate the matter to constitutional proportions. In finding for the defendant, he drew on *Ingraham* v. *Wright* in observing that adequate safeguards were available in the state's common law of torts to negate the need for due process protection (*Brooks* v. *School Board of City of Richmond,* 569 F. Supp. 1534 [1983]). Similarly, when a federal court was asked to uphold a student's claim that his due process rights were violated when a principal violated school-board policy by paddling him in a classroom rather than in his office, and without an adult witness present, the judge declined to do so. Pointing out that the board's policy was not required by the U.S. Constitution, the issue did not justify constitutional concern. Citing *Ingraham* v. *Wright,* the Alabama court suggested that remedies available through state civil or criminal law would be more appropriate (*Hale* v. *Pringle,* 562 F. Supp. 598 [1983]).

Determining the Extent of Procedural Due Process for Students

Clearly, the courts have decided that there are matters, particularly those involving suspension and expulsion, where students are entitled to the procedural protections of due process. The extent of due process required in any particular matter depends upon the court's judgment about how severe is the liberty or property restraint imposed upon the student as compared to the inconvenience to school operations and effect on its controlling and educative functions. Even given the generality of the due process concept, a general standard may be discerned through review of court decisions in representative cases.

In 1970, Tanya Tibbs was accused of assaulting other students outside of school. Based on unsigned student accusations (to protect them from reprisals), Tanya was expelled. In a subsequent court test of this action, Tanya's expulsion was invalidated because her due process rights were violated. Relying on cases such as *Dixon* v. *Alabama,* the court found that when the penalty was complete deprivation of schooling, as in this case, some due process was required. In this case, although there was a hearing, Tanya had not been afforded the right to know and cross-examine her accusers (*Tibbs et al.* v. *Board of Educ. of Township of Franklin,* 284 A. 2d 179 [1971]). Eleven years later, the California Supreme Court heard a case in which a student was expelled for the school year based on evidence supplied in signed statements of other students accusing the expelled student of fighting at a school athletic event. The witnesses, whose statements formed the basis of evidence for expulsion, were not brought into the hearing to present oral testimony and submit to cross-examination. Therefore, the expulsion was invalidated, even though the accusers were known (*John A.* v. *San Bernardino City Unified School Dist.,* 654 P. 2d 242 [1982]).

Where the penalty was only a short suspension, federal district courts in Virginia and Texas agreed that an informal conference in the principal's office was sufficient due process (*Hillman* v. *Elliott,* 436 F. Supp. 812 [1977]; *Coffman* v. *Keuhler,* 409 F. Supp. 546 [1976]). Thus, the *Goss* decision had not necessarily created complete legal restraint from applying relatively quick, informal disciplinary penalties when the deprivation of schooling was relatively minimal.

Defining the Scope of Substantive Due Process for Students

Substantive due process has been considered in a broad range of student behaviors, exposing the contrasting judicial attitudes of liberalism and conservatism, restraint and activism. The area of dress and grooming is illustrative. A New York court found an absolute prohibition against girls wearing slacks to school to be violative of substantive due process, as the rule was unrelated to safety or discipline, but rather just a preference of school authorities (*Scott* v. *Board of Education, Union Free School Dist. 117, Hicksville,* 305 N.Y.S. 2d 601 [1969]). In the same year, the issue of vague, overbroad rules was the basis for a California court's invalidating a school policy forbidding "extremes of dress or personal appearance." The judgment as to what constituted an extreme was left to school administrators. When a student challenged the rule in response to a demand that he cut his hair, the court declared the policy "void for vagueness" because the standards were left solely to the personal judgment of administrators (*Meyers* v. *Arcata Union High School Dist.,* 75 Cal. Rpts. 68 [1969]).

In a case that took pains to spell out the range of due process considerations in student dress and grooming (*Massie* v. *Henry* [1972]), a federal court invoked substantive due process to protect a student's right to wear his hair as he pleased, absent reasons of health or safety. The basis was not the rule's vagueness, as in *Meyers,* or the flat arbitrariness discovered in *Scott.* Rather, the basis was the lack of a rational relationship between the restriction and a legitimate school interest. After reviewing the great disparities in judicial opinion on the subject, the court concluded that hairstyle choice fell under the Fourth Amendment right to be secure in one's person incorporated into due process protection. In establishing the balancing test between the two competing interests, the court examined the school's justifications and how they measured up to due process standards:

> There was no evidence that considerations of health entered into the picture; the only claimed justifications were the need for discipline and considerations of safety. . . . Proof that jest, disgust, and amusement were evoked, and that there were threats of violence was insufficient. Moreover, there was no proof of the ineffectiveness of discipline of disrupters or a showing of any concerted effort to convey

the salutary teaching that there is little merit in conformity for the sake of conformity. . . . In short, we are inclined to think that faculty leadership in promoting and enforcing an attitude of tolerance rather than one of suppression or derision would obviate the relatively minor disruptions which have occurred. . . .

[T]he regulation lacks justification outweighing the minor plaintiff's rights. . . . [29]

While the federal panel's majority saw the case this way, the senior circuit judge dissented, based on the following reasoning:

The majority concludes that the constitutional right involved here is "an aspect of the right to be secure in one's person guaranteed by the due process clause." . . . I respectfully disagree. . . .

There is no hint here of an improper motivation or arbitrary procedure by the school officials in establishing the regulation or an uneven application thereof. Further, there is no specific clause in the Constitution which may be said to expressly prohibit regulation of a male student's hair length by local school authorities. Thus, the invalidation of the regulation on due process grounds would appear to be no more than a substitution of the majority's judgment concerning the reasonableness of the regulation for that of the local officials. [30]

This dissenting opinion proved a harbinger of growing court conservatism in student dress and grooming. In the same year, a federal court found a school rule forbidding girls from wearing tight skirts or "short shorts" to bear a rational relationship to the legitimate school objective of supporting modesty and decency (*Wallace* v. *Ford,* 346 F. Supp. 156 [1972]). Then, in 1984, when an Alabama high school enforced a policy prohibiting athletes from wearing moustaches and long sideburns, two ballplayers refused to shave, were dismissed from their school teams, and sued. The federal appellate court found the grooming policy a reasonable approach to the objectives of teaching hygiene, instilling discipline, imposing legitimate authority, and promoting appropriate uniformity (*Davenport* v. *Randolph County Board of Educ.,* 730 F. 2d 1395 [1984]). There was no criticism of "conformity for the sake of conformity" or demands to show safety or health justifications, as in *Massie.* In fact, imposing "legitimate" authority and uniformity were seen as desirable ends not triggering due process concerns.

Other areas of student behavior have been similarly affected by increased court restraint and conservativism, but it remains difficult to predict the positions that various jurists may take. In 1982, the U.S. Court of Appeals in New Hampshire upheld the action of a school board in suspending service on a school bus route plagued by student misbehavior and vandalism. The action had been taken after due warnings had been issued. In response to parental complaints that all students were being punished for behavior of a few (thus violating due process), the court ruled that the students' property interest in the bus route was too weak to override the state's interest in maintaining discipline and safety (*Rose* v. *Nashua Board of Educ.,* 679 F. 2d 279 [1982]).

In 1982, a student contended that his due process rights were violated when he was expelled for excessive absenteeism, because "excessive absenteeism" as grounds for expulsion had not been sufficiently defined. The Supreme Court of Arkansas denied the claim, as the action was based on so many absences as to preclude passing the courses in which the student was enrolled (*Williams* v. *Board of Educ. for the Marianna School Dist.,* 626 S.W. 2d 361 [1982]). Similarly, another student claimed that he was unconstitutionally denied membership in the National Honor Society because of anonymous teacher evaluations, even though his grades were high enough for membership. The court decided that not only was there an insufficient property interest, but that the rules for membership clearly allowed for requirements other than scholastic average (*Price* v. *Young,* 580 F. Supp. 1 [1983]).

The same general view of substantive due process obtained in a 1984 federal appellate court decision regarding the grade retention of a large percentage of black students. The plaintiffs argued that new standards were imposed without a sufficient phase-in period for black students who had experienced prior school segregation. The court disagreed, holding that there was no property right to expect promotion based on substandard performance. Further, it was held unreasonable to expect continued "social promotions" in the light of clear, reasonable board-promulgated promotion standards (*Bester* v. *Tuscaloosa City Board of Educ.,* 722 F. 2d 1514 [1984]).

A related issue has concerned the fairness and reasonableness of disciplining students by reducing their grades in school subjects. In examining the rational relationship of the action to school objectives and the inherent fairness of such action, an Illinois court found that when a student's grades were reduced one letter grade for unexcused absences as provided by school policy, there was no valid claim to substantive due process. Not only was the decision reached on reasoning that the *Goss*-imposed student property rights did not apply to grades, but public policy was best served by the court's not intervening in school grading decisions (*Knight* v. *Board of Educ.,* 348 N.E. 2d 299 [1976]). In contrast, when similar action was taken against a student in another Illinois district which did not have such a policy, the same court held that substantive due process required further consideration about the fairness and rationality of discipline by grade reduction where no prior authorizing policy existed (*Hamer* v. *Board of Educ.,* 382 N.E. 2d 231 [1978]). Such is the spread of opinion and applicable principles regarding substantive due process rights of students.

SUBSTANTIVE DUE PROCESS AND SEXUAL MORALITY

Under what conditions and to what extent may school authorities restrain teachers' or students' liberty to engage in that most personal area of conduct that includes such matters as marriage, pregnancy, and sexual relations? What aspects of moral conduct fall under the protection of due process liberty or property interests and related privacy rights?

The *Meyer* decision established that substantive due process included "not merely freedom from bodily restraint, but also the right of the individual to . . . marry, to establish a home . . . and generally to enjoy those privileges . . . essential to the orderly pursuit of happiness by free men."[31] The right to marry and establish a home implicates a wide range of sexual conduct. However, the individual's liberty to engage in private sexual conduct may collide with the public school's interest in maintaining high moral standing in the community, protecting community standards, and promoting conduct that stimulates high educational standards and attainment.

Courts no longer allow students to be barred from school because they are married. However, the extent to which married students may participate in extracurricular activities has been the subject of considerable litigation. Court attitudes have moved in the liberal direction in this regard, particularly since *Goss* established strong student property rights in their education. Two Texas cases indicate the trend. In *Kissick* v. *Garland Indep. School Dist.,* 330 S.W. 2d 708 (1959), a high-school boy was excluded from interscholastic-football participation because he married. This violated a school rule aimed at discouraging early marriage because of its negative effects on school performance. In answer to Kissick's claim that the rule was arbitrary and unreasonable, the court required only that the school rule bear a rational relationship to a legitimate school purpose. In the court's opinion, this rule met that test. However, fifteen years later, the same Texas court, influenced by liberal student-civil-rights decisions, raised exclusion of married students from athletic competition to the level of a compelling interest and found the rule to be an unconstitutional restraint on the student's liberty (*Bell* v. *Lone Oak Indep. School Dist.,* 507 S.W. 2d 636 [1974]).

After the *Goss* decision, federal courts followed suit in strengthening the right of married students to extracurricular participation. However, students were not allowed unlimited rights to participate in the extracurriculum. A federal court (*Aldbach* v. *Olde* [1976]) noted that, while "[t]he educational process is a broad and comprehensive concept with a variable and infinite meaning . . . [w]e do not read *Goss* to establish a property interest subject to constitutional protection in each of these separate components."[32] Further complexity in this balancing test was added by another federal court (*Pegram* v. *Nelson* [1979]), which held:

> Since there is not a property interest in each separate component of the "educational process," denial of the opportunity to participate in merely one of several extracurricular activities would not give rise to a right to due process. However, *total exclusion* from participation . . . for a *lengthy period of time* could, depending on the particular circumstances, be a sufficient deprivation to implicate due process.[33]

While barring teachers from marriage has long been established as a violation of their privacy rights without sufficient state justification, the court may remove that due process protection depending upon whom the teacher marries. Thus, when an Arizona high-school teacher married one of his students, the state appellate court found that his due process privacy rights must give way to the school's interests in maintaining teacher-student relations conducive to good discipline and learning (*Welch* v. *Board of Educ. of Chandler Unified School Dist.,* 667 P. 2d 746 [1983]). The key point was that the court found that there was a rational nexus between the teacher's conduct and his performance of duties, which was impaired by the conduct.

While student pregnancy was once sufficient cause for exclusion, this is no longer the case. Now the school must show compelling reasons for excluding pregnant students, such as wide notoriety for immorality. However, there is disagreement about the school's authority to limit attendance of pregnant students to special conditions. In 1973, a federal court held that substantive due process was not violated by limiting pregnant students and unwed mothers to nightschool attendance only (*Houston* v. *Posser,* 361 F. Supp. 295 [1973]). The difference between day- and night-school attendance did not present itself to the court as requiring the school to show a compelling interest in the rule; hence the court accepted it as bearing a rational relationship to school objectives. However, two years earlier, a Massachusetts court had reached the opposite conclusion (*Ordway* v. *Hargraves,* 323 F. Supp. 1155 [1971]).

When teachers are dismissed by school boards for sexual misconduct, the courts consider the question of the impact on community attitudes in addition to whether there is a rational nexus between the teacher's conduct and ability to satisfactorily acquit professional responsibilities. Thus, in a rural South Dakota case (*Sullivan* v. *Meade* [1976]), a teacher was dismissed because of community complaints that she was openly living with her boyfriend. She refused to change her behavior and was dismissed. A federal appellate court disallowed her due process privacy claims, holding that the school's interest in maintaining its moral position outweighed it. The court reasoned that: "Ms. Sullivan's conduct violated local mores, that her students were aware of this, and that because of the size of the town, this awareness would continue. . . . Ms. Sullivan was shown to have generated deep affection from her students, increasing the probability of emulation."[34]

The attitudes held by small-town residents do have their limits as justification for dismissing teachers for immoral conduct. Ms. Sullivan's behavior was patently clear. However, a different result occurred in a rural Nebraska case, when a divorced female teacher allowed her adult son's friend to stay overnight at her home on several occasions. The school board defended her dismissal as justified through inferences that her behavior implied potential for sexual misconduct. However, there was no other evidence of impropriety or character flaws, or of any community reaction. The federal appellate court concluded: "The school board's inference of misconduct was arbitrary and capricious and therefore constituted an impermissible reason for terminating her employment. . . ."[35]

Comparable reasoning was used in a case involving the dismissal of an unwed pregnant teacher from the school system of a medium-sized Nebraska city. Not only was there no community interest in the matter, but the school board did not even consider any less severe ways of handling the situation other than the extreme solution of dismissing the teacher. Therefore, the court decided that the teacher was entitled to the protection available through the concept of due process (*Brown* v. *Bathke,* 566 F. 2d 983 [1976]).

Similarly, when an Alabama school board fired an unwed teacher for being pregnant, the federal district court (*Drake* v. *Covington* [1974]) found the teacher's privacy rights required that the school board show it had a compelling interest that justified her dismissal. The court believed that: "If the right of privacy means anything, it is the right of the individual, married or single, to be free from unwarranted governmental intrusion into matters so fundamentally affecting a person as deciding whether to bear or beget a child."[36] Finding no compelling interest or even a rational nexus between the teacher's conduct and fitness to teach, the majority found for the teacher. In dissent, one judge on this federal panel believed that since the private affairs of this teacher had become public knowledge, this made for negative public attitude toward the school system and impaired the teacher's effectiveness. For this dissenter, these facts constituted a sufficiently compelling interest to justify her dismissal.

Sexual-Preference Rights

Another area of sexual conduct considered under substantive due process is that of homosexuality. The right of college students to advocate homosexuality through university-recognized organizations has been sustained by federal courts (*Gay Alliance of Students* v. *Matthews*, 544 F. Supp. 253 [1973]; *Gay Lib.* v. *Univ. of Missouri*, 558 F. 2d 848 [1977]), along with the right of a homosexual high-school student to take a male date to his high school prom (*Fricke* v. *Lynch,* 491 F. Supp. 381 [1980]). However, these decisions were based on First Amendment rights rather than due process protection. When due process claims are at issue, courts will not protect homosexual teachers from dismissal when their sexual conduct is public or otherwise affects their teaching, but homosexual teachers can find due process protection for their private homosexual conduct. The court's decision will be determined by the nexus between homosexuality and teaching effectiveness.

In a 1967 California case, a teacher convicted of disorderly conduct for homosexual advances on a public beach had his teaching certificate revoked. The court found a rational nexus between the out-of-school conduct and the teacher's fitness for service, and sustained his dismissal (*Sarac* v. *State Board of Education,* 57 Cal. Rptr. 69 [1967]). Two years later, the California Supreme Court disallowed the dismissal of a teacher for an isolated, brief homosexual liaison with another teacher. The court found no evidence of an impact on his teaching, or that his homosexuality was habitual, as was the case in *Sarac*. Therefore, no rational nexus justifying his dismissal was present (*Morrison* v. *State Board of Education,* 461 P. 2d 375 [1969]).

Later, in the Washington State case of *Gaylord* v. *Tacoma* (1977), student's knowledge of a teacher's homosexuality was considered to establish a sufficient nexus to justify his dismissal, even though he had been considered a good teacher. The court reasoned: "Such students could treat the retention of the high school teacher by the school board as indicating adult approval of his homosexuality."[37] Therefore, the school's interest in preserving accepted moral standards that it and the community wished students to accept, outweighed Gaylord's rights to privacy and liberty protected by due process.

Teacher-Student Sexual Relations

One of the least defensible moral areas in which teachers might seek protection in due process is that of sexual involvement with students. For example, when a teacher on a field trip with students engaged in sexual "horseplay" with them, he was dismissed. Although the teacher had a good reputation and claimed that there was no nexus between this conduct and his classroom effectiveness, the court sustained his dismissal (*Weissman* v. *Board of Educ. of Jefferson City School Dist.*, 547 P. 2d 1267 [1976]). While most other cases support this court attitude, there are examples of contrary decisions. Most extreme is the decision of a Michigan trial court. A female teacher had been conclusively shown to have engaged in a long-term sexual relationship with one of her male students, for which she was dismissed. The court reversed the dismissal because the board failed to establish a nexus between the teacher's conduct and its negative effect on other students or teachers. Upon appeal, this reasoning was rejected and the Michigan Court of Appeals upheld the dismissal because of the negative effects when teachers seduce or engage in sexual activity with students (*Clark* v. *Ann Arbor School Dist.*, 344 N.W. 2d 48 [1983]).

DUE PROCESS RESTRAINTS IN COMPETENCY TESTING

Is it fair to require passing a general test for promotion or graduation, regardless of performance in required courses? If so, are there substantive or procedural due process issues that might render the process unfair or unreasonable? What about requiring teachers to pass competency tests? Is it fair and reasonable to require them to pass a test even though they meet the usual teacher requirements? If such tests are generally permissible, what due process standards must attend their use?

The growing practice of requiring students to pass competency tests for graduation, regardless of whether all required courses have been passed, and parallel requirements for the professional practice of teaching, has become a dramatic issue in recent years. Born of the growing interest in educational accountability and concern for declining educational standards, this testing movement has encountered both equal protection and due process challenges, as well as the related statutory provisions found in the Civil Rights Act of 1964 and, when handicapped students are involved, the Rehabilitation Act of 1973 and the Education for All Handicapped Children Act, 1975. The due process issues may be obscured by these other points of law. Nevertheless, the concept of due process runs through the court challenges to competency testing. It takes the form of requiring that these tests be clearly and directly related to the skills and knowledge they are designed to measure and that they are fairly administered.

A case illustrating due process aspects of teacher competency tests is *Alba* v. *Los Angeles* (1983). Probationary high-school social-studies teachers were informed that their continued employment would be contingent upon passing a district competency test for social-studies teachers. The test had been prepared by a representative committee of district social-studies teachers, including geographic, racial, and sex balance. The test was validated by an independent agency. The committee determined the passing score based on its experience of required teacher knowledge. Eight teachers, who were not rehired because they failed, sued because sections of the test advertised to them, and for which they had studied, were not included, and the passing score had been raised from previous tests. Further, they complained that they had not been informed that the rules allowed them the alternative of qualifying by passing the social-studies section of the National Teachers Examination. The California appellate court reversed the trial court's finding that the school board had acted arbitrarily and capriciously in not including all the previously announced sections on the test and in not informing the teachers of the NTE alternative. In the opinion of the higher court, the missing sections did not render the test inherently unfair, as "[many examinations] . . . do not in fact test all possible subject matters that the examination administrators announce."[38] Further, it did not logically follow that the teachers would have passed if the missing sections had been included. As to the NTE alternative, the court found that the teachers' contract called for them to take the next test offered, which was the district examination. Finally, the overriding reason for finding for the district was that: "The failure bears directly on their competency as teachers. The welfare of . . . students would be affected by the retention of teachers who are unable to demonstrate their competency by successfully passing an examination in the field that they were engaged to teach."[39]

The due process issue of timely notice was raised (in addition to other claims) by black students who failed Florida's minimum competency test, because they had not been provided with timely notice, which should be before students entered high school, not after, as with the instant situation. The trial court agreed, and so ordered. Upon appeal, it was also decided that the district court should determine whether the test was fair; that is, whether it fairly assessed knowledge and information actually taught in the school. Thus, both procedural and substantive due process were implicated in the court's recognition of the property interest students had in their high-school diploma. Subsequent investigation led to the conclusion that the test was a reasonably valid measure of the curriculum (*Debra P.* v. *Turlington,* 644 F. 2d 397 [1981]).

A New York case involved claims of violation of due process, equal protection, and the Education for All Handicapped Children Act, when two handicapped students were denied their diplomas for failing the state's basic competency test. The state appeals court found no violations of equal protection or the Education for All Handicapped Children Act. However, it did find a violation of due process, in that these students had been studying according to individual education plans designed for special-education students who did not contemplate a general competency examination for receiving a diploma. This had been introduced just three years before the students were scheduled to complete their studies. Finding both property and liberty interests implicated in this issue, the court ordered the diplomas awarded without the requirement of passing the competency test (*Board of Educ. of Northport–East Northport Union Free Dist.* v. *Ambach,* 458 N.Y.S. 2d 680 [1982]).

The reasoning in *Ambach* was applied to *Brookhart* v. *Illinois State Board* (1983) by a federal appeals court. Handicapped students offered certificates of attendance rather than diplomas sued on statutory and constitutional grounds. All claims were set aside by the appellate court except that of due process, which was sustained because their individual education plans did not contemplate a competency test, hence a one-and-a-half-year notice of the test requirement was unfair. The court advised the school board of procedures that would meet the requirements of due process:

> The school district can, first, ensure that handicapped students are sufficiently exposed to most of the material that appears on the MCT, or second, they can produce evidence of a reasoned and well-informed decision by the parents and teachers involved that a particular high school student would be better off concentrating on educational objectives other than preparation for the MCT.[40]

Both *Ambach* and *Brookhart* rejected due process arguments challenging the validity of the competency tests. This issue, earlier raised in *Debra P.,* was renewed in *Anderson* v. *Banks* (1982). The challenge to the validity of competency tests influenced a federal court in Georgia to bar use of the California Achievement Test (CAT) as a graduation requirement unless the district could prove the CAT actually tested what the schools taught. If so, it could be equally applied to normal and handicapped students. District officials set out to do this and returned to court two years later. Plaintiffs argued that the reading level of the CAT was more difficult than the typical material to which these students were exposed. Testing officials responded that the test standardization process responded well to that type of problem. The court agreed with the testing officials, observing: "If a student is taught how to read in the first four grades, there is no failure of due process in asking reading comprehension questions of twelfth grade difficulty, even though when reading skills were actually taught in the curriculum, they were taught at a much simpler level."[41]

A final attack on the test was that the district students did worse on the more difficult test items than the norm group, showing that the material had not been taught. The judge countered that assuming the district students had simply not learned the material was an equally plausible explanation. In approving the use of the CAT as a competency test, the judge concluded that proving every test item reflected specific curricular content would be a "paralyzing burden" on the school, limiting its general educational effectiveness.

POLICY CONSIDERATIONS

Due process has become firmly imbedded into the administration of American education. Led by the decisions in *Meyer v. Nebraska, Board v. Roth, Perry v. Sindermann, Cleveland v. LaFleur, Goss v. Lopez, Hortonville v. Hortonville,* and *Ingraham v. Wright,* the role of due process in education has been strengthened, while some of its limits have been defined. State courts and lower federal courts have also played important roles in developing the concept. However, the essential vagueness and generality of the idea of due process has left the area as a fertile ground for liberal-conservative and activist-restraintist differences. There is hardly an area of litigation that has resulted in more severely split decisions and appellate-court reversals of lower-court decisions.

One reason for this is that the idea of fairness is easily subject to a variety of interpretations in specific situations. Another is that the benefits of providing liberal concepts of due process procedural and substantive fairness must be weighed against the costs it requires in school time, inconvenience, injury to others, and interruption of the educational process. Finally, this broad arena invites clashes between contrasting liberal and conservative educational philosophies about the effect of strong or weak administrative control on learning and student development. One critic of the liberal expansion of due process wrote: "I contend that the decline of adult authority in our schools, due to judicial decisions and the spread of legalistic relationships between students and faculty, are important causes for this disorder" (for instance, increased youthful suicides, homicides, and out-of-wedlock births).[42] A response to this argument countered: "I see it [increased court intervention] as part of the price we pay in a democratic society for continuing the political process of defining the relationship between the individual and government, and protecting the rights of all citizens, regardless of their position in society."[43]

There is evidence that the concept of due process may not be well understood by educators, which is not very surprising, given its generality, contrasting interpretations on the applicability to specific situations made by courts, and numerous vigorous dissents on important due process cases in education. Further, there is evidence that educators tend to be less liberal regarding court due process decisions affecting students than they are regarding their own rights.[44] These two factors combine to make Kirp's statement quoted in Chapter 1 a serious policy consideration: "If school authorities share the perception . . . that due process in the schools will undercut basic organizational patterns by radically altering administrators' and teachers' lives, the meaning of the concept is likely to be altered in a way that . . . strips due process of the very characteristics that imbue it with worth.''

Educators are left to ponder such philosophic concepts as the true nature of justice, and in so doing, attempt to anticipate whether their views will match those held by judges. General guidelines are available to help steer educational policy and decisions. The protections of due process procedures should be given to educators and students who appear to have reasonable property or liberty interests in threatened deprivations by school authorities. As the interests at stake (such as a teaching position, a teaching license, a teacher's transfer, a teacher's demotion, student suspension or expulsion, placement in a retarded track, grade reduction, denial of diploma, student's exclusion from extracurricular activities) increase, so should the due process protection afforded. While a one-day suspension may involve no more than an informal notice and a hearing involving no more than a few minutes of student-educator dialogue, the decision to expel a student should allow the student to be represented by an attorney in a hearing that has many of the procedural trappings of a courtroom trial. The same reasoning applies to educators threatened with liberty or property losses. The following list enumerates the elements of procedural due process, placed roughly in the order in which further due process elements are added to situations involving successively more severe sanctions:

1. A speedy and full notification of charges.
2. Provision of an opportunity to answer charges that allows time to prepare an adequate defense but does not unnecessarily delay a resolution and is held at a reasonable time and place.
3. The hearing should be conducted by an impartial tribunal; that is, the decision maker(s) should have no vested interest in the outcome.
4. The accused should be given the names of adverse witnesses, access to adverse evidence, and the right to introduce evidence.
5. The decision must be based on the rules and evidence adduced at the hearing.
6. A prompt finding, giving the reasons for the decision and the evidence supporting it, must be delivered at the conclusion of the hearing.
7. The accused (or his or her counsel) should have the right to cross-examine adverse witnesses and introduce witnesses in his or her defense.
8. The accused has a right to representation by legal counsel.
9. A written record of the proceedings must be maintained.
10. The accused has the right to appeal an adverse decision.

Controversies involving the substantive elements of due process are best managed by educational authorities considering the following questions before taking action against teachers, administrators, or students:

1. Does the rule bear a reasonable relationship to a legitimate educational interest? Where issues of race, free expression, or religion are implicated, is there a compelling interest in the school's restriction on teacher/student liberty or property interests?

2. Conversely, are the restrictions contained in the rule or regulation arbitrary or capricious? That is, are they based on personalistic, idiosyncratic attitudes, inconsiderate of equally legitimate opposing views for no better reason than that those in power prefer them?

3. Are the rules or regulations upon which actions against teachers or students are based so broad or vague as to obviate clear understanding of them?

4. Does the rule or regulation contain an "irrebuttable assumption"; that is, a conclusion that admits no possible contrary explanation?

5. Is the action taken against a student or teacher of a kind that would "literally shock the conscience" of the typical judge?

6. Does official action invade the area of privacy reserved to individuals by the due process concept?

These principles are much easier to state than to follow in practical situations. In particular, how might a school-board member, administrator, or teacher know what might "shock the conscience" of any particular judge? The circumstances in *Hall* v. *Tawney* shocked the conscience of that jurist, but would it be so for another? Further, Justice Rehnquist saw the whole concept of the "irrebuttable presumption" as defeating reasonable school administration in *Cleveland* v. *LaFleur,* as school boards must draw the line somewhere, "irrebuttable presumption" or not. Even in the seemingly more objective area of due process procedures, three dissenting justices in *Hortonville* v. *Hortonville* saw unconstitutional bias in allowing the school board to sit in judgment on teachers who had struck against it. Consider also that in *Goss* v. *Lopez,* four justices saw the entire application of procedural due process in student suspension as unwarranted.

It remains for educators to consider the weight of court opinions, supplemented by their own informed knowledge of what is reasonable in school governance. Obtaining legal advice is also necessary. Clearly, school authorities have no right to decide, without adequate justification, that a blind teacher, or an obese teacher, or a homosexual teacher, or a pregnant teacher, or a teacher who is an unwed mother, may not continue to teach. However, there are circumstances wherein termination of teachers in any of these categories, as well as others, may be justified. To do so requires that boards and administrators show the rational nexus and fairness of doing so, as the teacher's interest is weighed against educational interests. The same holds true for student control and discipline. School authorities are best served by "counting ten" before acting to impose sanctions against students or developing hasty restrictions against all students based on personal biases or the desire to be free of complications or irritations, regardless of the effects of the restrictions on all or some students.

Clearly, ten-day suspensions and expulsions require formal due process procedures, but none are required for administering corporal punishment. Extremes in corporal punishment might violate substantive due process, but that is also true of vague or overbroad regulations allowing administrators the authority to personally interpret a rule and decide when it has been broken, as well as the severity of the punishment to be meted out.

All of these decisions about educators and students require the exercise of judgment, not only to decide if due process applies, but also to decide what or how much "process is due." It is a mistake to assume that it applies to all situations. There must be a reasonably substantial property or liberty interest at stake. In *Madera* v. *Board,* the absence of any potential deprivation of liberty or property disallowed the student's claims for due process protection. The same was true for the teacher's claims in *Board* v. *Roth,* as he had not yet established a property interest in his teaching position, nor was his liberty interest affected by the dismissal.

In considering the propriety of their actions, school authorities are well advised not only to know the statutory and case law of due process applied to education, but to be sensitive to the political and social climate. When conservative opinion is dominant, the balancing test in due process will favor the school's interest in maintaining high standards over students' and teachers' due process claims, as illustrated by state and lower federal court decisions in *Debra P.* v. *Turlington* and *Alba* v. *Los Angeles.* The greater importance of maintaining authority in the school over the needs of privacy and various personal styles of behavior will also predominate, as illustrated by *Newman* v. *Board, Rose* v. *Nashua, Davenport* v. *Randolph, Williams* v. *Board,* and other cases cited earlier. During liberal periods, or in appearances before liberal judges, personal freedom, privacy, and tolerance of differences will predominate, as in *Brown* v. *Bathke, Steward* v. *Board, Scott* v. *Board, Meyers* v. *Arcata,* and other cases cited previously.

Community standards also are an important consideration, as are other questions of the unique conditions and needs found in any given set of circumstances. However, in this indefinite area in which applicable concepts are continually defined and redefined, interpreted and reinterpreted, school administrators must mainly rely on their understanding of the basic concepts underlying due process and their best judgment of how the balancing test illuminates what is fair action in controversies between due process rights and educational requirements. As Justice Frankfurter has noted: "It is a delicate process of adjustment inescapably involving the exercise of judgment."

Board of Regents of State Colleges v. Roth
408 U.S. 564 (1972)

MR. JUSTICE STEWART delivered the opinion of the Court.

In 1968 the respondent, David Roth, was hired for his first teaching job as assistant professor of political science at Wisconsin State University-Oshkosh. He was hired for a fixed term of one academic year. The notice of his faculty appointment specified that his employment would begin on September 1, 1968, and would end on June 30, 1969. The respondent completed that term. But he was informed that he would not be rehired for the next academic year.

The respondent had no tenure rights to continued employment. Under Wisconsin statutory law a state university teacher can acquire tenure as a "permanent" employee only after four years of year-to-year employment. Having acquired tenure, a teacher is entitled to continued employment "during efficiency and good behavior." A relatively new teacher without tenure, however, is under Wisconsin law entitled to nothing beyond his one-year appointment. There are no statutory or administrative standards defining eligibility for reemployment. State law thus clearly leaves the decision whether to rehire a nontenured teacher for another year to the unfettered discretion of university officials.

The respondent brought this action in Federal District Court alleging that the decision not to rehire him for the next year infringed his Fourteenth Amendment rights. He attacked the decision both in substance and procedure. First, he alleged that the true reason for the decision was to punish him for certain statements critical of the University administration, and that it therefore violated his right to freedom of speech. Second, he alleged that the failure of University officials to give him notice of any reason for nonretention and an opportunity for a hearing violated his right to procedural due process of law.

The only question presented to us at this stage in the case is whether the respondent had a constitutional right to a statement of reasons and a hearing on the University's decision not to rehire him for another year. We hold that he did not.

I

The requirements of procedural due process apply only to the deprivation of interests encompassed by the Fourteenth Amendment's protection of liberty and property. When protected interests are implicated, the right to some kind of prior hearing is paramount. But the range of interests protected by procedural due process is not infinite.

[T]o determine whether due process requirements apply in the first place, we must look not to the "weight" but to the *nature* of the interest at stake. We must look to see if the interest is within the Fourteenth Amendment's protection of liberty and property.

"Liberty" and "property" are broad and majestic terms. They are among the "[g]reat [constitutional] concepts . . . purposely left to gather meaning from experience. . . . [T]hey relate to the whole domain of social and economic fact, and the statesmen who founded this Nation knew too well that only a stagnant society remains unchanged."

Yet, while the Court has eschewed rigid or formalistic limitations on the protection of procedural due process, it has at the same time observed certain boundaries. For the words "liberty" and "property" in the Due Process Clause of the Fourteenth Amendment must be given some meaning.

II

In a Constitution for a free people, there can be no doubt that the meaning of "liberty" must be broad indeed.

There might be cases in which a State refused to re-employ a person under such circumstances that interests in liberty would be implicated. But this is not such a case.

The State, in declining to rehire the respondent, did not make any charge against him that might seriously damage his standing and associations in his community. It did not base the nonrenewal of his contract on a charge, for example, that he had been guilty of dishonesty, or immorality. Had it done so, this would be a different case. For "[w]here a person's good name, reputation, honor, or integrity is at stake because of what the government is doing to him, notice and an opportunity to be heard are essential."

Similarly, there is no suggestion that the State, in declining to re-employ the respondent, imposed on him a stigma or other disability that foreclosed his freedom to take advantage of other employment opportunities. The State, for example, did not invoke any regulations to bar the respondent from all other public employment in state universities. Had it done so, this, again, would be a different case. For "[t]o be deprived not only of present government employment but of future opportunity for it certainly is no small injury. . . . "

To be sure, the respondent has alleged that the nonrenewal of his contract was based on his exercise of right to freedom of speech. But this allegation is not now before us. The District Court stayed proceedings on this issue, and the respondent has yet to prove that the decision not to rehire him was, in fact, based on his free speech activities.

Hence, on the record before us, all that clearly appears is that the respondent was not rehired for one year at one university. It stretches the concept too far to suggest that a person is deprived of "liberty" when he simply is not rehired in one job but remains as free as before to seek another.

III

The Fourteenth Amendment's procedural protection of property is a safeguard of the security of interests that a person has already acquired in specific benefits. These interests—property interests—may take many forms.

To have a property interest in a benefit, a person clearly must have more than an abstract need or desire for it. He must have more than a unilateral expectation of it. He must, instead, have a legitimate claim of entitlement to it. It is a purpose of the ancient institution of property to protect those claims upon which people rely in their daily lives, reliance that must not be arbitrarily undermined. It is a purpose of the constitutional right to a hearing to provide an opportunity for a person to vindicate those claims.

Property interests, of course, are not created by the Constitution. Rather, they are created and their dimensions are defined by existing rules or understandings that stem from an independent source such as state law—rules or understandings that secure certain benefits and that support claims of entitlement to those benefits.

[T]he respondent's "property" interest in employment at Wisconsin State University-Oshkosh was created and defined by the terms of his appointment. Those terms secured his interest in employment up to June 30, 1969. But the important fact in this case is that they specifically provided that the respondent's employment was to terminate on June 30. They did not provide for contract renewal absent "sufficient cause." Indeed, they made no provision for renewal whatsoever.

Thus, the terms of the respondent's appointment secured absolutely no interest in re-employment for the next year. They supported absolutely no possible claim of entitlement to re-employment. Nor, significantly, was there any state statute or University rule or policy that secured his interest in re-employment or that created any legitimate claim to it. In these circumstances, the respondent surely had an abstract concern in being rehired, but he did not have a *property* interest sufficient to require the University authorities to give him a hearing when they declined to renew his contract of employment.

IV

Our analysis of the respondent's constitutional rights in this case in no way indicates a view that an opportunity for a hearing or a statement of reasons for nonretention would, or would not, be appropriate or wise in public colleges and universities. For it is a written Constitution that we apply. Our role is confined to interpretation of that Constitution.

We must conclude that the summary judgment for the respondent should not have been granted, since the respondent has not shown that he was deprived of liberty or property protected by the Fourteenth Amendment. The judgment of the Court of Appeals, accordingly, is reversed and the case is remanded for further proceedings consistent with this opinion.

Hortonville Dist. v. Hortonville Ed. Assn.
426 U.S. 482 (1976)

MR. CHIEF JUSTICE BURGER delivered the opinion of the Court.

We granted certiorari in this case to determine whether School Board members, vested by state law with the power to employ and dismiss teachers, could, consistent with the Due Process Clause of the Fourteenth Amendment, dismiss teachers engaged in a strike prohibited by state law.

I

The petitioners are a Wisconsin school district, the seven members of its School Board, and three administrative employees of the district. Respondents are teachers suing on behalf of all teachers in the district and the Hortonville Education Association (HEA), the collective-bargaining agent for the district's teachers.

During the 1972–1973 school year Hortonville teachers worked under a master collective-bargaining agreement; negotiations were conducted for renewal of the contract, but no agreement was reached for the 1973–1974 school year. The teachers continued to work while negotiations proceeded during the year without reaching agreement. On March 18, 1974, the members of the teachers' union went on strike, in direct violation of Wisconsin law. On March 20, the district superintendent sent all teachers a letter inviting them to return to work; a few did so. On March 23, he sent another letter, asking the 86 teachers still on strike to return, and reminding them that strikes by public employees were illegal; none of these teachers returned to work. After conducting classes with substitute teachers on March 26 and 27, the Board decided to conduct disciplinary hearings for each of the teachers on strike. Individual notices were sent to each teacher setting hearings for April 1, 2, and 3.

On April 1, most of the striking teachers appeared before the Board with counsel. Their attorney indicated that the teachers did not want individual hearings, but preferred to be treated as a group. He also argued that the Board was not sufficiently impartial to exercise discipline over the striking teachers and that the Due Process Clause of the Fourteenth Amendment required an independent, unbiased decisionmaker. An offer of proof was tendered to demonstrate that the strike had been provoked by the Board's failure to meet teachers' demands, and respondents' counsel asked to cross-examine Board members individually. The Board rejected the request, but permitted counsel to make the offer of proof, aimed at showing that the Board's contract offers were unsatisfactory, that the Board used coercive and illegal bargaining tactics, and that teachers in the district had been locked out by the Board.

On April 2, the Board voted to terminate the employment of striking teachers, and advised them by letter to that effect. However, the same letter invited all teachers on strike to reapply for teaching positions. One teacher accepted the invitation and returned to work; the Board hired replacements to fill the remaining positions.

II

The Hortonville School District is a common school district under Wisconsin law, financed by local property taxes and state school aid and governed by an elected seven-member School Board. The Board has broad power over "the possession, care, control and management of the property and affairs of the school district." The Board negotiates terms of employment with teachers under the Wisconsin Municipal Employment Relations Act, and contracts with individual teachers on behalf of the district. The Board is the only body vested by statute with the power to employ and dismiss teachers.

The sole issue in this case is whether the Due Process Clause of the Fourteenth Amendment prohibits this School Board from making the decision to dismiss teachers admittedly engaged in a strike and persistently refusing to return to their duties. The Wisconsin Supreme Court held that state law prohibited the strike and that termination of the striking teachers' employment was within the Board's statutory authority. The only decision remaining for the Board therefore involved the exercise of its discretion as to what should be done to carry out the duties the law placed on the Board.

Respondents argue, and the Wisconsin Supreme Court held, that the decision could be made only by an impartial decisionmaker, and that the Board was not impartial.

The Board cannot make a "reasonable" decision on this issue, the Wisconsin Supreme Court held and respondents argue, because its members are biased in some fashion that the due process guarantees of the Fourteenth Amendment prohibit.

Respondents' argument rests in part on doctrines that have no application to this case. They seem to argue that the Board members had some personal or official stake in the decision whether the teachers should be dismissed, and that the Board has manifested some personal bitterness toward the teachers, aroused by teacher criticism of the Board during the strike. [T]he teachers did not show, and the Wisconsin courts did not find, that the Board members had the kind of personal or financial stake in the decision that might create a conflict of interest, and there is nothing in the record to support charges of personal animosity. The Wisconsin Supreme Court was careful "not to suggest . . . that the board members were anything but dedicated public servants, trying to provide the district with quality education . . . within its limited budget." That court's analysis would seem to be confirmed by the Board's repeated invitations for striking teachers to return to work, the final invitation being contained in the letter that notified them of their discharge.

The only other factor suggested to support the claim of bias is that the School Board was involved in the negotiations that preceded and precipitated the striking teachers' discharge. Participation in those negotiations was a statutory duty of the Board. The Wisconsin Supreme Court held that this involvement, without more, disqualified the Board from deciding whether the teachers should be dismissed. Mere familiarity with the facts of a case gained by an agency in the performance of its statutory role does not, however, disqualify a decisionmaker. Nor is a decisionmaker disqualified simply because he has taken a position, even in public, on a policy issue related to the dispute, in the absence of a showing that he is not "capable of judging a particular controversy fairly on the basis of its own circumstances."

Respondents' claim and the Wisconsin Supreme Court's holding reduce to the argument that the Board was biased because it negotiated with the teachers on behalf of the school district without reaching agreement and learned about the reasons for the strike in the course of negotiating. From those premises the Wisconsin court concluded that the Board lost its statutory power to determine that the strike and persistent refusal to terminate it amounted to conduct serious enough to warrant discharge of the strikers. Wisconsin statutes vest in the Board the power to discharge its employees, a power of every employer, whether it has negotiated with the employees before discharge or not. The Fourteenth Amendment permits a court to strip the Board of the otherwise unremarkable power the Wisconsin Legislature has given it only if the Board's prior involvement in negotiating with the teachers means that it cannot act consistently with due process.

Due process, as this Court has repeatedly held, is a term that "negates any concept of inflexible procedures universally applicable to every imaginable situation." Determining what process is due in a given setting requires the Court to take into account the individual's stake in the decision at issue as well as the State's interest in a particular procedure for making it. Our assessment of the interests of the parties in this case leads to the conclusion that the Board's prior role as negotiator does not disqualify it to decide that the public interest in maintaining uninterrupted classroom work required that teachers striking in violation of state law be discharged.

The teachers' interest in these proceedings is, of course, self-evident. They wished to avoid termination of their employment, obviously an important interest, but one that must be examined in light of several factors. Since the teachers admitted that they were engaged in a work stoppage, there was no possibility of an erroneous factual determination on this critical threshold issue. Moreover, what the teachers claim as a property right was the expectation that the jobs they had left to go and remain on strike in violation of law would remain open to them. The Wisconsin court accepted at least the essence of that claim in defining the property right under state law, and we do not quarrel with its conclusion.

The Board's decision whether to dismiss striking teachers involves broad considerations, and does not in the main turn on the Board's view of the "seriousness" of the teachers' conduct or the factors they urge mitigated their violation of state law. It was not an adjudicative decision, for the Board had an obligation to make a decision based on its own answer to an important question of policy: What choice among the alternative responses to the teachers' strike will best serve the interests of the school system, the interests of the parents and children who depend on the system, and the interests of the citizens whose taxes support it? The Board's decision was only incidentally a disciplinary decision; it had significant governmental and public policy dimensions as well.

State law vests the governmental, or policymaking, function exclusively in the School Board and the State has two interests in keeping it there. First, the Board is the body with overall responsibility for the governance of the school district; it must cope with the myriad day-to-day problems of a modern public school system including the severe consequences of a teachers' strike; by virtue of electing them the constituents have declared the Board members qualified to deal with these problems, and they are accountable to the voters for the manner in which they perform. Second, the state legislature has given to the Board the power to employ and dismiss teachers, as a part of the balance it has struck in the area of municipal labor relations; altering those statutory powers as a matter of federal due process clearly changes that balance. Permitting the Board to make the decision at issue here preserves its control over school district affairs, leaves the balance of power in labor relations where the state legislature struck it, and assures that the decision whether to dismiss the teachers will be made by the body responsible for that decision under state law.

III

Respondents have failed to demonstrate that the decision to terminate their employment was infected by the sort of bias that we have held to disqualify other decisionmakers as a matter of federal due process. A showing that the Board was "involved" in the events preceding this decision, in light of the important interest in leaving with the Board the power given by the state legislature, is not enough to overcome the presumption of honesty and integrity in policymakers with decisionmaking power. Accordingly, we hold that the Due Process Clause of the Fourteenth Amendment did not guarantee respondents that the decision to terminate their employment would be made or reviewed by a body other than the School Board.

Reversed and remanded.

MR. JUSTICE STEWART, with whom MR. JUSTICE BRENNAN and MR. JUSTICE MARSHALL join, dissenting.

The issue in this case is whether the discharge of the respondent teachers by the petitioner School Board violated the Due Process Clause of the Fourteenth Amendment because the Board members were not impartial decisionmakers. It is now well established that "a biased decisionmaker [is] constitutionally unacceptable [and] 'our system of law has always endeavored to prevent even the probability of unfairness.' "

In order to ascertain whether there is a constitutionally unacceptable danger of partiality, both the nature of the particular decision and the interest of the decisionmaker in its outcome must be examined. Here, Wisconsin law controls the factors that must be found before a teacher may be discharged for striking. The parties present sharply divergent views of what the Wisconsin law requires.

Under the petitioners' view of the Wisconsin law, the discharge determination is purely a policy judgment involving an assessment of the best interest of the school system. Since that judgment does not require the Board to assess its own conduct during the negotiations, and since there is no indication that the Board members have a financial or personal interest in its outcome, the only basis for a claim of partiality rests on the Board's knowledge of the events leading to the strike acquired through its participation in the negotiation process. As the Court notes, however, "[m]ere familiarity with the facts of a case gained by an agency in the performance of its statutory role does not . . . disqualify a decisionmaker."

But a distinctly different constitutional claim is presented if, as the respondents contend, the School Board members must evaluate their own conduct in determining whether dismissal is a reasonable sanction to impose on the striking teachers. Apart from considerations of financial interest or personal hostility, the Court has found that officials "directly involved in making recommendations cannot always have complete objectivity in evaluating them."

"[U]nder a realistic appraisal of psychological tendencies and human weakness," I believe that there is a constitutionally unacceptable danger of bias where school board members are required to assess the reasonableness of their own actions during heated contract negotiations that have culminated in a teachers' strike. If, therefore, the respondents' interpretation of the state law is correct, then I would agree with the Wisconsin Supreme Court that "the board was not an impartial decision maker in a constitutional sense and that the [teachers] were denied due process of law."

Cleveland Board of Education v. LaFleur
414 U.S. 632 (1974)

MR. JUSTICE STEWART delivered the opinion of the Court.

The respondents are female public school teachers. During the 1970–1971 school year, each informed her local school board that she was pregnant; each was compelled by a mandatory maternity leave rule to quit her job without pay several months before the expected birth of her child. These cases call upon us to decide the constitutionality of the school boards' rules.

I

Jo Carol LaFleur and Ann Elizabeth Nelson are junior high school teachers employed by the Board of Education of Cleveland, Ohio. Pursuant to a rule first adopted in 1952, the school board requires every pregnant school teacher to take maternity leave without pay, beginning five months before the expected birth of her child. Application for such leave must be made no later than two weeks prior to the date of departure. A teacher on maternity leave is not allowed to return to work until the beginning of the next regular school semester which follows the date when her child attains the age of three months. A doctor's certificate attesting to the health of the teacher is a prerequisite to return; an additional physical examination may be required. The teacher on maternity leave is not promised re-employment after the birth of the child; she is merely given priority in reassignment to a position for which she is qualified. Failure to comply with the mandatory maternity leave provisions is ground for dismissal.

Neither Mrs. LaFleur nor Mrs. Nelson wished to take an unpaid maternity leave; each wanted to continue teaching until the end of the school year. Because of the mandatory maternity leave rule, however, each was required to leave her job in March 1971. The two women then filed separate suits in the United States District Court for the Northern District of Ohio, challenging the constitutionality of the maternity leave rule.

The petitioner Susan Cohen was employed by the School Board of Chesterfield County, Virginia. That school board's maternity leave regulation requires that a pregnant teacher leave work at least four months prior to the expected birth of her child. Notice in writing must be given to the school board at least six months prior to the expected birth date. A teacher on maternity leave is declared re-eligible for employment when she submits written notice from a physician that she is physically fit for re-employment, and when she can give assurance that care of the child will cause only minimal interference with her job responsibilities. The teacher is guaranteed re-employment no later than the first day of the school year following the date upon which she is declared re-eligible.

Mrs. Cohen informed the Chesterfield County School Board in November 1970, that she was pregnant and expected the birth of her child about April 28, 1971. She initially requested that she be permitted to continue teaching until April 1, 1971. The school board rejected the request, as it did Mrs. Cohen's subsequent suggestion that she be allowed to teach until January 21, 1971, the end of the first school semester. Instead, she was required to leave her teaching job on December 18, 1970. She subsequently filed this suit in the United States District Court for the Eastern District of Virginia.

We granted certiorari in both cases, in order to resolve the conflict between the Courts of Appeals regarding the constitutionality of such mandatory maternity leave rules for public school teachers.

II

This Court has long recognized that freedom of personal choice in matters of marriage and family life is one of the liberties protected by the Due Process Clause of the Fourteenth Amendment. [T]here is a right "to be free from unwarranted governmental intrusion into matters so fundamentally affecting a person as the decision whether to bear or beget a child."

By acting to penalize the pregnant teacher for deciding to bear a child, overly restrictive maternity leave regulations can constitute a heavy burden on the exercise of these protected freedoms. Because public school maternity leave rules directly affect "one of the basic civil rights of man," the Due Process Clause of the Fourteenth Amendment requires that such rules must not needlessly, arbitrarily, or capriciously impinge upon this vital area of a teacher's constitutional liberty. The question before us in these cases is whether the interests advanced in support of the rules of the Cleveland and Chesterfield County School Boards can justify the particular procedures they have adopted.

The school boards in these cases have offered two essentially overlapping explanations for their mandatory maternity leave rules. First, they contend that the firm cutoff dates are necessary to maintain continuity of classroom instruction, since advance knowledge of when a pregnant teacher must leave facilitates the finding and hiring of a qualified substitute. Secondly, the school boards seek to justify their maternity rules by arguing that at least some teachers become physically incapable of adequately performing certain of their duties during the latter part of pregnancy. By keeping the pregnant teacher out of the classroom during these final months, the maternity leave rules are said to protect the health of the teacher and her unborn child, while at the same time assuring that students have a physically capable instructor in the classroom at all times.

It cannot be denied that continuity of instruction is a significant and legitimate educational goal. Regulations requiring pregnant teachers to provide early notice of their condition to school authorities undoubtedly facilitate administrative planning toward the important objective of continuity.

Thus, while the advance-notice provisions in the Cleveland and Chesterfield County rules are wholly rational and may well be necessary to serve the objective of continuity of instruction, the absolute requirements of termination at the end of the fourth or fifth month of pregnancy are not. Were continuity the only goal, cutoff dates much later during pregnancy would serve as well as or better than the challenged rules, providing that ample advance notice requirements were retained. Indeed, continuity would seem just as well attained if the teacher herself were allowed to choose the date upon which to commence her leave, at least so long as the decision were required to be made and notice given of it well in advance of the date selected.

In fact, since the fifth or sixth month of pregnancy will obviously begin at different times in the school year for different teachers, the present Cleveland and Chesterfield County rules may serve to hinder attainment of the very continuity objectives that they are purportedly designed to promote. For example, the beginning of the fifth month of pregnancy for both Mrs. LaFleur and Mrs. Nelson occurred during March of 1971. Both were thus required to leave work with only a few months left in the school year, even though both were fully willing to serve through the end of the term. Similarly, if continuity were the only goal, it seems ironic that the Chesterfield County rule forced Mrs. Cohen to leave work in mid-December 1970 rather than at the end of the semester in January, as she requested.

We thus conclude that the arbitrary cutoff dates embodied in the mandatory leave rules before us have no rational relationship to the valid state interest of preserving continuity of instruction. As long as the teachers are required to give substantial advance notice of their condition, the choice of firm dates later in pregnancy would serve the boards' objectives just as well, while imposing a far lesser burden on the women's exercise of constitutionally protected freedom.

The question remains as to whether the cutoff dates at the beginning of the fifth and sixth months can be justified on the other ground advanced by the school boards—the necessity of keeping physically unfit teachers out of the classroom. There can be no doubt that such an objective is perfectly legitimate, both on educational and safety grounds. And, despite the plethora of conflicting medical testimony in these cases, we can assume, *arguendo,* that at least some teachers become physically disabled from effectively performing their duties during the latter stages of pregnancy.

The mandatory termination provisions of the Cleveland and Chesterfield County rules surely operate to insulate the classroom from the presence of potentially incapacitated pregnant teachers. But the question is whether the rules sweep too broadly. That question must be answered in the affirmative, for the provisions amount to a conclusive presumption that every pregnant teacher who reaches the fifth or sixth month of pregnancy is physically incapable of continuing. There is no individualized determination by the teacher's doctor—or the school board's—as to any particular teacher's ability to continue at her job. The rules contain an irrebuttable presumption of physical incompetency, and that presumption applies even when the medical evidence as to an individual woman's physical status might be wholly to the contrary.

While the medical experts in these cases differed on many points, they unanimously agreed on one—the ability of any particular pregnant woman to continue at work past any fixed time in her pregnancy is very much an individual matter. Even assuming, *arguendo,* that there are some women who would be physically unable to work past the particular cutoff dates embodied in the challenged rules, it is evident that there are large numbers of teachers who are fully capable of continuing work for longer than the Cleveland and Chesterfield County regulations will allow. Thus, the conclusive presumption embodied in these rules is neither "necessarily [nor] universally true," and is violative of the Due Process Clause.

The school boards have argued that the mandatory termination dates serve the interest of administrative convenience, since there are many instances of teacher pregnancy, and the rules obviate the necessity for case-by-case determinations.

While it might be easier for the school boards to conclusively presume that all pregnant women are unfit to teach past the fourth or fifth month or even the first month, of pregnancy, administrative convenience alone is insufficient to make valid what otherwise is a violation of due process of law. The Fourteenth Amendment requires the school boards to employ alternative administrative means, which do not so broadly infringe upon basic constitutional liberty, in support of their legitimate goals.

We conclude, therefore, that neither the necessity for continuity of instruction nor the state interest in keeping physically unfit teachers out of the classroom can justify the sweeping mandatory leave regulations that the Cleveland and Chesterfield County School Boards have adopted. While the regulations no doubt represent a good-faith attempt to achieve a laudable goal, they cannot pass muster under the Due Process Clause of the Fourteenth Amendment, because they employ irrebuttable presumptions that unduly penalize a female teacher for deciding to bear a child.

III

In addition to the mandatory termination provisions, both the Cleveland and Chesterfield County rules contain limitations upon a teacher's eligibility to return to work after giving birth. Again, the school boards offer two justifications for the return rules—continuity of instruction and the desire to be certain that the teacher is physically competent when she returns to work. As is the case with the leave provisions, the question is not whether the school board's goals are legitimate, but rather whether the particular means chosen to achieve those objectives unduly infringe upon the teacher's constitutional liberty.

Under the Cleveland rule, the teacher is not eligible to return to work until the beginning of the next regular school semester following the time when her child attains the age of three months. A doctor's certificate attesting to the teacher's health is required before return; an additional physical examination may be required at the option of the school board.

The Cleveland rule, however, does not simply contain these reasonable medical and next-semester eligibility provisions. In addition, the school board requires the mother to wait until her child reaches the age of three months before the return rules begin to operate. The school board has offered no reasonable justification for this supplemental limitation, and we can perceive none. To the extent that the three-month provision reflects the school board's thinking that no mother is fit to return until that point in time, it suffers from the same constitutional deficiencies that plague the irrebuttable presumption in the termination rules. The presumption, moreover, is patently unnecessary, since the requirement of a physician's certificate or a medical examination fully protects the school's interests in this regard. And finally, the three-month provision simply has nothing to do with continuity of instruction, since the precise point at which the child will reach the relevant age will obviously occur at a different point throughout the school year for each teacher.

Thus, we conclude that the Cleveland return rule, insofar as it embodies the three-month age provision, is wholly arbitrary and irrational, and hence violates the Due Process Clause of the Fourteenth Amendment. The age limitation serves no legitimate state interest, and unnecessarily penalizes the female teacher for asserting her right to bear children.

IV

For the reasons stated, we hold that the mandatory termination provisions of the Cleveland and Chesterfield County maternity regulations violate the Due Process Clause of the Fourteenth Amendment, because of their use of unwarranted conclusive presumptions that seriously burden the exercise of protected constitutional liberty. For similar reasons, we hold the three-month provision of the Cleveland return rule unconstitutional.

MR. JUSTICE REHNQUIST, with whom THE CHIEF JUSTICE joins, dissenting.

The Court rests its invalidation of the school regulations involved in these cases on the Due Process Clause of the Fourteenth Amendment, rather than on any claim of sexual discrimination under the Equal Protection Clause of that Amendment. My Brother Stewart thereby enlists the Court in another quixotic engagement in his apparently unending war on irrebuttable presumptions. In these cases we are told that although a regulation "requiring a termination of employment at some firm date during the last few weeks of pregnancy," might pass muster, the regulations here challenged requiring termination at the end of the fourth or fifth month of pregnancy violate due process of law.

As the Chief Justice pointed out in his dissent last year, "literally thousands of state statutes create classifications permanent in duration, which are less than perfect, as all legislative classifications are, and might be improved on by individualized determinations. . . . " Hundreds of years ago in England, before Parliament came to be thought of as a body having general lawmaking power, controversies were determined on an individualized basis without benefit of any general law. Most students of government consider the shift from this sort of determination, made on an *ad hoc* basis by the King's representative, to a relatively uniform body of rules enacted by a body exercising legislative authority, to have been a significant step forward in the achievement of a civilized political society. It seems to me a little late in the day for this Court to weigh in against such an established consensus.

It has been said before, but it bears repeating here: All legislation involves the drawing of lines, and the drawing of lines necessarily results in particular individuals who are disadvantaged by the line drawn being virtually indistinguishable for many purposes from those individuals who benefit from the legislative classification. The Court's disenchantment with "irrebuttable presumptions," and its preference for "individualized determination," is in the last analysis nothing less than an attack upon the very notion of lawmaking itself.

The lines drawn by the school boards in the city of Cleveland and Chesterfield County in these cases require pregnant teachers to take forced leave at a stage of their pregnancy when medical evidence seems to suggest that a majority of them might well be able to continue teaching without any significant possibility of physical impairment. But, so far as I am aware, the medical evidence also suggests that in some cases there may be physical impairment at the stage of pregnancy fastened on by the regulations in question, and that the probability of physical impairment increases as the pregnancy advances. If legislative bodies are to be permitted to draw a general line anywhere short of the delivery room, I can find no judicial standard of measurement which says the ones drawn here were invalid. I therefore dissent.

Goss v. Lopez
419 U.S. 565 (1975)

MR. JUSTICE WHITE delivered the opinion of the Court.

This appeal by various administrators of the Columbus, Ohio, Public School System (CPSS) challenges the judgment of a three-judge federal court, declaring that appellees—various high school students in the CPSS—were denied due process of law contrary to the command of the Fourteenth Amendment in that they were temporarily suspended from their high schools without a hearing either prior to suspension or within a reasonable time thereafter, and enjoining the administrators to remove all references to such suspensions from the students' records.

I

Ohio law, Rev. Code Ann. § 3313.64 (1972), provides for free education to all children between the ages of six and 21. Section 3313.66 of the Code empowers the principal of an Ohio public school to suspend a pupil for misconduct for up to 10 days or to expel him. In either case, he must notify the student's parents within 24 hours and state the reasons for his action. A pupil who is expelled, or his parents, may appeal the decision to the Board of Education and in connection therewith shall be permitted to be heard at the board meeting. The Board may reinstate the pupil following the hearing. No similar procedure is provided in § 3313.66 or any other provision of state law for a suspended student. Aside from a regulation tracking the statute, at the time of the imposition of the suspensions in this case the CPSS itself had not issued any written procedure applicable to suspensions. Nor, so far as the record reflects, had any of the individual high schools involved in this case. Each, however, had formally or informally described the conduct for which suspension could be imposed.

The proof below established that the suspensions arose out of a period of widespread student unrest in the CPSS during February and March 1971. Six of the named plaintiffs were students at the Marion-Franklin High School and were each suspended for 10 days on account of disruptive or disobedient conduct committed in the presence of the school administrator who ordered the suspension. None was given a hearing to determine the operative facts underlying the suspension, but each, together with his or her parents, was offered the opportunity to attend a conference, subsequent to the effective date of the suspension, to discuss the student's future.

Two named plaintiffs, Dwight Lopez and Betty Crome, were students at the Central High School and McGuffey Junior High School, respectively. The former was suspended in connection with a disturbance in the lunchroom which involved some physical damage to school property. Lopez testified that at least 75 other students were suspended from his school on the same day. He also testified below that he was not a party to the destructive conduct but was instead an innocent bystander. Because no one from the school testified with regard to this incident, there is no evidence in the record indicating the official basis for concluding otherwise. Lopez never had a hearing.

Betty Crome was present at a demonstration at a high school other than the one she was attending. There she was arrested together with others, taken to the police station, and released without being formally charged. Before she went to school on the following day, she was notified that she had been suspended for a 10-day period. Because no one from the school testified with respect to this incident, the record does not disclose how the McGuffey Junior High School principal went about making the decision to suspend Crome, nor does it disclose on what information the decision was based. It is clear from the record that no hearing was ever held.

On the basis of this evidence, the three-judge court declared that plaintiffs were denied due process of law because they were "suspended without hearing prior to suspension or within a reasonable time thereafter," and that Ohio Rev.

Code Ann. § 3313.66 (1972) and regulations issued pursuant thereto were unconstitutional in permitting such suspensions. It was ordered that all references to plaintiffs' suspensions be removed from school files.

II

At the outset, appellants contend that because there is no constitutional right to an education at public expense, the Due Process Clause does not protect against expulsions from the public school system. This position misconceives the nature of the issue and is refuted by prior decisions. The Fourteenth Amendment forbids the State to deprive any person of life, liberty, or property without due process of law. Protected interests in property are normally "not created by the Constitution. Rather, they are created and their dimensions are defined" by an independent source such as state statutes or rules entitling the citizen to certain benefits.

Here, on the basis of state law, appellees plainly had legitimate claims of entitlement to a public education. Having chosen to extend the right to an education to people of appellees' class generally. Ohio may not withdraw that right on grounds of misconduct, absent fundamentally fair procedures to determine whether the misconduct has occurred.

Although Ohio may not be constitutionally obligated to establish and maintain a public school system, it has nevertheless done so and has required its children to attend. Those young people do not "shed their constitutional rights" at the schoolhouse door. The authority possessed by the State to prescribe and enforce standards of conduct in its schools although concededly very broad, must be exercised consistently with constitutional safeguards. Among other things, the State is constrained to recognize a student's legitimate entitlement to a public education as a property interest which is protected by the Due Process Clause and which may not be taken away for misconduct without adherence to the minimum procedures required by that Clause.

The Due Process Clause also forbids arbitrary deprivations of liberty. "Where a person's good name, reputation, honor, or integrity is at stake because of what the government is doing to him," the minimal requirements of the Clause must be satisfied. School authorities here suspended appellees from school for periods of up to 10 days based on charges of misconduct. If sustained and recorded, those charges could seriously damage the students' standing with their fellow pupils and their teachers as well as interfere with later opportunities for higher education and employment. It is apparent that the claimed right of the State to determine unilaterally and without process whether that misconduct has occurred immediately collides with the requirements of the Constitution.

Appellants proceed to argue that even if there is a right to a public education protected by the Due Process Clause generally, the Clause comes into play only when the State subjects a student to a "severe detriment or grievous loss." The loss of 10 days, it is said, is neither severe nor grievous and the Due Process Clause is therefore of no relevance. Appellants' argument is again refuted by our prior decisions; for in determining "whether due process requirements apply in the first place, we must look not to the 'weight' but to the *nature* of the interest at stake." Appellees were excluded from school only temporarily, it is true, but the length and consequent severity of a deprivation, while another factor to weigh in determining the appropriate form of hearing, "is not decisive of the basic right" to a hearing of some kind. The Court's view has been that as long as a property deprivation is not *de minimis,* its gravity is irrelevant to the question whether account must be taken of the Due Process Clause. A 10-day suspension from school is not *de minimis* in our view and may not be imposed in complete disregard of the Due Process Clause.

A short suspension is, of course, a far milder deprivation than expulsion. But, "education is perhaps the most important function of state and local governments," and the total exclusion from the educational process for more than a trivial period, and certainly if the suspension is for 10 days, is a serious event in the life of the suspended child. Neither the property interest in educational benefits temporarily denied nor the liberty interest in reputation, which is also implicated, is so insubstantial that suspensions may constitutionally be imposed by any procedure the school chooses, no matter how arbitrary.

III

"Once it is determined that due process applies, the question remains what process is due." We turn to that question, fully realizing as our cases regularly do that the interpretation and application of the Due Process Clause are intensely practical matters and that "[t]he very nature of due process negates any concept of inflexible procedures universally applicable to every imaginable situation."

"[M]any controversies have raged about the cryptic and abstract words of the Due Process Clause but there can be no doubt that at a minimum they require that deprivation of life, liberty or property by adjudication be preceded by notice and opportunity for hearing appropriate to the nature of the case." "The fundamental requisite of due process of law is the opportunity to be heard," a right that "has little reality or worth unless one is informed that the matter is pending and can choose for himself whether to . . . contest." At the very minimum, therefore, students facing suspension and the consequent interference with a protected property interest must be given *some* kind of notice and afforded *some* kind of hearing. "Parties whose rights are to be affected are entitled to be heard; and in order that they may enjoy that right they must first be notified."

It also appears from our cases that the timing and content of the notice and the nature of the hearing will depend on appropriate accommodation of the competing interests involved. The student's interest is to avoid unfair or mistaken exclusion from the educational process, with all of its unfortunate consequences. The Due Process Clause will not shield him from suspensions properly imposed, but it disserves both his interest and the interest of the State if his suspension is in fact unwarranted. The concern would be mostly academic if the disciplinary process were a totally accurate, unerring process, never mistaken and never unfair. Unfortunately, that is not the case, and no one suggests that it is. Disciplinarians, although proceeding in utmost good faith, frequently act on the reports and advice of others; and the controlling facts and the nature of the conduct under challenge are often disputed. The risk of error is not at all trivial, and it should be guarded against if that may be done without prohibitive cost or interference with the educational process.

The difficulty is that our schools are vast and complex. Some modicum of discipline and order is essential if the educational function is to be performed. Events calling for discipline are frequent occurrences and sometimes require immediate, effective action. Suspension is considered not only to be a necessary tool to maintain order but a valuable educational device. The prospect of imposing elaborate hearing requirements in every suspension case is viewed with great concern, and many school authorities may well prefer the untrammeled power to act unilaterally, unhampered by rules about notice and hearing. But it would be a strange disciplinary system in an educational institution if no communication was sought by the disciplinarian with the student in an effort to inform him of his dereliction and to let him tell his side of the story in order to make sure that an injustice is not done. "[F]airness can rarely be obtained by secret, one-sided determination of facts decisive of rights. . . . " "Secrecy is not congenial to truth-seeking and self-righteousness gives too slender an assurance of rightness. No better instrument has been devised for arriving at truth than to give a person in jeopardy of serious loss notice of the case against him and opportunity to meet it."

We do not believe that school authorities must be totally free from notice and hearing requirements if their schools are to operate with acceptable efficiency. Students facing temporary suspension have interests qualifying for protection of the Due Process Clause, and due process requires, in connection with a suspension of 10 days or less, that the student be given oral or written notice of the charges against him and, if he denies them, an explanation of the evidence the authorities have and an opportunity to present his side of the story. The Clause requires at least these rudimentary precautions against unfair or mistaken findings of misconduct and arbitrary exclusion from school.

There need be no delay between the time "notice" is given and the time of the hearing. In the great majority of cases the disciplinarian may informally discuss the alleged misconduct with the student minutes after it has occurred. We hold only that, in being given an opportunity to explain his version of the facts at this discussion, the student first be told what he is accused of doing and what the basis of the accusation is. Since the hearing may occur almost immediately following the misconduct, it follows that as a general rule notice and hearing should precede removal of the student from school. We agree with the District Court, however, that there are recurring situations in which prior notice and hearing cannot be insisted upon. Students whose presence poses a continuing danger to persons or property or an ongoing threat of disrupting the academic process may be immediately removed from school. In such cases, the necessary notice and rudimentary hearing should follow as soon as practicable, as the District Court indicated.

In holding as we do, we do not believe that we have imposed procedures on school disciplinarians which are inappropriate in a classroom setting. Instead we have imposed requirements which are, if anything, less than a fair-minded school principal would impose upon himself in order to avoid unfair suspensions.

We stop short of construing the Due Process Clause to require, countrywide, that hearings in connection with short suspensions must afford the student the opportunity to secure counsel, to confront and cross-examine witnesses supporting the charge, or to call his own witnesses to verify his version of the incident. Brief disciplinary suspensions are almost countless. To impose in each such case even truncated trial-type procedures might well overwhelm administrative facilities in many places and, by diverting resources, cost more than it would save in educational effectiveness. Moreover, further formalizing the suspension process and escalating its formality and adversary nature may not only make it too costly as a regular disciplinary tool but also destroy its effectiveness as part of the teaching process.

On the other hand, requiring effective notice and informal hearing permitting the student to give his version of the events will provide a meaningful hedge against erroneous action. At least the disciplinarian will be alerted to the existence of disputes about facts and arguments about cause and effect. He may then determine himself to summon the accuser, permit cross-examination, and allow the student to present his own witnesses. In more difficult cases, he may permit counsel. In any event, his discretion will be more informed and we think the risk of error substantially reduced.

Requiring that there be at least an informal give-and-take between student and disciplinarian, preferably prior to the suspension, will add little to the fact-finding function where the disciplinarian himself has witnessed the conduct forming the basis for the charge. But things are not always as they seem to be, and the student will at least have the opportunity to characterize his conduct and put it in what he deems the proper context.

We should also make it clear that we have addressed ourselves solely to the short suspension, not exceeding 10 days. Longer suspensions or expulsions for the remainder of the school term, or permanently, may require more formal procedures. Nor do we put aside the possibility that in unusual situations, although involving only a short suspension, something more than the rudimentary procedures will be required.

IV

The District Court found each of the suspensions involved here to have occurred without a hearing, either before or after the suspension, and that each suspension was therefore invalid and the statute unconstitutional insofar as it permits such suspensions without notice or hearing. Accordingly, the judgment is

Affirmed.

MR. JUSTICE POWELL, with whom THE CHIEF JUSTICE, MR. JUSTICE BLACKMUN, and MR. JUSTICE REHNQUIST join, dissenting.

The Court today invalidates an Ohio statute that permits student suspensions from school without a hearing "for not more than ten days." The decision unnecessarily opens avenues for judicial intervention in the operation of our public schools that may affect adversely the quality of education. The Court holds for the first time that the federal courts, rather than educational officials and state legislatures, have the authority to determine the rules applicable to routine classroom discipline of children and teenagers in the public schools. It justifies this unprecedented intrusion into the process of elementary and secondary education by identifying a new constitutional right: the right of a student not to be suspended for as much as a single day without notice and a due process hearing either before or promptly following the suspension.

The Court's decision rests on the premise that, under Ohio law, education is a property interest protected by the Fourteenth Amendment's Due Process Clause and therefore that any suspension requires notice and a hearing. In my view, a student's interest in education is not infringed by a suspension within the limited period prescribed by Ohio law. Moreover, to the extent that there may be some arguable infringement, it is too speculative, transitory, and insubstantial to justify imposition of a *constitutional* rule.

I

In identifying property interests subject to due process protections, the Court's past opinions make clear that these interests "are created and their *dimensions are defined* by existing rules or understandings that stem from an independent source such as state law." The Ohio statute that creates the right to a "free" education also explicitly authorizes a principal to suspend a student for as much as 10 days. Thus the very legislation which "defines" the "dimension" of the student's entitlement, while providing a right to education generally, does not establish this right free of discipline imposed in accord with Ohio law. Rather, the right is encompassed in the entire package of statutory provisions governing education in Ohio—of which the power to suspend is one.

The Court thus disregards the basic structure of Ohio law in posturing this case as if Ohio had conferred an unqualified right to education, thereby compelling the school authorities to conform to due process procedures in imposing the most routine discipline.

But however one may define the entitlement to education provided by Ohio law, I would conclude that a deprivation of not more than 10 days' suspension from school, imposed as a routine disciplinary measure, does not assume constitutional dimensions. Contrary to the Court's assertion, our cases support rather than "refute" appellants' argument that "the Due Process Clause . . . comes into play only when the State subjects a student to a 'severe detriment or grievous loss.' "

The Ohio suspension statute allows no serious or significant infringement of education. It authorizes only a maximum suspension of eight school days, less than 5% of the normal 180-day school year. Absences of such limited duration will rarely affect a pupil's opportunity to learn or his scholastic performance. Indeed, the record in this case reflects no educational injury to appellees. Each completed the semester in which the suspension occurred and performed at least as well as he or she had in previous years. Despite the Court's unsupported speculation that a suspended student could be "seriously damage[d]," there is no factual showing of any such damage to appellees.

The Court also relies on a perceived deprivation of "liberty" resulting from any suspension, arguing—again without factual support in the record pertaining to these appellees—that a suspension harms a student's reputation. Underscoring the need for "serious damage" to reputation, the *Roth* Court held that a nontenured teacher who is not rehired by a public university could not claim to suffer sufficient reputational injury to require constitutional protections.

Surely a brief suspension is of less serious consequence to the reputation of a teenage student.

II

In prior decisions, this Court has explicitly recognized that school authorities must have broad discretionary authority in the daily operation of public schools. This includes wide latitude with respect to maintaining discipline and good order.

Moreover, the Court ignores the experience of mankind, as well as the long history of our law, recognizing that there *are* differences which must be accommodated in determining the rights and duties of children as compared with those of adults. Even with respect to the First Amendment, the rights of children have not been regarded as "co-extensive with those of adults."

I turn now to some of the considerations which support the Court's former view regarding the comprehensive authority of the States and school officials "to prescribe and control conduct in the schools." Unlike the divergent and even sharp conflict of interests usually present where due process rights are asserted, the interests here implicated—of the State through its schools and of the pupils— are essentially congruent.

The State's interest, broadly put, is in the proper functioning of its public school system for the benefit of *all* pupils and the public generally. Few rulings would interfere more extensively in the daily functioning of schools than subjecting routine discipline to the formalities and judicial oversight of due process. Suspensions are one of the traditional means—ranging from keeping a student after class to permanent expulsion—used to maintain discipline in the schools. It is common knowledge that maintaining order and reasonable decorum in school buildings and classrooms is a major educational problem, and one which has increased significantly in magnitude in recent years. Often the teacher, in protecting the rights of other children to an education (if not his or their safety), is compelled to rely on the power to suspend.

The State's generalized interest in maintaining an orderly school system is not incompatible with the individual interest of the student. Education in any meaningful sense includes the inculcation of an understanding in each pupil of the necessity of rules and obedience thereto. This understanding is no less important than learning to read and write. One who does not comprehend the meaning and necessity of discipline is handicapped not merely in his education but throughout his subsequent life. In an age when the home and church play a diminishing role in shaping the character and value judgments of the young, a heavier responsibility falls upon the schools. When an immature student merits censure for his conduct, he is rendered a disservice if appropriate sanctions are not applied or if procedures for their application are so formalized as to invite a challenge to the teacher's authority—an invitation which rebellious or even merely spirited teenagers are likely to accept.

In assessing in constitutional terms the need to protect pupils from unfair minor discipline by school authorities, the Court ignores the commonality of interest of the State and pupils in the public school system. Rather, it thinks in traditional judicial terms of an adversary situation. To be sure, there will be the occasional pupil innocent of any rule infringement who is mistakenly suspended or whose infraction is too minor to justify suspension. But, while there is no evidence indicating the frequency of unjust suspensions, common sense suggests that they will not be numerous in relation to the total number, and that mistakes or injustices will usually be righted by informal means.

One of the more disturbing aspects of today's decision is its indiscriminate reliance upon the judiciary, and the adversary process, as the means of resolving many of the most routine problems arising in the classroom. In mandating due process procedures the Court misapprehends the reality of the normal teacher-pupil relationship. There is an ongoing relationship, one in which the teacher must occupy many roles—educator, adviser, friend, and, at times, parent-substitute. It is rarely adversary in nature except with respect to the chronically disruptive or insubordinate pupil whom the teacher must be free to discipline without frustrating formalities.

The Ohio statute, providing as it does for due notice both to parents and the Board, is compatible with the teacher-pupil relationship and the informal resolution of mistaken disciplinary action. We have relied for generations upon the experience, good faith and dedication of those who staff our public schools, and the nonadversary means of airing grievances that always have been available to pupils and their parents. One would have thought before today's opinion that this informal method of resolving differences was more compatible with the interests of all concerned than resort to any constitutionalized procedure, however blandly it may be defined by the Court.

III

No one can foresee the ultimate frontiers of the new "thicket" the Court now enters. Today's ruling appears to sweep within the protected interest in education a multitude of discretionary decisions in the educational process. Teachers and other school authorities are required to make many decisions that may have serious consequences for the pupil. They must decide, for example, how to grade the student's work, whether a student passes or fails a course, whether he is to be promoted, whether he is required to take certain subjects, whether he may be excluded from interscholastic athletics or other extracurricular activities, whether he may be removed from one school and sent to another, whether he may be bused long distances when available schools are nearby, and whether he should be placed in a "general," "vocational," or "college-preparatory" track.

If, as seems apparent, the Court will now require due process procedures whenever such routine school decisions are challenged, the impact upon public education will be serious indeed. The discretion and judgment of federal courts across the land often will be substituted for that of the 50 state legislatures, the 14,000 school boards, and the 2,000,000 teachers who heretofore have been responsible for the administration of the American public school system. If the Court perceives a rational and analytically sound distinction between the discretionary decision by school authorities to suspend a pupil for a brief period, and the types of discretionary school decisions described above, it would be prudent to articulate it in today's opinion. Otherwise, the federal courts should prepare themselves for a vast new role in society.

Ingraham v. Wright
430 U.S. 651 (1977)

MR. JUSTICE POWELL delivered the opinion of the Court.

This case presents questions concerning the use of corporal punishment in public schools: First, whether the paddling of students as a means of maintaining school discipline constitutes cruel and unusual punishment in violation of the Eighth Amendment; and, second, to the extent that paddling is constitutionally permissible, whether the Due Process Clause of the Fourteenth Amendment requires prior notice and an opportunity to be heard.

I

Petitioners James Ingraham and Roosevelt Andrews filed the complaint in this case on January 7, 1971, in the United States District Court for the Southern District of Florida. At the time both were enrolled in the Charles R. Drew Junior High School in Dade County, Fla., Ingraham in the eighth grade and Andrews in the ninth.

Because he was slow to respond to his teacher's instructions, Ingraham was subjected to more than 20 licks with a paddle while being held over a table in the principal's office. The paddling was so severe that he suffered a hematoma requiring medical attention and keeping him out of school for several days. Andrews was paddled several times for minor infractions. On two occasions he was struck on his arms, once depriving him of the full use of his arm for a week.

The use of corporal punishment in this country as a means of disciplining schoolchildren dates back to the colonial period. It has survived the transformation of primary and secondary education from the colonials' reliance on optional private arrangements to our present system of compulsory education and dependence on public schools. Despite the general abandonment of corporal punishment as a means of punishing criminal offenders, the practice continues to play a role in the public education of schoolchildren in most parts of the country. Professional and public opinion is sharply divided on the practice, and has been for more than a century. Yet we can discern no trend toward its elimination.

At common law a single principle has governed the use of corporal punishment since before the American Revolution: Teachers may impose reasonable but not excessive force to discipline a child. The prevalent rule in this country today privileges such force as a teacher or administrator "reasonably believes to be necessary for [the child's] proper control, training, or education." To the extent that the force is excessive or unreasonable, the educator in virtually all States is subject to possible civil and criminal liability.

Although the early cases viewed the authority of the teacher as deriving from the parents, the concept of parental delegation has been replaced by the view—more consonant with compulsory education laws—that the State itself may impose such corporal punishment as is reasonably necessary "for the proper education of the child and for the maintenance of group discipline." All of the circumstances are to be taken into account in determining whether the punishment is reasonable in a particular case. Among the most important considerations are the seriousness of the offense, the attitude and past behavior of the child, the nature and severity of the punishment, the age and strength of the child, and the availability of less severe but equally effective means of discipline.

III

The Eighth Amendment provides: "Excessive bail shall not be required, nor excessive fines imposed, nor cruel and unusual punishments inflicted." Bail, fines, and punishment traditionally have been associated with the criminal process, and by subjecting the three to parallel limitations the text of the Amendment suggests an intention to limit the power of those entrusted with the criminal-law function of government. An examination of the history of the Amendment and the decisions of this Court construing the proscription against cruel and unusual punishment confirms that it was designed to protect those convicted of crimes. We adhere to this long-standing limitation and hold that the Eighth Amendment does not apply to the paddling of children as a means of maintaining discipline in public schools.

IV

The Fourteenth Amendment prohibits any state deprivation of life, liberty, or property without due process of law. Application of this prohibition requires the familiar two-stage analysis: We must first ask whether the asserted individual interests are encompassed within the Fourteenth Amendment's protection of "life, liberty or property"; if protected interests are implicated, we then must decide what procedures constitute "due process of law." Following that analysis here, we find that corporal punishment in public schools implicates a constitutionally protected liberty interest, but we hold that the traditional common-law remedies are fully adequate to afford due process.

"[T]he range of interests protected by procedural due process is not infinite." We have repeatedly rejected "the notion that *any* grievous loss visited upon a person by the State is sufficient to invoke the procedural protections of the Due Process Clause." Due process is required only when a decision of the State implicates an interest within the protection of the Fourteenth Amendment. And "to determine whether due process requirements apply in the first place, we must look not to the 'weight' but to the *nature* of the interest at stake."

While the contours of this historic liberty interest in the context of our federal system of government have not been defined precisely, they always have been thought to encompass freedom from bodily restraint and punishment. It is fundamental that the state cannot hold and physically punish an individual except in accordance with due process of law.

This constitutionally protected liberty interest is at stake in this case. There is, of course, a *de minimis* level of imposition with which the Constitution is not concerned. But at least where school authorities, acting under color of state law, deliberately decide to punish a child for misconduct by restraining the child and inflicting appreciable physical pain, we hold that Fourteenth Amendment liberty interests are implicated.

"[T]he question remains what process is due." Were it not for the common-law privilege permitting teachers to inflict reasonable corporal punishment on children in their care, and the availability of the traditional remedies for abuse, the case for requiring advance procedural safeguards would be strong indeed. But here we deal with a punishment—paddling—within that tradition, and the question is whether the common-law remedies are adequate to afford due process.

The concept that reasonable corporal punishment in school is justifiable continues to be recognized in the laws of most States. It represents "the balance struck by this country," between the child's interest in personal security and the traditional view that some limited corporal punishment may be necessary in the course of a child's education. Under that longstanding accommodation of interests, there can be no deprivation of substantive rights as long as disciplinary corporal punishment is within the limits of the common-law privilege.

This is not to say that the child's interest in procedural safeguards is insubstantial. The school disciplinary process is not "a totally accurate, unerring process, never mistaken and never unfair. . . . " In any deliberate infliction of corporal punishment on a child who is restrained for that purpose, there is some risk that the intrusion on the child's liberty will be unjustified and therefore unlawful. In these circumstances the child has a strong interest in procedural safeguards that minimize the risk of wrongful punishment and provide for the resolution of disputed questions of justification.

We turn now to a consideration of the safeguards that are available under applicable Florida law.

Florida has continued to recognize, and indeed has strengthened by statute, the common-law right of a child not to be subjected to excessive corporal punishment in school. Under Florida law the teacher and principal of the school decide in the first instance whether corporal punishment is reasonably necessary under the circumstances in order to discipline a child who has misbehaved. But they must exercise prudence and restraint. For Florida has preserved the traditional judicial proceedings for determining whether the punishment was justified. If the punishment inflicted is later found to have been excessive—not reasonably believed at the time to be necessary for the child's discipline or training—the school authorities inflicting it may be held liable in damages to the child and, if malice is shown, they may be subject to criminal penalties.

In those cases where severe punishment is contemplated, the available civil and criminal sanctions for abuse—considered in light of the openness of the school environment—afford significant protection against unjustified corporal punishment. Teachers and school authorities are unlikely to inflict corporal punishment unnecessarily or excessively when a possible consequence of doing so is the institution of civil or criminal proceedings against them.

It still may be argued, of course, that the child's liberty interest would be better protected if the common-law remedies were supplemented by the administrative safeguards of prior notice and a hearing. We have found frequently that some kind of prior hearing is necessary to guard against arbitrary impositions on interests protected by the Fourteenth Amendment. But where the State has preserved what "has always been the law of the land," the case for administrative safeguards is significantly less compelling.*

But even if the need for advance procedural safeguards were clear, the question would remain whether the incremental benefit could justify the cost. Acceptance of petitioners' claims would work a transformation in the law gov-

---

*We have no occasion in this case to decide whether or under what circumstances corporal punishment of a public school child may give rise to an independent federal cause of action to vindicate substantive rights under the Due Process Clause.

erning corporal punishment in Florida and most other States. Given the impracticability of formulating a rule of procedural due process that varies with the severity of the particular imposition, the prior hearing petitioners seek would have to precede *any* paddling, however moderate or trivial.

Such a universal constitutional requirement would significantly burden the use of corporal punishment as a disciplinary measure. Hearings—even informal hearings—require time, personnel, and a diversion of attention from normal school pursuits. School authorities may well choose to abandon corporal punishment rather than incur the burdens of complying with the procedural requirements. Teachers, properly concerned with maintaining authority in the classroom, may well prefer to rely on other disciplinary measures—which they may view as less effective—rather than confront the possible disruption that prior notice and a hearing may entail. Paradoxically, such an alteration of disciplinary policy is most likely to occur in the ordinary case where the contemplated punishment is well within the common-law privilege.

Elimination or curtailment of corporal punishment would be welcomed by many as a societal advance. But when such a policy choice may result from this Court's determination of an asserted right to due process, rather than from the normal processes of community debate and legislative action, the societal costs cannot be dismissed as insubstantial. We are reviewing here a legislative judgment, rooted in history and reaffirmed in the laws of many States, that corporal punishment serves important educational interests. This judgment must be viewed in light of the disciplinary problems commonplace in the schools. "Events calling for discipline are frequent occurrences and sometimes require immediate, effective action." Assessment of the need for, and the appropriate means of maintaining, school discipline is committed generally to the discretion of school authorities subject to state law. "[T]he Court has repeatedly emphasized the need for affirming the comprehensive authority of the States and of school officials, consistent with fundamental constitutional safeguards, to prescribe and control conduct in the schools."

"At some point the benefit of an additional safeguard to the individual affected . . . and to society in terms of increased assurance that the action is just, may be outweighed by the cost." We think that point has been reached in this case. In view of the low incidence of abuse, the openness of our schools, and the common-law safeguards that already exist, the risk of error that may result in violation of a schoolchild's substantive rights can only be regarded as minimal. Imposing additional administrative safeguards as a constitutional requirement might reduce that risk marginally, but would also entail a significant intrusion into an area of primary educational responsibility. We conclude that the Due Process Clause does not require notice and a hearing prior to the imposition of corporal punishment in the public schools, as that practice is authorized and limited by the common law.

V

Petitioners cannot prevail on either of the theories before us in this case. The Eighth Amendment's prohibition against cruel and unusual punishment is inapplicable to school paddlings, and the Fourteenth Amendment's requirement of procedural due process is satisfied by Florida's preservation of common-law constraints and remedies. We therefore agree with the Court of Appeals that petitioners' evidence affords no basis for injunctive relief, and that petitioners cannot recover damages on the basis of any Eighth Amendment or procedural due process violation.

Affirmed.

MR. JUSTICE WHITE, with whom MR. JUSTICE BRENNAN, MR. JUSTICE MARSHALL, and MR. JUSTICE STEVENS join, dissenting.

Today the Court holds that corporal punishment in public schools, no matter how severe, can never be the subject of the protections afforded by the Eighth Amendment. It also holds that students in the public school systems are not constitutionally entitled to a hearing of any sort before beatings can be inflicted on them. Because I believe that these holdings are inconsistent with the prior decisions of this Court and are contrary to a reasoned analysis of the constitutional provisions involved, I respectfully dissent.

I

The Eighth Amendment places a flat prohibition against the infliction of "cruel and unusual punishments." This reflects a societal judgment that there are some punishments that are so barbaric and inhumane that we will not permit them to be imposed on anyone, no matter how opprobrious the offense.

Nevertheless, the majority holds that the Eighth Amendment "was designed to protect [only] those convicted of crimes," relying on a vague and inconclusive recitation of the history of the Amendment. Yet the constitutional prohibition is against cruel and unusual *punishments;* nowhere is that prohibition limited or modified by the language of the Constitution.

In fact, as the Court recognizes, the Eighth Amendment has never been confined to criminal punishments. Nevertheless, the majority adheres to its view that any protections afforded by the Eighth Amendment must have something to do with criminals, and it would therefore confine any exceptions to its general rule that only criminal punishments are covered by the Eighth Amendment to abuses inflicted on prisoners. Thus, if a prisoner is beaten mercilessly for a breach of discipline, he is entitled to the protection of the Eighth Amendment, while a schoolchild who commits the same breach of discipline and is similarly beaten is simply not covered.

The purported explanation of this anomaly is the assertion that schoolchildren have no need for the Eighth Amendment. We are told that schools are open institutions, subject to constant public scrutiny; that schoolchildren have adequate remedies under state law; and that prisoners suffer the social stigma of being labeled as criminals. How any of these policy considerations got into the Constitution is difficult to discern, for the Court has never considered any of these factors in determining the scope of the Eighth Amendment.

By holding that the Eighth Amendment protects only criminals, the majority adopts the view that one is entitled to the protections afforded by the Eighth Amendment only if he is punished for acts that are sufficiently opprobrious for society to make them "criminal." This is a curious holding in view of the fact that the more culpable the offender the more likely it is that the punishment will not be disproportionate to the offense, and consequently, the less likely it is that punishment will be cruel and unusual. Conversely, a public school student who is spanked for a mere breach of discipline may sometimes have a strong argument that the punishment does not fit the offense, depending upon the severity of the beating, and therefore that it is cruel and unusual. Yet the majority would afford the student no protection no matter how inhumane and barbaric the punishment inflicted on him might be.

II

The majority concedes that corporal punishment in the public schools implicates an interest protected by the Due Process Clause—the liberty interest of the student to be free from "bodily restraint and punishment" involving "appreciable physical pain" inflicted by persons acting under color of state law. The question remaining, as the majority recognizes, is what process is due.

The reason that the Constitution requires a State to provide "due process of law" when it punishes an individual for misconduct is to protect the individual from erroneous or mistaken punishment that the State would not have inflicted had it found the facts in a more reliable way. In *Goss* v. *Lopez,* the Court applied this principle to the school disciplinary process, holding that a student must be given an informal opportunity to be heard before he is finally suspended from public school. To guard against the risk of punishing an innocent child, the Due Process Clause requires, not an "elaborate hearing" before a neutral party, but simply "an informal give-and-take between student and disciplinarian" which gives the student "an opportunity to explain his version of the facts."

The Court now holds that these "rudimentary precautions against unfair or mistaken findings of misconduct" are not required if the student is punished with "appreciable physical pain" rather than with a suspension, even though both punishments deprive the student of a constitutionally protected interest. Although the respondent school authorities provide absolutely *no* process to the student before the punishment is finally inflicted, the majority concludes that the student is nonetheless given due process because he can later sue the teacher and recover damages if the punishment was "excessive."

There is, in short, no basis in logic or authority for the majority's suggestion that an action to recover damages for excessive corporal punishment "afford[s] substantially greater protection to the child than the informal conference mandated by *Goss.*" The majority purports to follow the settled principle that what process is due depends on " 'the risk of an erroneous deprivation of [the protected] interest . . . and the probable value, if any, of additional or substitute procedural safeguards' "; it recognizes, as did *Goss,* the risk of error in the school disciplinary process and concedes that "the child has a strong interest in procedural safeguards that minimize the risk of wrongful punishment . . . ," but it somehow concludes that this risk is adequately reduced by a damages remedy that never has been recognized by a Florida court, that leaves unprotected the innocent student punished by mistake, and that allows the State to punish first and hear the student's version of events later. I cannot agree.

I would reverse the judgment below.

Hall v. Tawney
621 F. 2d 607 (1980)

Plaintiffs—Naomi Faye Hall, a minor, and her parents, appeal the dismissal of their action against various officials and employees of the school system of West Virginia, for alleged violation of their constitutional rights by the infliction of disciplinary corporal punishment upon Naomi, a student in the system. We affirm in part, reverse and remand in part.

The action arose from an incident occurring on December 6, 1974 in which Naomi, then a student at Left Hand Grade School in West Virginia, was paddled by a teacher in that school. [T]he complaint alleged resulting violations of Naomi's constitutional rights as secured by the Fourteenth Amendment to substantive due process.

In *Ingraham,* the Supreme Court denied review to the question, "Is the infliction of severe corporal punishment upon public school students arbitrary, capricious and unrelated to achieving any legitimate educational purpose and therefore violative of the Due Process Clause of the Fourteenth Amendment?" Therefore, the Court said, "[w]e have no occasion in this case . . . to decide whether or under what circumstances corporal punishment of a public school child may give rise to an independent federal cause of action to vindicate substantive rights under the Due Process Clause."

The Supreme Court's denial of review to the substantive due process issue in *Ingraham* presents an initial awkwardness to decision here that must frankly be recognized at the outset of our discussion. Without resolution of that issue, *Ingraham* of course stands directly only for the propositions that school paddlings of the kind there and here in issue violated neither procedural due process nor Eighth Amendment rights. But from the direct holding that these two rights were not violated it might be possible to imply a holding that neither could there have been violation of any substantive due process right. That this implication is not compelled, however, seems manifest to us from the fact and form of the Court's express reservation of the issue. Indeed, from this reservation the opposite implication seems compelled: that substantive due process rights *might* be implicated in school disciplinary punishments even though procedural due process is afforded by adequate state civil and criminal remedies, and though cruel and unusual punishment is not implicated at all. That question, unresolved and reserved in *Ingraham* is squarely presented for decision on this appeal. For reasons that follow we conclude that there may be circumstances under which specific corporal punishment administered by state school officials gives rise to an independent federal cause of action to vindicate substantive due process rights. We further conclude that whether those circumstances existed in the instant case could not properly be determined as to the defendants directly involved in the paddling on the motion to dismiss and that the case must therefore be remanded for further proceedings in respect of Naomi's substantive due process claim. Despite the dangers of expounding constitutional doctrine on the basis of barebones pleadings, we find it necessary in ordering remand here to give shape to the substantive due process right we recognize.

We start with the proposition that disciplinary corporal punishment does not *per se* violate the public school child's substantive due process rights. This is of course implicit in *Ingraham's* holding that the protectible liberty interest there recognized admits of some corporal punishment, which in turn is based upon a recognition that corporal punishment as such is reasonably related to a legitimate state interest in maintaining order in the schools—the critical inquiry in substantive due process analysis. Appellants here concede this much, but contend that the constitutional right is violated at the point where a specific punishment exceeds in severity that reasonably related to the interest.

We turn therefore to definition of the constitutionally protected substantive due process right we consider to exist here in addition to the substantive right and remedies provided by state law. First off, the substantive content is quite different than that defining state civil and criminal remedies. Instead, we find it grounded in those constitutional rights given protection under the rubric of substantive due process: the right to be free of state intrusions into realms of personal privacy and bodily security through means so brutal, demeaning, and harmful as literally to shock the conscience of a court. The existence of this right to ultimate bodily security—the most fundamental aspect of personal privacy—is unmistakably established in our constitutional decisions as an attribute of the ordered liberty that is the concern of substantive due process. Numerous cases in a variety of contexts recognize it as a last line of defense against those literally outrageous abuses of official power whose very variety makes formulation of a more precise standard impossible. Clearly recognized in persons charged with or suspected of crime and in the custody of police officers, we simply do not see how we can fail also to recognize it in public school children under the disciplinary control of public school teachers. Difficult as may be application of the resulting rule of constitutional law in the public school disciplinary context, it would seem no more difficult than in related realms already well established. In any event it is a difficulty that may not be avoided in the face of allegations or proof sufficient to raise the possibility that such an intolerable abuse of official power—no matter how aberrant and episodic—has occurred through disciplinary corporal punishment.

In the context of disciplinary corporal punishment in the public schools, we emphasize once more that the substantive due process claim is quite different than a claim of assault and battery under state tort law. In resolving a state tort claim, decision may well turn on whether "ten licks rather than five" were excessive, so that line-drawing this refined may be required. But substantive due process is concerned with violations of personal rights of privacy and bodily security of so different an order of magnitude that inquiry in a particular case simply need not start at the level of concern these distinctions imply. [T]he substantive due process inquiry in school corporal punishment cases must be whether the force applied caused injury so severe, was so disproportionate to the need presented, and was so inspired by malice or sadism rather than a merely careless or unwise excess of zeal that it amounted to a brutal and inhumane abuse of official power literally shocking to the conscience. Not every violation of state tort and criminal assault laws will be a violation of this constitutional right, but some of course may.

In ruling on the defendant's motion to dismiss, the district court considered Naomi's substantive due process claim only to the point of concluding, in reliance upon the Fifth Circuit's decision in *Ingraham* and the Supreme Court's denial of review on the issue, that because corporal punishment *per se* did not violate substantive due process no cognizable claim was stated. It did not analyze the allegations of the complaint to determine whether a cognizable claim based on the specific incident alleged might have been stated, presumably again relying on the Fifth Circuit's view in *Ingraham* that where state law provides adequate substantive remedies, merely episodic punishments that might violate state law do not give rise to a federal cause of action. As our opinion indicates, we disagree with that conclusion and have held instead that a cognizable claim based upon an episodic application of force not authorized by state law or policy may be stated under the substantive due process standard here recognized.

When we look to the complaint we cannot say that under that substantive standard it fails to state a claim for relief against Tawney and Claywell, the direct participants in the December 6 paddling incident. Of course, upon full development of a summary judgment or trial record, it may appear that the actual facts of the incident do not support a claim of substantive due process violation. But we cannot say from the bare pleading allegations that "it appears beyond doubt that the plaintiff can prove no set of facts in support of [her] claim which would entitle [her] to relief."

Though admittedly employing conclusory allegations in describing the incident, the complaint in pertinent part stated that Tawney "without apparent provocation" struck the minor plaintiff "with a homemade paddle, made of hard thick rubber and about five inches in width . . . across her left hip and thigh"; that in an ensuing struggle with the plaintiff he "violently shoved the minor plaintiff against a large stationary desk"; that he then "vehemently grasped and twisted the plaintiff's right arm and pushed her into" the presence of the defendant Claywell who then granted permission to Tawney to "again paddle the minor plaintiff"; that "the minor plaintiff was again stricken repeatedly and violently by the defendant Tawney with the rubber paddle, under the supervision and approval of defendant Claywell"; that as a result of this application of force "the minor plaintiff was taken that afternoon to the emergency room of [a nearby hospital] where she was admitted and kept for a period of ten (10) days for the treatment of traumatic injury to the soft tissue of the left hip and thigh, trauma to the skin and soft tissue of the left thigh, and trauma to the soft tissue with ecchyniosis of the left buttock"; that for the injuries inflicted the minor plaintiff was "receiving the treatment of specialists for possible permanent injuries to her lower back and spine and has suffered and will continue to suffer severe pain and discomfort, etc." There were also allegations respecting Tawney's demonstrated attitude toward Naomi and other student members of her family from which malicious motivation might be inferred if the events alleged were proven as fact.

As we have indicated, when exposed to the searching light of full discovery and other pre-trial procedures or eventually, if need be, to the testing of proof on trial, these bare allegations may be exposed as merely that in whole or substantial part, and the actual facts justifying a finding of substantive due process violation simply not present. We hold here only that they sufficed to state a claim for relief against Tawney and Claywell. . . . Accordingly it was error to dismiss the action against these two defendants as to the minor plaintiff's substantive due process claim.

NOTES

1. Joint Anti-Fascist Refugee Committee v. McGrath, 341 U.S. 123 (1951) at 162.
2. Meyer v. Nebraska, 262 U.S. 390 (1923) at 403.
3. Dixon v. Alabama State Board of Education, 294 F. 2d 150 (1961) (cert. denied 368 U.S. 390) at 155.
4. Id. at 157.
5. In re Gault, 387 U.S. 1 (1967) at 20–21.
6. Weimann v. Updegraff, 344 U.S. 183 (1952) at 192.
7. Board of Regents of State Colleges v. Roth, 408 U.S. 564 (1972) at 573–74.
8. Id. at 578.
9. Perry v. Sindermann, 408 U.S. 593 (1972) at 600.
10. Ambach v. Norwick, 441 U.S. 68 (1978) at 78–79.
11. H. C. Hudgins and Richard S. Vacca, *Law and Education: Contemporary Issues and Court Decisions* (Charlottesville, Va.: The Mitchie Co., 1979), p. 139.
12. Lane v. Board of Educ. of Fairbury-Cropsey Dist. 3, 348 N.E. 2d 470 (1976) at 472.
13. Mathews v. Eldridge, 424 U.S. 335 (1976) at 335.
14. Hortonville Joint School Dist. No. 1 v. Hortonville Educ. Assn., 426 U.S. 482 (1976) at 493.
15. Id. at 496.
16. Dike v. School Board of Orange County, Fla., 650 F. 2d 783 (1981) at 787.
17. Cleveland Board of Educ. et al. v. LaFleur et al., 414 U.S. 632 (1974) at 639.
18. Id. at 643.
19. Id. at 644.
20. Linwood v. Board of Education, 463 F. 2d 763 (1972) at 769.
21. Sullivan v. Houston Indep. School Dist., 307 F. Supp. 1328 (1969) at 1344–45.
22. Id. at 1345–46.
23. Goss v. Lopez, 419 U.S. 565 (1975) at 579.
24. Id. at 599.
25. Id. at 587–88.
26. Ingraham v. Wright, 430 U.S. 651 (1977) at 680.
27. Id. at 701.
28. Hall v. Tawney, 621 F. 2d 607 (1980) at 613.
29. Massie v. Henry, 455 F. 2d 779 (1972) at 783.
30. Id. at 784.
31. Meyer at 399.
32. Aldbach v. Olde, 531 F. 2d 983 (1976) at 985.
33. Pegram v. Nelson, 469 F. Supp. 1134 (1979) at 1140.
34. Sullivan v. Meade Indep. School Dist. No. 101, 530 F. 2d 799 (1976) at 804.
35. Fischer v. Snyder, 476 F. 2d 375 (1973) at 378.
36. Drake v. Covington City Board of Educ., 371 F. Supp. 974 (1974) at 979.
37. Gaylord v. Tacoma School Dist. No. 10, 559 P. 2d (1977) cert. denied, 434 U.S. 879 (1977) at 1347.
38. Alba v. Los Angeles Unified School District, 189 Cal Rptr. 897 (1983) at 902.
39. Id. at 905.
40. Brookhart v. Illinois State Board of Education, 697 F. 2d 179 (1983) at 187–88.
41. Anderson v. Banks, 540 F. Supp. 761 (1982) at 763.
42. Edward A. Wynne, "What are the courts doing to our children?" *The Public Interest,* 66 (Summer 1981), 3.
43. Julius Menacker and Edward A. Wynne, "Our Litigious Schools: A Controversy," *The Public Interest,* 67 (Spring 1982), 133.
44. Julius Menacker and Ernest Pascarella, "What attitudes do educators have about student and teacher civil rights?" *Urban Education,* 19, no. 2 (July 1984), 115–24.

SIX

Equal Protection:
Concepts of Equality
in Education

Equality before the law is an essential feature of a democratic society. The Declaration of Independence unequivocally holds that "all men are created equal." Yet, it remained for the Fourteenth Amendment's (1868) equal protection clause ("nor shall any State . . . deny to any person within its jurisdiction the equal protection of the laws") to demand that state governments abide by that principle. The general idea of equal protection is that the law does not favor or work against any classification of people for reasons of favoritism, prejudice, or bias. The law is to be impartially administered.

In its application to education, contrasting liberal and conservative views have developed as to how the equal protection concept is best served by government. The conservative view tends toward preference for a governmental role limited to insuring against official action favoring or penalizing particular categories of people. The liberal view supports a broader, more active government role, in which official steps are taken to insure substantial equality of opportunity, through the remedying of structural inequalities built into the racist premises of American society, inherited from the period of legal slavery. The difference in viewpoint may be clarified by analogizing government to the role of an official supervising a race. The conservative government official would confine the role to insuring that everyone starts at the same time and from the same place, regardless of individual condition or circumstance. The liberal official would view the role as requiring such intervention as giving the lame a head start so that they would have a realistic, practical opportunity to compete successfully. As a result, jurists with liberal equal protection attitudes tended to be activists in the fifties, sixties, and early seventies. After the great liberal equal protection advances of those decades, conservatives seeking to redress the equal protection balance now tend to be the activists.

The equal protection concept was introjected into educational litigation even before the Civil War. In *Roberts* v. *City of Boston* (59 Mass. 5 Cush. 198 [1849]), Charles Sumner argued that forcing a Negro child to travel past five elementary schools to attend the rundown black elementary school violated the "great principle" of equality before the law. Further, it stigmatized and degraded blacks and injured whites in the process. Sumner went on to contend that the Massachusetts Constitution was violated by allowing official classifications of people that bore no reasonable relationship to legitimate government purpose. Classification of students by age or intellect seemed reasonable and legitimate to Sumner, but not classification by race.

While the Massachusetts Supreme Court sympathized with Sumner's "great principle" of equality before the law, the court decided that the rights due particular people were determined by an infinite variety of societal circumstances. In this case, school segregation appeared in the best interests of both races and society generally.

With passage of the Fourteenth Amendment, the U.S. Supreme Court initially applied conservative, restraintist interpretations to the equal protection clause. The most significant decision for its application to the developing national public-education system concerned segregation on railroad cars. In *Plessy* v. *Ferguson* (1896) an eight-justice majority approved state passenger segregation laws on the grounds that since the statute required separate, substantially equal facilities for Negroes, the demands of equal protection were satisfied. Conservative influence is evident in the decision's reliance on tradition and accepted practice, and wariness of social change. This combined with the restraintist tendency to defer matters regarding what constituted good social policy to local legislative authorities. As to the issue of the policy officially sanctioning inferior status for blacks, the majority reasoned that "the underlying fallacy . . . [is] the assumption that the enforced separation of the races stamps the colored race with a badge of inferiority. If this be so, it is . . . solely because the colored race chooses to put that construction on it."[1]

It was left to the lone dissenter, Justice Harlan, to expound the liberal position in his advocacy of social change promoting greater individual choice and freedom. For him, the "Constitution is color-blind, and neither knows nor tolerates classes among citizens."[2]

The majority view paved the way for legal race segregation in public education, under the theory that separate-but-equal facilities satisfied the requirements of the equal protection clause. The principle was confirmed for education in a decision showing the extremes to which judicial restraint can carry. *Cumming*

v. *Richmond County Board of Education* (175 U.S. 528 [1899]) considered the constitutionality of a Georgia school-board decision to solve overcrowding at Negro elementary schools by converting the black high school to an elementary school, foreclosing black secondary education while it was available for whites. The Court saw no reason to interfere, seeing its role as confined to insuring that the school-tax burden was equitably distributed.

THE LEGAL STRUGGLE TO END SCHOOL RACE SEGREGATION

By the 1930s, the Legal Defense Fund of the National Association of Colored People (NAACP) had been established to combat judicial interpretations of equal protection applied to education. Rather than directly challenging the constitutionality of the separate-but-equal doctrine, the strategy was to expose its fallacies and impracticality in a variety of higher-education situations. The NAACP recognized that the prevailing judicial attitude reflected the larger society, and that a piecemeal, gradual erosion of the doctrine would best serve its interests. The first victory came in *Missouri ex rel. Gaines* v. *Canada* (305 U.S. 337 [1938]), in which a Supreme Court majority ruled that when a law school was not available for blacks, equal protection prohibited the state's barring blacks admission to the state university's law school. Most encouraging from the liberal perspective was the strengthened view of equal protection, encouraged by the seven-to-one majority's finding that the option of paying for a legal education at an integrated out-of-state law school was improper, as the state must provide equal protection *within its jurisdiction.*

The rapid social change following the Second World War quickened the growing pace of liberalism, bringing further successes. In *Sipuel* v. *Board* (1948), the Supreme Court turned aside Oklahoma's defense that a black law-school applicant had not given it sufficient time to establish separate facilities, holding instead that such facilities must be provided for blacks "as soon as . . . for applicants of any other group."[3] Two years later, a unanimous Supreme Court rejected the device of admitting a black to the University of Oklahoma graduate program in education but segregating him within the school. *McLaurin* v. *Oklahoma* (399 U.S. 637 [1950]) provided a significant expansion in the Court's interpretation of equal protection cases, as here it recognized the importance of "intangible" factors that could affect educational equality. On the same day, this issue was more forcefully presented in another unanimous opinion further eroding the separate-but-equal doctrine. In *Sweatt* v. *Painter* (1950) the Court found the public law school for blacks unconstitutionally below the necessary standards of separate-but-equal on such objective criteria as library resources and faculty. More significant, it also found that, in comparison, the University of Texas law school had "to a far greater degree those qualities which are incapable of measurement but which make for greatness in a law school."[4] These qualities included factors such as faculty reputation, administrative experience, alumni influence, community standing, and prestige. While separate-but-equal was not directly attacked, consideration of these intangibles boded ill for the concept under this expanded and strengthened view of equal protection.

The stage was now set for a direct assault on the separate-but-equal doctrine. In 1951 and 1952 four cases were heard by lower federal courts and the Supreme Court of Delaware that directly challenged the separate-but-equal doctrine applied to public schools.[5] The decisions variously upheld or struck down segregated public-school education and were collectively accepted by the Supreme Court. Proceeding cautiously, the Court heard arguments in 1952, and then ordered reargument in 1953. This laborious approach indicated the Court's sensitivity to the great emotional importance of its impending decision, and the need for it to be clear and free of internal dispute. The Court asked litigants to help it decide the intent and meaning of the Fourteenth Amendment's equal protection clause, as well as how they saw the Court's power to resolve the basic issue, and if it decided against "separate but equal," how it should move to dismantle the concept in public education.

Liberalism and change were in the nation's spirit, and on May 17, 1954 the Supreme Court issued what surely was its most important, far-reaching decision in education. Using *Brown* v. *Board of Education of Topeka, Kansas* as the model on which the other cases* would be resolved, the Court issued a clear, unequivocal statement: "We conclude that in the field of public education, the doctrine of 'separate-but-equal' has no place. Separate educational facilities are inherently unequal. . . . [P]laintiffs . . . are, by reason of the segregation complained of, deprived of the equal protection of the laws guaranteed by the Fourteenth Amendment."[6]

This unanimous decision was liberal, but as restraintist of Court policy making as possible. It did little more than declare segregated public schools violative of the equal protection clause. There was no extended dissertation on the evils of racism or the like. It is doubtful if unanimity could otherwise have been secured. In fact, the decision did not even directly order the southern schools to desegregate. That was put over to a rehearing scheduled for the following year. Even clearly liberal attitudes were avoided, the Court contenting itself to note that: "Today, education is perhaps the most important function of state and local governments. . . . Today it is a principal instrument in awakening the child to cultural values, in preparing him for later professional training, and in helping him to adjust normally to his environment."[7] However, the implicit liberalism behind a decision that promoted dramatic change in the southern way of life was patently evident, and for many analysts it was a precipitous change, taken without the care and caution that conservatism would have preferred.

In another sense, the decision brought court activism to a new high. It considered the issue of public-school segregation ripe for adjudication at a time when there was little support or interest in change among the states practicing

*A companion case (*Bolling* v. *Sharpe,* 347 U.S. 497 [1954]) concerned the District of Columbia, to which the Fourteenth Amendment did not apply. However, the Court found District school segregation to violate the due process clause of the Fifth Amendment.

it. The willingness to overrule the long-standing position of several state legislatures (as well as Congress in *Bolling* v. *Sharpe*) was a very activist stance, as was
the easy Court acceptance of a variety of social-science data and opinion allowed
to influence its opinion. This led the Court to decide that for black children,
segregation "generates a feeling of inferiority as to their status in the community
that may affect their hearts and minds in a way unlikely to be undone."[8] This
conclusion could be reached because: "Whatever may have been the extent of
psychological knowledge at the time of *Plessy* v. *Ferguson* this finding is amply
supported by modern authority."[9] This modern psychological knowledge allowed the Court to further accept as fact that "[a] sense of inferiority affects the
motivation of a child to learn."[10] Yet, in recognition of the profoundly personal
and deep values involved, Court activists were constrained by the more restraintist members from doing anything more than asking the litigating parties to provide it with advice on how to proceed in the following years.

In Brown II (*Brown* v. *Board of Educ.*, 349 U.S. 294 [1955]) the Court con-
tented itself with assigning lower federal courts the task of supervising the dis-
mantling of segregated schooling "with all deliberate speed." Gradually, in
subsequent cases, liberal and conservative views on equal protection applied to
education became more distinct and pronounced, as did the restraintist-activist
positions. Liberal activism was successful in developing an enlarged scope for
equal protection as the range of issues applicable to equal protection review increased, and stiffer review standards were developed to evaluate desegregation
policies and activities in formerly segregated school districts. In particular, the
more difficult to sustain "compelling interest" test was applied to state and local
actions in place of the traditional "rational basis" test for issues involving "suspect classifications," particularly that of race. In opposition to these rapid liberal, activist developments, conservative restraintists urged the need to give
formerly segregated districts sufficient time to adjust, and to be allowed to do
so through local decision making.

The liberal view of equal opportunity held by the Warren Court predom-
inated. The role of government, including the courts, was seen as actively intervening in state and local school policies to redress the inequities created by
past racial discrimination. This approach was epitomized by the concept of "affirmative action"; that is, the requirement that schools not only desegregate, but
take positive steps to redress the negative effects of past discrimination for those
"suspect classifications" that the courts must carefully protect because of the
history of official discrimination against them.

In the years following *Brown I* and *Brown II,* the Supreme Court beat back
southern efforts to retain segregation. These efforts included state and district
closing of public schools in favor of providing public financial aid to private
segregated schools (*Griffin* v. *Board of Prince Edward County,* 377 U.S. 218 [1964])
and freedom-of-choice plans for integration, which, lacking government force,
failed to further desegregation (*Green* v. *New Kent County,* 391 U.S. 430 [1968]).
Finally, in 1969, an exasperated Supreme Court in *Alexander* v. *Holmes* declared

that "the obligation of every school district is to terminate dual school systems at once and to operate now and hereafter only unitary schools."[11] Meanwhile, the Supreme Court was making it clear that desegration applied to the faculty as well as the student body (*Bradley* v. *School Board, City of Richmond,* 382 U.S. 103 [1965]). Less than a month later, it granted students standing to sue on the basis of equal protection denied when faculty desegregation did not parallel student desegregation (*Rogers* v. *Paul,* 382 U.S. 198 [1965]).

The liberal activism regarding equal protection embraced the inherently tentative and contradictory nature of social-science research to support its positions in equal protection decisions. The early years of the seventies saw the continued consolidation of liberal activism in strengthening equal protection standards designed to combat school segregation through unanimous Supreme Court decisions. Among the most sharply activist decisions was *Swann* v. *Charlotte-Mecklenburg Board of Educ.* (1971), in which the High Court decided that upon finding desegregation plans proposed by school authorities to be inadequate, courts could exercise discretionary power to implement their own plans for desegregation. In this case, the Court sanctioned a lower federal court's device of forced busing to achieve student integration, regardless of the inconvenience such plans posed for local authorities. In the Court's opinion: "The remedy for such segregation may be administratively awkward, inconvenient, and even bizarre in some situations and may impose burdens on some; but all awkwardness and inconvenience cannot be avoided in the interim period when remedial adjustments are being made to eliminate the dual school systems."[12]

The liberal attitude shown in this decision for rapid, sweeping change was buttressed by exposition of the "strict scrutiny" standard to be applied to formerly segregated school systems:

> [I]n a system with a history of segregation the need for remedial criteria of sufficient specificity to assure . . . compliance with its constitutional duty warrants a presumption against schools that are substantially disproportionate in their racial composition. . . . [T]hey have the burden of showing that such school assignments are genuinely nondiscriminatory. The court should scrutinize such schools, and the burden upon the school authorities will be to satisfy the court that their racial composition is not the result of present or past discriminatory action on their part.[13]

Liberal activism was continued in the same year with High Court decisions: (1) striking down a state statute forbidding student assignment on the basis of race and instituting the use of involuntary busing to create racial balance (*North Carolina State Board of Educ.* v. *Swann,* 402 U.S. 43 [1971]); (2) approving the use of ratios for student and faculty desegregation plans and encouraging busing (*Davis* v. *Board of Commissioners of Mobile City,* 402 U.S. 33 [1971]); and (3) reversing the Georgia Supreme Court's disapproval of a desegregation plan because it treated students differently based on race, since that was the only way to combat the status quo (*McDaniel* v. *Barresi,* 402 U.S. 39 [1971]).

Conservatism and Restraint Introduced Into School Segregation

In the next year, the Supreme Court's unprecedented unanimity under the liberal-activist banner ended as signs of conservatism regarding equal protection surfaced. Four justices dissented in a decision forbidding local authorities to create a separate school district from an existing one because the lower court thought this might contribute to future segregation. The majority did not require proof of a discriminatory motive for its holding, but the minority believed it should not interfere with local statutory authority when there was no proof of discriminatory effect, and only conjecture about future effects (*Wright* v. *Council of City of Emporia,* 407 U.S. 451 [1972]).

In *Keyes* v. *Denver* (1973), the Supreme Court first addressed northern school segregation, raising the issue of the difference between *de jure* (through deliberate government action) and *de facto* (arising without governmental intent) segregation. While the Denver schools had never operated under segregation laws, the Court found that actions of the Denver Board of Education had the effect of creating segregated black and Hispanic schools, and thus was *de jure* segregation subject to Court remedy under the equal protection clause. New liberal-activist principles were added to the judicial equation; that is, Hispanics were considered a suspect class regarding school segregation, and where government policy creates segregation in just some of its schools, the whole school system must be considered suspect. However, the Court showed a glimmering of conservative restraint by noting that it could not become involved in issues of *de facto* segregation: "We emphasize that the differentiating factor between *de jure* and so-called de facto segregation . . . is *purpose* or *intent* to segregate."[14]

Another northern school segregation case in the year after *Keyes* (*Milliken* v. *Bradley,* [1974]) finally produced a High Court majority for conservative restraint in an equal protection case involving racial segregation. In order to remedy the typical northern urban pattern of school segregation whereby central-city schools were populated by minority students and white students attended suburban public schools, a lower federal court ordered interdistrict student integration. By a five-to-four vote the Supreme Court overturned the lower court, holding that since the suburban districts had not committed segregative acts, they could not be compelled to be unwilling parties to solve segregation problems in other districts. The decision showed respect for conservative principles of upholding traditional authority and practice and distrust of unique, untried solutions to problems, as well as restraintist deference to the positions of legislatures and local authorities. Regarding local authority and tradition, the majority believed that:

> the notion that school district lives may be casually ignored or treated as a mere administrative convenience is contrary to the history of public education in our country. No single tradition in public education is more deeply rooted than local control over the operation of schools; local autonomy has long been thought essential both to the maintenance of community concern and support for public schools and to quality of the educational process.[15]

As for novel, untried solutions such as the one proposed, the Court observed that "a review of the scope and character of these local powers indicates the extent to which the inter-district remedy . . . could disrupt and alter the structure of public education in Michigan."[16] Finally, the majority indicated a restraintist view of the judicial role in a controversy such as presented in this case:

> [I]t is obvious from the scope of the inter-district remedy itself that absent a complete restructuring of the laws of Michigan relating to school districts the district Court will become first, a *de facto* "legislative authority" to resolve these complex questions, and then the "school superintendent" for the entire area. This is a task which few, if any judges are qualified to perform and one which would deprive the people of control of schools through their elected representatives.[17]

Another conservative victory occurred in 1976 (*Pasadena* v. *Spangler*), when students who had participated in court-ordered desegregation of the Pasadena schools sued after they graduated, because population shifts had disturbed the standard set by the lower court. The standard was that no school could have a majority of the minority population. Since the district had followed the guideline in implementing desegregation, the Court considered it excessive for lower courts continually to demand adherence to that standard, regardless of population movement. Further, the plaintiffs had already graduated from the Pasadena schools; thus, restraintist denial of standing to sue was invoked.

Justice Marshall, the most liberally activist justice on desegregation matters, vigorously protested this restraint on court scope and authority to impose continuing supervision of the desegregation process. In his dissent, he said:

> In insisting that the District Court largely abandon its scrutiny of attendance patterns, the Court might well be assuring that a unitary system in which segregation has been eliminated "root and branch" . . . will never be achieved in Pasadena. . . . Particularly, given the breadth of discretion normally accorded a district court in fashioning equitable remedies, I see no reason to require the District Court in a case such as this to modify its order prior to the time that it is clear that the entire violation has been remedied and a unitary system achieved. . . .[18]

Balance and Expansion in Equal Protection Applied to Desegregation

Decisions such as *Milliken* and *Pasadena* did not develop a conservative equal protection trend comparable to the liberal trend initiated with *Brown*. Rather, a greater liberal-conservative, activist-restraintist balance was achieved. Continued adjudication caused certain principles, as the distinction between *de jure-de facto* segregation, to become blurred and lose their value (*Columbus Board of Education* v. *Penick*, 443 U.S. 449 [1979]; *Dayton Board of Education* v. *Brinkman*, 443 U.S. 526 [1979]). New concepts and principles emerged gathering new objects of equal protection scrutiny; some of them adjudicated on the narrower grounds of federal statutes embodying the concept of equal protection (for instance, the

Civil Rights Act of 1964, The Education for All Handicapped Children Act, and Title IX). Illustrative of this trend was Supreme Court adjudication of the equal protection rights of non-English-speaking students to supplementary compensatory instruction. A divided Court decided the issue on the basis of Title VI of the Civil Rights Act, which bans discrimination based on race, color, or national origin, rather than on the Fourteenth Amendment. The majority held that such extraschool effort was required by the Act (*Lau* v. *Nichols*, 414 U.S. 563 [1974]). While this is a liberal interpretation of the Act's equal protection emphasis, the decision was restrained by applying the issue to a statute rather than to the broader sweep of the Constitution.

Led by the Supreme Court, the judiciary continues to struggle to find an adequate liberal-conservative balance in defining the meaning and scope of equal protection. In the process, issues would develop that focused equal protection upon such areas as school testing and placement, the public-education rights of aliens, public-education financing policy, and the question of reverse discrimination. These examples show the range of possibilities for application of equal protection by liberals and activists. The manner in which they were resolved illustrates the companion roles of conservatism and restraint. These controversies, as well as the center-stage issue of school desegregation, are governed by the following basic principles:

Principles of Equal Protection Applied to Education

1. The general concept behind the equal protection clause is that government should not invidiously discriminate among classes of persons within its jurisdiction. All should be considered equal before the law.

2. In education, equal protection means, at a minimum, that all students should be provided with equal educational opportunity. In the words of the *Brown* decision: "Such an opportunity, where the state has undertaken to provide it, is a right which must be made available to all on equal terms."[19] This does not mean education is a constitutionally guaranteed right. It is not. However, once a state provides it, it must be accorded on a basis of equality.

3. Discrimination based on race is unconstitutional. However, schools may discriminate when a rational basis for it is established, such as by intellect or age. When discrimination involves a "suspect classification," such as race or ethnicity, the school must show a "compelling interest" served by it, under the Supreme Court's "strict scrutiny" test. This applies to staff as well as students.

4. Intangible social and psychological effects of discrimination may be considered by courts as evidence in reaching determinations of equal protection violations.

5. While courts have acquired broad power to impose desegregation upon recalcitrant districts, there are definable limits to court authority. Among

these limits are that inter-district desegregation remedies are impermissible when the district forced to participate did not contribute to the segregation problem. Another limit is that courts may not force continuing adherence to desegregation standards after initial desegregation levels have eroded because of factors beyond the district's control.

6. The Supreme Court has established that the Constitution is violated by discriminatory intent, not by discriminatory effect. However, discriminatory effect caused by benign official action may be violative of statutes such as the Civil Rights Act. Like the related *de jure–de facto* distinction, this prevents court action on segregation that was not promoted by official action, unless there is a contrary legislative mandate.

7. Courts will apply "strict scrutiny" to the actions of districts found to have previously practiced unconstitutional discrimination. In such cases, courts may require affirmative action to compensate for the effects of past discrimination. However, these positive steps may not trample on the rights of others.

8. The Fourteenth Amendment protects "persons" rather than just citizens, bringing aliens within its scope.

9. Such benign matters as school tests used for placement, state school-finance formulas, and school policies to help disadvantaged students achieve parity may fall afoul of equal protection, depending on the facts of the specific case and the attitudes of the judges hearing the cases.

TESTING, PLACEMENT, AND EQUAL PROTECTION

To what extent can (should) courts become involved in such technical educational matters as student testing, and placement decisions stemming from test results? Does equal protection require schools to insure against bias in tests and resultant placement? If so, how can the existence of such bias be proven and then corrected?

In *Hobson* v. *Hansen* (1967), a federal judge in the District of Columbia applied the equal protection concept implicit in the Fifth Amendment's due process clause to the federal capital, as had been done in *Bolling* v. *Sharpe*. One issue was whether equal protection was denied to minority and poor students placed in the lowest school tracks because of low scores on standardized tests, which were claimed to be biased in favor of the white middle class. The decision reached by Judge J. Skelly Wright stands as an exemplar of the liberal activist tradition. His "parting word" revealed his activist attitude, albeit with an apology:

> It is regrettable, of course, that in deciding this case this court must act in an area so alien to its expertise. It would be far better indeed for these great social and political problems to be resolved in the political arena by other branches of government. But these are social and political problems which seem at times to defy such resolution. In such situations, under our system, the judiciary must bear a hand and accept its responsibility to assist in the solution where constitutional rights hang in the balance.[20]

A restraintist court would not act in an area "alien to its expertise," nor would it suggest that political and social problems could not be solved by the executive and legislative authorities constituted to deal with them. The activist bent of Judge Wright is also seen in his willingness to accept as unassailable truth liberal social-science generalizations such as those found in the following passage of his decision:

> [A]ctual integration of students and faculty . . . by setting the stage for meaningful and continuous exchanges . . . educates white and Negro students equally in the fundamentals of racial tolerance and understanding . . . Negro and white children playing innocently together in the schoolyard are the primary liberating promise in a society imprisoned by racial consciousness. If stereotypic racial thinking does set in, it can best be overcome by the reciprocal racial exposure which school integration entails.[21]

This is his notion of right behavior; in the liberal tradition, he acted deliberately to adopt judicial techniques to move the schools in the direction he considered proper. Those institutions had to be adjusted to free the individuals (teachers and students) involved to attain the practical advantages of education implicit in the liberal, realist, pragmatic education philosophy. Judge Wright identified a number of arbitrary, unjustified restraints placed upon minority and all lower-class children by the District of Columbia School System. He found black schools physically inferior, overcrowded, and poorly staffed. Staff assignments followed the same patterns of race segregation as with students, and program opportunities such as kindergarten were much more limited in black attendance areas than in white ones. Of particular interest here was Wright's finding that the system of tracking students into ability groupings on the basis of standardized test results was really a system of assigning minority and other lower-class students to the least-desirable range of educational experiences for learning and career opportunities. This judgment was supported by a finding that the basis for classification "depends essentially on standardized aptitude tests which . . . are completely inappropriate . . . [b]ecause these tests are standardized primarily on and are relevant to a white, middle-class group of students."[22] Further, little retesting or remedial assistance is offered those assigned to the lowest, dead-end tracks.

In his elaboration on these findings, Judge Wright marshaled liberal social and educational theory to his defense:

On kindergartens: "[T]he children of the slums must be brought into the culturally rich atmosphere of the school at the earliest age—three or four, if possible."[23]

On the social benefits of integration: "[S]egregation in the schools precludes the kind of social encounter . . . which is an indispensible attribute of education for mature citizenship in an interracial and democratic society."[24]

On the psychological harm of segregation: "[W]hat . . . can we expect the Negro to think and feel when almost all the adult faces they see at their predominantly Negro schools are black by virtue of a process of deliberate selection? . . . These circumstances . . . conspire to inflict the entire emotional hurt crippling to academic motivation set out in *Brown*."[25]

On teacher attitude and approach: "[T]eachers acting under false assumptions because of low test scores will treat the disadvantaged student in such a way as to make him conform to their low expectations; this acting out process—the self-fulfilling prophecy—makes it appear that the false assumptions were correct, and the student's talent is wasted."[26]

On the track system: "Even in concept, the track system is undemocratic and discriminatory . . . [as] it is designed to prepare some children for white-collar, and other children for blue-collar, jobs."[27]

Judge Wright found that the District of Columbia School System violated the equal protection rights of its poor and black students in regard to pupil assignment, teacher assignment, and the track system. Consequently, he ordered: (1) the abolition of the tracking system; (2) the submission of a district plan of student school-assignment policies that would, through a variety of measures including transportation of students, promote integration; and (3) that the Board provide "substantial" faculty integration by a specified date.

Throughout this decision, Judge Wright demonstrates the liberal's faith in the resources of all people to continually improve themselves when freed from arbitrary government restraints, replaced by supportive techniques that are grounded in the conviction that education must serve the material enhancement of students. Common-sense reasoning was all Judge Wright apparently deemed necessary to fashion appropriate remedies to the restraints imposed on the poor and minorities by those having a less optimistic view of human capacity.

Judicial activism and the liberal's interest in relatively fast and large-scale change is also evident in this decision. His decision, albeit with regret that "this court must act in an area so alien to its expertise," nevertheless swept aside broad areas of professional education policy and practice. In its place, the judge fashioned his own remedies, according to his personal assessment of and judgment about the issues. Student and teacher assignment policies were completely and quickly changed, and a student testing-tracking policy that had existed for many years was summarily dismantled. This is the epitome of judicial liberalism—broad, sweeping application of legal principles to implement a judge's notion of social justice. The concept of equal protection, in Judge Wright's court, was used to create fast, large-scale changes to the presumed benefit of minority and poor students, who were judged victims of abuse because of discrimination against them.

Judge Wright's decision sent shock waves through much of the public-school community, causing many districts to reassess their testing and tracking practices. The next front for the liberal-activist challenge to intelligence testing and consequent tracking was in California, in *Diana* v. *State Board of Education* (Civil No. C–70–37 RFR N.D. Cal. [1970]). Parents of Spanish-speaking students classified as mentally retarded on the basis of intelligence-test results claimed an equal protection violation. The basis of the claim was that English, the language of the test, was not the student's primary language. Further, the tests were accused of being culturally biased against Mexican-American students, as that group was not represented in the normalizing sample. The California Board of Education agreed to an out-of-court settlement in which tests used would be renormalized to reflect Mexican-Americans, and they would be tested in their primary language as well as English.

In the same year, the issue of bias in tests and their uses was considered by the U.S. Supreme Court (*Griggs* v. *Duke Power Co.* [1971]) in a business case argued under Title VII of the Civil Rights Act of 1964, which bars employment classifications, limiting job opportunities that are based on race, color, religion, sex, or national origin. The company had a policy requiring high-school graduation for assignments other than unskilled labor, once the company discontinued its policy of assigning only blacks to its labor department; however, whites already assigned to other departments were not subjected to that qualification. Then the company added the further requirement of satisfactory performance on two professionally prepared aptitude tests for assignment to departments other than labor. Both were general tests unrelated to specific job requirements.

The Court found unanimously that these requirements had a disproportionate negative effect on the hiring and promotion of blacks, without showing any valid relationship to predicting job performance. It concluded that, on the basis of Title VII: "If an employment practice which operates to exclude Negroes cannot be shown to be related to job performance, the practice is prohibited."[28] Five years later, in another noneducation case, the Supreme Court considered whether a District of Columbia examination for police applicants, which blacks failed in disproportionate numbers, violated the equal protection rights conferred on District residents through the Fifth Amendment. The Court decided that while the police test had a disproportionate *effect,* it did not have discriminatory *intent.* Because of that and the demonstrated relationship of the test to the valid interest of verbal facility for policemen, a divided Court decided that equal protection had not been violated. *Washington* v. *Davis,* 426 U.S. 229 (1976), established a principle for adjudicating discrimination cases brought under the Civil Rights Act and those claiming Fourteenth Amendment violations. Title VII of the Civil Rights Act "may focus solely on the racially different impact," but the Fourteenth Amendment may only be invoked for "the prevention of official conduct discriminating on the basis of race, regardless of impact."[29] Thus, a more limited scope was set for the equal protection clause than for a statute, which is more amenable to change or repeal.

These issues would surface in school testing cases. Following *Diana, Larry P.* v. *Riles* emerged to occupy California schools' testing policy from 1972 to 1984. The case shuttled back and forth between the federal district and appellate courts on the question of whether the major standardized IQ tests, and policies and procedures associated with them, discriminated against black students classified as Educable Mentally Retarded (EMR) primarily on the basis of these tests.

District court Judge Peckham eventually ruled that the IQ tests were culturally biased. Compounding the problem, test results played too powerful a role in the placement decision. These were judged the causes of disproportionately high black EMR enrollment, which violated the Civil Rights Act, the Rehabilitation Act, the Education for All Handicapped Children Act, and the equal protection clause of the California Constitution. Judge Peckham had listened to the testimony of experts about the relative merits of IQ testing and the placement procedures used, and decided that school officials had "a desire to perpetuate the segregation of minorities in inferior, dead end, and stigmatizing classes for the retarded."[30] He also felt that some test experts accepted the idea of the inherent intellectual inferiority of blacks. In contrast, Peckham accepted the theory that abilities are normally distributed among groups of the total population. This helped convince him that it was the cultural bias of the tests and overreliance on them for placement decisions that caused the disproportionate black EMR enrollment. Therefore, he enjoined the California schools from using their standardized IQ tests unless they could satisfy the court that: (1) the tests were not racially or culturally discriminatory, (2) the tests would be administered in a nondiscriminatory manner, (3) black and white test results supported nondiscrimination claims, and (4) proof was available of the tests' validation for the uses to which they are claimed to be put.

This strongly liberal and activist decision was subsequently affirmed by the ninth circuit on the basis of various federal statutes and the California Constitution's equal protection provision. The court ordered California schools to stop using the tests, reevaluate currently enrolled black EMR students, and to develop plans within three years to eliminate racial disproportion in black EMR enrollment. This result was based on the court's finding that IQ scores were the main criterion for placement but the tests were not validated for EMR placement for black children.

In direct contrast to the *Larry P.* case was the finding in *Parents in Action on Special Education (PASE)* v. *Hannon* (1980). The case had the same issues as presented in *Larry P.,* but Judge Grady of the seventh circuit district court arrived at the opposite conclusion. He did so by bringing to the issue a more conservative attitude toward education and a more activist approach than Peckham. Judge Grady ignored the testimony of experts, upon which Peckham had relied, and decided to enter the professional controversy directly and judge the bias or its absence in the tests by his personal review and judgment of each item of the Wechsler and Stanford-Binet tests. After doing so, he decided that the small number of items he judged to be biased was insufficient to seriously affect a student's score and subsequent placement, especially since it was not the only basis for placement. This was a conservative, activist decision. Traditional practice and authority were upheld, and judicial judgment was not substituted for educator judgment. However, the process through which this was accomplished represented taking great liberties with the traditional judicial role when Judge Grady set himself up as an expert on test bias, in contrast to Peckham's more accepted role of relying on expert testimony. Thus, as Judge Grady proceeded with his analysis, he remarked:

> This testimony, standing alone, does not preponderate in either direction . . . [n]one of the witnesses in this case has so impressed me with his or her credibility or expertise that I would feel secure in basing a decision simply upon his or her opinion. In some instances, I am satisfied that the opinions expressed are more the result of doctrinaire commitment to a preconceived idea than they are the result of scientific inquiry. I need something more than the conclusions of the witnesses in order to arrive at my own conclusions . . .
>
> It is obvious to me that I must examine the tests themselves . . . I do not see how an informed decision on the question of bias could be reached in any other way.[31]

Judge Grady went on to reach his independent decision, allowing the testing practices to remain. However, the Chicago School District entered into an out-of-court settlement in which they agreed to discontinue test use for special-education placement of black children in exchange for the plaintiffs' promise not to appeal the decision. Thus, the issue of test bias remains cloudy, with contradictory decisions in two federal circuits.

EQUAL SCHOOLING RIGHTS OF ALIENS

Are aliens entitled to the same access to public education as citizens? Do illegal-alien children have equal protection in securing a public education? Can an American citizen leave his or her foreign parents in a different country and claim access to a public education under the equal protection clause?

In 1970, a federal district court in the U.S. Virgin Islands decided a case dealing with the equal protection rights of alien West Indian children to receive public-education benefits in this American territory. Due to the remoteness of the locale, the case received little attention. Yet, it was a harbinger of an issue that would eventually reach the Supreme Court. In *Hosier* v. *Evans* (1970), the Fourteenth Amendment was directly applied to a territory by virtue of the Virgin Islands Organic Act, and the judge noted that the amendment protected "persons," not just citizens. Therefore, he found ripe the issue of whether the public schools could exclude alien children from free public education because of the financial and administrative pressures this large, quickly accumulated student group brought upon the school system. Judge Christian decided that the requirements of equal protection mandated that the alien children be admitted to school on the same basis as citizen students in the Virgin Islands. To the school district's defense that educational facilities were already inadequate and admission of the aliens would render the system "so chaotic as to totally destroy public education," Judge Christian responded: "The short answer to that argument is that fundamental rights guaranteed by the Constitution may be neither denied nor abridged solely because their implementation requires the expenditure of public funds. For such purposes, the Government must raise the funds."[32]

The Virgin Islands students were wards of aliens legally residing on American territory. What of the equal protection rights of children of illegal aliens? This was the question before the Supreme Court in *Plyler* v. *Doe* (1982). Texas had passed legislation excluding undocumented alien children from public education. Plaintiffs claimed the statute violated the equal protection rights of those children; that is, no state shall "deny to any person within its jurisdiction the equal protection of the laws." Texas claimed that illegal aliens were not technically within its jurisdiction, and that the classification had a rational relationship to the state's interest, which was to preserve limited resources for its legal residents. The latter argument was dismissed as easily as it had been in the Virgin Islands case a decade earlier, but for a different reason: "There is no evidence . . . that illegal entrants impose any significant burden on the State's economy. To the contrary . . . illegal aliens underutilize public services, while contributing their labor to the local economy and tax money to the state."[33] As to the issue of jurisdiction, the fact that the children were in Texas evidenced that they were "within that jurisdiction," legal or not.

The more pressing question considered was whether the Texas statute should be held to the strict-scrutiny standard rather than merely the rational-basis one. The former requires that a suspect class or fundamental interest be found. Even though illegal-alien children were not considered entitled to strict scrutiny under either concept, a bare five-member majority decided that even so, the law worked to consign innocent children to a lifetime of hardship in an "underclass" without showing the justification of a substantial state interest. In its words: "If the State is to deny a discrete group of innocent children the free public education that it offers to other children . . . that denial must be justified by a showing that it furthers some substantial state interest. No such showing was made here."[34]

This decision was partly based on the passive role of the children, whose parents had made the decision to become illegal aliens. The liberal activist majority expressed its particular sense of morality and good policy by holding that:

> the record is clear that many of the undocumented children disabled by this classification will remain in the country indefinitely, and that some will become lawful residents or citizens of the United States. It is difficult to understand precisely what the State hopes to achieve by promoting the creation and perpetuation of a subclass of illiterates within our boundaries, surely adding to the problems and costs of unemployment, welfare, and crime. It is thus clear that whatever savings might be achieved by denying these children an education, they are wholly insubstantial in light of the costs involved to these children, the State and the Nation.[35]

This instance of judicial judgment and policy formulation was balanced by a more restrained, conservative decision the following year in another Texas case adjudicated by the Supreme Court (*Martinez* v. *Bynum* [1983]). This case represented still another variant of school policy involving equal opportunity and an aspect of alienage. Roberto Morales was born in the United States to Mexican parents, thus making him a United States citizen. After living with his parents in Mexico, he returned to Texas to live with his sister, Oralia Martinez, and attend public school. This violated a Texas statute that denied free schooling for minors living apart from their parents or guardian primarily to benefit from free public schooling. The Court majority turned aside the equal protection argument of the plaintiffs on the grounds that residence requirements of school districts represented a substantial state interest. With only liberal Justice Marshall dissenting, the Court reasoned as follows:

> A bona fide residence requirement, appropriately defined and uniformly applied, furthers the substantial state interest in assuring that services provided for its residents are enjoyed only by residents. Such a requirement with respect to attendance in public free schools does not violate the Equal Protection Clause of the Fourteenth Amendment. It does not burden or penalize the constitutional right of interstate travel, for any person is free to move to a State and to establish residence there. A bona fide residence requirement simply requires that the person *does* establish residence before demanding the services that are restricted to residents.[36]

Marshall saw the issue differently:

> The State of Texas does not attempt to justify the classification by reference to its interests in the safety and well-being of children within its boundaries. The State instead contends that the principle purpose of the classification is to preserve educational and financial resources for those most closely connected to the State. The classification of children according to their motive for residing in the State cannot be justified . . . [37]

The contrasting views on aliens' equal protection rights to an education illustrate the complexities of policy to which case law can bring educational administration. Illegal as well as legal aliens may be entitled to free public education, but an American citizen residing away from the foreign home of his alien parents may not be so entitled.

THE ISSUE OF FISCAL EQUITY

Does equal protection require that state school finances provide each student with the same school-funding levels? Is education a constitutionally guaranteed right, or at least a fundamental interest, requiring strict scrutiny over such matters as equity in school-funding policies? Should courts supersede traditional state legislative programs of school finance, to impose their notions of the demands of equality in school finance? Should the level of school funding for students be a function of local district wealth or of the state's wealth as a whole?

The liberal concept of equal opportunity has extended to the point where it has challenged the traditionally independent sphere of state tax and fiscal policies. Liberal theorists in the sixties challenged the traditional approaches to state school finance, which courts generally viewed as beyond the reaches of the equal protection clause provided that they appeared reasonable and in the state's best interests. Courts tended to accept state interpretations of what was reasonable and in the state's interest. This changed with the development of a line of reasoning, supported by strong evidence, that the traditional practice of emphasizing local property-tax resources for school finance created school fiscal inequities based on "accidents of geography." The level of school funding was primarily a function of the wealth of a local district rather than that of the state as a whole. This, the critics contended, violated equal protection. One of the first challenges to reach the Supreme Court on this issue was *McInnis v. Shapiro,* 377 U.S. 533 (1964). The Supreme Court rejected the challenge that the Illinois system that allowed for wide disparities of funding among public-school districts violated equal protection. Clearly not wishing to substitute its notions of proper school-finance policy for those of the Illinois legislature, the Court concluded that unequal expenditures did not constitute invidious discrimination and were not unreasonable. The Court's restraintist attitude on the matter was captured by its conclusion that the problem defied "discoverable and manageable standards" by which it could usefully intervene. Similarly, in a later challenge to the Virginia school-finance system, the Supreme Court declined to make new policy, holding that: "the courts have neither the knowledge, nor the means, nor the power to tailor public moneys to fit the varying needs of these students throughout the state. We can only see to it that the outlays on one group are not invidiously greater or less than that of another. No such arbitrariness is manifest here."[38]

It remained for the California Supreme Court, applying the equal protection clause of the state constitution rather than that of the Fourteenth Amendment, to decide that equal protection was violated when the state fiscal system allowed wide per-pupil expenditure disparities among the state's public school districts. This was considered especially invidious when some districts taxed themselves more heavily than richer districts and still ended up with lower per-pupil expenditure levels. Also, the California court saw a pattern in which poorer people suffered the brunt of these resulting disparities. The court saw a compelling interest here, justifying strict scrutiny, causing it to declare the state school-finance system violative of equal protection. In the words of the *Serrano v. Priest* (1971) decision:

> [S]ince it deals with education, [it] obviously touches upon a fundamental interest . . . [T]his system conditions the full entitlement to such interest on wealth, classifies its recipients on the basis of their collective affluence and makes the quality of a child's education depend upon the pocketbook of his parents. We find that such financing . . . is not necessary to the attainment of any compelling state interest. Since it does not withstand the requisite "strict scrutiny," it denies to the plaintiffs and others similarly situated the equal protection of the laws.[39]

This California decision had a strong impact on the acceptance by other state courts and even lower federal courts of the idea that education was a "fundamental interest" and wealth a "suspect classification," triggering the application of the equal protection clause to the systems of state-school finance.

In recognition of the administrative turmoil becoming rampant throughout the country on this issue, the Supreme Court accepted a Texas school-finance equal protection case to establish case law on the matter. In *San Antonio* v. *Rodriguez* (1973), the Supreme Court reviewed a federal court decision invalidating the Texas system of school finance. The Court approached the issue as follows:

> We must decide, first, whether the Texas system of financing public education operates to the disadvantage of some suspect class or impinges upon a fundamental right explicitly or implicitly protected by the Constitution, thereby requiring strict judicial scrutiny. If so, the judgment of the District Court should be affirmed. If not, the Texas scheme must still be examined to determine whether it rationally furthers some legitimate, articulated state purpose and therefore does not constitute an invidious discrimination in violation of the Equal Protection Clause of the Fourteenth Amendment.[40]

The five-justice majority found that those receiving less per-pupil funding did not constitute a suspect class, as there was "no definitive description of the classifying facts or delineation of the disfavored class."[41] Poor people lived in tax-rich districts and rich ones in tax-poor districts. Further, education quality as determined by funding was difficult to assess. Finally, the Constitution does not explicitly or implicitly create a fundamental right to education. "It is not the province of this Court to create substantive constitutional rights in the name of guaranteeing equal protection of the laws," and "the undisputed importance of education will not alone cause this Court to depart from the usual standard of reviewing a state's social and economic legislation."[42] In this case, the proper standard was found to be the rational relationship test, and such a relationship was found to exist.

The decision closed with evidence of the struggle of the justices between some apparent liberal sentiment, checked by their notions of the need to exercise judicial restraint. "We hardly need add that this Court's action today is not to be viewed as placing its judicial imprimatur on the status quo. The need is apparent for reform in tax systems which may well have relied too long and too heavily on the local property tax."[43]

This parting *obiter dictum* stands as interesting evidence of court strain about imposing its notions of good policy when such a matter is best left, in its view, to the province of state legislatures. In *Rodriguez,* the attitude that the Court should limit itself to interpreting the Constitution, rather than making new law (however much it felt it was needed), prevailed. While this decision may have slowed the process of national school-fiscal reform, it did not reverse it. The parting *obiter dictum* must be viewed as instrumental in the continuance of reform, illustrating that the Supreme Court teaches, in addition to deciding legal issues.

For example, since *Rodriguez,* New Jersey, New York, and Maryland courts have approved local property-tax systems, but fifteen states have declared invalid the systems challenged in *Serrano* and *Rodriguez.*

REVERSE DISCRIMINATION

Is the Constitution "color blind" in applying equal protection, as Justice Harlan said it should be in his dissent to *Plessy?* Does the fact that white males constitute anything but a suspect class deprive them of fair consideration under the equal protection clause? Should the primary goal of remediating past racial injustice allow affirmative action to take precedence over the aspirations of those who have not suffered from discrimination?

In *Plessy* v. *Ferguson,* Harlan's dissent had expressed the opinion that applying equal protection or any other constitutional principle should be done without reference to race. This point was made to help blacks receive the protection of the Fourteenth Amendment. By the seventies, liberal, activist decisions had moved so far to remediate past discrimination against minorities that voices were raised to protest an opposite problem; that is, giving minorities preferred equal-protection treatment as compared to members of the majority. The result of decisions supporting affirmative action had left many whites feeling that they had been placed in an unfair competitive position, giving rise to judicial inquiry as to whether or not equal protection forbid discrimination against the dominant, advantaged class.

The initial challenge came from a white applicant to the University of Washington law school. He was denied admission, while several minority-group students with lower qualifications had been admitted, under the provisions of a special program to encourage and support the production of minority-group attorneys. *De Funis* v. *Odegaard* was initially argued in 1971 on the constitutionality of using race as an admission criterion. The lower state court saw the practice as unconstitutional and ordered De Funis admitted to law school pending appeal. The Washington Supreme Court reversed, holding: "The consideration of race in the law school admission policy meets the test of necessity here because racial imbalance in the law school and the legal profession is the evil to be corrected, and it can only be corrected by providing legal education to those minority groups which have been previously deprived."[44] The Washington court held that there can be compelling state interest permitting racial classification, as in this instance, where the state was promoting the full societal participation of minority members.

Three years would pass between the *De Funis* decision and the Supreme Court review of the case in 1974. In the interim, national resentment of affirmative action grew, as did a general public and judicial conservatism regarding equal protection issues. While the required four justices agreed to grant certiorari, the decision suggested that the majority deemed that the issue of reverse discrimination was not ripe for judicial consideration. Over the vigorous dissent of Justice Douglas, the majority observed that De Funis was now in his final term of law school. Since he had filed an individual rather than a class action, the Court declared the case moot; that is, there was nothing to decide (*De Funis* v. *Odegaard*, 409 U.S. 75 [1974]). Article III of the Constitution requires that the courts decide active controversies, and De Funis's academic situation removed it from that category. Perhaps the majority considered the 1974 social and political climate unfavorable to the type of decision it wished to render. In any event, the decision was delayed until the Supreme Court considered *Regents of the University of California* v. *Bakke* (1978).

This case involved the Davis campus medical school's use of a quota system favoring the admission of a particular number of minority students who had lesser qualifications than Bakke. Bakke saw this as a violation of his Fourteenth Amendment rights as well as of Title VI of the Civil Rights Act of 1964. Bakke won in the state courts, and in a series of split votes involving three main opinions supported by different majorities, he gained Supreme Court support for his admission. However, the complex split votes rendered the decision less than a complete victory for the opponents of reverse discrimination. In painstaking fashion the Court divided itself among the answers to four main questions: (1) Is equal protection violated when majority students are denied admission in preference to minority students solely on the basis of race? (2) Is it constitutionally permissible to grant groups "preferred status" for competitive advantage in public programs? (3) May race be considered a factor in public-university admission? (4) May an individual bring a personal Title VI action before the Court?

In answer to the first question, the majority decided that admission preference based solely on the basis of race offended the equal protection clause:

> The guarantee of equal protection cannot mean one thing when applied to one individual and something else when applied to a person of another color [319–320].
> . . . If both are not accorded the same protection, then it is not equal . . . [The program] tells applicants who are not Negro, Asian, or Chicano that they are totally excluded from a specific percentage of the seats in an entering class. No matter how strong their qualifications . . . they are never afforded the chance to compete with applicants from the preferred groups for the special admission seats. At the same time, the preferred applicants have the opportunity to compete for every seat in the class. The fatal flaw in [the University] preferential program is the disregard of individual rights as guaranteed by the Fourteenth Amendment.[45]

As to the concept of assigning "preferred status" to groups recognized as historically victimized by past discrimination, one majority rejected that principle as imposing an unfair burden on current members of the white majority, who had no role in or responsibility for past inequities: "It is far too late to argue that the guarantee of equal protection to *all* persons permits the recognition of special wards entitled to a degree of protection greater than that accorded others . . . The concepts of "majority" and "minority" necessarily reflect temporary arrangements and political judgments . . . "[46]

The Court required a different coalescence of justices to decide that race may be considered as a factor in determining admission (along with other factors), in recognition of the diverse interests and considerations that attend admission policy at a state-supported institution of higher education:

> In such an admissions program [as Harvard's, cited with approval by this majority] race or ethnic background may be deemed a "plus" in a particular applicant's file, yet it does not insulate him from comparison with all other candidates for the available seats . . . This kind of program treats each applicant as an individual in the admission process . . . [T]he State has a substantial interest that legitimately may be served by a properly devised admissions program involving the competitive consideration of race and ethnic origins . . . [47]

The issue regarding Bakke's right to bring an action under the Civil Rights Act as an individual was avoided by still another majority, notwithstanding a vigorous protest by Justice White that the Title VI claim should be addressed and disallowed. The majority's reason for avoiding this decision was: "The question of respondent's right to bring an action under Title VI was neither argued nor decided in either of the courts below . . . We therefore do not address this difficult issue . . . We assume only for the purpose of this case that [Bakke] has a right of action under Title VI."[48]

The majority's unwillingness to decide the question of access for an individual to sue under the Civil Rights Act evidences the equally balanced liberal and conservative strengths that interplayed on this decision. The majority's lack of clarity on this matter was matched by its position on the more central issue of whether or not race could be used as a factor in granting access or other advantages in educational programs. This issue was resolved on very narrow grounds, specific to the precise, unique characteristics of the University of California at Davis Medical School's admission program. Race could be used as *one* factor in determining admission, but not to the point where it served as an exclusive bar to competition for spaces by members of the majority race. The constitutionality of using race to discriminate in favor of previously injured minority groups would depend on the precise, unique characteristics of any new case. The same would be true for the uncertain application of the Civil Rights Act to new "reverse discrimination" cases.

POLICY CONSIDERATIONS

The struggle to eliminate racism and other forms of undemocratic discrimination from American society has been largely focused upon public schools. While we have advanced to the point where the equity of forbidding legal school segregation is accepted, the history of *Brown* and its progeny indicate the difficulty of adequate policy resolutions to the complex, wide variety of issues falling within the purview of the equal protection clause. At the time *Brown* was decided, the moral direction required for the equal protection clause was relatively simple and clear, even if violently opposed in the bastions of segregation. However, as equal protection has been strengthened and expanded, it has been revealed that altering societal arrangements and relationships is fraught with unanticipated problems and negative side effects. Enforced busing to achieve integration is a good example of this. No better way of creating integration could be found than forcibly transporting students (many unwillingly) far from their homes to satisfy the court mandates for desegregation. Such "solutions" illustrate the difficulty of translating abstractions of judicial decisions into reality, regardless of their morality and ethical correctness, to say nothing of their legal appropriateness.

An important reason for this problem is that the courts have found the schools to be the most vulnerable and tractable agency of society for establishing more complex and forceful notions of equal protection. Courts make little progress in reducing the racial isolation of residential patterns, and even their impact on the workplace pales in comparison to their impact on schooling. Thus, the major arena for working out the problems of prejudice and discrimination in American society continues to be the schools.

The early need for judicial activism in fashioning desegregation remedies for recalcitrant districts encouraged courts to explore such diverse areas of possible equal protection applicability as the characteristics of standardized IQ tests, school-funding policies, policies for the schooling of aliens, and college-admission policies. It has become clear that the courts have not been able to devise any magic formulas that create educational equity without affecting the corresponding rights of groups other than the "suspect class," or without producing serious educational inconvenience and limitations. While one can sympathize with the plight of Judge Grady in trying to decide which experts were right about the bias or nonbias of IQ tests, the judicial device of simply rendering a personal judgment on a very technical matter does not bode well for professional use of expertise in education, even though he supported the educational establishment. His action, if repeated in other educational areas, might produce changes more deep and sweeping than those rendered by Judges Wright and Peckham, extreme as they were.

The less definite, qualified decisions rendered in cases like *Bakke* produce different but equally difficult educational-policy problems. Then school boards and administrators are unsure of exactly what is required and what is proscribed. Confusion reigns, and the frequent approach becomes to ignore the courts and hope that no one sues.

It would appear that the best route for educational-policy formulation is to understand well the theory and intent of equal protection as generally defined by the courts, and act accordingly. In matters of equal protection, this certainly means satisfying oneself that official policy intended to create classifications based on noneducational considerations is avoided and that efforts are taken to anticipate the discriminatory effects of benign policies as well.

A policy test for equal-protection conformance can take the form of the following questions for each policy area, which should all be answered in the affirmative to conform with general protection guidelines discerned from court decisions.

In the area of school desegregation, the questions might be:

1. Are there alternative approaches available to school organization and administration that better avoid present or potential racial and other suspect class imbalances without impairing school quality and operation?
2. Is adequate attention paid to the special needs of students suffering from past or present discrimination? Is this done in a way that minimizes any disregard of the needs of the more advantaged class?
3. Is constant vigilance applied to insure that benign policies that allow or even encourage race/ethnic segregation are identified and then removed?

Regarding the issue of discrimination through testing and placement decisions based on them, the questions could take a form similar to the following:

1. Is there assurance that the tests used are reasonably free of biases created by failure to include minority groups in the normalizing sample? Similarly, are test items scrutinized to remove those that relate to cultural/environmental factors with which minority/poor students would be unfamiliar because of their life conditions?
2. Is the test clearly relevant to the curriculum and school programs for which classifications will be made, carefully avoiding items that are irrelevant to the educational process but penalize students because of differences in social background?
3. Are placement decisions, and all other forms of student labeling, made on the basis of a variety of data that balance possibly biased test scores with other evidence more directly applicable to the students' environmental circumstances?

Court decisions in the educational-finance area might include the following:

1. Does that state pattern of school finance avoid funding inequities imposed on particular classes of people?
2. Is the school-finance burden equitably distributed among districts, so that achieving a standard funding level does not require a greater tax burden for one district's residents than for another's?
3. Are efforts made to avoid an overreliance on the local property tax for educational finance, so that the level of school financial support is more a function of the wealth of the state as a whole than it is of any local district?

When a school district is confronted by a group as legally distinctive as aliens, the relevant questions might be:

1. Is it clear that the constitutional protection for all *persons* within the state's (or school district subdivision's) jurisdiction is not restricted to only citizens?
2. Is care taken not to penalize the children of law violators in the educational opportunity afforded them because of the misbehavior of their parents?
3. Are decisions limiting service to noncitizens or those of foreign origin justified on better grounds than that of inadequate financial resources?

When schools encounter situations where admission to particular types of schools or school programs involves questions of race or equally suspect classifications, positive answers to the following questions would indicate observance of equal protection guidelines:

1. Is the policy so constructed as to insure that the discrimination the policy is intended to remedy does not do so at the expense of the equal opportunity to which all persons are entitled?

2. Has the policy been so constructed as to avoid reliance on race as the sole criterion on which selection preference is based?

3. When race is used as a selection factor to redress past disadvantages suffered by a minority group, is care taken to provide additional qualification standards to allow those outside of that category to successfully compete, if they can overcome their initial competitive disadvantage through very high qualifications on the additional standards?

Brown v. Board of Education of Topeka
347 U.S. 483 (1954)

MR. CHIEF JUSTICE WARREN delivered the opinion of the Court.

These cases come to us from the States of Kansas, South Carolina, Virginia, and Delaware. They are premised on different facts and different local conditions, but a common legal question justifies their consideration together in this consolidated opinion.

In each of the cases, minors of the Negro race, through their legal representatives, seek the aid of the courts in obtaining admission to the public schools of their community on a nonsegregated basis. In each instance, they had been denied admission to schools attended by white children under laws requiring or permitting segregation according to race. This segregation was alleged to deprive the plaintiffs of the equal protection of the laws under the Fourteenth Amendment. In each of the cases other than the Delaware case, a three-judge federal district court denied relief to the plaintiffs on the so-called "separate but equal" doctrine announced by this Court in *Plessy* v. *Ferguson.* Under that doctrine, equality of treatment is accorded when the races are provided substantially equal facilities, even though these facilities be separate. In the Delaware case, the Supreme Court of Delaware adhered to that doctrine, but ordered that the plaintiffs be admitted to the white schools because of their superiority to the Negro schools.

The plaintiffs contend that segregated public schools are not "equal" and cannot be made "equal," and that hence they are deprived of the equal protection of the laws.

In the first cases in this Court construing the Fourteenth Amendment, decided shortly after its adoption, the Court interpreted it as proscribing all state-imposed discriminations against the Negro race. The doctrine of "separate but equal" did not make its appearance in this Court until 1896 in the case of *Plessy* v. *Ferguson,* involving not education but transportation. American courts have since labored with the doctrine for over half a century. In this Court, there have been six cases involving the "separate but equal" doctrine in the field of public education. In *Cumming* v. *County Board of Education* and *Gong Lum* v. *Rice,* the validity of the doctrine itself was not challenged. In more recent cases, all on the graduate school level, inequality was found in that specific benefits enjoyed by white students were denied to Negro students of the same educational qualifications. In none of these cases was it necessary to re-examine the doctrine to grant relief to the Negro plaintiff. And in *Sweatt* v. *Painter,* the Court expressly reserved decision on the question whether *Plessy* v. *Ferguson* should be held inapplicable to public education.

In the instant cases, that question is directly presented. Here, unlike *Sweatt* v. *Painter,* there are findings below that the Negro and white schools involved have been equalized, or are being equalized, with respect to buildings, curricula, qualifications and salaries of teachers, and other "tangible" factors. Our decision, therefore, cannot turn on merely a comparison of these tangible factors in the Negro and white schools involved in each of the cases. We must look instead to the effect of segregation itself on public education.

In approaching this problem, we cannot turn the clock back to 1868 when the Amendment was adopted, or even to 1896 when *Plessy* v. *Ferguson* was written. We must consider public education in the light of its full development and its present place in American life throughout the Nation. Only in this way can it be determined if segregation in public schools deprives these plaintiffs of the equal protection of the laws.

Today, education is perhaps the most important function of state and local governments. Compulsory school attendance laws and the great expenditures for education both demonstrate our recognition of the importance of education to our democratic society. It is required in the performance of our most basic public responsibilities, even service in the armed forces. It is the very foundation of good citizenship. Today it is a principal instrument in awakening the child to cultural values, in preparing him for later professional training, and in helping him to adjust normally to his environment. In these days, it is doubtful that any child may reasonably be expected to succeed in life if he is denied the opportunity of an education. Such an opportunity, where the state has undertaken to provide it, is a right which must be made available to all on equal terms.

We come then to the question presented: Does segregation of children in public schools solely on the basis of race, even though the physical facilities and other "tangible" factors may be equal, deprive the children of the minority group of equal educational opportunities? We believe that it does.

In *Sweatt* v. *Painter,* in finding that a segregated law school for Negroes could not provide them equal educational opportunities, this Court relied in large part on "those qualities which are incapable of objective measurement but which make for greatness in a law school." In *McLaurin* v. *Oklahoma State Regents,* the Court, in requiring that a Negro admitted to a white graduate school be treated like all other students, again resorted to intangible considerations: ". . . his ability to study, to engage in discussions and exchange views with other students, and, in general, to learn his profession." Such considerations apply with added force to children in grade and high schools. To separate them from others of similar age and qualifications solely because of their race generates a feeling of inferiority as to their status in the community that may affect their hearts and minds in a way unlikely ever to be undone. The effect of this separation on their educational opportunities was well stated by a finding in the Kansas case by a court which nevertheless felt compelled to rule against the Negro plaintiffs:

"Segregation of white and colored children in public schools has a detrimental effect upon the colored children. The impact is greater when it has the sanction of the law; for the policy of separating the races is usually interpreted as denoting the inferiority of the negro group. A sense of inferiority affects the motivation of a child to learn. Segregation with the sanction of law, therefore, has a tendency to [retard] the educational and mental development of negro children and to deprive them of some of the benefits they would receive in a racial[ly] integrated school system."

Whatever may have been the extent of psychological knowledge at the time of *Plessy* v. *Ferguson,* this finding is amply supported by modern authority. Any language in *Plessy* v. *Ferguson* contrary to this finding is rejected.

We conclude that in the field of public education the doctrine of "separate but equal" has no place. Separate educational facilities are inherently unequal. Therefore, we hold that the plaintiffs and others similarly situated for whom the actions have been brought are, by reason of the segregation complained of, deprived of the equal protection of the laws guaranteed by the Fourteenth Amendment.

Because these are class actions, because of the wide applicability of this decision, and because of the great variety of local conditions, the formulation of decrees in these cases presents problems of considerable complexity. On reargument, the consideration of appropriate relief was necessarily subordinated to the primary question—the constitutionality of segregation in public education. We have now announced that such segregation is a denial of the equal protection of the laws. In order that we may have the full assistance of the parties in formulating decrees, the cases will be restored to the docket, and the parties are requested to present further argument.

Pasadena City Bd. of Education v. Spangler
427 U.S. 424 (1976)

MR. JUSTICE REHNQUIST delivered the opinion of the Court.

In 1968, several students in the public schools of Pasadena, Cal., joined by their parents, instituted an action in the United States District Court for the Central District of California seeking injunctive relief from allegedly unconstitutional segregation of the high schools of the Pasadena Unified School District (PUSD). This action named as defendants the Pasadena City Board of Education, which operates the PUSD, and several of its officials.

II

Petitioners requested the District Court to dissolve its injunctive order requiring that there be no school in the PUSD with a majority of any minority students enrolled. The District Court refused this request, and ordered the injunction continued. The court apparently based this decision in large part upon its view that petitioners had failed properly to comply with its original order. This conclusion was in turn premised upon the fact that although the School

Board had reorganized PUSD attendance patterns in conformity with the court-approved Pasadena Plan, literal compliance with the terms of the court's order had been obtained in only the initial year of the plan's operation. Following the 1970–1971 school year, black student enrollment at one Pasadena school exceeded 50% of that school's total enrollment. The next year, four Pasadena schools exceeded this 50% black enrollment figure; and at the time of the hearing on petitioners' motion some five schools, in a system of 32 regular schools, were ostensibly in violation of the District Court's "no majority of any minority" requirement. It was apparently the view of the majority of the Court of Appeals' panel that this failure to maintain literal compliance with the 1970 injunction indicated that the District Court had not abused its discretion in refusing to grant so much of petitioner's motion for modification as pertained to this aspect of the order. We think this view was wrong.

We do not have before us any issue as to the validity of the District Court's original judgment, since petitioners' predecessors did not appeal from it. All that is now before us are the questions of whether the District Court was correct in denying relief when petitioners in 1974 sought to modify the "no majority" requirement as then interpreted by the District Court.

The meaning of this requirement, as originally established by the District Court, was apparently unclear even to the parties. In opposing the petitioners' request for relief in 1974, counsel for the original individual plaintiffs and counsel for the Government jointly stipulated that they were aware "of no violations of the Pasadena Plan up to and including the present." These parties were, of course, aware that some of the Pasadena schools had "slipped out of compliance" with the literal terms of the order. The stipulation was based upon the fact that the plaintiffs never understood the District Court's order to require annual reassignment of pupils in order to accommodate changing demographic residential patterns in Pasadena from year to year, as the Government candidly admits in its brief here.

Petitioners have argued that they never understood the injunction, or the provisions of the plan which they drafted to implement that order, to contain such a requirement either. But at the hearing on petitioners' motion for relief the District Court made it clear that *its* understanding of the decree was quite different from that of the parties. In response to the arguments of petitioners' counsel, the judge stated that his 1970 order "meant to me that at least during my lifetime there would be no majority of any minority in any school in Pasadena."

When the District Court's order in this case, as interpreted and applied by that court, is measured against what this Court said in its intervening decision in *Swann* v. *Board of Education* regarding the scope of the judicially created relief which might be available to remedy violations of the Fourteenth Amendment, we think the inconsistency between the two is clear. The District Court's interpretation of the order appears to contemplate the "substantive constitutional right [to a] particular degree of racial balance or mixing" which the Court in *Swann* expressly disapproved. It became apparent, at least by the time of the 1974 hearing, that the District Court viewed this portion of its order not merely as a "starting point in the process of shaping a remedy," which *Swann* indicated would be appropriate, but instead as an "inflexible requirement," to be applied anew each year to the school population within the attendance zone of each school.

The District Court apparently believed it had authority to impose this requirement even though subsequent changes in the racial mix in the Pasadena schools might be caused by factors for which the defendants could not be considered responsible. Whatever may have been the basis for such a belief in 1970, in *Swann* the Court cautioned that "it must be recognized that there are limits" beyond which a court may not go in seeking to dismantle a dual school system. These limits are in part tied to the necessity of establishing that school authorities have in some manner caused unconstitutional segregation, for "[a]bsent a constitutional violation there would be no basis for judicially ordering assignment of students on a racial basis." While the District Court found such a violation in 1970, and while this unappealed finding afforded a basis for its initial requirement that the defendants prepare a plan to remedy such racial segregation, its adoption of the Pasadena Plan in 1970 established a racially neutral system of student assignment in the PUSD. Having done that, we think that in enforcing its order so as to require annual readjustment of attendance zones so that there would not be a majority of any minority in any Pasadena public school, the District Court exceeded its authority.

There was also no showing in this case that those post-1971 changes in the racial mix of some Pasadena schools which were focused upon by the lower courts were in any manner caused by segregative actions chargeable to the defendants. The District Court rejected petitioners' assertion that the movement was caused by so-called "white flight" traceable to the decree itself. It stated that the "trends evidenced in Pasadena closely approximate the state-wide trends in California schools, both segregated and desegregated." The fact that black student enrollment at 5 out of 32 of the regular Pasadena schools came to exceed 50% during the 4-year period from 1970 to 1974 apparently resulted from people randomly moving into, out of, and around the PUSD area. This quite normal pattern of human migration resulted in some changes in the demographics of Pasadena's residential patterns, with resultant shifts in the racial makeup of some of the schools.

In this case the District Court approved a plan designed to obtain racial neutrality in the attendance of students at Pasadena's public schools. No one disputes that the initial implementation of this plan accomplished *that* objective. That being the case, the District Court was not entitled to require the PUSD to rearrange its attendance zones each year so as to ensure that the racial mix desired by the court was maintained in perpetuity. For having once implemented a racially neutral attendance pattern in order to remedy the perceived constitutional violations on the part of the defendants, the District Court had fully performed its function of providing the appropriate remedy for previous racially discriminatory attendance patterns.

Even had the District Court's decree been unambiguous and clearly understood by the parties to mean what that court declared it to mean in 1974, the "no majority of any minority" provision would, as we have indicated previously, be contrary to the intervening decision of this Court in *Swann, supra*. The ambiguity of the provision itself, and the fact that the parties to the decree interpreted it in a manner contrary to the interpretation ultimately placed upon it by the District Court, is an added factor in support of modification. The two factors taken together make a sufficiently compelling case so that such modification should have been ordered by the District Court.

Petitioners have plainly established that they were entitled to relief from the District Court's injunction insofar as it required them to alter school attendance zones in response to shifts in demographics within the PUSD. The order of the District Court which was affirmed by the Court of Appeals equally plainly envisioned the continuation of such a requirement. We do not think petitioners must be satisfied with what may have been the implicit assumption of the Court of Appeals that the District Court would heed the "disapproval" expressed by each member of the panel of that court in his opinion. Instead, we think petitioners were entitled on this phase of the case to a judgment of the Court of Appeals reversing the District Court with respect to its treatment of that portion of the order.

Accordingly the judgment of the Court of Appeals is vacated, and the case is remanded to that court for further proceedings not inconsistent with this opinion.

So ordered.

MR. JUSTICE MARSHALL, with whom MR. JUSTICE BRENNAN joins, dissenting.

I cannot agree with the Court that the District Court's refusal to modify the "no majority of any minority" provision of its order was erroneous. Because at the time of the refusal "racial discrimination through official action" had apparently not yet been eliminated from the Pasadena school system, it is my view that the District Court did not abuse its discretion in refusing to dissolve a major part of its order.

In denying petitioners' motion for modification of the 1970 desegregation order, the District Court described a 3-year pattern of opposition by a number of the members of the Board of Education to both the spirit and letter of the Pasadena Plan. It found that "the Pasadena Plan has not had the cooperation from the Board that permits a realistic measurement of its educational success or failure." Moreover, the 1974 Board of Education submitted to the District Court an alternative to the Pasadena Plan, which, at least in the mind of one member of the Court of Appeals, "would very likely result in rapid resegregation." I agree with Judge Ely that there is "abundant evidence upon which the district judge, in the reasonable exercise of his discretion, could rightly determine that the 'dangers' which induced the original determination of constitutional infringements in Pasadena have not diminished sufficiently to require modification or dissolution of the original Order."

The Court's conclusion that modification of the District Court's order is mandated is apparently largely founded on the fact that during the Pasadena Plan's first year, its implementation did result in no school's having a majority of minority students. According to the Court, it follows from our decision in *Swann, supra,* that as soon as the school attendance zone scheme had been successful, even for a very short period, in fulfilling its objectives, the District Court should have relaxed its supervision over that aspect of the desegregation plan.

It is irrelevant to the Court that the system may not have achieved "'unitary' status in all other respects such as the hiring and promoting of teachers and administrators."

In my view, the Court, in so ruling, has unwarrantedly extended our statement in *Swann* that "[n]either school authorities nor district courts are constitutionally required to make year-by-year adjustments of the racial composition of student bodies *once the affirmative duty to desegregate has been accomplished and racial discrimination through official action is eliminated from the system.*" That statement recognizes on the one hand that a fully desegregated school system may not be compelled to adjust its attendance zones to conform to changing demographic patterns. But on the other hand, it also appears to recognize that *until* such a unitary system is established, a district court may act with broad discretion—discretion which includes the adjustment of attendance zones—so that the goal of a wholly unitary system might be sooner achieved.

In insisting that the District Court largely abandon its scrutiny of attendance patterns, the Court might well be insuring that a unitary school system in which segregation has been eliminated "root and branch" will never be achieved in Pasadena. For at the point that the Pasadena system is in compliance with the aspects of the plan specifying procedures for hiring and promoting teachers and administrators, it may be that the attendance patterns within the system will be such as to once again manifest substantial aspects of a segregated system. It seems to me singularly unwise for the Court to risk such a result.

We have held that "[o]nce a right and a violation have been shown, the scope of a district court's equitable powers to remedy past wrongs is broad, for breadth and flexibility are inherent in equitable remedies." As the Court recognizes, there is no issue before us as to the validity of the District Court's original judgment that unconstitutional segregation existed in the Pasadena school system. Thus, there is no question as to there being both a "right and a violation." Moreover, at least as of the time that the District Court acted on the request for modification, the violation had not yet been entirely remedied. Particularly, given the breadth of discretion normally accorded a district court in fashioning equitable remedies, I see no reason to require the District Court in a case such as this to modify its order prior to the time that it is clear that the entire violation has been remedied and a unitary system has been achieved. We should not compel the District Court to modify its order unless conditions have changed so much that "dangers, once substantial, have become attenuated to a shadow." I, for one, cannot say that the District Court was in error in determining that such attenuation had not yet taken place and that modification of the order would "surely be to sign the death warrant of the Pasadena Plan and its objectives." Accordingly, I dissent.

Parents in Action on Special Ed. (Pase) v. Hannon
506 F. Supp. 831 (1980)

GRADY, District Judge.

This case presents the question whether standard intelligence tests administered by the Chicago Board of Education are culturally biased against black children. The action is brought on behalf of all black children who have been or will be placed in special classes for the educable mentally handicapped ("EMH") in the Chicago school system. The defendants are the Chicago Board of Education and its officers responsible for administration of the relevant programs. The named plaintiffs are two black children who were placed in EMH classes after achieving low scores on standard intelligence tests.

An erroneous assessment of mental retardation, leading to an inappropriate placement of a child in an EMH class, is clearly an educational tragedy. However beneficial such classes may be for those who truly need them, they are likely to be almost totally harmful to those who do not. The two named plaintiffs in this case are examples of what can happen. Each of these children had learning disabilities but was erroneously diagnosed as being mentally retarded. Each of them scored low on a standard intelligence test administered as part of the assessment process. The two plaintiffs were assigned to EMH classes, where they spent several years. As a result of a belated re-evaluation, it was determined that these two children were not mentally retarded but rather were children in the normal range of intelligence whose learning was hampered by disabilities which are remediable.

The two named plaintiffs claim that their misassessment as retarded children was caused by racial bias in the standard intelligence tests they took, causing them to achieve low scores. It is claimed on behalf of the two named plaintiffs and the class they represent, consisting of all black children in the Chicago school system who are or might be assigned to EMH classes, that the use of racially biased intelligence tests in EMH placement violates the Equal Protection Clause of the Fourteenth Amendment as well as various federal statutes. Plaintiffs seek declaratory and injunctive relief. The principal relief sought is a permanent injunction against the use of standard IQ tests in the evaluation of black children for EMH placement.

The disagreement between the parties can be summarized briefly. It has been known since the early days of standard intelligence tests, around the time of World War I, that blacks as a group score about one standard deviation—15 points—lower than whites. On the Stanford-Binet test, for instance, the mean white score is 100 and the mean black score is 85. While there is no disagreement as to the existence of this phenomenon, there is considerable disagreement about what causes it.

The psychologists who developed the Stanford-Binet test in this country, Terman, Yerkes and Goddard, believed that they were measuring innate mental abilities which were not subject to change. This was their concept of "intelligence." They explained the relatively poor performance of blacks, as well as that of many other groups such as recent immigrants to this country from southern and eastern Europe, on the basis of genetic inferiority.

The current view of most psychologists is that IQ tests measure something which is changeable rather than something that is fixed for all time, something which can be increased and improved. The parties in this case agree on that much.

The question remains, what does the IQ score measure? Dr. Kamin is the country's leading exponent of the view that the tests measure nothing innate. He testified that in his opinion differences in performance on the tests are due solely to differences in exposure to "information" called for by the tests.

Defendants contend that the tests measure the child's current level of abilities which correlate significantly with his prospects of succeeding in school. [T]he IQ tests afford an indication of the areas of the child's mental strengths and weaknesses. According to Mr. Smith, the tests give an indication of the child's ability to retain factual information, to attend, to concentrate, to formulate new associative learning, and to perform simple arithmetic processes. These abilities are called for by the regular school curriculum, and accordingly the test results have some predictive value. Defendants' witnesses concede a slight amount of cultural bias in the tests but deny that this results in erroneous placements or deprives the tests of their usefulness. They point out that a diagnosis of retardation is not based solely upon an IQ score but upon a combination of relevant factors. These witnesses also emphasized that the IQ score affords a criterion that is relatively objective. They fear that, lacking the student's score on a standardized test, they would be forced to make the assessment upon a largely subjective basis.

This testimony, standing alone, does not preponderate in either direction. I have seen cases in which one set of experts is clearly more credible than the other and will, by their demeanor, appearance, credentials, and the reasonableness of their testimony, carry the day. This is not such a case. None of the witnesses in this case has so impressed me with his or her credibility or expertise that I would feel secure in basing a decision simply upon his or her opinion. In some instances, I am satisfied that the opinions expressed are more the result of doctrinaire commitment to a preconceived idea than they are the result of scientific inquiry. I need something more than the conclusions of the witnesses in order to arrive at my own conclusions.

The Evidence Concerning Bias

The focus is on the question of whether the WISC–R, the WISC and the Stanford-Binet are culturally biased against black children so that it is unfair to use these tests in the determination of whether a black child is mentally retarded.

[Neither] Dr. Kamin nor any other witness attempted to demonstrate any bias in the test items traceable to the racist notions of Goddard, Yerkes, Terman and their followers. If evidence concerning their racial attitudes was offered only to show why they misinterpreted the test results, the evidence bears upon something which is not an issue in this case. Defendants agree with plaintiffs that there is no evidence to support a hypothesis that blacks have less innate mental capacities than whites.

Dr. Kamin testified that blacks have had different experiences than whites, which account for the differences in their performance on the test, but said that he does not know what these experiences are.

Dr. Williams described the characteristics of black culture which he believes are pertinent to this case. He stated that black culture is rooted in African philosophy, whereas ''Anglo-Saxon culture'' is rooted in European philosophy. He stated that these two cultures are ''diametrically opposed.'' Blacks also share a common language, different from the language used by whites. This is sometimes referred to as non-standard English. Dr. Williams gave two examples of "standard" English which he says black children have difficulty understanding in test situations.

As was noted during the description of the various test items, Dr. Williams addressed himself to very few of them. Many children, white and black, would never have worked a maze or a coding-type problem before confronting it on the IQ test.

Some test items, on the other hand, are quite similar to the material both black and white children are exposed to in the classroom before they would be asked to take an IQ test. This is true of the arithmetic items. Generally, black and white children are exposed to such material in school to the same degree, and there is no evidence that arithmetic plays a bigger role in the nonschool environment of a white child than of a black child.

Dr. Kamin's argument that the black child does not obtain the same "information," and Dr. Albee's argument that the black child does not share in the dominant white culture, seem inapplicable to most items on all three of the tests in question. As already noted, many of the categories of test items have no precise counterpart in the experience of *any* children, of whatever race. Others have almost precise counterparts in the everyday experience of American children of all races.

The evidence does not establish how the use of non-standard English would interfere with performance on the Wechsler and Stanford-Binet tests.

The vocabulary items on the tests should have drawn more fire from plaintiffs' witnesses if "non-standard English" presents a real problem. Yet, the only plaintiffs' witness who testified about any test items, Dr. Williams, did not refer to a single one of the vocabulary items on any of the three tests. At the levels where a school child suspected of retardation would be tested, which the parties agree would be fairly early in the child's school experience, the vocabulary items are words of ordinary, common usage.

Dr. Williams' criticism of many test items appears unrelated to the question of racial bias. In fact, of the relatively few items he did discuss, most of them were criticized as inappropriate tests of any child's intelligence, not simply a black child's intelligence.

Dr. Williams did criticize some specific items on the ground that they were culturally biased against black children. I believe there is a substantial basis for some of these criticisms, and I have indicated in the preceding section of this opinion some of those items as to which I agree. On the WISC and WISC–R, I believe the following items are either racially biased or so subject to suspicion of bias that they should not be used:

1. "What is the color of rubies?"
2. "What does C.O.D. mean?"
3. "Why is it better to pay bills by check than by cash?"
4. "What would you do if you were sent to buy a loaf of bread and the grocer said that he did not have any more?"
5. "What does a stomach do?"

6. "Why is it generally better to give money to an organized charity than to a street beggar?"

7. "What are you supposed to do if you find someone's wallet or pocket book in a store?"

8. "What is the thing to do if a boy (girl) much smaller than yourself starts to fight with you?"

On the Stanford-Binet, I believe the one item which is racially inappropriate is the "aesthetic comparison" on the 4½ year old sub-test, where the child is asked to tell which of two persons is "prettier."

The importance of missing a particular item is, of course, magnified if indeed the difference between being sent to a class for the mentally retarded and not being sent there could rest on so slim a basis. However, there are factors which tend to protect against such an occurrence. First, as far as the WISC and WISC–R tests are concerned, the importance of an individual item is lessened by the fact that the child continues with the sub-test until he has a certain number of consecutive misses. No one is expected to answer all items correctly, and the fact that a child misses one item does not prevent him from accumulating points on others.

The third factor which mitigates the impact of missing any particular question is the fact that the IQ score is not the sole determinant of whether a child is placed in an EMH class. First, the score itself is evaluated by the psychologist who administers the test. The child's responses are recorded verbatim, and the significance of his numerical score is a matter involving judgment and interpretation. Dr. Terrence Hines testified that as a school psychologist in the Chicago system he finds that clinical judgment plays a large role in the interpretation of IQ test results.

In short, Dr. Hines testified that the examiner who knows the milieu of the child can correct for cultural bias by asking the questions in a sensitive and intelligent way.

It is relevant to note that 44 of the 193 school psychologists in the Chicago system are black and that defendants' witnesses testified without contradiction that the likelihood of a black child being placed in an EMH class without at least one black professional having participated in the evaluation is very slight.

Finally, the IQ test and the psychologist's evaluation of the child in the light of that test is only one component of several which forms the basis for an EMH referral. We will deal with this aspect of the case in a later section of this opinion.

I conclude that the possibility of the few biased items on these tests causing an EMH placement that would not otherwise occur is practically nonexistent.

Plaintiffs argue that the racial bias of the IQ tests is shown circumstantially by the fact that blacks, although possessing the same innate mental ability as whites, do not score as well as whites on the tests. Plaintiffs say this of itself shows the tests must be measuring the amount of culture-specific information acquired by whites and not by blacks. There is no dispute in this case about the equality of innate intellectual capacity. Defendants assert no less strongly than plaintiffs that there are no genetic differences in mental capacity. However, the rest of plaintiffs' argument sidesteps their inability to point to any actual racial bias in the test items. All but a few of the items on their face appear racially neutral. It is not valid to draw an inference of unfairness if that can be done only by ignoring direct evidence of fairness. A preferable analysis would seek to account for all the data.

The IQ tests do not purport to measure innate intelligence. What the tests appear to measure is the extent to which one utilizes his innate abilities in the performance of certain general categories of learned intellectual tasks. Performance on the tests reflects, for instance, the extent to which one has learned to observe, to see similarities and differences, to notice causal relationships, to remember, to draw inferences, to generalize, and to concentrate. The tests also indicate how well one has used those abilities to acquire certain specific knowledge, such as language and arithmetical concepts.

The acquisition and development of these mental skills is, according to defendants' witnesses greatly affected by the child's early experiences. Early intellectual stimulation is essential. If the child does not receive it, or if he receives it to an insufficient degree, his intellectual development—his ability to use his innate capacity to deal with intellectual problems—will be delayed. Lack of opportunity for cognitive stimulation is, according to these witnesses and some of the literature received in evidence, often due to factors associated with economic poverty in the home. Defendants offered a collection of census data documenting the fact that poverty and reduced socio-economic status is far more often a condition of black families than of white families in Chicago.

Plaintiffs totally reject this suggestion that the performance of black children on IQ tests can be explained by deficiencies in their cognitive environment. Dr. Williams and Dr. Gloria Powell strongly contended that the mental stimulation received by poor black children in the inner city is adequate and in all respects equal to the intellectual stimulation received by middle class white children. Dr. Powell's explanation for the disproportionate placement of black children in EMH classes is the "[f]ailure of the school to adequately assess the intellectual function of children who are culturally different." This failure, in the view of Drs. Powell and Williams, is caused by use of the culturally biased IQ tests.

Dr. Powell's explanation does not satisfy me. She seemed ill-prepared to discuss the question of cognitive stimulation. I believe the defendants have presented the more persuasive argument.

Defendants' explanation of the IQ difference, that it is caused by socio-economic factors which interfere with the development of intellectual skills, is consistent with other circumstances not accounted for by plaintiffs' theory of cultural bias. It is uncontradicted that most of the children in the EMH classes do in fact come from the poverty pockets of the city. This tends to suggest that what is involved is not simply race but something associated with poverty. It is also significant that many black children who take the tests score at levels high enough to preclude EMH placement. Plaintiffs have not explained why the alleged cultural bias of the tests did not result in EMH level scores for these children. Plaintiffs' theory of cultural bias simply ignores the fact that black children perform differently from each other on the tests. It also fails to explain the fact that some black children perform better than most whites. Nationally, 15 to 20 per cent of the blacks who take the tests score above the white mean of 100.

I conclude that plaintiffs' have failed to prove their contention that the Wechsler and Stanford-Binet IQ tests are culturally unfair to black children, resulting in discriminatory placement of black children in classes for the educable mentally handicapped.

The Assessment Process

Defendants' system for the identification and placement of mentally handicapped children, which is spelled out in manuals and printed regulations, involves several levels of investigation. It is important to understand that an IQ test is not the first level, nor is an IQ score the catalyst for the assessment process. The first level of investigation is the classroom. Unless the child is having difficulty with his studies in the classroom, the question of EMH placement will never arise and there is no occasion for an IQ test. Individually administered IQ tests of the kind involved in this case have never been given routinely in the Chicago school system, and the former practice of giving group-administered general intelligence tests to all students was discontinued some years ago.

No child can be placed in an EMH class unless the placement is recommended by a psychologist who has evaluated the child. While the conference can decline an EMH placement recommended by the psychologist, it cannot make such a placement without the psychologist's recommendation.

The evaluation and placement process is not carried out hastily. There are more children in need of placement than there are available seats in the EMH classrooms. Sometimes the decision is against placement even though the parent desires it. A motive for unnecessary placement is nonexistent, since the cost to the local system of administering the program far exceeds the state and federal aid received for it.

Plaintiffs claim that, despite the various steps involved in EMH placement, the placement decision is really made primarily on the basis of the child's IQ score. They argue that the IQ score has a "hypnotic effect" on the participants in the multidisciplinary staffing, so that a child with an IQ of less than 80 stands a high chance of being put in an EMH class on that basis alone.

Dr. Berk concluded that the most constant characteristic of all children who were placed in EMH classes was the fact that they had low IQ scores. He concluded from this that there is a strong relationship between low IQ and placement in an EMH class.

I fail to see how this testimony proves plaintiffs' contention that IQ scores are given undue weight in the placement decision. One thing I would expect of a mentally retarded child is that he would have difficulty with an IQ test. While there may be reasons other than mental retardation that would account for a low IQ score, it is difficult to see how a high IQ could be reconciled with a finding of mental retardation.

In the circumstances of this case, where defendants have shown that IQ scores are only one factor which enters into the EMH assessment and that a low IQ score frequently does not result in such placement, I believe the burden of showing an absence of racial bias in the tests does not rest on the defendants.

It is apparently plaintiffs' position that the tests in question could be vindicated only by a showing that blacks do as well on them as whites. Plaintiffs regard any differential performance between the races as evidence of cultural bias.

Plaintiffs believe that their theory of the case accounts for the fact that the mean black score on each and every item is lower than the mean white score. They contend that the difference is entirely due to cultural bias. The implications of the argument are striking. Plaintiffs' hypothesis implies, for instance, that of the 328 items on the WISC–R, spread across twelve sub-tests of different kinds of subject matter and standardized on a sample that included representative numbers of blacks, there is not a single item which is not culturally biased against blacks. That such a thing could happen by chance, or because of simple inadvertence on the part of the psychologists who devised the test, is difficult to believe. No statistical evidence was presented on the question, but it seems highly unlikely that if mere inadvertence were involved, at least a few culturally fair items would not have found their way onto the test simply by chance.

It is unfortunately true that, despite what I believe are sincere efforts on the part of the defendants to avoid erroneous placements, some children are placed in EMH classes who should not be there.

These erroneous placements have not been shown to be due to racial bias in the IQ tests. The situations of the two named plaintiffs illustrate this failure of proof. These two black children, Barbara B. and Angela J., were each evaluated as being mentally retarded and were transferred out of their regular classes to EMH classes. Each child was evaluated by a school psychologist and achieved a low score on one of the WISC tests or the Stanford-Binet.

Later reevaluation of these children disclosed that they are not mentally retarded. They have normal intelligence but suffer from learning disabilities which make it difficult for them to perform well in certain kinds of learning situations. One of plaintiffs' witnesses was Robert E. Stoner, a clinical psychologist who examined and evaluated each of the named plaintiffs in connection with this case. He gave each of them a variety of tests, including the WISC. He found that each of these children had perceptual problems which interfered with their visual and auditory discrimination between different shapes and sounds. This accounted for their difficulty with such items as picture completion and picture arrangement. Incorrect answers to some of the verbal items may have been caused by the fact that the child did not correctly perceive the words spoken by the examiner.

Mr. Stoner testified that Barbara and Angela should have been placed in special classes for the learning disabled rather than classes for the mentally retarded. He pointed out that an educational handicap should have been suspected by reason of the profiles these two children show on their IQ tests. If there is a significant difference in the level of performance on the various sub-tests, this suggests a learning disability rather than mental retardation. Such differences did appear on the WISC tests Mr. Stoner administered to Barbara and Angela, and his interpretation of this data was a primary basis for his conclusion that these children are learning disabled.

The problems these two children had with the tests were caused by their learning disabilities, not by any bias in the test items. On the sub-tests where their perceptual problems did not inhibit performance, these children scored within the normal range. Had their test results been properly interpreted in the first instance they would not have been assigned to EMH classes.

Plaintiffs seem not to realize that their own evidence shows the two class representatives, Barbara and Angela, do not have claims which are typical of the class they purport to represent.

The Larry P. Case

This is not a case of first impression. The exact issue of racial bias in the WISC, WISC–R and Stanford-Binet tests has been decided by Judge Robert F. Peckham of the United States District Court for the Northern District of California in the case of *Larry P. et al.* v. *Wilson Riles* (1979). Plaintiffs rely upon that decision heavily, since Judge Peckham held that the tests are culturally biased against black children. Judge Peckham heard a number of the same witnesses who testified here. He found their testimony persuasive. Judge Peckham's lengthy and scholarly opinion is largely devoted to the question of what legal consequences flow from a finding of racial bias in the tests. There is relatively little analysis of the threshold question of whether test bias in fact exists, and Judge Peckham even remarked that the cultural bias of the tests ''. . . is hardly disputed in this litigation. . . .'' I find reference to specific test items on only one page of the opinion. Judge Peckham mentions the WISC ''fight'' item, finds that it is culturally biased against blacks and then remarks, ''Similarly, it may be that such questions as who wrote Romeo and Juliet, who discovered America, and who invented the lightbulb, are culturally biased.'' Finally, Judge Peckham noted that ''. . . such skills as 'picture arrangement' may be tested in a biased fashion if the pictures, which generally are of caucasian persons, relate to situations more typical of white, middle class, life than the experiences of many black children.''

As is by now obvious, the witnesses and the arguments which persuaded Judge Peckham have not persuaded me. Moreover, I believe the issue in the case cannot properly be analyzed without a detailed examination of the items on the tests. It is clear that this was not undertaken in the *Larry P.* case.

Conclusion

I have found one item on the Stanford-Binet and a total of eight items on the WISC and WISC–R to be culturally biased against black children, or at least sufficiently suspect that their use is in my view inappropriate. These few items do not render the tests unfair and would not significantly affect the score of an individual taking the test. The evidence fails to show that any additional test items are racially or culturally unfair or suspect.

I believe and today hold that the WISC, WISC–R and Stanford-Binet tests, when used in conjunction with the statutorily mandated [''other criteria] for determining an appropriate educational program for a child'' do not discriminate against black children in the Chicago public schools. Defendants are complying with that statutory mandate.

Intelligent administration of the IQ tests by qualified psychologists, followed by the evaluation procedures defendants use, should rarely result in the misassessment of a child of normal intelligence as one who is mentally retarded. There is no evidence in this record that such misassessments as do occur are the result of racial bias in test items or in any other aspect of the assessment process currently in use in the Chicago public school system.

I find the issues in favor of the defendants and against the plaintiffs.

San Antonio Indep. School Dist. v. Rodriguez
411 U.S. 1 (1973)

MR. JUSTICE POWELL delivered the opinion of the Court.

This suit attacking the Texas system of financing public education was initiated by Mexican-American parents whose children attend the elementary and secondary schools in the Edgewood Independent School District, an urban school district in San Antonio, Texas. They brought a class action on behalf of school children throughout the State who are members of minority groups or who are poor and reside in school districts having a low property tax base. In December 1971 the panel rendered its judgment in a *per curiam* opinion holding the Texas school finance system unconstitutional under the Equal Protection Clause of the Fourteenth Amendment. The State appealed, and we noted probable jurisdiction to consider the far-reaching constitutional questions presented. For the reasons stated in this opinion, we reverse the decision of the District Court.

I

The school district in which appellees reside, the Edgewood Independent School District, has been compared throughout this litigation with the Alamo Heights Independent School District. This comparison between the least and most affluent districts in the San Antonio area serves to illustrate the manner in which the dual system of finance operates and to indicate the extent to which substantial disparities exist despite the State's impressive progress in recent years.

[S]ubstantial interdistrict disparities in school expenditures found by the District Court to prevail in San Antonio and in varying degrees throughout the State still exist. And it was these disparities, largely attributable to differences in the amounts of money collected through local property taxation, that led the District Court to conclude that Texas' dual system of public school financing violated the Equal Protection Clause. The District Court held that the Texas system discriminates on the basis of wealth in the manner in which education is provided for its people. Finding that wealth is a "suspect" classification and that education is a "fundamental" interest, the District Court held that the Texas system could be sustained only if the State could show that it was premised upon some compelling state interest. On this issue the court concluded that "[n]ot only are defendants unable to demonstrate compelling state interests . . . they fail even to establish a reasonable basis for these classifications."

This, then, establishes the framework for our analysis. We must decide, first, whether the Texas system of financing public education operates to the disadvantage of some suspect class or impinges upon a fundamental right explicitly or implicitly protected by the Constitution, thereby requiring strict judicial scrutiny. If so, the judgment of the District Court should be affirmed. If not, the Texas scheme must still be examined to determine whether it rationally furthers some legitimate, articulated state purpose and therefore does not constitute an invidious discrimination in violation of the Equal Protection Clause of the Fourteenth Amendment.

II

The wealth discrimination discovered by the District Court in this case, and by several other courts that have recently struck down school-financing laws in other States, is quite unlike any of the forms of wealth discrimination heretofore reviewed by this Court. Rather than focusing on the unique features of the alleged discrimination, the courts in these cases have virtually assumed their findings of a suspect classification through a simplistic process of analysis: since, under the traditional systems of financing public schools, some poorer people receive less expensive educations than other more affluent people, these systems discriminate on the basis of wealth. This approach largely ignores the hard threshold questions, including whether it makes a difference for purposes of consideration under the Constitution that the class of disadvantaged "poor" cannot be identified or defined in customary equal protection terms, and whether the relative—rather than absolute—nature of the asserted deprivation is of significant consequence. Before a State's laws and the justifications for the classifications they create are subjected to strict judicial scrutiny, we think these threshold considerations must be analyzed more closely than they were in the court below.

The case comes to us with no definitive description of the classifying facts or delineation of the disfavored class. The Texas system of school financing might be regarded as discriminating (1) against "poor" persons whose incomes fall below some identifiable level of poverty or who might be characterized as functionally "indigent," or (2) against those who are relatively poorer than others, or (3) against all those who, irrespective of their personal incomes, happen to reside in relatively poorer school districts. Our task must be to ascertain whether, in fact, the Texas system has been shown to discriminate on any of these possible bases and, if so, whether the resulting classification may be regarded as suspect.

The precedents of this Court provide the proper starting point. The individuals, or groups of individuals, who constituted the class discriminated against in our prior cases shared two distinguishing characteristics: because of their impecunity they were completely unable to pay for some desired benefit, and as a consequence, they sustained an absolute deprivation of a meaningful opportunity to enjoy that benefit.

Only appellees' first possible basis for describing the class disadvantaged by the Texas school-financing system—discrimination against a class of definably "poor" persons—might arguably meet the criteria established in these prior cases. Even a cursory examination, however, demonstrates that neither of the two distinguishing characteristics of wealth classifications can be found here. First, in support of their charge that the system discriminates against the "poor," appellees have made no effort to demonstrate that it operates to the peculiar disadvantage of any class fairly definable as indigent, or as composed of persons whose incomes are beneath any designated poverty level. Indeed, there is reason to believe that the poorest families are not necessarily clustered in the poorest property districts.

Second, neither appellees nor the District Court addressed the fact that lack of personal resources has not occasioned an absolute deprivation of the desired benefit. The argument here is not that the children in districts having relatively low assessable property values are receiving no public education; rather, it is that they are receiving a poorer quality education than that available to children in districts having more assessable wealth. Apart from the unsettled and disputed question whether the quality of education may be determined by the amount of money expended for it, a sufficient answer to appellees' argument is that, at least where wealth is involved, the Equal Protection Clause does not require absolute equality or precisely equal advantages. Nor, indeed, in view of the infinite variables affecting the educational process, can any system assure equal quality of education except in the most relative sense.

For these two reasons—the absence of any evidence that the financing system discriminates against any definable category of "poor" people or that it results in the absolute deprivation of education—the disadvantaged class is not susceptible of identification in traditional terms.

As suggested above, appellees and the District Court may have embraced a second or third approach, the second of which might be characterized as a theory of relative or comparative discrimination based on family income. Appellees sought to prove that a direct correlation exists between the wealth of families within each district and the expenditures therein for education. That is, along a continuum, the poorer the family the lower the dollar amount of education received by the family's children.

For almost 90% of the sample, the districts that spend next to the most money on education are populated by families having next to the lowest median family incomes while the districts spending the least have the highest median family incomes. It is evident that, even if the conceptual questions were answered favorably to appellees, no factual basis exists upon which to found a claim of comparative wealth discrimination.

This brings us, then, to the third way in which the classification scheme might be defined—*district* wealth discrimination. Since the only correlation indicated by the evidence is between district property wealth and expenditures, it may be argued that discrimination might be found without regard to the individual income characteristics of district residents. Assuming a perfect correlation between district property wealth and expenditures from top to bottom, the disadvantaged class might be viewed as encompassing every child in every district except the district that has the most assessable wealth and spends the most on education. Alternatively, as suggested in Mr. Justice Marshall's dissenting opinion, the class might be defined more restrictively to include children in districts with assessable property which falls below the statewide average, or median, or below some other artificially defined level.

However described, it is clear that appellees' suit asks this Court to extend its most exacting scrutiny to review a system that allegedly discriminates against a large, diverse, and amorphous class, unified only by the common factor of residence in districts that happen to have less taxable wealth than other districts. The system of alleged discrimination and the class it defines have none of the traditional indicia of suspectness: the class is not saddled with such disabilities, or subjected to such a history of purposeful unequal treatment, or relegated to such a position of political powerlessness as to command extraordinary protection from the majoritarian political process.

We thus conclude that the Texas system does not operate to the peculiar disadvantage of any suspect class. But in recognition of the fact that this Court has never heretofore held that wealth discrimination alone provides an adequate basis for invoking strict scrutiny, appellees have not relied solely on this contention. They also assert that the State's system impermissibly interferes with the exercise of a "fundamental" right and that accordingly the prior decisions of this Court require the application of the strict standard of judicial review. It is this question—whether education is a fundamental right, in the sense that it is among the rights and liberties protected by the Constitution—which has so consumed the attention of courts and commentators in recent years.

B

In *Brown* v. *Board of Education,* a unanimous Court recognized that "education is perhaps the most important function of state and local governments." What was said there in the context of racial discrimination has lost none of its vitality with the passage of time.

Nothing this Court holds today in any way detracts from our historic dedication to public education. We are in complete agreement with the conclusion of the three-judge panel below that "the grave significance of education both to the individual and to our society" cannot be doubted. But the importance of a service performed by the State does not determine whether it must be regarded as fundamental for purposes of examination under the Equal Protection Clause.

It is not the province of this Court to create substantive constitutional rights in the name of guaranteeing equal protection of the laws. Thus, the key to discovering whether education is "fundamental" is not to be found in comparisons of the relative societal significance of education as opposed to subsistence or housing. Nor is it to be found by weighing whether education is as important as the right to travel. Rather, the answer lies in assessing whether there is a right to education explicitly or implicitly guaranteed by the Constitution. . . .

Education, of course, is not among the rights afforded explicit protection under our Federal Constitution. Nor do we find any basis for saying it is implicitly so protected. As we have said, the undisputed importance of education will not alone cause this Court to depart from the usual standard for reviewing a State's social and economic legislation. It is appellees' contention, however, that education is distinguishable from other services and benefits provided by the State because it bears a peculiarly close relationship to other rights and liberties accorded protection under the Constitution. Specifically, they insist that education is itself a fundamental personal right because it is essential to the effective exercise of First Amendment freedoms and to intelligent utilization of the right to vote. In asserting a nexus between speech and education, appellees urge that the right to speak is meaningless unless the speaker is capable of articulating his thoughts intelligently and persuasively. The "market-place of ideas" is an empty forum for those lacking basic communicative tools. Likewise, they argue that the corollary right to receive information becomes little more than a hollow privilege when the recipient has not been taught to read, assimilate, and utilize available knowledge.

Even if it were conceded that some identifiable quantum of education is a constitutionally protected prerequisite to the meaningful exercise of either right, we have no indication that the present levels of educational expenditures in Texas provide an education that falls short. Whatever merit appellees' argument might have if a State's financing system occasioned an absolute denial of educational opportunities to any of its children, that argument provides no basis for finding an interference with fundamental rights where only relative differences in spending levels are involved and where—as is true in the present case—no charge fairly could be made that the system fails to provide each child with an opportunity to acquire the basic minimal skills necessary for the enjoyment of the rights of speech and of full participation in the political process.

We have carefully considered each of the arguments supportive of the District Court's finding that education is a fundamental right or liberty and have found those arguments unpersuasive.

C

It should be clear, for the reasons stated above and in accord with the prior decisions of this Court, that this is not a case in which the challenged state action must be subjected to the searching judicial scrutiny reserved for laws that create suspect classifications or impinge upon constitutionally protected rights.

We need not rest our decision, however, solely on the inappropriateness of the strict-scrutiny test. A century of Supreme Court adjudication under the Equal Protection Clause affirmatively supports the application of the traditional standard of review, which requires only that the State's system be shown to bear some rational relationship to legitimate state purposes. This case represents far more than a challenge to the manner in which Texas provides for the education of its children. We have here nothing less than a direct attack on the way in which Texas has chosen to raise and disburse state and local tax revenues. We are asked to condemn the State's judgment in conferring on political subdivisions the power to tax local property to supply revenues for local interests. In so doing, appellees would have the Court intrude in an area in which it has traditionally deferred to state legislatures. This Court has often admonished against such interferences with the State's fiscal policies under the Equal Protection Clause.

Thus, we stand on familiar ground when we continue to acknowledge that the Justices of this Court lack both the expertise and the familiarity with local problems so necessary to the making of wise decisions with respect to the raising and disposition of public revenues. Yet, we are urged to direct the States either to alter drastically the present system or to throw out the property tax altogether in favor of some other form of taxation. No scheme of taxation, whether the tax is imposed on property, income, or purchases of goods and services, has yet been devised which is free of all discriminatory impact. In such a complex arena in which no perfect alternatives exist, the Court does well not to impose too rigorous a standard of scrutiny lest all local fiscal schemes become subjects of criticism under the Equal Protection Clause.

The foregoing considerations buttress our conclusion that Texas' system of public school finance is an inappropriate candidate for strict judicial scrutiny. These same considerations are relevant to the determination whether that system, with its conceded imperfections, nevertheless bears some rational relationship to a legitimate state purpose. It is to this question that we next turn our attention.

III

The Texas system of school finance is responsive. While assuring a basic education for every child in the State, it permits and encourages a large measure of participation in and control of each district's schools at the local level. In an era that has witnessed a consistent trend toward centralization oif the functions of government, local sharing of responsibility for public education has survived.

The persistence of attachment to government at the lowest level where education is concerned reflects the depth of commitment of its supporters. In part, local control means the freedom to devote more money to the education of one's children. Equally important, however, is the opportunity it offers for participation in the decisionmaking process that determines how those local tax dollars will be spent. Each locality is free to tailor local programs to local needs. Pluralism also affords some opportunity for experimentation, innovation, and a healthy competition for educational excellence. No area of social concern stands to profit more from a multiplicity of viewpoints and from a diversity of approaches than does public education.

Appellees do not question the propriety of Texas' dedication to local control of education. To the contrary, they attack the school-financing system precisely because, in their view, it does not provide the same level of local control and fiscal flexibility in all districts. Appellees suggest that local control could be preserved and promoted under other financing systems that resulted in more equality in educational expenditures. While it is no doubt true that reliance on local property taxation for school revenues provides less freedom of choice with respect to expenditures for some districts than for others, the existence of "some inequality" in the manner in which the State's rationale is achieved is not alone a sufficient basis for striking down the entire system. Nor must the financing system fail because, as appellees suggest, other methods of satisfying the State's interest, which occasion "less drastic" disparities in expenditures, might be conceived. Only where state action impinges on the exercise of fundamental constitutional rights or liberties must it be found to have chosen the least restrictive alternative.

Appellees further urge that the Texas system is unconstitutionally arbitrary because it allows the availability of local taxable resources to turn on "happenstance." They see no justification for a system that allows, as they contend, the quality of education to fluctuate on the basis of the fortuitous positioning of the boundary lines of political subdivisions and the location of valuable commercial and industrial property. But any scheme of local taxation—indeed the very existence of identifiable local governmental units—requires the establishment of jurisdictional boundaries that are inevitably arbitrary. It is equally inevitable that some localities are going to be blessed with more taxable assets than others. Nor is local wealth a static quantity. Changes in the level of taxable wealth within any district may result from any number of events, some of which local residents can and do influence.

In sum, to the extent that the Texas system of school financing results in unequal expenditures between children who happen to reside in different districts, we cannot say that such disparities are the product of a system that is so irrational as to be invidiously discriminatory. Texas has acknowledged its shortcomings and has persistently endeavored—not without some success—to ameliorate the differences in levels of expenditures without sacrificing the benefits of local participation. One also must remember that the system here challenged is not peculiar to Texas or to any other State. In its essential characteristics, the Texas plan for financing public education reflects what many educators for a half century have thought was an enlightened approach to a problem for which there is no perfect solution. We are unwilling to assume for ourselves a level of wisdom superior to that of legislators, scholars, and educational authorities in 50 States, especially where the alternatives proposed are only recently conceived and nowhere yet tested. The constitutional standard under the Equal Protection Clause is whether the challenged state action rationally furthers a legitimate state purpose or interest. We hold that the Texas plan abundantly satisfies this standard.

IV

In light of the considerable attention that has focused on the District Court opinion in this case and on its California predecessor, *Serrano* v. *Priest* (1971), a cautionary postscript seems appropriate. It cannot be questioned that the constitutional judgment reached by the District Court and approved by our dissenting Brothers today would occasion in Texas and elsewhere an unprecedented upheaval in public education. Those who have devoted the most thoughtful attention to the practical ramifications of these cases have found no clear or dependable answers and their scholarship reflects no such unqualified confidence in the desirability of completely uprooting the existing system.

The complexity of these problems is demonstrated by the lack of consensus with respect to whether it may be said with any assurance that the poor, the racial minorities, or the children in overburdened core-city school districts would be benefited by abrogation of traditional modes of financing education. Unless there is to be a substantial increase in state expenditures on education across the board—an event the likelihood of which is open to considerable question—these groups stand to realize gains in terms of increased per-pupil expenditures only if they reside in districts that presently spend at relatively low levels, *i. e.,* in those districts that would benefit from the redistribution of existing resources. Yet, recent studies have indicated that the poorest families are not invariably clustered in the most impecunious school districts. Nor does it now appear that there is any more than a random chance that racial minorities are concentrated in property-poor districts. Additionally, several research projects have concluded that any financing alternative designed to achieve a greater equality of expenditures is likely to lead to higher taxation and lower educational expenditures in the major urban centers, a result that would exacerbate rather than ameliorate existing conditions in those areas.

These practical considerations, of course, play no role in the adjudication of the constitutional issues presented here. But they serve to highlight the wisdom of the traditional limitations on this Court's function. The consideration and initiation of fundamental reforms with respect to state taxation and education are matters reserved for the legislative processes of the various States, and we do no violence to the values of federalism and separation of powers by staying our hand. We hardly need add that this Court's action today is not to be viewed as placing its judicial imprimatur on the status quo. The need is apparent for reform in tax systems which may well have relied too long and too heavily on the local property tax. And certainly innovative thinking as to public education, its methods, and its funding is necessary to assure both a higher level of quality and greater uniformity of opportunity. These matters merit the continued attention of the scholars who already have contributed much by their challenges. But the ultimate solutions must come from the lawmakers and from the democratic pressures of those who elect them.

Reversed.

MR. JUSTICE STEWART, concurring.

The method of financing public schools in Texas, as in almost every other State, has resulted in a system of public education that can fairly be described as chaotic and unjust. It does not follow, however, and I cannot find, that this system violates the Constitution of the United States. I join the opinion and judgment of the Court because I am convinced that any other course would mark an extraordinary departure from principled adjudication under the Equal Protection Clause of the Fourteenth Amendment. The uncharted directions of such a departure are suggested, I think, by the imaginative dissenting opinion my Brother Marshall has filed today.

Unlike other provisions of the Constitution, the Equal Protection Clause confers no substantive rights and creates no substantive liberties. The function of the Equal Protection Clause, rather, is simply to measure the validity of *classifications* created by state laws.

Plyler v. Doe
457 U.S. 202 (1982)

JUSTICE BRENNAN delivered the opinion of the Court.

The question presented by these cases is whether, consistent with the Equal Protection Clause of the Fourteenth Amendment, Texas may deny to undocumented school-age children the free public education that it provides to children who are citizens of the United States or legally admitted aliens.

I

Since the late 19th century, the United States has restricted immigration into this country. Unsanctioned entry into the United States is a crime, and those who have entered unlawfully are subject to deportation. But despite the existence of these legal restrictions, a substantial number of persons have succeeded in unlawfully entering the United States, and now live within various States, including the State of Texas.

In May 1975, the Texas Legislature revised its education laws to withhold from local school districts any state funds for the education of children who were not "legally admitted" into the United States. The 1975 revision also authorized local school districts to deny enrollment in their public schools to children not "legally admitted" to the country. Tex. Educ. Code Ann. § 21.031. These cases involve constitutional challenges to those provisions.

II

The Fourteenth Amendment provides that "[n]o State shall . . . deprive any person of life, liberty, or property, without due process of law; nor deny to *any person within its jurisdiction* the equal protection of the laws." Appellants argue at the outset that undocumented aliens, because of their immigration status, are not "persons within the jurisdiction" of the State of Texas, and that they therefore have no right to the equal protection of Texas law. We reject this argument. Whatever his status under the immigration laws, an alien is surely a "person" in any ordinary sense of that term. Aliens, even aliens whose presence in this country is unlawful, have long been recognized as "persons" guaranteed due process of law by the Fifth and Fourteenth Amendments.

Appellants seek to distinguish our prior cases, emphasizing that the Equal Protection Clause directs a State to afford its protection to persons *within its jurisdiction* while the Due Process Clauses of the Fifth and Fourteenth Amendments contain no such assertedly limiting phrase. In appellants' view, persons who have entered the United States illegally are not "within the jurisdiction" of a State even if they are present within a State's boundaries and subject to its laws. Neither our cases nor the logic of the Fourteenth Amendment supports that constricting construction of the phrase "within its jurisdiction." We have never suggested that the class of persons who might avail themselves of the equal protection guarantee is less than coextensive with that entitled to due process. To the contrary, we have recognized that both provisions were fashioned to protect an identical class of persons, and to reach every exercise of state authority.

To permit a State to employ the phrase "within its jurisdiction" in order to identify subclasses of persons whom it would define as beyond its jurisdiction, thereby relieving itself of the obligation to assure that its laws are designed and applied equally to those persons, would undermine the principal purpose for which the Equal Protection Clause was incorporated in the Fourteenth Amendment. The Equal Protection Clause was intended to work nothing less than the abolition of all caste-based and invidious class-based legislation. That objective is fundamentally at odds with the power the State asserts here to classify persons subject to its laws as nonetheless excepted from its protection.

Our conclusion that the illegal aliens who are plaintiffs in these cases may claim the benefit of the Fourteenth Amendment's guarantee of equal protection only begins the inquiry. The more difficult question is whether the Equal Protection Clause has been violated by the refusal of the State of Texas to reimburse local school boards for the education of children who cannot demonstrate that their presence within the United States is lawful, or by the imposition by those school boards of the burden of tuition on those children. It is to this question that we now turn.

III

The Equal Protection Clause directs that "all persons similarly circumstanced shall be treated alike." But so too, "[t]he Constitution does not require things which are different in fact or opinion to be treated in law as though they were the same." The initial discretion to determine what is "different" and what is "the same" resides in the legislatures of the States. A legislature must have substantial latitude to establish classifications that roughly approximate the nature of the problem perceived, that accommodate competing concerns both public and private, and that account for limitations on the practical ability of the State to remedy every ill. In applying the Equal Protection Clause to most forms of state action, we thus seek only the assurance that the classification at issue bears some fair relationship to a legitimate public purpose.

But we would not be faithful to our obligations under the Fourteenth Amendment if we applied so deferential a standard to every classification. The Equal Protection Clause was intended as a restriction on state legislative action inconsistent with elemental constitutional premises. Thus we have treated as presumptively invidious those classifications that disadvantage a "suspect class," or that impinge upon the exercise of a "fundamental right." With respect to such classifications, it is appropriate to enforce the mandate of equal protection by requiring the State to demonstrate that its classification has been precisely tailored to serve a compelling governmental interest. In addition, we have recognized that certain forms of legislative classification, while not facially invidious, nonetheless give rise to recurring constitutional difficulties; in these limited circumstances we have sought the assurance that the classification reflects a reasoned judgment consistent with the ideal of equal protection by inquiring whether it may fairly be viewed as furthering a substantial interest of the State. We turn to a consideration of the standard appropriate for the evaluation of § 21.031.

A

Sheer incapability or lax enforcement of the laws barring entry into this country, coupled with the failure to establish an effective bar to the employment of undocumented aliens, has resulted in the creation of a substantial "shadow population" of illegal migrants—numbering in the millions—within our borders. This situation raises the specter of a permanent caste of undocumented resident aliens, encouraged by some to remain here as a source of cheap labor, but nevertheless denied the benefits that our society makes available to citizens and lawful residents. The existence of such an underclass presents most difficult problems for a Nation that prides itself on adherence to principles of equality under law.

The children who are plaintiffs in these cases are special members of this underclass. Persuasive arguments support the view that a State may withhold its beneficence from those whose very presence within the United States is the product of their own unlawful conduct. These arguments do not apply with the same force to classifications imposing disabilities on the minor *children* of such illegal entrants. At the least, those who elect to enter our territory by stealth and in violation of our law should be prepared to bear the consequences, including, but not limited to, deportation. But the children of those illegal entrants are not comparably situated. Their "parents have the ability to conform their conduct to societal norms," and presumably the ability to remove themselves from the State's jurisdiction; but the children who are plaintiffs in these cases "can affect neither their parents' conduct nor their own status." Even if the State found it expedient to control the conduct of adults by acting against their children, legislation directing the onus of a parent's misconduct against his children does not comport with fundamental conceptions of justice.

Of course, undocumented status is not irrelevant to any proper legislative goal. Nor is undocumented status an absolutely immutable characteristic since it is the product of conscious, indeed unlawful, action. But § 21.031 is directed against children, and imposes its discriminatory burden on the basis of a legal characteristic over which children can have little control. It is thus difficult to conceive of a rational justification for penalizing these children for their presence within the United States. Yet that appears to be precisely the effect of § 21.031.

Public education is not a "right" granted to individuals by the Constitution. But neither is it merely some governmental "benefit" indistinguishable from other forms of social welfare legislation. Both the importance of education in maintaining our basic institutions, and the lasting impact of its deprivation on the life of the child, mark the distinction. [E]ducation has a fundamental role in maintaining the fabric of our society. We cannot ignore the significant social costs borne by our Nation when select groups are denied the means to absorb the values and skills upon which our social order rests.

In addition to the pivotal role of education in sustaining our political and cultural heritage, denial of education to some isolated group of children poses an affront to one of the goals of the Equal Protection Clause: the abolition of governmental barriers presenting unreasonable obstacles to advancement on the basis of individual merit. Paradoxically, by depriving the children of any disfavored group of an education, we foreclose the means by which that group might raise the level of esteem in which it is held by the majority. But more directly, "education prepares individuals to be self-reliant and self-sufficient participants in society." Illiteracy is an enduring disability. The inability to read and write will handicap the individual deprived of a basic education each and every day of his life. The inestimable toll of that deprivation on the social, economic, intellectual, and psychological well-being of the individual, and the obstacle it poses to individual achievement, make it most difficult to reconcile the cost or the principle of a status-based denial of basic education with the framework of equality embodied in the Equal Protection Clause.

B

Undocumented aliens cannot be treated as a suspect class because their presence in this country in violation of federal law is not a "constitutional irrelevancy." Nor is education a fundamental right; a State need not justify by compelling necessity every variation in the manner in which education is provided to its population. But more is involved in these cases than the abstract question whether § 21.031 discriminates against a suspect class, or whether education is a fundamental right. Section 21.031 imposes a lifetime hardship on a discrete class of children not accountable for their disabling status. The stigma of illiteracy will mark them for the rest of their lives. By denying these children a basic education, we deny them the ability to live within the structure of our civic institutions, and foreclose any realistic possibility that they will contribute in even the smallest way to the progress of our Nation. In determining the rationality of § 21.031, we may appropriately take into account its costs to the Nation and to the innocent children who are its victims. In light of these countervailing costs, the discrimination contained in § 21.031 can hardly be considered rational unless it furthers some substantial goal of the State.

IV

It is the State's principal argument, and apparently the view of the dissenting Justices, that the undocumented status of these children establishes a sufficient rational basis for denying them benefits that a State might choose to afford other residents. The State notes that while other aliens are admitted "on an equality of legal privileges with all citizens under non-discriminatory laws," the asserted right of these children to an education can claim no implicit congressional imprimatur. Indeed, in the State's view, Congress' apparent disapproval of the presence of these children within the United States, and the evasion of the federal regulatory program that is the mark of undocumented status, provides authority for its decision to impose upon them special disabilities. But we are unable to find in the congressional immigration scheme any statement of policy that might weigh significantly in arriving at an equal protection balance concerning the State's authority to deprive these children of an education.

V

Appellants argue that the classification at issue furthers an interest in the "preservation of the state's limited resources for the education of its lawful residents." Of course, a concern for the preservation of resources standing alone can hardly justify the classification used in allocating those resources. The State must do more than justify its classification with a concise expression of an intention to discriminate. Apart from the asserted state prerogative to act against undocumented children solely on the basis of their undocumented status—an asserted prerogative that carries only minimal force in the circumstances of these cases—we discern three colorable state interests that might support § 21.031.

First, appellants appear to suggest that the State may seek to protect itself from an influx of illegal immigrants. While a State might have an interest in mitigating the potentially harsh economic effects of sudden shifts in population, § 21.031 hardly offers an effective method of dealing with an urgent demographic or economic problem. There is no evidence in the record suggesting that illegal entrants impose any significant burden on the State's economy. To the contrary, the available evidence suggests that illegal aliens underutilize public services, while contributing their labor to the local economy and tax money to the state. The dominant incentive for illegal entry into the State of Texas is the availability of employment; few if any illegal immigrants come to this country, or presumably to the State of Texas, in order to avail themselves of a free education. Thus, even making the doubtful assumption that the net impact of illegal aliens on the economy of the State is negative, we think it clear that "[c]harging tuition to undocumented children constitutes a ludicrously ineffectual attempt to stem the tide of illegal immigration," at least when compared with the alternative of prohibiting the employment of illegal aliens.

Second, while it is apparent that a State may "not . . . reduce expenditures for education by barring [some arbitrarily chosen class of] children from its schools," appellants suggest that undocumented children are appropriately singled out for exclusion because of the special burdens they impose on the State's ability to provide high quality public education. But the record in no way supports the claim that exclusion of undocumented children is likely to improve the overall quality of education in the State.

Finally, appellants suggest that undocumented children are appropriately singled out because their unlawful presence within the United States renders them less likely than other children to remain within the boundaries of the State, and to put their education to productive social or political use within the State. Even assuming that such an interest is legitimate, it is an interest that is most difficult to quantify. The State has no assurance that any child, citizen or not, will employ the education provided by the State within the confines of the State's borders. In any event, the record is clear that many of the undocumented children disabled by this classification will remain in this country indefinitely, and that some will become lawful residents or citizens of the United States. It is difficult to understand precisely what the State hopes to achieve by promoting the creation and perpetuation of a subclass of illiterates within our boundaries, surely adding to the problems and costs of unemployment, welfare, and crime. It is thus clear that whatever savings might be achieved by denying these children an education, they are wholly insubstantial in light of the costs involved to these children, the State, and the Nation.

VI

If the State is to deny a discrete group of innocent children the free public education that it offers to other children residing within its borders, that denial must be justified by a showing that it furthers some substantial state interest. No such showing was made here.

CHIEF JUSTICE BURGER, with whom JUSTICE WHITE, JUSTICE REHNQUIST, and JUSTICE O'CONNOR join, dissenting.

Were it our business to set the Nation's social policy, I would agree without hesitation that it is senseless for an enlightened society to deprive any children—including illegal aliens—of an elementary education. I fully agree that it would be folly—and wrong—to tolerate creation of a segment of society made up of illiterate persons, many having a limited or no command of our language. However, the Constitution does not constitute us as "Platonic Guardians" nor does it vest in this Court the authority to strike down laws because they do not meet our standards of desirable social policy, "wisdom," or "common sense." We trespass on the assigned function of the political branches under our structure of limited and separated powers when we assume a policymaking role as the Court does today.

The Court makes no attempt to disguise that it is acting to make up for Congress' lack of "effective leadership" in dealing with the serious national problems caused by the influx of uncountable millions of illegal aliens across our borders. The failure of enforcement of the immigration laws over more than a decade and the inherent difficulty and expense of sealing our vast borders have combined to create a grave socioeconomic dilemma. It is a dilemma that has not yet even been fully assessed, let alone addressed. However, it is not the function of the judiciary to provide "effective leadership" simply because the political branches of government fail to do so.

The Court's holding today manifests the justly criticized judicial tendency to attempt speedy and wholesale formulation of "remedies" for the failures—or simply the laggard pace—of the political processes of our system of government. The Court employs, and in my view abuses, the Fourteenth Amendment in an effort to become an omnipotent and omniscient problem solver. That the motives for doing so are noble and compassionate does not alter the fact that the Court distorts our constitutional function to make amends for the defaults of others.

In a sense, the Court's opinion rests on such a unique confluence of theories and rationales that it will likely stand for little beyond the results in these particular cases. Yet the extent to which the Court departs from principled constitutional adjudication is nonetheless disturbing.

I have no quarrel with the conclusion that the Equal Protection Clause of the Fourteenth Amendment *applies* to aliens who, after their illegal entry into this country, are indeed physically "within the jurisdiction" of a state. However, as the Court concedes, this "only begins the inquiry." The Equal Protection Clause does not mandate identical treatment of different categories of persons.

The dispositive issue in these cases, simply put, is whether, for purposes of allocating its finite resources, a state has a legitimate reason to differentiate between persons who are lawfully within the state and those who are unlawfully there. The distinction the State of Texas has drawn—based not only upon its own legitimate interests but on classifications established by the Federal Government in its immigration laws and policies—is not unconstitutional.

Denying a free education to illegal alien children is not a choice I would make were I a legislator. Apart from compassionate considerations, the long-range costs of excluding any children from the public schools may well outweigh the costs of educating them. But that is not the issue; the fact that there are sound *policy* arguments against the Texas Legislature's choice does not render that choice an unconstitutional one.

The Constitution does not provide a cure for every social ill, nor does it vest judges with a mandate to try to remedy every social problem. Moreover, when this Court rushes in to remedy what it perceives to be the failings of the political processes, it deprives those processes of an opportunity to function. When the political institutions are not forced to exercise consitutionally allocated powers and responsibilities, those powers, like muscles not used, tend to atrophy. Today's cases, I regret to say, present yet another example of unwarranted judicial action which in the long run tends to contribute to the weakening of our political processes.

NOTES

1. Plessy v. Ferguson, 163 U.S. 537 (1896) at 544.
2. Id. at 559.
3. Sipuel v. Board of Regents of University of Oklahoma, 332 U.S. 631 (1948) at 633.
4. Sweatt v. Painter, 339 U.S. 629 (1950) at 634.
5. Brown v. Board of Education, 98 F. Supp. 797 (1951); Davis v. County School Board, 103 F. Supp. 337 (1952); Belton v. Gebhart, 87 A. 2d 862 (1952); Briggs v. Elliot, 98 F. Supp. 529 (1951).
6. Brown v. Board of Education of Topeka, Kansas, 347 U.S. 483 (1954) at 495.
7. Id. at 493.
8. Id. at 494.
9. Id.
10. Id.
11. Alexander v. Holmes, 396 U.S. 19 (1969) at 19.
12. Swann v. Charlotte-Mecklenburg Board of Education, 402 U.S. 1 (1971) at 24.
13. Id. at 26.
14. Keyes v. School District No. 1, Denver, Colorado, 413 U.S. 189 (1973) at 208.
15. Millikin v. Bradley, 418 U.S. 717 (1974) at 741-42.
16. Id. at 743.
17. Id. at 744.
18. Pasadena City Board of Education v. Spangler, 427 U.S. 424 (1976) at 443-44.
19. Brown at 493.
20. Hobson v. Hansen, 269 F. Supp. 401 (1967) at 517 aff'd sub nom, Smuck v. Hobson, 408 F. 2d. 175 (1969) (en banc).
21. Id. at 419.
22. Id. at 514.
23. Id. at 496.
24. Id. at 504.
25. Id. at 506.
26. Id. at 514.
27. Id. at 515.
28. Griggs v. Duke Power Co., 401 U.S. 424 (1971) at 431.
29. Washington v. Davis, 426 U.S. 229 (1976) at 238-39.
30. Larry P. v. Riles, 495 F. Supp. 926 (1979) at 983, aff, d (9th Cir. 1984).
31. Parents in Action on Special Education v. Hannon, 506 F. Supp. 831 (1980) at 836-37.
32. Hosier v. Evans, 314 F. Supp. 316 (1970) at 320.
33. Plyler v. Doe, 457 U.S. 202 (1982) at 228.
34. Id. at 230.
35. Id.
36. Martinez v. Bynum, Slip Opinion No. 81-857 (1983) at 7.
37. Id. at 15.
38. Burruss v. Wilkerson, 397 U.S. 44 (1970) at 44.
39. Serrano v. Priest, 487 p. 2d 1241 (1971) at 1263.
40. San Antonio Independent School District v. Rodriguez, 411 U.S. 1 (1973) at 17.
41. Id. at 19.
42. Id. at 35.
43. Id. at 58.
44. De Funis v. Odegaard, 507 P. 2d. 1169 (1971) at 1184.
45. Regents of the University of California v. Bakke, 438 U.S. 265 (1978) at 289-90 and 319-20.
46. Id. at 295-96.
47. Id. at 317-20.
48. Id. at 283-84.

SEVEN

Student Rights to Privacy

FOURTH AMENDMENT RIGHTS OF STUDENTS

The Fourth Amendment to the U.S. Constitution reads: "The rights of the people to be secure in their persons, papers and effects, against unreasonable searches, and seizures, shall not be violated, and no warrants shall issue, but upon probable cause. . . . " The issue of student protection against unreasonable searches and related privacy rights did not emerge until the Fourth Amendment was incorporated as among the rights applying to the relationship between states and the people under the Fourteenth Amendment (*Mapp* v. *Ohio,* 367 U.S. 643 [1961]). This decision, combined with the liberal expansion of rights for minors in such decisions as *Gault* and *Tinker,* opened the area of school search and privacy rights to litigation, fueled by heightened efforts of educators to combat growing student crime and drug abuse.

The Fourth Amendment is based on the English common-law principle that "a man's home is his castle." It was enacted to confer general rights to an expectation of reasonable privacy for people in relation to government and protect people from the unrestrained power of government officials to unfairly obtain and use information and evidence against them.

As this relatively recent area of school litigation developed, state and federal courts devised a variety of standards for the application of the Fourth

Amendment to schools, illustrating contrasting liberal and conservative attitudes. A generally accepted distinction in deciding such cases is whether the educator acted in an official or a private capacity. The conservative tendency is to view the educators' search action as related to private action, thus conferring *in loco parentis* rights, in which the school personnel are acting as parents, unfettered by strict adherence to constitutional standards of "probable cause" for a search, and not requiring the constitutional mandate of obtaining a warrant prior to the search. Liberals, less concerned with maintaining adult authority and more solicitous of protecting student freedom against "big brother" school authorities, tend to see educators conducting school searches as public officials, requiring stricter standards of justification and action. Thus, one area of judicial dispute centers on whether the required search justification is probable cause, or whether it is the more relaxed, easier justified standard of reasonable suspicion, under which a warrant would not be required and where personal privacy is more easily invaded. It is important to note that a legal search occurs when a student is told to reveal what is hidden as well as when he or she is physically searched.

The Reasonable Suspicion and Probable Cause Standards

A 1983 Florida decision provided a clear description of its reasonable suspicion standards in a case in which a teacher searched for and found marijuana in a student's purse on the basis of overhearing another student say that the searched student "had something." According to the Florida District Court of Appeal, a teacher is not justified in searching a student just because the teacher feels "something is wrong." In finding for the student, this liberal decision expounded the following standards for reasonable suspicion: (1) consideration of the student's age, history, and school record; (2) the seriousness of the problem in the school; (3) the need to search without delay and further investigation; (4) the value and reliability of evidence used to justify the search; (5) the educator's experience with the student; and (6) the educator's experience with the type of problem the search involves. The school was found wanting on all of these tests, invalidating its reliance on the reasonable suspicion standard (*A.B.* v. *State,* 440 So. 2d 500 [1983]).

The following general definition of what constitutes probable cause was put forth in a 1931 noneducation case: Probable cause involves reasonable grounds for suspicion, supported by sufficient evidence, to cause a cautious person to believe that the individual is guilty of the offense in question (*Shore* v. *United States,* 49 F. 2d 519 [1931]). This definition is persuasive on other courts as well. Generally, if the school conducts a warrantless search under conditions that would have justified a search warrant, courts will not invalidate the search. When a student, in response to the assistant principal's demand, emptied his pockets, revealing a pipe containing marijuana residue, he was subsequently expelled. He sued, claiming his Fourth Amendment rights were violated. The court decided for the school district, finding that information provided to the assistant principal by another student constituted probable cause. The validity of the search was further strengthened by the absence of police involvement and the slight extent of intrusion; that is, merely being required to empty his pockets (*M.* v. *Board of Educ., Ball-Chatham Dist. No. 5,* 429 F. Supp. 288 [1977]).

The Illinois Supreme Court considered a case in which police were called in to assist school officials in searching a student, whom an anonymous informant had said was carrying a gun in school. The student was searched by the police and a gun was found. The search was conducted without the benefit of a search warrant, leading to a Fourth Amendment challenge. The challenge was strengthened by the involvement of police, which tends to lead courts to incline toward the probable cause standard. However, the Illinois high court found for the school and the police, judging the school administrator to be the appropriate person to weigh the immediate danger presented, as he was responsible for discipline and safety within the school, and he properly availed himself of the police, who did not overstep their role (*In re Boykin,* 237 N.E. 2d 460 [1968]).

A Maryland decision illustrates a more liberal bent than the foregoing decisions. A wristwatch and ten dollars were stolen from a gymnasium locker. The students suffering the loss reported to the assistant principal that they had seen some students hanging around the locker. The administrator searched one of the suspects and found the wristwatch and the money. The Maryland court voided the search because it was not initiated with probable cause to believe the suspect guilty. Mere suspicion is not tantamount to probable cause, which is the required standard when theft—a criminal matter—is involved (*In re Dominic W.,* 426 A. 2d [1981]).

Similarly, when a New York student was convicted of drug dealing, based on evidence secured by school officials acting without a warrant, the conviction was overturned. The educators based their search on observing the student meeting with other students in the same toilet stall. Given the gravity of the result, the court held that the search had not been based on probable cause. Students are protected by the probable cause standard, even if the suspicion occurs in the school and the search is conducted by educators. This is particularly so when the evidence seized is used in subsequent criminal proceedings (*New York* v. *Scott,* 385 NYS 2d 403 [1974]).

In regard to the reasonable suspicion standard, a Florida court found that a teacher did not have reasonable suspicion to search students merely because they acted suspicious when she looked at them (*W.J.S.* v. *State of Florida,* 409 So. 2d 1209 [1982]). In *Jones* v. *Latexo* (1980), a federal court explained what falls beyond the scope of reasonable suspicion justification: "The blanket search or dragnet is, except in the most unusual or compelling circumstances, anathema to the protection afforded citizens under the fourth amendment. The state may not constitutionally use its authority to fish for evidence of wrongdoing."[1] Similarly, another federal court (*Bellnier* v. *Lund,* 438 F. Supp. 47 [1977]) found that even probable cause did not justify an intrusive and blanket search of all members of a fifth-grade class because one class member reported three dollars missing from his coat. All students were indiscriminately searched to their undergarments. The court decided that while there was probable cause that someone in the class had stolen the money, that did not justify such an intrusive, undifferentiated search.

The *In Loco Parentis* Standard

Liberal and conservative jurists struggle over the determination of when the probable cause or reasonable suspicion standard should apply. However, there is some general agreement that when school personnel cooperate with police to obtain evidence for criminal prosecutions, they shed their *in loco parentis* status, and that their actions must be judged according to the stricter probable cause standard. There is also general agreement that the basic issue to be decided is the ultimate question of whether school search-and-seizure action conforms—in the final analysis—to the constitutional injunction that it be reasonable. It is accepted that school authorities have a responsibility to maintain discipline and protect school health and safety, which confers the right to search students, but the nub of controversy becomes whether action pursuant to such responsibilities is "reasonable" or not. Here, the attitudes of liberals wanting to encourage a free school atmosphere conflict with conservative views that good schooling requires effective control of students.

The determination of reasonableness in Fourth Amendment school cases depends upon the circumstances of each case, and balances the duty of school personnel to provide a safe environment, along with the type of danger anticipated, against the privacy right of students as determined by their past conduct, age, sex, or other applicable characteristics. The training and prior knowledge of the educator conducting the search may also be an important factor. Finally, to be reasonable, a search must conform to the schools' accepted educational function and role.

In support of the *in loco parentis* justification for the reasonable suspicion standard, a conservative New York decision (*State* v. *Baccino* [1971]) held: "The *in loco parentis* doctrine is so compelling in light of public necessity and as a social concept antedating the Fourth Amendment, that any action, including a search, taken thereunder upon reasonable suspicion, should be accepted as necessary and reasonable."[2] Support of *in loco parentis* search authority extends outside the school as well as within it. In *New York* v. *Jackson*, 319 N.Y.S. 2d 731 (1971), a school administrator received a tip that student Jackson was carrying illegal drugs in the school. Upon being asked by the administrator to accompany him to the office, Jackson ran out of the school. The administrator pursued him, and caught Jackson with the aid of a policeman assigned to the school. Narcotics paraphernalia were found on Jackson, and the policeman took the evidence for court use. Jackson claimed the evidence was seized unconstitutionally. The court disagreed, relying on the *in loco parentis* doctrine to hold that the responsibility of school officials, as with parents, does not stop at the school door. Jackson's act of running out of the school extended the school's authority to the streets.

The liberal view of *in loco parentis* search authority was provided in *Picha* v. *Wielgos* (1976), which strengthened students' Fourth Amendment rights. Here, on the basis of a telephone tip that certain students possessed illicit drugs, school officials in contact with the police searched the students. No drugs were found. The court ruled that when school personnel search in conjunction with the police, they lose their status as private citizens and become public officials, requiring them to justify a search on the standard of probable cause. This federal judge noted that "the *in loco parentis* authority of a school official cannot transcend constitutional rights."[3]

The Introduction of a U.S. Supreme Court Standard for School Searches

Until 1985, the U.S. Supreme Court had not ruled on school search cases. This changed when the Supreme Court granted certiorari to the New Jersey case of *State in the Interest of T.L.O.* in 1984. It originally involved two cases (*T.L.O.* and *Engerud* v. *State*), which were combined into one by the New Jersey Supreme Court. In the initial *T.L.O.* case, a teacher reported to the assistant principal that a fourteen-year-old student (T.L.O.) was smoking in the school washroom. T.L.O. was confronted with the charge and denied it, whereupon the administrator opened her purse, which she had surrendered at his request, and found cigarettes. Even so, he continued searching the purse and found evidence of marijuana trafficking. The administrator notified the student's home and turned T.L.O. over to the police. This led to her being convicted of delinquency. T.L.O. moved to suppress the evidence used, because she contended it was obtained through an unlawful search. Both the trial court and the appellate court denied the motion to suppress, on the grounds that the vice-principal had reasonable ground for searching the purse to enforce the school's prohibition against smoking. Once this was done, the remaining contents of the purse were plainly exposed and subject to inspection. Evidence of involvement with illegal drugs justified continuation of the search.

The *Engerud* case involved an anonymous tip to a high-school assistant principal that a student (Engerud) was selling illegal drugs in the school. Two administrators opened Engerud's locker and found amphetamine pills and related illegal drug products. Her home and the police were notified, and Engerud was subsequently convicted of unlawful possession of a controlled dangerous substance with intent to distribute it.

Upon appeal, the New Jersey Supreme Court reversed both decisions, holding that they violated the Fourth Amendment rights of the respective students. Regarding T.L.O., it was reasoned that the assistant principal did not have reasonable grounds to search the purse, as carrying cigarettes was not a school violation, nor were there grounds to suspect that T.L.O. was carrying material related to drug trafficking. The court saw the search as motivated by the administrator's "good hunch," and pronounced: "No doubt good hunches would unearth much more evidence of crime on the persons of students and citizens as a whole. But more is required to sustain a search.''[4] As for Engerud, the court found that an anonymous tip, absent of any independent investigation by school officials to corroborate it, was an insufficient basis for justifying the search.

This decision was more liberal than those of most other jurisdictions, as it ignored *in loco parentis* justification and the responsibility imposed on school authorities to promote health and safety. While the criminal proceedings to which both searches led would tend toward stricter court scrutiny of the Fourth Amendment rights of the students, the standards imposed by this court were so liberal that they led the Supreme Court to grant certiorari for review of the *T.L.O.* decision.

In January 1985, the U.S. Supreme Court announced its six-to-three decision in *New Jersey* v. *T.L.O.* While turning aside state claims that school personnel should be exempt from Fourth Amendment standards, the majority reversed the New Jersey Supreme Court's finding that the evidence of drug trafficking was obtained in violation of the Fourth Amendment and required its exclusion as evidence in criminal charges against T.L.O. The Court held that search requirements of warrants and a probable cause standard did not apply to public schools. Instead, the general requirement for schools is that the search simply be "reasonable." According to this standard, the vice-principal's extensive search for evidence of drug trafficking was held permissible. The reasonableness standard requires balancing student privacy interests against the needs of school authorities to maintain order and discipline. The standard for striking the balance is found "when there are reasonable grounds for suspecting that a search will turn up evidence that the student has violated or is violating either the law or the rules of the school."[5] The standard was seen as a good balance between student rights and societal interests because:

> By focusing attention on the question of reasonableness, the standard will spare teachers and school administrators the necessity of schooling themselves in the niceties of probable cause and permit them to regulate their conduct according to the dictates of reason and common sense. At the same time, the reasonableness standard should ensure that the interests of students will be invaded no more than is necessary to achieve the legitimate end of preserving order in the schools.[6]

Two points made in dissent deserve special notice. One was that the vagueness of this balancing test, which amounted to a "conceptual free-for-all," would increase both administrative uncertainty among school personnel and subsequent litigation. The other was a charge of unwarranted conservative activism aimed at strengthening government authority at the expense of individual rights in order to weaken the power to exclude from criminal cases evidence secured unconstitutionally. Noting that the case had not raised the question of whether the search of T.L.O's purse violated the Fourth Amendment, but only whether the exclusionary rule applied to searches by school officials, Justice Stevens remonstrated that "with characteristic disregard of the doctrine of judicial restraint":

> [t]he Court has unnecessarily . . . reached out to decide a constitutional question.
> . . . More importantly, I fear that the concerns that motivated the Court's activism
> have produced a holding that will permit school administrators to search students
> suspected of violating only the most trivial school regulations and guidelines for
> behavior.[7]

Privacy of Personal School Records

Due process has also been invoked as related to privacy protection, as an aspect of personal liberty (*Griswold* v. *Connecticut,* 381 U.S. 479 [1965]). The Fourteenth Amendment concept of privacy and the Fourth Amendment type of privacy were combined in a federal statute named the Family Educational Rights and Privacy Act of 1974 (FERPA). It responded to a problem previously addressed by statutes in over a score of states, which was the unrestricted control of student records often exercised by schools. Court cases illustrated the need for legislation to allow students and parents access to school records, to be aware of information in them, and to challenge suspect entries. The dangers of records that were kept from the scrutiny of their subjects was revealed in cases such as *Dixon* v. *Alabama* (1961) (see Chapter 5), where disciplinary actions against students were attended by inaccurate, damaging entries on student records; and *Mills* v. *Board of Educ.* (1972) (see Chapter 2), where the right of parents to examine their children's records was shown to be required to prevent school abuse of the interests of handicapped children. More directly, in *Van Allen* v. *Mc Cleary* (211 N.Y.S. 2d 501 [1961]), a New York court held that the common-law principle of giving people access to public records in which they have a clear interest required schools to be more open with their records to concerned students and parents. In this case, the parent was told that his son required psychological treatment, but was denied access to evidence supporting that judgment. The court held that no legal authority was needed to establish the obvious interest that parents had in their children's school records.

The Family Rights and Privacy Act, popularly known as the Buckley Amendment, protects the privacy interests of students and their parents in regard to school records—whether grades, psychological assessments, test results, or other types of personal data that may affect the student's future. Students (or parents when the student is under age eighteen) are given the right to inspect and challenge information, and personally identifiable information may not be released without either the student's or the parent's permission. Violators of the Act risk loss of federal funding.

This statutory extension of privacy rights has been combined with expanded Fourth Amendment concerns that respond to intensified school search activity designed to combat violence, drug abuse, and other forms of crime in the school to enlarge the scope of privacy litigation. Most prominent have been the adjudication of school uses of smell-sensitive sniffing dogs and strip searches to uncover concealed illegal drugs in the school, as well as the more traditional issue of school locker searches. These legal controversies balance the responsibilities of educators to maintain discipline, health, and safety standards of the school against the constitutional and statutory protections of students for a reasonable degree of privacy and unwarranted invasion of their persons and belongings.

Principles Governing Student Privacy

1. The school's interest in conducting a search is weighed against the student's right to privacy under the Fourth Amendment's prohibition against unreasonable search and seizure.
2. The intrusiveness of the type of search used is balanced against the severity of the problem it is designed to combat, as well as matters of student age, sex, and physical and emotional condition. For example, strip searches require strong justification.
3. Courts have generally distinguished between whether a search requires probable cause (suspicion of wrongdoing backed by evidence sufficient to convince a cautious person that the individual is likely to be guilty) or reasonable suspicion (good knowledge of the student and the nature of the transgression and a reasonable anticipation of uncovering evidence). Courts tended to apply the easier reasonable suspicion standard to school personnel, except where the educator was acting as a public official rather than a private person covered by *in loco parentis* standing. The stricter standard would also be applied when school personnel acted in concert with the police or when search evidence would be used in criminal proceedings. These rules have been altered by the *T.L.O.* decision, which allows school authorities to set aside the complexities of deciding between probable cause and reasonable suspicion in favor of a standard based upon "reason and common sense." While schools' authority to search has clearly been strengthened, the vagueness of the standard leaves its translation into school policy unclear.
4. Mass searches and other forms of undifferentiated search will generally be invalidated, unless justified by compelling interests of health or safety.
5. The Family Rights and Privacy Act provides that students and their parents (for students under eighteen) have privacy rights giving them access to their records, restricting the access to others without their permission, and giving them the right to challenge information contained in school records.

CONFLICTS OVER SHARED CONTROL OF SCHOOL RECORDS

Where is the balance between individual rights to privacy of records and the public's need for knowledge contained in personal school records? Where should the balance rest between the competing interests of the school and the student/parent for control of school records?

The purpose of the Family Rights and Privacy Act was to protect students against abuses of their welfare caused by the school's unrestricted control of student records. However, one immediate policy problem encountered was that teachers were hesitant to provide honest letters of assessment to prospective higher-education institutions or employers. The Act addressed this problem by allowing students to waive the right to see the particular letters for which waivers were given. This issue was anticipated by FERPA, but it remained for the courts to decide a number of other questions about how the Act applied to the balance between student/parent rights and school interests. A New York court considered whether FERPA required the public schools to release names of bilingual students with English deficiencies. The complainants held that this was required under the Act, while the school held the opposite view, that the Act forbids release of the names without the consent of the parents of all affected students. Only some of them were represented in the complaining group. The court ruled that the information could be released because the complainants had demonstrated a genuine need for the information, which "outweighs the privacy interests of the student." This court saw FERPA as not allowing an absolute privacy privilege when an overriding public interest was served that did not result in obvious harm to affected students (*Rios* v. *Read,* 73 F.R.D. 589 [1977]).

Three years later, another New York court considered the request of a parent for release of all third-grade test scores so that he could compare his child's performance with that of his classmates. In this case, the state's Freedom of Information Act was counterposed against the Buckley Amendment. The court reasoned that both the privacy of records demanded by FERPA and disclosure of public information required by freedom-of-information legislation could be served by publication of student test results not identified by name (*Kryston* v. *Board of Education, East Rampano,* 77 A.D. 2d. 896 [1980]).

What if a grand jury requests student records? A federal court confronted this issue and decided that the records could only be withheld if the student could show that they bore no relevance to the subject under investigation. The student was not able to sustain this burden, and his records were ordered released (*Frasca* v. *Andrews,* 463 F. Supp. 1043 [1979]).

Another apparent conflict between FERPA and competing privacy legislation occurred in North Carolina, where a university faculty contended that its meetings must be exempt from the requirements of Open Meetings legislation, because they included discussion of student records, which must be kept restricted by FERPA. The court held that FERPA did not negate open meetings, but required that disclosure of personal information about students be handled with care, as an injudicious release of personal information about students could run afoul of FERPA (*Student Bar Association Board of Governors* v. *Byrd,* 239 S.E. 2d. 415 [1977]).

A different focus on FERPA was provided in a case where a student claimed the Act required a college to release certified copies of his record even though he owed the college money. A federal court ruled that the Act only required that the records be open to his inspection. It did not require that his records be released to outside parties (*Girardier* v. *Webster College,* 563 F. 2d 1267 [1977]).

In interpreting FERPA, courts attempt to balance the institutional needs for control of records with the public's right to know and personal-privacy rights. In the process, the main intent of the law, to prevent the inclusion of unsubstantiated, personally derogatory information being placed in student records, appears to have been well-served. When parents are apprised of FERPA, the objective of allowing for fuller parental awareness and understanding of the school's procedures is also served. It is interesting to see how the Act has been used to combat Freedom of Information requirements and other types of policies. Courts resolve these questions by focusing on the intent of the legislation and the effects of particular actions on legitimate school, private, and public interests.

PRIVACY OF SCHOOL LOCKERS

Is the student's expectation of privacy in his or her school locker sufficiently strong to prevent unwarranted locker searches? If not, is there at least a sufficient expectation of privacy to prevent searches when school officials have no clear suspicion that students are concealing contraband? Does the judicial standard applied differ when police are involved in a locker search?

In *Katz* v. *U.S.* (1967), the Supreme Court emphasized that "the Fourth Amendment protects people, not places."[8] The point was that people have Fourth Amendment protection in places or things where they have an expectation of privacy. They do not have to establish ownership to be so protected. Thus, privacy rights in telephone booths and automobiles have been held to fall under the Fourth Amendment's protection. Yet, when it comes to school lockers, which are not owned by students, but are assigned to them by the school, courts have generally not considered them a sanctuary for student privacy.

In *People* v. *Overton* (1967), police showed a warrant to the vice-principal, who allowed them to search Overton's locker, wherein four marijuana cigarettes were found. Overton sued to invalidate the search on the grounds that the search warrant was defective, but the defendants claimed that even if that was so, school authorities had the right to grant permission to search Overton's locker. The lower New York court held that the vice-principal's consent could not justify an otherwise illegal search, but the higher court overruled. It held that, while lockers were protected from unreasonable searches, school officials did not require presentation of a warrant to allow a locker search. Their power to search lockers upon their discretion was based both on their *in loco parentis* relationship to students and on their basic control over school lockers. School regulations were cited in defense of the school's right to unrestricted locker searches:

> The students at Mount Vernon are well aware that the school authorities possess the combinations of their lockers. It appears understood that the lock and combination are provided in order that each student may have exclusive possession of the locker vis-a-vis other students but the student does not have such exclusivity . . . as against the school authorities. In fact, the school issues regulations regarding what may and what may not be kept in the lockers and presumably can spot check to insure compliance.[9]

The court then, in a conservative, activist mode, went on to express its unsolicited opinion about the obligations of school officials in regard to locker searches:

> Indeed, it is doubtful if a school would be properly discharging its duty of supervision over the students, if it failed to retain control over the lockers. Not only have the school authorities a right to inspect, but this right becomes a duty when suspicion arises that something of an illegal nature may be secreted there. When Dr. Panitz learned of the detectives' suspicion, he was obligated to inspect the locker. This interest, together with the nonexclusive nature of the locker, empowered him to consent to the search by the officers.[10]

Upon a rehearing justified by a nonschool U.S. Supreme Court decision on Fourth Amendment rights (*Bumper* v. *North Carolina,* 391 U.S. 543 [1968]), the New York Appellate Court reaffirmed its decision, with one judge dissenting. The dissent held that the search warrant was bad, and the principal was coerced into opening the locker. "The result is unlawful even though the principal gave his 'consent' to the search and had a general authority in the school premises."[11]

Subsequent to the *Overton* decision, the Supreme Court of Kansas agreed that a school locker, unlike a car, house, or a private locker, does not afford a student the exclusive possession that would trigger Fourth Amendment protection. This judgment in *State* v. *Stein* (1969) did imply that the ruling pertained to searches initiated by school personnel having reasonable suspicion. Thus it did not go as far as *Overton* in making school officials obligated to cooperate with police. However, its basic agreement with *Overton* regarding the school's right to virtually unrestricted searches of student lockers is made clear in the following passage from the decision:

> Although a student may have control of his locker as against fellow students, his possession is not exclusive against the school and its officials. A school does not supply its students with lockers for illicit use in harboring pilfered property or harmful substances. We deem it a proper function of school authorities to inspect the lockers under their control to prevent their use in illicit ways or for illegal purposes. We believe this right of inspection is inherent in the authority vested in school administrators and that the same must be retained and exercised in the management of our schools if their educational functions are to be maintained and the welfare of the student bodies preserved.[12]

While the law seems settled regarding the lack of Fourth Amendment protection for school locker searches by school personnel, such searches must at least conform to the minimum standards of reasonableness. For example, in a Louisiana case, the Fourth Amendment was extended to locker searches. A teacher seized a boy's wallet that had been locked in safekeeping during gym class. The reason for the search was that the teacher thought that the boy looked suspicious. Even though the wallet proved to contain narcotics, the evidence was excluded because the search was deemed illegal (*State* v. *Mora,* 330 So. 2d 900 [1976]). The clearest inhibition to unrestricted school locker search is that police may not initiate such a search without a warrant or cause. However, when school personnel initiate the search, particularly when acting as private citizens rather than school officials, the courts will tend to support most justifications for locker searches.

DEFINING THE LIMITS OF SCHOOL SEARCHES:
THE USE OF STRIP SEARCHES AND SNIFFING DOGS

How far can school authorities go in devising methods to ferret out student contraband carried into the school? How strong must the cause of search be to justify the embarrassment of a strip search? What of the use of smell-sensitive dogs to discover students hiding drugs on their person? Does that represent an unwarranted intrusion of the basic rights to personal privacy in the school? What level of justification does a school need to use such extreme search techniques?

The judicial principle that the extent and severity of official action must be justified by the corresponding seriousness of the problem being combatted has been applied to the use of sniffing dogs in the classroom and conducting student-strip searches. Unlike locker searches and searches of student clothing, these devices have been viewed with greater scrutiny by the courts than traditional search cases in regard to balancing the need for such devices against the problem encountered and the age, sex, and other characteristics of the students involved.

An Indiana case (*Doe* v. *Renfrow* [1979]) combined the uses of sniffing dogs and strip searches. Joint police-school planning resulted in the unannounced introduction of dogs trained to smell drugs into junior- and senior-high-school classrooms to combat school drug abuse. While concealed drugs were found on the persons, pockets, or desks of several students to whom the dogs alerted authorities, no drugs were found on the persons or effects of others identified by the dogs. Miss Doe was in this latter group. She was strip-searched, but still no contraband was uncovered. It was subsequently noted that in the morning, Doe had played with her dog, which was in heat. Her parents sued, claiming that her Fourth Amendment rights were violated, both by the use of sniffing dogs and by the strip search.

The decision of the federal district court, subsequently approved by the appellate court, was that the use of sniffing dogs did not violate the Fourth

Amendment. The court reached this conclusion by first noting that school drug abuse was a recognized problem at the school. Also considered important was the prior agreement between the school and police that evidence obtained by the use of the dogs would not be used in criminal prosecutions, but only for school-discipline purposes. The court decided that the use of uniformed police and the dogs was not unconstitutional. In particular, claims against the use of the dogs were set aside. The dogs were simply aiding the staff and the police by sniffing the air (which is not protected by the Fourth Amendment) to detect drugs. Further, the court believed that "students did not have a justifiable expectation of privacy that would preclude a school administrator from sniffing the air . . . with the aid of a trained drug-detecting canine . . . Any expectation of privacy necessarily diminishes in light of a student's constant supervision while in school."[13]

As for the standard to be applied, even if this would have been considered a search, the court believed that only a "reasonable cause to believe" was necessary. "School officials fulfilling their state empowered duties will not be held to the same standards as law enforcement officials when determining if the use of canines is necessary . . . This lesser standard applies only when the purpose of the dog's use is to fulfill the school's duty to provide a safe, ordered and healthy educational environment."[14] Concerning pocket searches, the court saw probable cause as the proper standard, but this problem was solved by judicial reasoning that the Fourth Amendment standard was modified by the school's *in loco parentis* standing, as the object of the search was discipline and health, not criminal prosecution. Further, the pocket search was made upon reasonable cause provided by the dog's alert, thus making it constitutional.

The court's support of the school ended when the issue of the strip search was considered. Here the court concluded that strip-searching a thirteen-year-old girl, solely upon evidence provided by an alerting dog, was not warranted even under the more easily justified "reasonable cause to believe" standard. This action was "an intrusion into an individual's basic justifiable expectation of privacy. Before such a search can be performed, the school administrators must articulate some facts that provide a reasonable cause to believe the student possesses the contraband sought. . . . The alert of the dog alone does not provide the necessary reasonable cause. . . . "[15]

The appellate court modified the decision only to the extent that it reversed the trial court's finding that the school district was not liable for damages stemming from the strip search. While the Supreme Court refused to grant certiorari, it did so only over the vigorous objections of the liberal Justice Brennan, who believed that the use of unannounced, dragnet canine searches violated the Fourth Amendment rights of the students involved. For Brennan, the use of dogs did constitute a search, and the search violated the Fourth Amendment.

Three years later, another federal search case involving sniffing dogs was decided from the liberal viewpoint (*Horton* v. *Goose Creek Independent School District* [1982]). A Texas district had used sniffing dogs for several years to discover hidden drugs by smelling students, their lockers, and their cars. Parents sued, claiming the practice violated the Fourth Amendment rights of their children. Here, a different federal appellate court reversed a district court finding consistent with *Doe* and found the dragnet use of sniffing dogs to violate the Fourth Amendment. The decision cited with approval a lower court ruling in its circuit (*Jones* v. *Latexo,* cited earlier). In that case, a federal court found that the absence of individualized suspicion, the use of large and fearsome animals, and the intrusiveness of the search combined to render the use of sniffing dogs unreasonable. That decision, and the invalidation of dragnet sniffing in California (*People* v. *Mayberry,* 172 Cal. Rptr. 629 [1981]), lent support to the liberal decision in *Horton.*

As to whether the dogs sniffing the air constituted a search, the court concluded that it did, particularly when dogs sniffed students. "The students' persons certainly are not the subject of lowered expectation of privacy. On the contrary . . . the Fourth Amendment applies with its fullest vigor against any indecent or indelicate intrusion on the human body."[16] When such intrusions occur as part of dragnet searches, without direct suspicion of particular individuals, the Fourth Amendment must bear even more heavily in the matter. "When there is *no* reason to believe that a search will produce evidence of crime . . . the Constitution does not tolerate intrusions on protected privacy"[17] even in the form of "limited searches." School administrators involved in these searches were clearly seen as government officials, requiring at least a minimal standard of reasonableness to justify canine sniff searches. In this case there was "too great an intrusion on the privacy of the students to be justified by the need to prevent abuse of drugs and alcohol when there is no individualized suspicion, and we hold it unconstitutional."[18]

While the undifferentiated sniffing of persons by dogs, without reasonable suspicion, was declared violative of the Fourth Amendment, the same was not true for the sniffing of lockers and cars, which, because of the lesser Fourth Amendment standards applied in the light of school-discipline and safety needs, was permissible. This was especially so because of the minimal intrusion of locker and car sniffing. Even here, however, the appellate court remanded the case to the district court to determine the reliability of dog alerts. The dogs must be reasonably reliable, and if so, only minimal justification of reasonableness was needed. As with *Doe,* the Supreme Court refused review of *Horton,* thus allowing the two contradictory decisions to stand as controlling precedents in their respective districts.

Two 1983 cases decided subsequent to the holding of the unconstitutionality of the strip search in *Doe* have found such searches justified by the particular facts presented. In *Tartar* v. *Raybuck* (556 F. Supp. 625 [1983]), administrators concealed themselves and observed Tartar dealing marijuana cigarettes in the school. When confronted, Tartar denied the charge and was searched, revealing no marijuana. He was then requested to drop his trousers, but refused to do so. His parents arrived, and he left with them. He was subsequently expelled from high school, whereupon he filed a Fourth Amendment complaint. The court found that a strip search would have been reasonable in this case, given the evidence motivating the attempt at strip searching.

In a Kentucky case, a fifteen-year-old boy confessed to smoking marijuana, but claimed to have none in his possession. School administrators nevertheless insisted on strip-searching him to obtain additional evidence. The subsequent Fourth Amendment suit was decided in favor of the school, on the basis of the school's *in loco parentis* standing as well as the existence of reasonable suspicion in the instant situation (*Rone* v. *Daviess County Board of Education,* 655 S.W. 2d. 28 [1983]). The Kentucky court did not see the need to have strip searches justified by either the "extreme emergency" or probable cause standards that courts usually apply in such cases. Yet, the following year, a U.S. appellate court in Oregon found that when a fifth-grader was strip-searched because a school bus driver had seen him exchange packages with another student, his Fourth Amendment rights were violated. The driver had suspected that the exchange was drug-related. In fact, the students had exchanged bubble gum. Neither the bus driver nor the principal who conducted the strip search was entitled to "good faith" immunity, as neither reasonable suspicion nor probable cause existed to justify the search (*Bilbrey* v. *Brown,* 738 F. 2d 1462 [1984]).

Conservative and liberal interpretations of what constitutes a search continue to vacillate in this unsettled area. Equally troublesome is determining how the school's *in loco parentis* standing, or the official or private action of a school administrator, should affect the standard of reasonableness of cause needed to justify strip searches and/or the use of sniffing dogs.

POLICY CONSIDERATIONS

The U.S. Supreme Court's first decision regarding student Fourth Amendment rights in *T.L.O.* has shifted the balance between government authority and student-privacy rights in favor of school authority. However, in doing so, the High Court made clear that school officials must act within the confines of the Fourth Amendment, even in light of their *in loco parentis* status. In the words of the decision: "In carrying out searches . . . school officials act as representatives of the state . . . and they cannot claim the parents' immunity from the strictures of the Fourth Amendment."[19] Therefore, while school officials may find comfort in the relaxed "reason and common sense" standard articulated by the Court, they have not been provided with unlimited discretion or license in conducting student searches. The balancing test still applies to the area of student privacy.

Nothing in *T.L.O.* suggests that limitations of schools' search authority announced in *Doe* or *Horton* regarding strip searches or dragnet searching has been overturned. However, the decision does suggest that justifications for such activities would be judged by more relaxed standards by the present Supreme Court, and consequently the same way by lower federal and state courts. The almost complete exemption for obtaining search warrants granted to school officials by the *T.L.O.* decision ("The warrant requirement in particular, is unsuited to the school environment"[20]) further adds to the strengthened schools' search authority. Along with traditional support of strong school authority to search school lockers, the balancing test, while still applicable, is strongly weighted in favor of school officials.

School personnel are thus given greater authority, but also greater responsibility. Historic distinctions drawn by American courts between probable cause and reasonable suspicion cannot be entirely dismissed in regard to school searches. Courts will not entirely set aside these concepts when judging whether or not school actions conform to "reason and common sense." Even in that strongest area of schools' search authority, the school locker, reason and common sense would stand as a bar to school officials invading even that relatively defenseless sanctuary without some adequate reason as noted earlier in *State* v. *Mora.* Courts consider the conditions that stimulate search actions, and where school crime, drug abuse, and the like are problems, searches are justified. But when such justifications are not present, it is unlikely that courts would approve searches. The Florida *A.B.* v. *State* decision (discussed earlier in the chapter), which invalidated a student search based merely on vague suspicion that something was wrong, still stands as good law. Similarly, when school officials act in concert with police in order to obtain evidence for criminal proceedings, "reason and common sense" would dictate judicial distinctions between probable cause and reasonable suspicion. Finally, considerations of student age, sex, and emotional condition are still directly applicable as inhibitions to searches that must be justified by reason and common sense. The reason and common sense applicable to strip-searching a thirteen-year-old girl is not a casual matter.

The Supreme Court has invested school officials with greater latitude for making judgments in the area of the Fourth Amendment. It remains to be seen how well that judgment will be exercised. If educators conduct themselves in ways that show a balanced concern for accepted concepts of privacy that should be afforded students when weighed against the school's need for information, the views of the Court will be vindicated. The danger is that educators will see this broad, vague loosening of official restraint against searching students as license to make extensive intrusions based on the merest justifications. If this occurs, the historical record suggests that the Court will limit schools' search authority by providing stricter, clear guidelines.

In charting its course through this constitutional area, the school establishment is well advised to observe how the rights of students and teachers usually operate in tandem. There is a tendency for educators to see the wisdom and necessity of strong court support of their civil rights, but they do not see a need for corresponding support of students' civil rights.[21] Courts have not made such sharp distinctions of liberalism toward teachers' rights simultaneously with conservatism toward students' rights. Thus, evidence of a need for judicial conservative activism or restraint or liberal activism or restraint will be generally applied to all elements of the school community, Justice Black's distinctions drawn between the status of students and teachers in his *Tinker* dissent notwith-standing.

The tensions between notions of students' and teachers' rights and search authority expressed in *T.L.O., Doe, Overton,* and *Horton* are not the only strains in the area of privacy. There are also the inherent strains and contradictions between freedom-of-information laws and privacy-rights legislation. Which is more important—the right of the public for information about public-school operations or the right of individuals to control access of others to information about themselves? The answer, of course, is that both considerations are important, and administrative policy must balance one against the other in carrying out its responsibilities. Solutions such as arrived at in *Kryston* (discussed in this chapter), in which general student information is released without identifying each student, is one way to resolve this issue. Other situations may not lend themselves to such clear disposition. Values and attitudes of educators and jurists will then decide the resolution.

As with other areas of constitutional rights applied to education, privacy rights in the school demand that educators apply the classic balancing test between rights and protection of the individual against the needs and interests of government. Current views about the need for stronger control over students in light of school problems of violence, drug abuse, and similar issues have led to judicial strengthening of educators' search authority. This authority must be exercised with care and consideration for the interests and rights of students.

Picha v. Wielgos
410 F. Supp. 1214 (1976)

It is undisputed in the testimony given at trial that the defendant school principal, Raymond Wielgos, received a phone call which led him to suspect that the thirteen year old plaintiff and two other girls in his school possessed illegal drugs. The principal was advised by his superintendent to call the police, which he did. When the police arrived each of the girls was separately searched by the school nurse and the school psychologist in order to establish whether any of the three students possessed drugs. No drugs were found. A conflict in the testimony exists as to what the plaintiff's state of undress was at each particular point of the search, and as to the duration of the search. The plaintiff, Renee Picha, brought this suit against the three school officials and the two policemen on the theory that in the course of the incident the defendants violated her civil rights.

On the basis of the foregoing discussion, it is evident that the *in loco parentis* authority of a school official cannot transcend constitutional rights. However, the student-teacher relationship out of which such statutory or common law authority readily flows does have an impact on the application of constitutional doctrine to the rights of students.

As its constitutional maximum, an *in loco parentis* statute merely codifies a substantial state interest against which constitutional rights must be balanced. There are no reported cases discovered or suggested by counsel in this case which show a civil rights action for damages arising from a search conducted by a school principal. However, there is a considerable body of case law, mostly state court, discussing what Fourth Amendment protection is required for a student when he or his possessions are searched by a school official. The official may be acting alone, or in conjunction with law enforcement officials.

At the time of the search of Renee Picha, the Fourth Amendment to the Constitution was in effect. It was clear, in view of the cases earlier discussed, that students in public schools were not relieved of the protection of that amendment except to the extent that a compelling state interest in the maintenance of school activities, particularly discipline, required. It was clear, from the cases that searches motivated by something other than the prospect of obtaining evidence of crime were subject to the general Fourth Amendment standard of reasonableness, and that where the interest in making the search competed with the privacy interest of the individual, the scope of the search had to be appropriately limited, in order to be constitutionally permissible.

Although not explicitly articulating the parameters of reasonableness in this situation, the Illinois Supreme Court, in *In Re Boykin* (1968) applied the reasonableness standard to a search conducted by police in the course of an appraisal of danger by the school principal. This court thus concludes that the settled law indicated that as a minimum, Renee Picha could not be subject to an intrusion of her privacy unless that intrusion was reasonably justified in terms of the school's legitimate interests, which are set forth in the statutory codification of *in loco parentis*. Those interests are the ones which the officials are vested with *in loco parentis* authority to carry out, namely matters relating to discipline, safety, supervision, and activities connection with school programs. This standard is consistent with and required by the one set in *In Re Boykin, supra.* It is also consistent with the thrust of most state and federal decisions that have considered searches carried out jointly by police and school officials.

School officials cannot claim immunity when they violate the well settled rights of their students. The court recognizes the novelty of the fact situation, both from a legal standpoint, and from the experimental standpoint of the school officials. However, no case can be found contradicting the notion that when a government official works with the police to conduct a search which is, at least in part, in the nature of a criminal investigation, and which occasions such an invasion of privacy as in the present case, that search is subject to the reasonableness of the Fourth Amendment.

The court now considers the standard, under the facts presented at trial, to which police must adhere to protect the rights of a student under the Fourth Amendment. From the very beginning of this episode, when the principal of the school received information as to the possible presence of drugs, there was police involvement. Indeed, although the school officials continued to act under the color of their statutory school authority, the matter became at least partly a quest for illegal items. As far as the police are concerned, such an investigation cannot come under the ambit of the state interest that dwells under the banner of "*in loco parentis.*" Although the school may have an interest in the safety of its charges, either with regard to one student possessing drugs, or with regard to the possibility that that student would transfer possession of drugs to another student, all it can do in furtherance of that interest is to locate and perhaps confiscate the drugs. In the course of such a procedure, evidence may be acquired which may ultimately be considered to have been reasonably obtained and therefore usable in a criminal prosecution or in an adjudication of delinquency. However, the evidence here could not support a jury finding that the police were called merely in furtherance of this interest. Consequently, the substantial state interest in the provision of education and the maintenance of school discipline cannot be here said to temper the application of the Constitution to a search caused by police for evidence of crime. Moreover, whatever may be the consent to the discretion of the school officials deemed constructively made by parent or student, it cannot vitiate the constitutional expectation of privacy which creates the need for levels of suspicion and/or exigency in the conduct of a criminal investigation.

The nature of the intrusion occasioned by a search, in this case, is such that it can only be accomplished by a detention of the person. It is not a mere pat-down, but requires as total, if brief, a seizure of the person as possible. Given the responsibility of the police to find evidence of crime, in this case, the standard of probable cause for an actual arrest must be met to justify the search under the Fourth Amendment. Therefore, the jury must be instructed that a civil rights violation may occur if the police proximately caused Renee Picha to be searched without their having probable cause to believe she was then breaking the law by possessing an illegal substance on her person.

Conclusion

The law was settled, that when Renee Picha was searched, that she had a constitutional right not to be searched by school officials who were in contact with the police unless the extent of the intrusion occasioned by the search was justified in terms of the state interest of maintaining the order, discipline, safety, supervision, and education of the students within the school. This court further holds that in the circumstances of this case, Renee Picha had a constitutional right not to have the police cause a search in the absence of probable cause that she possessed an illegal material at the time of the search.

New Jersey v. T.L.O.
83–712 (1985) U.S. Supreme Court

MR. JUSTICE WHITE delivered the opinion of the court.

*   *   *   *   *

In determining whether the search at issue in this case violated the Fourth Amendment, we are faced initially with the question whether that Amendment's prohibition on unreasonable searches and seizures applies to searches conducted by public school officials. We hold that it does.

It is now beyond dispute that "the Federal Constitution, by virtue of the

Fourteenth Amendment, prohibits unreasonable searches and seizures by state officers.'' Equally indisputable is the proposition that the Fourteenth Amendment protects the rights of students against encroachment by public school officials.

These two propositions—that the Fourth Amendment applies to the States through the Fourteenth Amendment, and that the actions of public school officials are subject to the limits placed on state action by the Fourteenth Amendment—might appear sufficient to answer the suggestion that the Fourth Amendment does not proscribe unreasonable searches by school officials. On reargument, however, the State of New Jersey has argued that the history of the Fourth Amendment indicates that the Amendment was intended to regulate only searches and seizures carried out by law enforcement officers; accordingly, although public school officials are concededly state agents for purposes of the Fourteenth Amendment, the Fourth Amendment creates no rights enforceable against them.

Notwithstanding the general applicability of the Fourth Amendment to the activities of civil authorities, a few courts have concluded that school officials are exempt from the dictates of the Fourth Amendment by virtue of the special nature of their authority over schoolchildren. Teachers and school administrators, it is said, act *in loco parentis* in their dealings with students: their authority is that of the parent, not the State, and is therefore not subject to the limits of the Fourth Amendment.

Such reasoning is in tension with contemporary reality and the teachings of this Court. We have held school officials subject to the commands of the First Amendment and the Due Process Clause of the Fourteenth Amendment. If school authorities are state actors for purposes of the constitutional guarantees of freedom of expression and due process, it is difficult to understand why they should be deemed to be exercising parental rather than public authority when conducting searches of their students. More generally, the Court has recognized that ''the concept of parental delegation'' as a source of school authority is not entirely ''consonant with compulsory education laws.'' Today's public school officials do not merely exercise authority voluntarily conferred on them by individual parents; rather, they act in furtherance of publicly mandated educational and disciplinary policies. In carrying out searches and other disciplinary functions pursuant to such policies, school officials act as representatives of the State, not merely as surrogates for the parents, and they cannot claim the parents' immunity from the strictures of the Fourth Amendment.

III

To hold that the Fourth Amendment applies to searches conducted by authorities is only to begin the inquiry into the standards governing such searches. Although the underlying command of the Fourth Amendment is always that searches and seizures be reasonable, what is reasonable depends on the context within which a search takes place. The determination of the standard of reasonableness governing any specific class of searches requires ''balancing the need to search against the invasion which the search entails.'' On one side of the balance are arrayed the individual's legitimate expectations of privacy and personal security; on the other, the government's need for effective methods to deal with breaches of public order.

To receive the protection of the Fourth Amendment, an expectation of privacy must be one that society is "prepared to recognize as legitimate." The State of New Jersey has argued that because of the pervasive supervision to which children in the schools are necessarily subject, a child has virtually no legitimate expectation of privacy in articles of personal property "unnecessarily" carried into a school. This argument has two factual premises: (1) the fundamental incompatibility of expectations of privacy with the maintenance of a sound educational environment; and (2) the minimal interest of the child in bringing any items of personal property into the school. Both premises are severely flawed.

Students at a minimum must bring to school not only the supplies needed for their studies, but also keys, money, and the necessaries of personal hygiene and grooming. In addition, students may carry on their persons or in purses or wallets such nondisruptive yet highly personal items as photographs, letters, and diaries. Finally, students may have perfectly legitimate reasons to carry with them articles of property needed in connection with extracurricular or recreational activities. In short, schoolchildren may find it necessary to carry with them a variety of legitimate, noncontraband items, and there is no reason to conclude that they have necessarily waived all rights to privacy in such items merely by bringing them onto school grounds.

Against the child's interest in privacy must be set the substantial interest of teachers and administrators in maintaining discipline in the classroom and on school grounds. Maintaining order in the classroom has never been easy, but in recent years, school disorder has often taken particularly ugly forms: drug use and violent crime in the schools have become major social problems. Even in schools that have been spared the most severe disciplinary problems, the preservation of order and a proper educational environment requires close supervision of schoolchildren, as well as the enforcement of rules against conduct that would be perfectly permissible if undertaken by an adult. Accordingly, we have recognized that maintaining security and order in the schools requires a certain degree of flexibility in school disciplinary procedures, and we have respected the value of preserving the informality of the student-teacher relationship.

How, then, should we strike the balance between the schoolchild's legitimate expectations of privacy and the school's equally legitimate need to maintain an environment in which learning can take place? It is evident that the school setting requires some easing of the restrictions to which searches by public authorities are ordinarily subject. The warrant requirement, in particular, is unsuited to the school environment: requiring a teacher to obtain a warrant before searching a child suspected of an infraction of school rules (or of the criminal law) would unduly interfere with the maintenance of the swift and informal disciplinary procedures needed in the schools. Just as we have in other cases dispensed with the warrant requirement when "the burden of obtaining a warrant is likely to frustrate the governmental purpose behind the search," we hold today that school officials need not obtain a warrant before searching a student who is under their authority.

The school setting also requires some modification of the level of suspicion of illicit activity needed to justify a search. Ordinarily, a search—even one that may permissibly be carried out without a warrant—must be based upon "probable cause" to believe that a violation of the law has occurred. However, "probable cause" is not an irreducible requirement of a valid search. The fundamental command of the Fourth Amendment is that searches and seizures be reasonable, and although "both the concept of probable cause and the requirement of a warrant bear on the reasonableness of a search, . . . in certain limited circumstances neither is required." Where a careful balancing of governmental and private interests suggests that the public interest is best served by a Fourth Amendment standard of reasonableness that stops short of probable cause, we have not hesitated to adopt such a standard.

We join the majority of courts that have examined this issue in concluding that the accommodation of the privacy interests of schoolchildren with the substantial need of teachers and administrators for freedom to maintain order in the schools does not require strict adherence to the requirement that searches be based on probable cause to believe that the subject of the search has violated or is violating the law. Rather, the legality of a search of a student should depend simply on the reasonableness, under all the circumstances, of the search. Determining the reasonableness of any search involves a twofold inquiry: first, one must consider "whether the . . . action was justified at its inception"; second, one must determine whether the search as actually conducted "was reasonably related in scope to the circumstances which justified the interference in the first place." Under ordinary circumstances, a search of a student by a teacher or other school official* will be "justified at its inception" when there are reasonable grounds for suspecting that the search will turn up evidence that the student has violated or is violating either the law or the rules of the school. Such a search will be permissible in its scope when the measures adopted are reasonably related to the objectives of the search and not excessively intrusive in light of the age and sex of the student and the nature of the infraction.

This standard will, we trust, neither unduly burden the efforts of school authorities to maintain order in their schools nor authorize unrestrained intrusions upon the privacy of schoolchildren. By focusing attention on the question of reasonableness, the standard will spare teachers and school administrators the necessity of schooling themselves in the niceties of probable cause and permit them to regulate their conduct according to the dictates of reason and common sense. At the same time, the reasonableness standard should ensure that the interests of students will be invaded no more than is necessary to achieve the legitimate end of preserving order in the schools.

IV

There remains the question of the legality of the search in this case. We recognize that the "reasonable grounds" standard applied by the New Jersey Supreme Court in its consideration of this question is not substantially different

---

*We here consider only searches carried out by school authorities acting alone and on their own authority. This case does not present the question of the appropriate standard for assessing the legality of searches conducted by school officials in conjunction with or at the behest of law enforcement agencies, and we express no opinion on that question.

from the standard that we have adopted today. Nonetheless, we believe that the New Jersey court's application of that standard to strike down the search of T.L.O.'s purse reflects a somewhat crabbed notion of reasonableness. Our review of the facts surrounding the search leads us to conclude that the search was in no sense unreasonable for Fourth Amendment purposes.

The incident that gave rise to this case actually involved two separate searches, with the first—the search for cigarettes—providing the suspicion that gave rise to the second—the search for marijuana. Although it is the fruits of the second search that are at issue here, the validity of the search for marihuana must depend on the reasonableness of the initial search for cigarettes, as there would have been no reason to suspect that T.L.O. possessed marihuana had the first search not taken place. Accordingly, it is to the search for cigarettes that we first turn our attention.

The New Jersey Supreme Court pointed to two grounds for its holding that the search for cigarettes was unreasonable. First, the court observed that possession of cigarettes was not in itself illegal or a violation of school rules. Because the contents of T.L.O.'s purse would therefore have "no direct bearing on the infraction" of which she was accused (smoking in a lavatory where smoking was prohibited), there was no reason to search her purse. Second, even assuming that a search of T.L.O.'s purse might under some circumstances be reasonable in light of the accusation made against T.L.O., the New Jersey court concluded that Mr. Choplick in this particular case had no reasonable grounds to suspect that T.L.O. had cigarettes in her purse. At best, according to the court, Mr. Choplick had "a good hunch."

Both these conclusions are implausible.

Because the hypothesis that T.L.O. was carrying cigarettes in her purse was itself not unreasonable, it is irrelevant that other hypotheses were also consistent with the teacher's accusation. Accordingly, it cannot be said that Mr. Choplick acted unreasonably when he examined T.L.O.'s purse to see if it contained cigarettes.

Our conclusion that Mr. Choplick's decision to open T.L.O.'s purse was reasonable brings us to the question of the further search for marihuana once the pack of cigarettes was located. The suspicion upon which the search for marihuana was founded was provided when Mr. Choplick observed a package of rolling papers in the purse as he removed the pack of cigarettes. Although T.L.O. does not dispute the reasonableness of Mr. Choplick's belief that the rolling papers indicated the presence of marihuana, she does contend that the scope of the search Mr. Choplick conducted exceeded permissible bounds when he seized and read certain letters that implicated T.L.O. in drug dealing. This argument, too, is unpersuasive. The discovery of the rolling papers concededly gave rise to a reasonable suspicion that T.L.O. was carrying marihuana as well as cigarettes in her purse. This suspicion justified further exploration of T.L.O.'s purse, which turned up more evidence of drug-related activities: a pipe, a number of plastic bags of the type commonly used to store marihuana, a small quantity of marihuana, and a fairly substantial amount of money. Under these circumstances, it was not unreasonable to extend the search to a separate zippered compartment of the purse; and when a search of that compartment revealed an index card containing a list of "people who owe me money" as well as two letters, the inference that T.L.O. was involved in marihuana trafficking was substantial enough to justify Mr. Choplick in examining the letters to determine whether they contained any further evidence. In short, we cannot conclude that the search for marihuana was unreasonable in any respect.

Because the search resulting in the discovery of the evidence of marihuana dealing by T.L.O. was reasonable, the New Jersey Supreme Court's decision to exclude that evidence from T.L.O.'s juvenile delinquency proceedings on Fourth Amendment grounds was erroneous. Accordingly, the judgment of the Supreme Court of New Jersey is

Reversed.

JUSTICE BRENNAN, with whom JUSTICE MARSHALL joins, concurring in part and dissenting in part.

Today's decision sanctions school officials to conduct full-scale searches on a "reasonableness" standard whose only definite content is that it is *not* the same test as the "probable cause" standard found in the text of the Fourth Amendment. In adopting this unclear, unprecedented, and unnecessary departure from generally applicable Fourth Amendment standards, the Court carves out a broad exception to standards that this Court has developed over years of considering Fourth Amendment problems. Its decision is supported neither by precedent nor even by a fair application of the "balancing test" it proclaims in this very opinion.

I emphatically disagree with the Court's decision to cast aside the constitutional probable-cause standard when assessing the constitutional validity of a schoolhouse search. The Court's decision jettisons the probable-cause standard—the only standard that finds support in the text of the Fourth Amendment—on the basis of its Rohrschach-like "balancing test." Use of such a "balancing test" to determine the standard for evaluating the validity of a full-scale search represents a sizable innovation in Fourth Amendment analysis. This innovation finds support neither in precedent nor policy and portends a dangerous weakening of the purpose of the Fourth Amendment to protect the privacy and security of our citizens. Moreover, even if this Court's historic understanding of the Fourth Amendment were mistaken and a balancing test of some kind were appropriate, any such test that gave adequate weight to the privacy and security interests protected by the Fourth Amendment would not reach the preordained result the Court's conclusory analysis reaches today.

I thus do not accept the majority's premise that "[t]o hold that the Fourth Amendment applies to searches conducted by school authorities is only to begin the inquiry into the standards governing such searches." For me, the finding that the Fourth Amendment applies, coupled with the observation that what is at issue is a full-scale search, is the end of the inquiry. But even if I believed that a "balancing test" appropriately replaces the judgment of the Framers of the Fourth Amendment, I would nonetheless object to the cursory and short-sighted "test" that the Court employs to justify its predictable weakening of Fourth Amendment protections. In particular, the test employed by the Court vastly overstates the social costs that a probable-cause standard entails and, though it plausibly articulates the serious privacy interests at stake, inexplicably fails to accord them adequate weight in striking the balance.

It is not the government's need for effective enforcement methods that should weigh in the balance. Rather, it is the costs of applying probable cause as opposed to applying some lesser standard that should be weighed on the government's side.

A legitimate balancing test whose function was something more substantial than reaching a predetermined conclusion acceptable to this Court's impressions of what authority teachers need would therefore reach rather a different result than that reached by the Court today. On one side of the balance would be the costs of applying traditional Fourth Amendment standards—the "practical" and "flexible" probable-cause standard where a full-scale intrusion is sought, a lesser standard in situations where the intrusion is much less severe and the need for greater authority compelling. Whatever costs were toted upon this side would have to be discounted by the costs of applying an unprecedented and ill-defined "reasonableness under all the circumstances" test that will leave teachers and administrators uncertain as to their authority and will encourage excessive fact-based litigation.

On the other side of the balance would be the serious privacy interests of the student, interests that the Court admirably articulates in its opinion, but which the Court's new ambiguous standard places in serious jeopardy. I have no doubt that a fair assessment of the two sides of the balance would necessarily reach the same conclusion that, as I have argued above, the Fourth Amendment's language compels—that school searches like that conducted in this case are valid only if supported by probable cause.

On my view, the presence of the word "unreasonable" in the text of the Fourth Amendment does not grant a shifting majority of this Court the authority to answer *all* Fourth Amendment questions by consulting its momentary vision of the social good. Full-scale searches unaccompanied by probable cause violate the Fourth Amendment. I do not pretend that our traditional Fourth Amendment doctrine automatically answers all of the difficult legal questions that occasionally arise. I do contend, however, that this Court has an obligation to provide some coherent framework to resolve such questions on the basis of more than a conclusory recitation of the results of a "balancing test." The Fourth Amendment itself supplies that framework and, because the Court today fails to heed its message, I must respectfully dissent.

People v. Overton
229 N.E. 2d 596 (1967)

Three detectives of the Mount Vernon Police Department having obtained a search warrant went to the Mount Vernon High School. The warrant directed a search of the persons of two students and, also, of their lockers.

The detectives presented the warrant to the vice-principal, Dr. Panitz, who sent for the two students, one of whom was the defendant, Carlos Overton. The detectives searched them and found nothing. A subsequent search of Overton's locker, however, revealed four marijuana cigarettes.

The defendant moved to invalidate that portion of the search warrant which directed a search of his locker, on the ground that the papers were defective upon which it was based. This motion was granted. The court denied the motion to suppress, however, on the grounds that the vice-principal had consented to the search and that he had a right to do so. The Appellate Term reversed and dismissed the information, holding that the consent of the vice-principal could not justify an otherwise illegal search. The People have appealed from this order of the Appellate Term.

[1] It is axiomatic that the protection of the Fourth Amendment is not restricted to dwellings. A depository such as a locker or even a desk is safeguarded from unreasonable searches for evidence of a crime.

There are situations, however, where someone other than the defendant in possession of a depository may consent to what otherwise would have been an illegal search. Dr. Panitz, in this case, gave his consent to the search of Overton's locker. The dissenting opinion suggests, however, that Dr. Panitz' consent was not freely given, because he acted under compulsion of the invalid search warrant. If this were the case, his consent might be rendered somewhat questionable. However, Dr. Panitz testified that: "Being responsible for the order, assignment, and maintenance of the physical facilities, if *any* report were given to me by *anyone* of an article or item of the nature that does not belong there, or of an illegal nature, I would inspect the locker."

This testimony demonstrates beyond doubt that Dr. Panitz would have consented as he did regardless of the presence of the invalid search warrant.

The power of Dr. Panitz to give his consent to this search arises out of the distinct relationship between school authorities and students.

The school authorities have an obligation to maintain discipline over the students. It is recognized that, when large numbers of teenagers are gathered together in such an environment, their inexperience and lack of mature judgment can often create hazards to each other. Parents, who surrender their children to this type of environment, in order that they may continue developing both intellectually and socially, have a right to expect certain safeguards.

It is in the high school years particularly that parents are justifiably concerned that their children not become accustomed to antisocial behavior, such as the use of illegal drugs. The susceptibility to suggestion of students of high school age increases the danger. Thus, it is the affirmative obligation of the school authorities to investigate any charge that a student is using or possessing narcotics and to take appropriate steps, if the charge is substantiated.

When Overton was assigned his locker, he, like all the other students at Mount Vernon High School, gave the combination to his home room teacher who, in turn, returned it to an office where it was kept on file. The students at Mount Vernon are well aware that the school authorities possess the combinations of their lockers. It appears understood that the lock and the combination are provided in order that each student may have exclusive possession of the locker vis-à-vis other students, but the student does not have such exclusivity over the locker as against the school authorities. In fact, the school issues regulations regarding what may and may not be kept in the lockers and presumably can spot check to insure compliance. The vice-principal testified that he had, on occasion, inspected the lockers of students.

[2] Indeed, it is doubtful if a school would be properly discharging its duty of supervision over the students, if it failed to retain control over the lockers. Not only have the school authorities a right to inspect but this right becomes a duty when suspicion arises that something of an illegal nature may be secreted there. When Dr. Panitz learned of the detectives' suspicion, he was obligated to

inspect the locker. This interest, together with the nonexclusive nature of the locker, empowered him to consent to the search by the officers.

Accordingly, the order of the Appellate Term should be reversed.

BERGAN, Judge (dissenting).

The District Attorney concedes the search warrant was bad, i.e., "We acknowledge, to take as many issues out of the case as possible, that the search warrant was properly vacated." Defendant had paid for personal use of the locker and, as far as he was concerned, the People also admit, a search of the locker by police without a warrant "would be invalid."

No doubt the principal of the school had a supervisory power to inspect the locker. But if an invalid warrant was used to compel him to exercise this power, and if it adversely affected the constitutional right of the defendant to be secure against unlawful search and seizure, this invalid compulsion under a bad search warrant was as much an invasion of defendant's rights as if the police, under the purported authority of the warrant, had broken the door of the locker or compelled the defendant himself to open it.

There can be no doubt, reading this record, that the principal opened the door, not because he was exercising a free supervisory control over the locker in the interest of the school program, but because he felt the invalid search warrant compelled him to do so. He affirmatively answered the question that in opening the door he was "honoring the search warrant."

The order should be affirmed.

Horton v. Goose Creek Indep. School Dist.
677 F. 2d 471 (1982)

This case presents a question of first impression in this circuit: as a matter of constitutional law, can a school district, acting in good faith in an effort to deal with a serious drug and alcohol problem, subject students, their lockers, and their automobiles to the exploratory sniffing of dogs trained to detect certain contraband? We must consider the special circumstances peculiar to the public school environment, the duty of school officials to protect the minors in their care, the growing problem of drug and alcohol abuse in the schools, the students' interest in the integrity of their persons and effects, and the importance of demonstrating to the young that constitutional guarantees are not only lofty theories but do in practice control our government. Bearing in mind all these considerations, we hold that the dogs' sniffing of the children was unconstitutional. We conclude, however, that the dogs' sniffing of cars and lockers does not rise to the same level of intrusiveness, and we hold that, in the school environment, such sniffing operations are permissible.

I

The defendant, GCISD, adopted the challenged program in response to a growing drug and alcohol abuse problem in the schools. It contracted with a security services firm, Securities Associates International, Inc. (SAI), that provides dogs trained to alert their handlers to the presence of any one of approximately sixty different substances, including alcohol and drugs, both over-the-counter and controlled. The defendant conducted assemblies in the elementary schools to acquaint the children with the dogs and informed students in the junior and senior high schools of the program. On a random and unannounced basis, the dogs are taken to the various schools in the district, where they sniff students' lockers and automobiles. They also go into the classrooms, on leashes, to sniff the students themselves. During their "playtime" at the schools, the dogs are sometimes taken off their leashes. If the student proves to possess substances that violate school policy, he may agree to seek outside counseling; otherwise, the administrator may recommend to the superintendent that the student be suspended. Second-time violators do not have the option of counseling.

The named plaintiffs were all subjected to the sniffing of the canine drug detectors. Two of them, Robby Horton and Sandra Sanchez, triggered alerts. School officials questioned Sandra, took her purse, and searched it without her consent. They found a small bottle of perfume, which they returned to her. Robby was asked to empty his pockets, which he did. When nothing incriminating was found, the school officials searched his socks and lower pants legs but again found no contraband.

The plaintiffs brought this action, alleging a violation of the fourth amendment prohibition of unreasonable searches and seizures.

II

The problem presented in this case is the convergence of two troubling questions. First, is the sniff of a drug-detecting dog a "search" within the purview of the fourth amendment? Second, to what extent does the fourth amendment protect students against searches by school administrators seeking to maintain a safe environment conducive to education?

A. The Canine Sniff as a Search

Frequent use of drug-detecting dogs by law enforcement officials has led to a great number of cases challenging the admissibility of the fruits of a canine sniff. From these cases, one proposition is clear and universally accepted: if the police have some basis for suspecting an individual of possessing contraband, they may, consonant with the fourth amendment, use a drug-detecting dog to sniff. The theory of these cases, however, is not at all clear. The majority view is that the sniffing of the dog is not a search. Almost without exception, even in those cases in which the court does not condition its holding on the existence of a reasonable suspicion, either the court concludes that there was, or the facts of the case reveal the existence of, some level of reasonable, individualized suspicion.

The problem with these cases, of course, is that if canine sniffing truly is not a search within the fourth amendment, it is constitutionally irrelevant whether there is any basis for suspicion of the individual searched. To detect something in "open view", the police officer need have no probable or reasonable cause or even a particularized suspicion. Thus is it difficult to square the holding that canine sniffing is not a search with the reliance on the existence of some level of individualized suspicion. Given that theoretical inconsistency, the dragnet sniffing case now before us could be resolved either way—in relying on precedent, we could focus either on the requirement of grounds for suspicion or on the statement that canine sniffing is not a search. Unsurprisingly, the three states that have decided the issue of dragnet canine sniffing have split. In the face of this confusion, we are hesitant to extend the rule that canine sniffing is not a search to dragnet sniffing operations simply on the basis of precedent. Instead, we must analyze the problem afresh and determine whether the sniffing offends reasonable expectations of privacy.

Both the general characteristics of a canine sniffing investigation and the specific features of the object of the investigation—car, locker, or person—are relevant in determining the constitutionality of the search. The argument raised most frequently against viewing canine sniffing as a search is that a person has no legitimate expectation of privacy in the air surrounding his property. From this proposition courts have concluded that the sniffing of a dog is "no different" or that the dog's olfactory sense merely "enhances" that of the police officer in the same way that a flashlight enhances the officer's sight.

[1] We find this reasoning unpersuasive. The sniffing of a dog is unquestionably "different" from the sniffing of a human being; otherwise a rational law enforcement agency would not invest resources in training the animals but would simply send the handlers to sniff. The trained dogs—occasionally described as "giant olfactory nerve[s]"—detect odors well outside the range of human senses. Nor do we think that the distinction between "enhancement" and "replacement" resolves the question: a dog's olfactory sense enhances that of the police officer in the same way that an electronic listening device, picking up sound waves in the air, enhances his hearing. The latter case, however, is clearly a search. Of course, the use of an aid to perception does not always render an investigation a "search". For instance, the use of a flashlight does not change an otherwise permissible visual scan into a search. The proper way to determine whether the use of a given aid to perception renders an investigation a search, we think, is to consider both whether the aid permits an officer to detect data otherwise imperceptible to human senses and whether the aid is one generally in use in society. One should not be able to prevent an officer from using a more efficient means to detect what he could detect by using his own senses. But the converse is not true: the individual's legitimate expectation of privacy does not extend to every datum imperceptible to unaided human senses, for life in society carries with it a significant risk that certain widely used sensory aids will reveal some otherwise imperceptible data.

[2] The application of these principles to the sniff of a drug-detecting dog suggests that there was a search in this case. The trained dog can detect odors that no human investigator could possibly perceive. And the use of such dogs is not widespread in society; we cannot say that the revelation of these undetectable odors is a concomitant of life in society.

In addition to these considerations, though, we must evaluate also the nature of the object of the investigation. Here, the dogs sniffed lockers, automobiles, and persons. Certain minimal intrusions, though perhaps not expected, cannot be completely *un*expected. Nor are they intolerable. But the run of the mill intrusion does not reveal much information and certainly would not reveal the scent of one seed of marijuana, as would the sniff of the trained dog. We conclude that the intrusion on the cars and lockers here is different from those acceptable and unremarkable intrusions and must be recognized as a search governed by the fourth amendment.

The use of the dogs to sniff the students presents an even clearer instance of a search within the fourth amendment. The students' persons certainly are not the subject of lowered expectations of privacy. On the contrary, society recognizes the interest in the integrity of one's person, and the fourth amendment applies with its fullest vigor against any indecent or indelicate intrusion on the human body. Ours is a society that would not tolerate the widespread use of dogs in dragnet sniffing of property; even less is it a society that would tolerate the use of dogs in dragnet intrusions into the physical integrity of our people, unrestrained by the fourth amendment.

Our decision that the procedures employed by GCISD constitute searches does not, however, compel the conclusion that they were constitutionally impermissible. The fourth amendment does not prohibit all searches; it only restricts the government to ''reasonable'' searches.

[3] Although we recognize significant drawbacks to the adoption of a ''sliding scale'' approach to fourth amendment analysis, we cannot ignore the vast body of precedent denying the full array of fourth amendment safeguards in canine sniffing cases. And we think that canine sniffing of property is a good candidate for inclusion in the category of ''limited searches.'' It is minimally intrusive, involving no inconvenience or humiliation. The information is nevertheless of great value, for it aids in the detection of otherwise easily hidden contraband. Under the balancing procedure, when there is some level of articulable individualized suspicion, we think that the need for the search outweighs the intrusiveness, and canine sniffing of property is a reasonable procedure under the fourth amendment. When there is no individualized suspicion, though, the balance tips in the opposite direction. The intrusiveness of the search is unchanged, but the justification is diminished, if not eliminated. When there is *no* reason to believe that a search will produce evidence of crime, beyond the knowledge that some people are criminals and that searching everyone's property will identify the criminal few, the Constitution does not tolerate intrusions on protected privacy, even when those intrusions are only ''limited searches.''

Similarly, when the object of the search is a person, the balance permits the search only if there is a reasonable suspicion. When a dog inspects the human body, we cannot ignore the indignity inflicted upon the person. Yet the indignity is no more than that inflicted by a frisk. Consequently, the intrusion may be permissible when justified by reasonable cause. Again, though, when there is no individualized cause to justify the sniffing, the Constitution prohibits the intrusion.

The preceding discussion, however, does not resolve the case currently before us. We have established that dragnet searches of persons and property by sniffing dogs are ordinarily prohibited. But the fourth amendment does not always require the same results in the schools as it does in ordinary circumstances.

As a result, we must consider the extent to which the public school setting affects fourth amendment analysis.

B. The Fourth Amendment in the Public Schools

The courts have encountered substantial difficulty in accommodating the fourth amendment to the special situation presented by the public schools, where school officials have both a right and a duty to provide a safe environment conducive to education. At one time, it was not uncommon for a court to view the school official who searched a student as acting under authority derived from the parent and therefore as a private party not subject to the constraints of the fourth amendment. As courts in most recent cases have decided, we think it beyond question that the school official, employed and paid by the state and supervising children who are, for the most part, compelled to attend, is an agent of the government and is constrained by the fourth amendment.

[4] But the decision that school officials are governed by the fourth amendment does not dictate a holding that their activity in this case was unconstitutional. The basic concern of the fourth amendment is reasonableness, and reasonableness depends on the circumstances. Often the ordinary requirements of the fourth amendment are modified to deal with special situations. The public school presents special circumstances that demand similar accommodations of the usual fourth amendment requirements. When society requires large groups of students, too young to be considered capable of mature restraint in their use of illegal substances or dangerous instrumentalities, to congregate in the public schools, it assumes a duty to protect them from dangers posed by anti-social activities—their own and those of other students—and to provide them with an environment in which education is possible. To fulfill that duty, teachers and school administrators must have broad supervisory and disciplinary powers. At the same time, though, we must protect the fourth amendment rights of students. Indeed, constitutional rights in the schools take on a special importance.

[5] When the school official acts in furtherance of his duty to maintain a safe environment conducive to education, the usual accommodation is to require that the school official have "reasonable cause" for his action. Although the standard is less stringent than that applicable to law enforcement officers, it requires more of the school official than good faith or minimal restraint. The Constitution does not permit good intentions to justify objectively outrageous intrusions on student privacy. Thus, though we do not question the good faith of the GCISD officials in their attempt to eradicate a serious and menacing drug and alcohol abuse problem, we cannot approve the program on that basis; we must examine its objective reasonableness.

In some circumstances, the seriousness of the threat to safety or the limited nature of the intrusion may render a dragnet school search a reasonable means of dealing with a problem. Indeed, relatively nonintrusive administrative searches outside the schools need not be justified by individualized suspicion, if there is sufficient suspicion of a violation somewhere in the area covered by the dragnet. Dragnet sniffing of lockers and cars, carried out for the administrative purpose of maintaining a safe school environment conducive to education, is, therefore, reasonable.

[6] The analogy to the administrative searches, then, breaks down when we consider the dragnet sniffing of the children. In resolving that problem, we must consider the significant intrusion on dignity and personal security that goes with a canine inspection of the student's person. That aspect of the GCISD program entails too great an intrusion on the privacy of the students to be justified by the need to prevent abuse of drugs and alcohol when there is no individualized suspicion, and we hold it unconstitutional.

One hurdle remains to the validation of the dragnet sniffing of lockers and cars—the failure to obtain a warrant. The usual fourth amendment rule is that, even if supported by probable cause, a warrantless search is unreasonable, subject to a few well-delineated exceptions. The ordinary administrative search, even though not supported by individualized cause, also requires a warrant. The warrant serves a useful function because it assures the person whose property is to be searched that the official is authorized to search, alerts both the official and the citizen to the lawful limits of the search, and prevents discriminatory searches.

[7] In the schools, however, as discussed above, blanket rules are of little use, for the proper inquiry is the overall reasonableness of the search. In considering the reasonableness of warrantless sniffing, it is instructive to note that, in this circuit, a canine sniff of property based on some individualized suspicion does not require a warrant, even in the absence of exigent circumstances. Furthermore, we perceive little reason to anticipate that school officials will exceed the bounds of their authority or will use the procedure to harass individuals—if for no other reason, because the intrusion is so minimal that it would not be an effective harassment technique. The limited scope of the intrusion lends further support for excusing the warrant requirement. Consequently, we conclude that this searching technique is reasonable, even without a warrant.

[8] The plaintiffs urge that, even if the initial sniffing of the cars and lockers by the dogs is permissible, the dogs' reactions do not give the defendant a sufficiently strong basis for suspicion to justify a further search. The district court stated that the "generalized perception of a problem of drug and alcohol abuse" along with the positive reaction of the dog gave the school sufficient cause to believe that the student occupant or driver had violated school policy to justify opening the locker or car and searching it. The court did not, however, make any finding on the reliability of the dogs, and there was no evidence in the record to support such a finding. In fact, although the representative of the SAI asserted that the dogs were quite reliable, he admitted that there were no comprehensive records kept of those incidents when the dogs reacted positively in the absence of contraband. On this record, then, we cannot say whether the reaction of the dogs provided adequate cause for more intrusive searches, and summary judgment is inappropriate. GCISD need not show that the dogs are infallible or even that they are reliable enough to give the defendant probable cause; instead, the dogs must be reasonably reliable.

V

We conclude that the use of dogs in dragnet sniff-searches of the students of GCISD is unconstitutional, and we direct the district court to grant relief by appropriate declaration and injunction. Although the use of the dogs in similar dragnet sniffing of lockers and cars is permissible, we must remand to the district court for the case to proceed to trial on the reliability of the dogs' reactions as the basis for further searches.

Reversed and Remanded.

NOTES

1. Jones v. Latexo Independent School Dist., 499 F. Supp. 223 (1980) at 234.
2. State v. Baccino, 282 A. 2d 869 (1971) at 872.
3. Picha v. Wielgos, 410 F. Supp. 1214 (1976) at 1218.
4. State in Interest of T.L.O., 463 A. 2d 934 (1983) at 942–43.
5. New Jersey v. T.L.O., Slip Opinion No. 83–712 (1985) at 15.
6. Id. at 16.
7. Id., Stevens dissent at 2–3.
8. Katz v. United States, 389 U.S. 347 (1967) at 351.
9. People v. Overton, 229 N.E. 2d 596 (1967) at 351.
10. Id.
11. People v. Overton, 249 N.E. 2d 366 (1969) at 369.
12. State v. Stein, 456 P. 2d 1 (1969) at 3, cert. denied 90 U.S. 966 (1970).
13. Doe v. Renfrow, 475 F. Supp. 1012 (1979), modified 635 F. 2d 582 (1980), cert. denied 451 U.S. 1022 (1981) at 1022.
14. Id. at 1021.
15. Id. at 1024.
16. Horton v. Goose Creek Indep. School Dist., 677 F. 2d 471 (1982) at 480.
17. Id. at 482.
18. Id. at 485.
19. T.L.O. at 10.
20. Id. at 13.
21. Julius Menacker and Ernest Pascarella, "What Attitudes Do Educators Have About Student and Teacher Civil Rights?" *Urban Education* 19(2) (July 1984), 115–124.

EIGHT

Torts in Education:
School Responsibility for Harm

A tort is a civil wrong committed by one person against another, for which courts may provide monetary compensation, provided that injury resulted from unreasonable conduct. While general principles of tort law are accepted throughout all judicial jurisdictions, state policies may vary as to special immunities, liabilities, and related standards. Tort law developed as common law, with judicial precedent being more predominant than state statutes. Tort law is primarily a matter of state legal policy, but the constitutional tort, activated by federal civil-rights legislation, is an exception to that rule.

Torts affecting education may be classified into the categories of (1) strict liability; (2) intentional interference; (3) negligence; (4) professional negligence; that is, educational malpractice; and (5) constitutional civil-rights torts. The major tort area concerning education is that of negligence. Each area will be described briefly.

CLASSIFICATIONS OF TORTS

Strict Liability

Strict liability involves intentional behavior by someone (for example, a teacher) taken in regard to another (for instance, a student) that causes harm in an area creating automatic liability. There is no need to prove fault. Injuries related to fire protection, experiments with dangerous chemicals, shop work with dangerous power saws, field trips, and the care of very young children might be classified by one state or another as producing strict liability. This is presently a relatively unimportant area of educational tort liability, but it appears to be growing.

Intentional Interference

Intentional interference torts occur when one person deliberately interferes with another, leading to harm. Intent to harm is not necessary for establishing liability. False imprisonment, defamation (libel or slander), assault, and battery are examples of intentional interference torts.

False imprisonment occurs when someone is injured as the result of un-lawful restriction of movement. The keys to false imprisonment are intent to restrict movement, regardless of intent to harm, and the reasonableness of the restriction. Thus, keeping a pupil in the classroom, or even detaining him after school, would not be considered false imprisonment in the event that injury oc-curred. However, if the student were placed in a closet for discipline and locked in it for hours, any subsequent injury would be related to false imprisonment. Such restriction is unreasonable.

Assault occurs when one is reasonably put in fear of harm through the actions of another; for instance, shaking one's fist and threatening to punch another person. The damage shown prior to recovery from an assault charge may be emotional as well as physical. Battery is physical harm inflicted wrong-fully by one person against another.

Defamation occurs when information is transmitted by one person to an-other about a third person that brings the third person into disrepute or causes him or her to be ridiculed or hated by others. When the information is passed on orally, the charge of slander is raised. If it is written, it is called libel. In order for defamation to be actionable regarding school personnel or students, it must be shown that the information harms the individual in pursuing his or her ed-ucation or profession. The information in question may involve skill, qualifi-cation, ethics, or any other area related to a person's standing as a student, teacher, or administrator.

The major defenses of educators against intentional interference torts of assault, battery, or false imprisonment charged by students is the teacher's *in loco parentis* disciplinary authority established in common-law and state statutes. The obligation of educators to control schools and classrooms is uniformly rec-ognized by courts, and damages will be awarded to students only when corporal punishment or various forms of assault, battery, and false imprisonment are con-sidered malicious or excessive. The severity of the offense, the pupil's prior be-havior, age, sex, and physical/emotional condition all will be weighed in the balance against the action taken by the educator. The decision reached will de-pend on precedent within the state, as well as on the attitude of the judge or jury.

In *Frank* v. *Orleans Parish School Bd.*, 195 So. 2d 451 (1967), a Louisiana court awarded a student damages for assault and battery when a teacher shook him so hard that he fell and broke his arm. This was considered excessive force, as such action was unnecessary in the circumstances. In contrast, when an Ohio assistant superintendent angrily shook a student very vigorously while shouting threats, the Ohio Court of Appeals rejected the lower court's finding of assault (battery charges had been disallowed by the lower court because any injury sustained did not cause interruption of school attendance), because the action was not proven to be unreasonable corporal punishment or unrelated to maintaining discipline (*State* v. *Hoover*, 450 N.E. 2d 710 [1982]). In a later Ohio case, a principal struck a nine-year-old girl with a thick paddle, in response to reports that the girl had been disruptive in class. The blow produced a red welt on her buttock that her physician called "reasonably severe," requiring some treatment for soreness. The court decided to dismiss charges against the principal, as Ohio law allowed moderate corporal punishment and there was no "substantial suffering" by the child (*State* v. *Albert*, 456 N.E. 2d 594 [1983]).

Assault and battery is not just a one-way path allowing students to sue teachers. The reverse is also possible, as illustrated in a Wisconsin case awarding punitive damages to a teacher bringing assault and battery charges against a student. A seventeen-year-old boy was smoking in front of the school, in violation of a school rule. A teacher grabbed the student's arm in attempting to bring him to the school office. The boy fell, got up, and punched the teacher. The judgment in favor of the teacher took into account the student's record of past misbehavior, his age, and the strong public policy against student violence directed at teachers (*Anello* v. *Savignac*, 342 N.W. 2d 440 [1983]).

The major defenses in defamation charges are (1) conditional or qualified privilege afforded public officials, including school personnel, to use information accompanied by special protection against liability, provided malice is not present, and (2) the truth of the information conveyed.

The Supreme Court of Wisconsin rejected a teacher's defamation charge against a board member whose letter to school administrators accused the teacher of intemperate behavior with his eighth-grade class. The court's decision was based on the qualified privilege the board member had in discussing school personnel with school administrators who had a right to the information. The board member was absolved of liability even though the court observed that the letter was sent without formal board approval (*Ranous* v. *Hughes*, 141 N.W. 2d 251 [1966]). Parents also have qualified privilege when communicating about matters affecting their children, provided malice is not found. A parent complaining to a school principal about a male teacher's fondling female students was found to be protected also by qualified privilege (*Deselle* v. *Guillory*, 407 So. 2d 79 [1982]).

A similar finding occurred in a New York case. The court held that a parent's defamatory petition about a teacher was cloaked with "absolute privilege," precluding a lawsuit. The finding that the parent's communication was intended to stimulate official action led to this conclusion. To find otherwise, in the court's view, would discourage citizens' complaints to school boards, which was poor public policy. It is better to allow the school board, rather than courts, to decide the merits of parents' criticisms to the school board (*Weissman* v. *Mogul*, 462 N.Y.S. 2d 383 [1983]).

Constitutional Torts and Related Civil-Rights Statutory Torts

The constitutional tort was introduced in the Civil Rights Act of 1871. In response to concerns about controlling potential abuse of newly freed blacks, Section 1983 of the Act stipulated that persons whose civil rights were violated may institute a suit to recover damages from the offender. This legal avenue was rarely used until the advent of the Civil Rights movement of the fifties and sixties. While Section 1983 of the Civil Rights Act of 1871 remains the broadest, least restrictive avenue of damage recovery for violating civil rights, more recent federal statutes, based on constitutionally related civil rights, have increased the available options.

Title VII (employment discrimination) of the Civil Rights Act of 1964 authorizes plaintiffs to receive monetary damages for violations, provided all other nonjudicial remedies have been exhausted. The Equal Pay Act and the Age Discrimination Act have similiar provisions. Also, while Title IX (sex discrimination) of the Education Amendments of 1972 does not specifically provide a right to recover money for violations, the Supreme Court has held that the Act implies that right (*Cannon* v. *U. of Chicago*, 441 U.S. 677 [1979]). That decision has also raised the possibility of recovery of damages under Title VI (race, national-origin discrimination) of the Civil Rights Act of 1964.

The Supreme Court has created an absolute-immunity defense for prosecutors and legislators accused of constitutional torts (for instance, *Imbler* v. *Pachtman*, 424 U.S. 409 [1976]). Other state officials have been granted qualified or conditional immunity; that is, they are immune provided they acted clearly within the scope of their authority and in the interests of those being served. More recent conservative, restraintist limitations on the availability of monetary compensation for successful litigants in civil-rights statutory suits has occurred in the 1984 Supreme Court decisions of *Irving Indep. School Dist.* v. *Tatro*, 104 S. Ct. 3371 (1984), and *Smith* v. *Robinson*, 52 U.S.L.W. 5179 (1984). Even in civil-rights statutes not specifically authorizing monetary damages, the award of substantial attorneys' fees was permitted under the Civil Rights Attorney's Fees Award Act of 1976. This alone could serve as a deterrent against actions that might violate federal civil-rights statutes. However in *Irving* v. *Tatro* and *Smith* v. *Robinson*, the Supreme Court denied attorneys' fees to the successful plaintiffs who were found to have had their rights violated under the Education For All Handicapped Children Act. While these decisions are a considerable discouragement to those considering suits based on a civil-rights statute, the potential effect of these various statutes on providing monetary compensation to successful plaintiffs remains to be settled.

Educational Malpractice

The concept of educational malpractice, like the more well known medical malpractice, is based on negligence in the application of professional skills and knowledge. The plaintiff attempts to show that the practices and/or professional decisions of the educator caused injury to the plaintiff's educational development through conduct falling below the standard expected from educators. Thus, passing an illiterate student from grade to grade and awarding him or her a high-school diploma would be such a course of action. Another example would be the misplacement of a normal student in a track for mentally handicapped students or vice versa. In all cases, the malpractice claim would involve the exercise of professional education techniques, procedures, or judgments, rather than the matters of health and safety that govern traditional negligence suits.

This area of litigation has not yet developed a strong place in tort law. Courts are reluctant to allow it to develop because of the negative public-policy effects of developing a potential source for draining treasuries of school districts. Another inhibition to judicial acceptance of the tort of educational malpractice is the unsettled professional standards and knowledge governing teaching, learning, and related school practices. Even so, the development of competency testing standards and demands for educational accountability may yet see this area explode into prominence.

Negligence

The great preponderance of tort litigation in education concerns the tort of negligence. Negligence is conduct falling below an established standard that results in injury. The conduct in question may involve something the accused did or failed to do that he or she should have done. The standard by which the conduct is judged is that of prudence or reasonableness. The court considers whether the educator acted in a manner expected of a reasonably prudent teacher. This hypothetic reasonable teacher is assumed to possess at least average intelligence, physical capacity appropriate to his or her role, at least average perception and memory, and the skills and knowledge expected of a qualified teacher or administrator. These factors are applied to the question of foreseeability; that is, should a reasonable educator have been expected to foresee and, consequently, have taken action to prevent the injury that occurred? If the anser is yes, liability looms large; if the answer is no, the educator would most likely be absolved of negligence. Final determination of the question of liability would involve the answers derived from the following questions the court will consider in school-negligence cases:

1. The educator should observe a standard of care for protecting students against unreasonable risk. Did the educator's behavior meet or fall below the expected standard of care?
2. Was the action or inaction of the educator the "proximate cause" of the student's

injury; that is, was what the educator did or failed to do closely connected to the injury sustained?

3. Was there an actual injury to the student of such magnitude that financial damages should be awarded to compensate for the injury?

In considering the first two questions, courts pay particular attention to the educators' responsibilities regarding the provision of responsible supervision, proper instruction, and adequate maintenance of equipment. The extent of scrutiny given to any of these areas will depend on the ages and physical and psychological condition of the students involved, as well as the type of activity and conditions under which the activity took place. Physical-education and shop teachers are expected to exercise greater caution and care than, say, a history or English teacher, given the risks involved in athletic activities or working with such inherently dangerous equipment as revolving saws. Younger children are considered to require greater care and protection than older children, given their relative lack of knowledge, experience, and understanding. An elementary-school science teacher providing students with their first experience in working with chemicals that might be dangerous when mixed would be held to a higher standard of care than would a high-school teacher instructing an honors class in advanced chemistry. Similarly, a teacher of behavior-disordered teenagers would be expected to provide closer supervision that that required for an honors class. Also, a physical-education teacher managing fifty students using several trampolines in a gym has a greater responsibility for careful supervision, instruction, and equipment maintenance than when instructing ten students in how to sit in the Yoga lotus position. Finally, children seven or younger place teachers in a particularly vulnerable positon. They are not legally responsible for their actions, and require extreme care by teachers.

Educators defending against charges of negligence have several traditional defenses available to them. These include:

1. *Assumption of Risk*: The injured party understood and accepted the risks involved in the activity under the conditions in which it took place. A high-school player on an interscholastic football team would fall into this category. While this does not absolve the educator of reasonable care for supervision, instruction, and equipment maintenance, it does reduce the educator's legal duty of care and places considerable responsibility for personal care and protection on the student.

2. *Contributory Negligence*: In the few jurisdictions still allowing this defense, defendants must show that the injury resulted from the injured person's own neglect of personal safety, which could reasonably have been expected. While this defense cannot easily apply to very young children, it might be viable for older students whose behavior was rash, impulsive, or reckless.

3. *Comparative Negligence*: This defense is viable when it can be shown that the injury was partly the fault of several persons. In states allowing comparative negligence, damages would be apportioned according to the assessed degrees of fault of all parties.

4. *Sovereign Immunity*: While this defense is disappearing, it once was prominent. It is grounded in the ancient concept that "the king can do no wrong." This translated

into a policy exempting school districts and the state from liability for tort damages, although teachers and administrators could be sued.

5. *Act of God*: Here the defendant claims the injury was caused by an unforseeable natural event, such as a sudden storm, an earthquake, or a rockslide, rather than by what the educator did or failed to do.

THE INFLUENCE OF JUDICIAL ATTITUDES

Regardless of the type of tort at issue, the influence of judicial attitudes will play an important role in the policies established controlling the outcomes of tort suits. Conservative jurists will tend to protect the interests of government in order to insure the fiscal stability of public education. Equally important to the conservative view is guarding against inhibiting and confusing school authority by eager, broad assignments of liability for tort damages to educators, board members, and school districts. Thus, the conservative tends to be a restraintist in the field of tort law. There will be reluctance to easily grant standing to sue, and discouragement of developing new areas of tort liability, such as educational malpractice or civil-rights statutory tort liability.

The liberal will be quicker to take the side of the individual claiming a tort grievance against the school or its agents, in order to protect the individual against the states' potential for unbridled behavior when sanctions do not exist to restrain it. Accordingly, liberals tend toward granting easy court access for tort action, activist expansions of tort areas, and erosion of schools' tort immunity and other tort defenses.

School-District Tort-Immunity/Liability Policies

The tendency of liberal jurists to incline toward the plaintiff as opposed to the conservative support of government is best illustrated in regard to the tort defense of sovereign immunity for school districts. The conservative would see this common-law rule as needed to preserve the strength and viability of government, and as part of the needed historic continuity of law. The liberal would favor change, especially since the principle would be seen as inhibiting the role of reason in settling disputes, and an unfair restriction on the individual's rights and liberties.

In striking down the doctrine of the sovereign immunity of public-school districts to tort suits in Illinois, the state supreme court displayed the attitudes of the liberal, accompanied by the activists' tendency to make public policy through court decisions:

> It is almost incredible that in this modern age of comparative sociological enlightenment, and in a republic, the medieval absolutism supposed to be implicit in the maxim, ''the King can do no wrong,'' should exempt the various branches of the government from liability for their torts. . . .
> The other chief reason advanced in support of the immunity rule . . . is the

protection of public funds and public property . . . . This reasoning seems to follow the line that it is better for the individual to suffer than for the public to be inconvenienced. . . .

We conclude that the rule of school district tort immunity is unjust, unsupported by any valid reason, and has no rightful place in modern day society.

Defendant strongly urges that if said immunity is to be abolished, it should be done by the legislature, not by this court. With this contention we must disagree. The doctrine of school district immunity was created by this court alone. Having found that doctrine to be unsound and unjust under present conditions, we consider that we have not only the power, but the duty, to abolish that immunity . . . .

We have repeatedly held that the doctrine of *stare decisis* is not an inflexible rule requiring this court to blindly follow precedents . . . . When it appears that public policy and social needs require a departure from prior decisions, it is our duty . . . to overrule those decisions and establish a rule consonant with our present day concepts of right and justice . . . . [1]

The Illinois high court was able to change policy on tort immunity in that state because it was based on common law. In Texas, school-district tort immunity was supported by state statute. While the court sympathized with the views of the Illinois court, it took a restraintist position, refusing to make law when it saw its role confined to interpreting law. The decision noted:

Appellants make a frontal attack on the doctrine of governmental immunity. We agree that this doctrine . . . has little, if any justification in these times. Essentially the doctrine arose out of judge-made law and can be abrogated or modified by court decision. Many courts without legislative intervention have abolished the immunity effective immediately or prospectively. Other jurisdictions had adhered to the doctrine treating the problem as one for the legislature . . . .

The legislature is in a better position than the judicial branch of government to establish procedures, limits of liability and exclusions, and make provision for insurance or other methods of funding tort payment of tort claims against school districts. . . . [2]

Since the Texas legislature had passed a Tort Claims Act allowing immunity, the court was loath to substitute its judgment for that of the legislature. Presently, most states have abandoned the governmental-immunity doctrine, with some states allowing limited immunity by setting financial limits on the amount of recovery.

Another state policy distinction concerns district insurance for tort liability. For example, in Minnesota, where statutory limits are set for recovery, school districts are required to have insurance coverage, and can be liable for the difference between its coverage and the statutory limit (*Scott* v. *School Dist. No. 709, Duluth,* 256 N.W. 2d 485 [1977]). In contrast, West Virginia provides district tort immunity and consequently bars purchase of liability insurance as an unnecessary expenditure of public funds. Still other states (such as Michigan and Missouri) allow the purchase of insurance without affecting district immunity.[3]

Tort-Immunity Policy for School Employees

In most states, a distinction is made for tort liability purposes between whether the educator was performing a ministerial function or a discretionary one. Most states will allow immunity for torts committed while performing discretionary (judgmental) functions, but hold personnel liable for their ministerial activities, which are mandated and prescribed by state law. There are also a growing number of states that have enacted "save harmless" statutes, which provide varying levels of immunity to educators from tort suits or require districts to pay the legal expenses or damage claims assessed against them.

Another distinction some states make that strengthens educators' protection against tort liability is applying the "willful and wanton" standard usually reserved to protect parents against tort claims for injury to their children. In Georgia, a principal had allowed a slippery rug to be placed near a glass door, causing a student to fall through the glass, severely cutting himself. The Georgia Supreme Court held that since the principal was acting within the scope of his duty and had not acted in a willful or wanton manner, he was not liable (*Hennessy* v. *Webb*, 264 S.E. 2d 878 [1980]). To understand the logic behind this distinction, the development of this doctrine in Illinois is examined.

In the 1976 companion cases of *Kobylanski* v. *Chicago Board of Education* and *Chilton* v. *Cook County School Dist. 207*, teachers were sued for negligence when, in gym classes, they failed to provide spotters for students exercising on a hanging rope and a trampoline, respectively, resulting in severe injuries to the two students. In searching for protection against liability, a defense was developed based on the Illinois statutes governing the teachers' *in loco parentis* standing. The Illinois law provided that: "In all matters related to the discipline and conduct of the schools and school children, they [teachers] stand in the relation of parents and guardians to the pupils."[4] The defense argued that this provision of *in loco parentis* standing accepted for discipline also applied to supervision and other nondisciplinary matters. Illinois law, as with other states, provided that parents were not liable to their children for ordinary negligence, but only for conduct that was "willful and wanton." To be so, the injury must result from intent or a reckless disregard for the safety of the injured person.

The Illinois Supreme Court accepted this reasoning by a bare four-to-three majority, stating:

> Reviewing the language of the statutes, we find that they were intended to confer the status of *in loco parentis*, in nondisciplinary as well as disciplinary matters. . . . The statutes . . . confer upon teachers and other certified educational employees immunity from suits of negligence arising out of matters relating to the discipline in and conduct of the schools and school children. In order to impose liability against such educators, the plaintiffs must prove willful and wanton misconduct.[5]

Subsequent Illinois Supreme Court decisions would create exceptions to the "willful and wanton" standard of protection against teacher tort liability. In

Gerrity v. *Beatty* (1978), the court held that a student's injury sustained because the school provided him with a defective football helmet allowed for using the standard of ordinary negligence, since "public policy argues rather strongly against . . . relax[ing] a school district's obligation to insure that equipment . . . is fit for the purpose. . . . We therefore conclude that *Kobylanski* is not controlling here."[6]

Court Judgments Protecting Teachers

The conservative judicial view works to protect educators against the diminution of their authority caused by increasing fear and apprehension of liability for negligence. Upholding sovereign immunity is one policy in this direction; another is generally holding for defendants when the proper decision is unclear. In a 1972 Wyoming case, a seven-year-old threw a small rock, which put out the eye of another one during noon recess. The supervising teacher and district were sued for negligence (substandard supervision and unsafe grounds, respectively). In disallowing these negligence charges, the Superme Court of Wyoming observed that neither the teacher's supervision nor the rocks on the playground could be considered proximate causes of the injury. The proximate cause of the injury was the other child picking up and throwing the stone:

> A teacher cannot anticipate the varied and unexpected acts which occur daily in and about the school premises. When the time between an act of a student and injury to a fellow student is so short that the teacher has no opportunity to prevent injury, it cannot be said that negligence of the teacher is the proximate cause of the injury. . . .
> We realize there are cases in which a school district can be held liable for injury resulting from a dangerous and defective condition of a playground. We have found no case, however, which holds rocks on the ground to be a dangerous and defective condition. Left on the ground, a rock will hurt no one. . . . [A]ppellants cite no authority for the proposition that such a result was reasonably foreseeable.
> It is apparent from all we have said that the proximate cause of George Fagan's injury was the act of his fellow student in throwing a rock. It was not the failure of the Park County School District No. 1 to maintain the playground in a safe condition.[7]

While educators entrusted with the care of retarded children are held to a stricter duty of care than for normal children, even here, a conservative view can reasonably defend the authority and protect the liability of the school. A retarded student was landscaping near a pond. He entered the pond to retrieve a tool that had fallen into it, and drowned. The supervisor was not present at the time. The plaintiff parents claimed a breach of the school's duty of care, particularly because they claimed the pond was an "attractive nuisance"—that is, an inherently dangerous element to which children are attracted—which required special measures by educators to prevent harm.

The Louisiana Court of Appeals found that the Evergreen School was not negligent. In the words of the decision:

Evergreen's duty to use reasonable care in this instance did not dictate continuous supervision. The school's policy to allow its students a certain amount of freedom consistent with their mental capacities was reasonable and necessary to the accomplishment of the school's purposes. . . .

The educational advantages of providing the students some freedom and opportunity to learn self-reliance, and the quality-of-life advantages of the open-space rural environment in which the students lived and worked, far outweigh the risks of harm attendant thereto. The risks were minimal and were not unreasonable under the circumstances.

The duty of the school to provide reasonable care to protect the retarded student from harm did not include the duty of providing continuous supervision or the duty of enclosing the pond. The school's conduct did not create an unreasonable risk of harm . . . nor was the school's conduct substandard. There was no breach of the duty of reasonable care.[8]

The field of tort litigation, particularly as focused upon the major area of negligence, has created more fear among educators than is probably warranted. Some states have legislation offering varying degrees of protection for educators facing tort suits. Most state courts will give educators the benefit of the doubt when liability is cloudy. Even so, educators will be held responsible for adhering to an expected standard of care for children.

Principles of Tort Liability in Education

Negligence

1. The most common tort in education is negligence, defined as conduct falling below an established standard of care that results in injury to another person.
2. Educators have a duty to care for students in their charge.
3. The standard of care to which educators are held is based on the expectation of the care a reasonably prudent teacher would exercise. This standard assumes at least average intelligence, perception, and memory, sufficient physical capacity, and requisite educational skill and knowledge.
4. A primary test of whether an acceptable standard of care was used is whether students were protected from unreasonable risk.
5. An important factor in determining whether an educator is liable for an injury is the determination of whether the circumstance causing injury was foreseeable, and hence could have been guarded against by prudent action or judgment.
6. Even in areas where courts might not require school supervision, if the school decides to accept responsibility, it will then be held accountable for properly executing that duty of care.
7. For liability to be proven, it must be established that what the educator did or failed to do was the proximate cause of the injury; that is, that it had a close causal connection to the injury.

8. In considering whether a charge of negligence against an educator is valid, particular attention is paid to standards of supervision, instruction, and maintenance of equipment.

9. Among the defenses available to educators and school districts charged with negligence are:

   a. assumption of risk (student was aware of and accepted the special risks involved)

   b. contributory negligence (the student contributed to his or her own injury)

   c. comparative negligence (several parties hold varying degrees of responsibility for the injury

   d. sovereign immunity (school-district immunity from tort liability)

   e. act of God (unforseeable, unpreventable natural cause of injury)

Other Torts

10. Intentional-interference torts, such as false imprisonment and assault and battery, occur when there is an intent to interfere, even if not to harm another. This may take the forms of unreasonably preventing movement (false imprisonment), threats of harm (assault), or physical action causing injury (battery).

11. The main defense of educators against intentional-interference charges is their *in loco parentis* standing. The *in loco parentis* status of educators has also strengthened teachers' defenses against negligence charges in some jurisdictions.

12. Tort suits for defamation (libel or slander) must prove actual injury to an individual by information transmitted from one person to another about the individual.

13. There are two main defenses against defamation suits in education: (a) the truth of the information and (b) privilege accorded to educators to transmit information about others of concern to educational policy and decisions without fear of tort suits.

14. Certain federal statutes have created the opportunity to sue for damages arising from civil-rights violations. Section 1983 of the Civil Rights Act of 1871 allows the greatest latitude for constitutional torts. Title VII of the Civil Rights Act of 1964 and Title IX of the Education Amendments of 1972 offer more restricted tort-claim opportunities, as do more focused legislations, such as the Equal Pay Act and Age Discrimination Act.

15. Educational malpractice—that is, negligence in the performance of professional tasks and the exercise of professional judgment—may be a new class of tort applied to education. Its status is currently unclear, but courts have generally disallowed educational malpractice claims.

General

16. In order for a tort claim to be valid, actual injury must be proven for which monetary damages are an appropriate remedy. An exception to this rule

is the violation of a civil-rights tort, for which nominal damages may be awarded, even without a showing of injury.

17. Some states protect school districts from tort suits through sovereign immunity. Some further protect school personnel through "save harmless" legislation. Other states do neither.

18. In deciding tort claims against educators, courts weigh the age, size, sex, physical, intellectual, and emotional condition of the plaintiffs against the obligations of educators to maintain order and control.

THE SEARCH FOR CLEAR POLICY IN SCHOOL-NEGLIGENCE SUITS

What considerations determine whether the educator's "standard of care" is proper or has been breached? How vulnerable or protected are educators in regard to negligence charges? What legal reasoning allows students and parents or school personnel and school districts to be favored in negligence tort suits?

The judgment as to whether educational policy or action meets or breaches an acceptable standard of care is central to negligence cases. While state statute or judicial precedent may vary, there is general agreement about the appropriate standard of conduct. This standard was articulated as follows by Judge Learned Hand: "The degree of care demanded . . . is the resultant of three factors: the likelihood that his conduct will injure others, taken with the seriousness of the injury if it happens, and balanced against the interest he must sacrifice to avoid the risk."[9] The concept of the hypothetical prudent or reasonable teacher is related to the standard of care appropriate in particular educational circumstances. It is the particular set of circumstances that determines the standard of care applicable and the conduct, especially regarding foreseeability, expected of the reasonably prudent teacher. The scope of potential circumstances is extremely broad, ranging from classrooms to halls, lunchrooms, and athletic fields, as well as out-of-school activities, both supervised and unsupervised, authorized and unauthorized. The following discussion of cases illustrates the general variety of court judgments that occur in negligence cases.

The type of student and inherent danger of the activity undertaken is important in determining the required standard of care. A fourteen-year-old boy considered "slow" was injured when using a power saw without a blade guard. He sued, claiming teacher negligence. It was established that while the teacher instructed students to use the guard, he himself occasionally did not, and often failed to reprimand students who did not. In his defense, the teacher claimed the student was injured through his own negligence; that is, he allowed sawdust to accumulate, on which he slipped. The court found for the student, holding that the teacher's duty of care was high, and it was breached by his imprudent behavior. The potential for an accident occurring because of lax enforcement of the rule to use a blade guard was foreseeable (*Matteucci* v. *High School Dist. 208*, 281 N.E. 2d 383 [1972]). Here, the burden of requiring students to use a blade guard was far outweighed by the magnitude of the potential harm.

In contrast, when a normal high-school student cut fingers off his hand while using a power saw soon after receiving safety instructions including a demonstration by the teacher, a North Carolina court found for the school. The teacher had even offered to do the cutting for any student not wishing to do the work. The standard of care applied was warning students of hazards, particularly those of which inexperienced students would be unaware. The prudence dictated by the situation was demonstrated by the teacher. Indeed, the boy admitted that he knew better than to take the action that led to his injury (*Izard* v. *Hickory City Schools Board of Education*, 315 S.E. 2d 756 [1984]).

When a six-year-old boy got sick at school, his older brother, who was sick at home, was called to take his brother home. This eleven-year-old rode his bike to school and rode double with his brother on the way home, whereupon the bike tipped and the older boy was injured. The school was sued for negligence, but the court found for the defendant. The California school code did not hold the school accountable for pupil travel to and from school. Further, the school did not know the older boy was ill, did not know about the double-riding on the bike, and the injured boy was not enrolled at the school in question. Thus, the school did not owe him a duty of care (*Kerwin* v. *County of San Mateo*, 1 Cal. Rptr. 437 [1959]).

That decision is contrasted by a California case in which a six-year-old, without his parents' knowledge, rode his bike to school after missing the school bus, although school regulations forbade this for students below fourth grade. Teachers were posted in front of the school at the end of classes to enforce the rule and supervise safe exiting. The boy was allowed to ride home and was hit by a car. The court found the school negligent, as it had assumed a duty of care to prevent bicycle travel by very young students, and that duty had been breached. The eventuality of a six-year-old traveling on busy streets being injured was foreseeable by a reasonably prudent teacher, in the judgment of this court (*Justus* v. *Jefferson County School Dist. R-1*, 683 P. 2d 805 [1984]). Had the school not assumed this duty, it might not have been considered negligent. Once it assumed supervision and enforcement of the rule, it became accountable under it.

The issue of whether a teacher's absence from class violated the standard of care and prudence owed to students has been the subject of a great deal of litigation. On the affirmative side are cases such as *Schnell* v. *Travelers Ins. Co.*, 264 So 2d 346 (1972), in which a first-grade teacher was found liable for negligence when she assigned a sixth-grader to monitor her class. The monitor's hand, greasy from potato chips, slipped on a door and was injured when it broke through glass in the door. The teacher was found to have breached the duty of care owed to the sixth-grader by exposing her to unreasonable risk. The school board also was found liable for having such weak glass put in the door. In another case, when a high-school gym teacher left his class of fifty boys, some of them became rowdy, resulting in injury to one of the rowdies. The teacher was gone for a half hour. The appellate court considered that while the student's rowdiness might have been contributory, requiring apportionment of damages through comparative negligence, the teacher's absence in an environment conducive to rowdiness for so long was not prudent, and falls below the expected standard of care (*Cirillo* v. *City of Milwaukee*, 150 N.W. 2d 460 [1967]).

On the negative side, there is the case of the fifth-grade student injured by a pencil thrown by a classmate while the teacher was outside in the hall supervising a class returning to its room. The Pennsylvania court ruled that the teacher's absence was not negligence. She acted reasonably in making a choice about supervisory priorities. A teacher cannot be expected to be in two places at one time, nor can she be expected to anticipate all possible student acts (*Simonetti* v. *School Dist. of Philadelphia*, 454 F. 2d 1038 [1982]). In a related case (*Segerman* v. *Jones* [1969]), a fourth-grade teacher left her class while pupils were doing physical exercises. During her brief absence, a boy moved from his assigned place to one next to a girl and, while doing an exercise, kicked out some of her teeth. The Maryland court rejected the contention that the teacher's absence was the proximate cause of injury, stating: "A teacher's absence from the classroom, or failure properly to supervise students' activities, is not likely to give rise to a cause of action for injury to a student unless under all circumstances the possibility of injury is reasonably foreseeable."[10] Finally, there is the Louisiana case in which a teacher left some elementary-school students alone after school to clean the room. A pupil found the teacher's paring knife in her desk and cut another student with it. The court found no negligence, as the knife had not been placed in possession of the student. In fact, students were forbidden to go near the desk (*Richard* v. *St. Landry Parish School Board*, 344 So. 2d 1116 [1977]).

In the matter of out-of-class supervision within the school, the same standards apply. When a girl was injured because a boy threw an object into the girls' washroom at an elementary school, a Louisiana court found the school board, through its principal and teachers, to be negligent for failing to provide supervision, given a history of washroom disorders that made injury foreseeable and supervision the prudent response (*Carson* v. *Orleans Parish School Board*, 432 So 2d 956 [1983]). Similarly, when chemicals stolen by students from an unlocked school storeroom were hidden in bushes outside the school and found by an eight-year-old who injured himself by igniting them, the school was found negligent. The New York court decided the school had a duty of care to better protect the dangerous chemicals, and it breached that duty. This was the proximate cause of injury (*Kush* v. *City of Buffalo*, 462 N.Y.S. 2d 831 [1983]).

Contrasting attitudes were expressed in *Ferreira* v. *Sanchez* (449 P. 2d 784 [1969]). A pistol capable of shooting real bullets was used as a prop in a school play. A student put live ammunition in it and shot another student. He was sued, along with the supervising teacher and principal. The New Mexico Supreme Court dismissed charges of negligence against the teacher and principal, as normal supervision and care was proper here and had been exercised. The substitution of live ammunition in the gun could not have been reasonably foreseen.

School personnel are responsible for out-of-school care and supervision that they elect to assume. A nine-year-old arrived on school grounds shortly before classes began and was injured by a paper clip shot into his eye by a thirteen-year-old boy waiting for a bus to another school. The principal was on the premises but was in the building when the injury occurred. The New Jersey Supreme Court found the principal negligent, since he had assumed responsibility by being at the school, and by staying within the school he had breached his duty of care. The school board was also found negligent for not providing regular supervision, given the heavy traffic and presence of students, such as the one inflicting damage, known to be behavior problems (*Titus* v. *Lindberg*, 228 A. 2d 65 [1967]). However, when a California student was stabbed on school grounds by a non-student, the court did not find the school negligent in failing to provide supervision, even though the area was known to be dangerous. The school was held to have no duty to protect against general criminal activity. "Foreseeable victims are not themselves sufficient to establish a special relationship imposing upon the school district a duty to warn or protect" (*Rodriguez* v. *Inglewood Unified School Dist.*, 199 Cal. Rptr. 524 [1984]).

Duty of care also extends to field trips, extracurricular activities such as athletics, school buses, and similar areas of activity. As indicated in the following discussion, court policy making can strengthen or weaken school-tort liability to a considerable degree.

THE CONSTITUTIONAL TORT AND SECTION 1983

Under what circumstances can educators be liable for damages arising out of claims of violating civil rights? What defenses are available to educators threatened with civil-rights damage suits? How vulnerable are board members and districts to civil-rights damage suits? What protection do board members and districts have against damage claims based on violations of constitutional rights?

The Civil Rights Act of 1871, designed as one form of legal protection and recourse for blacks experiencing violations of their civil rights in the postemancipation South, lay dormant following the end of the reconstruction period. Its use was revived during the Civil Rights movement of the fifties and sixties. Section 1983 of the Act states:

> Every person who, under color of any statute, ordinance, regulation, custom, or usage, of any State or Territory, subjects or causes to be subjected, any citizen of the United States or other person within the jurisdiction thereof to the deprivation of any rights, privileges or immunities secured by the Constitution and laws, shall be liable to the party injured in an action at law, suit in equity, or other proper proceeding for redress.[11]

During the sixties and early seventies, the lack of any procedural barriers to initiating Section 1983 monetary damage suits for constitutional tort claims saw liberal court acceptance of these suits applied to the areas of free expression (*Needleman* v. *Bohlen*, 386 F. Supp. 741 [1974]), due process (*Strickland* v. *Inlow*,

519 F. 2d 744 [1975]), and equal protection (*Williams* v. *Albemarle Board of Educ.*, 508 F. 2d 1242 [1974]).

In 1975, the Superme Court expanded the reach of Section 1983 to include school-board members, who traditionally had been considered immune from this form of liability when acting within the scope of their authority, unless their actions were motivated by malice. In *Wood* v. *Strickland* (1975), the Supreme Court reduced this protection to a qualified immunity. A school board was found to have violated the due process rights of students suspended without a hearing for "spiking" the punch at a high-school function. The students sought monetary damages from the school-board members. A divided (five-to-four) Court decided that under Section 1983 a board member's immunity depended not only on the absence of malice. The majority held that a board member could be liable for damages within the context of school discipline if "he knew or reasonably should have known that the action he took within his sphere of official responsibility would violate the constitutional rights of the student affected. . . . "[12]

The scope of educational liability under Section 1983 was further extended in *Monell* v. *Department of Social Services of City of N.Y.* (1978). Here, the U.S. Supreme Court reversed its prior ruling (*Monroe* v. *Pape*, 365 U.S. 167 [1961]) holding local governments, including school districts, to be wholly immune from Section 1983 suits. In *Monell*, the seven-to-two majority held that while "a local government may not be sued for an injury inflicted solely by its employees or agents" it could be sued "when execution of a government's policy or custom . . . inflicts the injury that the government as an entity is responsible under Section 1983."[13]

In the same year that *Monell* was decided, the Supreme Court issued another ruling that placed effective limits on money damage recovery for Section 1983 suits. In *Carey* v. *Piphus*, 435 U.S. 247 (1978), two students were found to have been denied due process in their suspension. They sued the school board for monetary damages under Section 1983. In considering the extent to which monetary damages would be collectable, the Court decided that for a violation such as not providing proper procedural due process, only nominal damages were allowable, not more costly punitive or compensatory damages, unless actual injury could be proven. The plaintiff who had been suspended without procedural due process was awarded damages "not to exceed one dollar." Thus, any civil-rights violation is actionable under Section 1983, but actual injury must be proven to receive anything more than nominal compensation.

By 1978, the vulnerability of school board members (*Wood* v. *Strickland*) and school districts (*Monell* v. *Department*) to Section 1983 suits had been established, but limitations on damage awards had been established by *Carey* v. *Piphus*. In 1980, the Supreme Court addressed the matter of what limited immunity from civil-rights suits still remained to protect school districts. Specifically, the issue focused on the traditional "good faith" immunity defense; that is, districts and their agents were immune from civil-rights damage when the agents were acting in good faith. In *Owen* v. *City of Independence* (1980), the Court stripped away that defense from local governments. While local government officials could claim protection by that defense, government bodies, which include school districts, could not. The Court explained its constitutional tort policy as follows:

> We believe that today's decision, together with prior precedents in the area, properly allocates these costs among the three principals in the scenario of the Section 1983 cause of action: the victim of the constitutional deprivation; the officer whose conduct caused the injury; and the public, as represented by the municipal entity. The innocent individual who is harmed by an abuse of government authority is assured that he will be compensated for his injury. The offending official, so long as he conducts himself in good faith, may go about his business secure in the knowledge that a qualified immunity will protect him from personal liability from damages that are more appropriately chargeable to the populace as a whole. And the public will be forced to bear only the costs of the injury inflicted by the "execution of a government's policy or custom, whether made by its lawmakers or by those whose edicts or acts may fairly be said to represent official policy."[14]

Thus, while school employees or officials have a limited "good faith" immunity from constitutional tort damages, they are liable when they "knew or reasonably should have known" that their actions violated civil rights. Districts, however, enjoy no such immunity. Even so, only nominal damages will be awarded unless actual injury is proven.

EDUCATIONAL MALPRACTICE

Is the public interest served by holding educators accountable for negligence in performing their educational functions? What standards of professional practice have students and their parents a right to expect from educators? Do they have a right to expect certain educational outcomes? How can expected levels of professional educational practice be determined?

The precedent established for tort suits based on professional negligence in medicine and law entered the schooling arena with the California case of *Peter W.* v. *San Francisco School Dist.* (1976). Peter was passed from grade to grade and graduated from high school even though his reading ability was at the fifth-grade level and his mathematics ability was similarly retarded. This occurred even in the face of a California statute requiring that high-school graduates read above the eighth-grade level. Recognizing his inability to perform adequately in society according to expectations for a high-school graduate, Peter sued the school district for tort damages, claiming that the school "negligently and carelessly" failed to respond to his reading disability, assigned him to inappropriate classes, and allowed him to pass classes and be graduated without adequate instruction. He sought damages sufficient to compensate him for permanent disability and inability to gain meaningful employment caused by the school's failure to exercise its duty of care.

The California Court of Appeals rejected Peter's claim on the grounds that to do otherwise would open the door to a new, judicially unmanageable area of litigation and would create a public policy destructive of public education. These restraintist views were defended by noting, in regard to court competency to adequately deal with this area, that:

> Unlike the activity of the highway or marketplace, classroom methodology affords no readily acceptable standards of care, of cause, or injury. The science of pedagogy itself is fraught with different and conflicting theories of how or what a child should be taught . . . Substantial professional authority attests that the achievement of literacy in the schools, or its failure, is influenced by a host of factors which affect the student subjectively, from outside the formal teaching process, and beyond the control of its ministers. They may be physical, neurological, emotional, cultural, environmental; they may be present but not perceived, recognized, but not identified.[15]

As to the issue of public policy, the court believed that holding schools accountable to a professional duty of care

> would expose them to the tort claims—real or imagined—of disaffected students and parents in countless numbers. They are already beset by social and financial problems which have gone to major litigation, but for which no permanent solution has yet appeared. The ultimate consequences, in terms of public time and money, would burden them—and society—beyond calculation.[16]

The question of providing Peter with a diploma in violation of state legal standards was held not actionable for negligence in the form of misrepresentation.

New York was the scene of the next attempts to establish the legal standing of the tort of educational malpractice. The New York appellate court considered the claim that a school district breached its duty of care by failing to meet a student's various educational needs but nevertheless awarded him a certificate of graduation (*Donohue* v. *Copiague Dist.*, [1978]). The student, Donohue, was subsequently unable to keep a job, read want ads, or properly complete a job application. Therefore, Donohue sought damages from the school district for the alleged educational malpractice.

In rejecting Donohue's claim, the Court repeated the public policy and judicial unmanageability arguments used in *Peter W*. It further pointed out that the school did not have total responsibility for Donohue's education; he and his parents shared that responsibility, as "[t]he failure to learn does not bespeak a failure to teach. It is not alleged that the plaintiff's classmates, who were exposed to the identical classroom instruction, also failed to learn."[17] Further, the Court noted that:

> The grades of the plaintiff's periodic report cards gave notice both to his parents and to himself that he had failed in two or more subjects. . . . Having this knowledge, the plaintiff could properly have demanded the special testing and evaluation . . .[18]

While the New York court rejected this attempt at establishing educational malpractice, it did hold that educators "may be held to answer for the failure to faithfully perform their duties."[19] This left enough encouragement for another suit argued in the same year (*Hoffman* v. *Board of New York* [1978]). Danny Hoffman had a speech defect, but at age four was given a nonverbal intelligence test at a hospital and scored in the average range. Upon entering school, he scored 74 on a verbal IQ test and was placed in a retarded program, even though he missed the cutoff score by just one point. The examiner recommended retesting, but it never took place. Eleven years later, he was retested and found to have an IQ of 94, rendering him ineligible for continuation in the vocational training program for retarded students in which he was enrolled. Subsequently, independent testing confirmed his normal intelligence. However, psychiatric opinion held that his long stay in programs for the retarded had imposed retarded behavior on Danny, which could not be corrected by his newly discovered normal intelligence.

In considering Hoffman's claim of damages due to school malpractice, the trial court found the school system negligent and awarded him $750,000. The decision was affirmed on first appeal, although the award was reduced to $500,000. The court reasoned:

> Had plaintiff been improperly diagnosed or treated by medical or psychological personnel in a municipal hospital, the municipality would be liable for the ensuing injuries. There is no reason for any different rule here because the personnel were employed by government entity other than a hospital. Negligence is negligence even if . . . [called] educational malpractice.[20]

However, upon appeal to the state's highest court, the judgment finding malpractice was reversed. Relying on the earlier decision in *Donohue*, the court, by a four-to-three vote, reiterated its restraintist, conservative attitude on this area of school law:

> [T]he courts of this State may not substitute their judgment . . . for the professional judgment of educators and government officials actually engaged in the complex and often delicate process of educating. . . . Indeed, we have previously stated that the courts will intervene in the administration of the public school system only in the most exceptional circumstances involving "gross violations of defined public policy." . . . Clearly, no such circumstances are present here.[21]

The issue of educational malpractice has been blunted thus far, but it does not appear too fanciful to speculate that when a strong case appears in a more receptive judicial climate, the results may be different than for the cases discussed herein.

POLICY CONSIDERATIONS

In the area of tort liability, courts are confronted with the public-policy question of how to balance the interests of persons injured by the action or inaction of educators against the need to provide school personnel with a relatively secure environment in which to act, unfettered by fears of tort liability. The growth of education liability insurance in recent years suggest that school personnel, whether board members, teachers, or administrators, consider themselves put at risk by court tort liability policy. However, a close analysis of this area of litigation reveals that courts are more inclined to take the side of educators. It is the growth of tort litigation and societal litigiousness, and the attendant stripping away of some of the traditional tort-immunity protections of school boards and districts, that has caused the heightened apprehension within the educational community.

It is commonplace for teachers to fear leaving their classrooms for any reason at all, or not to take students on field trips without parental permission for fear of suit, to cite just two examples. Reference to cases involving teachers' absences from class show that such absence is not a *prima facie* reason for finding a teacher negligent. Similarly, parental permission for field trips is not held to be a determining factor in finding teachers liable for field-trip injuries in most jurisdictions. Also, board members hesitate to suspend or expel students because of fears about tort litigation, even though liability beyond nominal damages is relatively difficult to establish. Principals also have become hesitant to allow practices or programs that might suggest a tort cause of action, restricting the adaptiveness and responsiveness to student needs and interests that would otherwise be the case.

Some of this apprehension is justified because of the difficulty of determining how the precise facts in one case may or may not measure up to standards applied to similar, but not exactly alike, related cases. Another area of concern is the potential difference in how various judges, while using the same basic principle of law, may arrive at varying conclusions based on contrasting attitudes of liberalism or conservatism, restraintism or activism. The unpredictability of cases decided by juries is even more problematic.

Even given these problems, there are a number of overarching policy guidelines that provide relatively clear direction for educators negotiating the thicket of tort law, especially regarding the most prominent area of negligence. Most important are the related concepts of reasonableness, prudence, and foreseeability. The educator involved in either policy development or teaching practice must balance considerations of discipline, order, useful school activities for students, testing and placing students, and related educational concerns against the standard of care owed to those in their charge. They must ask themselves whether or not any potential risks involved in their decisions, actions, or inactions are justified by the results intended. There are few activities that are completely free of any and all potential injury due to accident or some natural cause that cannot be anticipated. The key to resolution of this matter is whether due care was taken, as would be expected from a reasonably prudent educator. School personnel must consider such questions as:

1. Is the student protected from unreasonable risk; that is, risks that might foreseeably lead to injury, given the age, sex, or mental, emotional, or physical condition of the student?
2. Has prudent care been exercised by the educator, particularly in regard to adequate instruction, supervision, and maintenance of equipment? Were the standards applied to each appropriate to the type of activity and type of student?
3. Is there a possibility that an action or lack of action in regard to students was influenced by malice or was so reckless that it amounts to willful and wanton behavior?
4. Is it possible that threats or physical punishment are so extreme as to render the educator liable to charges of assault or battery?
5. Are professional skills and judgment responsibly exercised, so that educational harm is precluded?

The law of torts is based upon the rule of reason. The grounding of tort law in common law renders it relatively easy to change or to undergo various modifications of interpretation. It behooves educational personnel to keep pace with the precedents and general judicial thinking within their jurisdiction. It is even more important to understand and follow the concepts governing the reasonable behavior of teachers that have been developed by the courts.

Ferreira v. Sanchez
449 P. 2d 784 (1969)

Jackie Ferreira, a minor and high-school student, and her mother sued George Chavez, a student at the Mora high school, Gilbert Sanchez, a teacher, and Max A. Valdez, principal of the high school, for personal injuries to Jackie resulting from an alleged negligent discharge of a pistol. The case, tried on its merits without a jury, resulted in a judgment against Chavez and dismissal of the action as to Sanchez and Valdez. Chavez has not appealed. The plaintiffs have appealed from the dismissal of the action against Sanchez and Valdez.

The court found that Kenneth Medina, Gabriel Bustos, George Chavez and Jackie Ferreira were Mora high school seniors and members of the cast of the senior play; that Gilbert Sanchez directed the play; that the script called for a blank cartridge to be fired at one place in the play by Gabriel Bustos, and for this purpose Bustos furnished his own gun. The court further found that the gun was kept in a safe in the principal's office when not used in the play, and that only Medina and Bustos were to have access to the gun. Just prior to the final performance of the play George Chavez, a member of the cast, without the knowledge of either Valdez or Sanchez, got the gun, inserted a live bullet in it and fired the pistol, injuring Jackie Ferreira. While there was no finding to that effect, it appears undisputed that while Sanchez was helping put "makeup" on the cast, the weapon was lying on a table on the stage.

The plaintiffs assert that error arose because a pistol is a dangerous weapon, and its use on school premises created an artificial condition involving an unreasonable risk requiring the exercise of a high degree of care by the school authorities. They argue that the court applied the ordinary care test and, accordingly, applied an erroneous rule of law requiring reversal. The correct test to be applied in the law of negligence was explained in Archuleta v. Jacobs, where we said there are no degrees of duty; that the test is not whether in degree the care to be exercised should be slight, ordinary, or extreme care, but commensurate care, due care under the circumstances. We defined it thus:

> "By the great weight of authority the legal measure of duty, except that made absolute by law, in nearly all legal relations, is better expressed by the phrases 'due care', 'reasonable care', or 'ordinary care', terms used interchangeably. * *
>
> "The degree of care does not vary with the increase or diminution of danger. It continues to be ordinary in degree, but the quantum of diligence to be used differs under different conditions. * *"

[W]e said that the person charged with the duty must exercise that degree of care which a reasonably prudent person would use under the same or similar circumstances. We recognize, as was said in Archuleta, that even though the degree of care continues to be ordinary care under the circumstances, "the quantum of diligence to be used differs under different conditions," and that because of the position of these defendants in the school system and of their knowledge of the presence of the gun, a greater quantum of diligence was required to constitute due, reasonable or ordinary care under these circumstances, than would have been required in the absence of a dangerous instrumentality. Nevertheless, we measure the care required by the one standard, i. e., "what would a reasonably prudent person do under like circumstances?" Our review of the record and of the findings makes it apparent that the court applied a correct test as defined by our decisions.

The harm to Jackie was not caused by the direct act of the principal or teacher, but by the intervening act of a third person—George Chavez. The plaintiffs, accordingly, seek to impose liability for negligence upon Valdez and Sanchez by the assertion that in the exercise of the degree of care cast upon them by reason of their positions, they should have foreseen that unauthorized persons might inflict harm with the pistol. Following that theory of negligence, the following findings made by the trial court are challenged as lacking support in the evidence:

> "The cast of the play was composed of Mora High School seniors all of whom, including Gabriel Bustos and George Chavez, were responsible and dependable persons who at all times conducted themselves in an exemplary manner."
>
> "Defendants Max A. Valdez and Gilbert Sanchez did not know or have reason to believe a live bullet would be brought on the premises by George Chavez or by any other person."

"The injury to Plaintiff Jackie Ferreira was caused solely by the conduct of Defendant George Chavez."

"Defendants Max A. Valdez and Gilbert Sanchez could not have anticipated or foreseen the conduct of Defendant George Chavez which caused injury to Plaintiff Jackie Ferreira."

"Defendants Max A. Valdez and Gilbert Sanchez did not cause or contribute to the injury sustained by Plaintiff Jackie Ferreira."

It is true that the mere fact that the injury stemmed from such an intervening act does not of itself exonerate these defendants from negligence, if under the facts of this case the intervening force is reasonably foreseeable.

There appears to be no dispute that the play had been rehearsed over a period of time and that two actual performances had been given on preceding nights. The court expressly found that all of the students comprising the cast were responsible and dependable and conducted themselves in an exemplary manner at all times. The record substantially supports that finding. Nothing has been pointed out to us to indicate that any person except those members of the cast having authority to use the weapon had ever before touched it, nor has anything been pointed out to us to cause even a suspicion that anyone would bring a live bullet into the building, much less that any person would under any circumstances point and discharge the weapon at another, whether loaded with a live or blank cartridge. We must recognize the impossibility of a teacher supervising every minute detail of every activity during the preparation and presentation of the class play. After reading the entire record we cannot say, as a matter of law, that the intervening act of George Chavez was reasonably foreseeable by the teachers. Even if the facts would support an inference that harm was foreseeable, they likewise support the findings made. The court, as trier of the facts, has resolved the issue and this court, on review, is bound by those findings which are the facts before us on appeal.

It follows that the court's conclusion that Sanchez and Valdez were not negligent is supported by the findings. The judgment appealed from should be affirmed.

Kobylanski v. Chicago Board of Education
63 Ill. 2d 165 (1976)

This appeal involves two consolidated cases presenting the common issue of whether teachers and school districts can be held liable for injuries to students resulting from their allegedly negligent conduct, or whether the greater burden of wilful and wanton misconduct must be proved in order to impose liability. Subsidiary issues raised by the various parties will be considered where they are necessary for a resolution of these cases.

In cause No. 47084, plaintiff, the father of Barbara Kobylanski, brought suit on her behalf against the Chicago Board of Education and James Lecos, a physical education instructor, for injuries she sustained during her seventh grade gymnasium class. Kobylanski, who was 13 years old at the time of the accident on November 18, 1968, suffered spinal injuries when she fell while attempting to perform a "knee hang" on steel rings suspended from the ceiling of the gymnasium. Prior to the accident, Lecos had instructed the students on the performance of this exercise. Kobylanski's amended complaint alleged, *inter alia*, that the defendants negligently failed to provide proper instruction and supervision. The defendants answered the complaint, denying the allegations of negligence and setting forth as an affirmative defense section 34—84a of the School Code, which, they maintained, required a plaintiff to prove wilful and wanton misconduct in order to recover. Following the presentation of plaintiff's case, the trial court directed a verdict in favor of the defendants. The trial court found that Kobylanski had failed to prove the defendants were guilty of wilful and wanton misconduct. On appeal to the appellate court, the judgment of the circuit court was affirmed, and we granted plaintiff's petition for leave to appeal. There is no contention made that the evidence presented at trial was sufficient to establish wilful and wanton misconduct.

Cause No. 47454 involves a suit initially filed by the father of the then minor Suzanne Chilton against Cook County School District 207 and Linda Walton, a physical education instructor, for injuries she sustained on April 25, 1968. Chilton was a 15-year-old freshman at Maine Township High School East and was injured during her physical education class while performing a trampoline maneuver known as a "front drop." As in the Kobylanski case, Chilton suffered spinal injuries. Prior to the accident, Chilton received personal instructions from Walton on the performance of this maneuver, since she had previously experienced difficulty in performing it. The second amended complaint, which was predicated upon negligence, alleged, basically, that District 207 failed to provide proper supervision, failed to require increased supervision as trampoline accidents occurred more frequently, and failed to test beginners in order to determine who was capable of taking a trampoline course. Count II charged that Walton failed to properly supervise the class, and forced Chilton to perform the maneuver after it became obvious that she lacked confidence and had considerable difficulty in performing it. The jury returned a verdict in favor of Chilton only against District 207. The trial court refused to instruct the jury that a wilful and wanton standard was applicable rather than a negligence standard, and expressed the belief that section 24—24 applied only to teacher-student disciplinary situations. On appeal to the appellate court, the judgment of the circuit court was affirmed, and we granted the District's petition for leave to appeal. Chilton does not contend that the evidence was sufficient for the jury to find wilful and wanton misconduct had it been instructed as to the applicability of that standard.

The statutes relevant to these appeals are sections 24—24 and 34—84a of the School Code. The pertinent parts of ther two statutes are identical, and they provide:

"Teachers and other certificated educational employees shall maintain discipline in the schools. In all matters relating to the discipline in and conduct of the schools and the school children, they stand in the relation of parents and guardians to the pupils. This relationship shall extend to all activities connected with the school program and may be exercised at any time for the safety and supervision of the pupils in the absence of their parents or guardians."

These statutes confer upon educators the status of parent or guardian to the students. None of the parties to these appeals disputes the fact that a parent is not liable for injuries to his child absent wilful and wanton misconduct.

Kobylanski and Chilton concede that the statutes confer the status of parent or guardian upon teachers, but they maintain that they apply solely in disciplinary situations and not to the facts of the present appeals, which arose from nondisciplinary matters. In support of this position, they point out that the pertinent statutes are found in those portions of the School Code which deal with the employment and duties of teachers, and that the statutes are titled "Maintenance of discipline" and "Teachers shall maintain discipline." Defendants, Chicago Board of Education, Lecos and District 207, contest this interpretation of the statutes and argue that the statutes clearly apply to the present situations, as illustrated by the third sentence of sections 24—24 and 34—84a, which provide that "[t]his relationship shall extend to all activities connected with the school program."

Reviewing the language of the statutes, we find that they were intended to confer the status *in loco parentis* in nondisciplinary as well as disciplinary matters. The second sentence in each of the two statutes provides that "[i]n all matters relating to the discipline in *and conduct of the schools* and the school children, [teachers] stand in the relation of parents and guardians to the pupils." The statutes further indicate that this relationship applies to all activities in the school program. Since physical education is a required part of the academic curriculum, the classes in which Kobylanski and Chilton were injured are clearly "activities connected with the school program."

Furthermore, we note that in *People* v. *Ball*, this court held that, in situations involving the imposition of corporal punishment, teachers enjoy no greater rights nor are they entitled to any greater protection than parents. Conversely, it logically follows that teachers, standing *in loco parentis*, should not be subjected to any greater liability than parents, who are liable to their children for wilful and wanton misconduct, but not for mere negligence.

We conclude, therefore, that sections 24—24 and 34—84a confer upon teachers and other certificated educational employees immunity from suits for negligence arising out of "matters relating to the discipline in and conduct of the schools and the school children." In order to impose liability against such educators, a plaintiff must prove wilful and wanton misconduct.

MR. CHIEF JUSTICE WARD, MR. JUSTICE SCHAEFER and I dissent and would reverse the judgment in 47084 (Kobylanski) and affirm the judgment in 47454 (Chilton).

It seems clear that the statutes apply only to discipline. To reach a contrary interpretation requires a distortion of the language of the second sentence of these sections. Properly construed, that sentence refers to "all matters related to the discipline in the schools and the conduct of the school children." The phrase "and conduct of the schools," which is emphasized by the majority opinion, does not stand alone. The words "discipline in" can not refer to "school children"; those words refer to the "schools." Similarly, the words "conduct of" do not relate to "the schools"; they refer to "the school children." If the phrase "conduct of the schools" is to be torn from its context and given independent significance, the following sentence, which provides that "[t]his relationship shall extend to all activities connected with the school program," is rendered redundant.

Wood v. Strickland
420 U.S. 308 (1975)

MR. JUSTICE WHITE delivered the opinion of the Court.

Respondents Peggy Strickland and Virginia Crain brought this lawsuit against petitioners, who were members of the school board at the time in question, two school administrators, and the Special School District of Mena, Ark., purporting to assert a cause of action under 42 U.S.C.§ 1983, and claiming that their federal constitutional rights to due process were infringed under color of state law by their expulsion from the Mena Public High School on the grounds of their violation of a school regulation prohibiting the use or possession of intoxicating beverages at school or school activities. The complaint as amended prayed for compensatory and punitive damages against all petitioners, injunctive relief allowing respondents to resume attendance, preventing petitioners from imposing any sanctions as a result of the expulsion, and restraining enforcement of the challenged regulation, declaratory relief as to the constitutional invalidity of the regulation, and expunction of any record of their expulsion.

I

The violation of the school regulation prohibiting the use or possession of intoxicating beverages at school or school activities with which respondents were charged concerned their "spiking" of the punch served at a meeting of an extracurricular school organization attended by parents and students. At the time in question, respondents were 16 years old and were in the 10th grade. The relevant facts begin with their discovery that the punch had not been prepared for the meeting as previously planned. The girls then agreed to "spike" it. Since the county in which the school is located is "dry," respondents and a third girl drove across the state border into Oklahoma and purchased two 12-ounce bottles of "Right Time," a malt liquor. They then bought six 10-ounce bottles of a soft drink, and, after having mixed the contents of the eight bottles in an empty milk carton, returned to school. Prior to the meeting, the girls experienced second thoughts about the wisdom of their prank, but by then they were caught up in the force of events and the intervention of other girls prevented them from disposing of the illicit punch. The punch was served at the meeting, without apparent effect.

Ten days later, the teacher in charge of the extracurricular group and meeting, Mrs. Curtis Powell, having heard something about the "spiking," questioned the girls about it. Although first denying any knowledge, the girls admitted their involvement after the teacher said that she would handle the punishment herself. The next day, however, she told the girls that the incident was becoming increasingly the subject of talk in the school and that the principal, P. T. Waller, would probably hear about it. She told them that her job was in jeopardy but that she would not force them to admit to Waller what they had done. If they did not go to him then, however, she would not be able to help them if the incident became "distorted." The three girls then went to Waller and admitted their role in the affair. He suspended them from school for a maximum two-week period, subject to the decision of the school board. Waller also told them that the board would meet that night, that the girls could tell their parents about the meeting, but that the parents should not contact any members of the board.

Neither the girls nor their parents attended the school board meeting that night. Both Mrs. Powell and Waller, after making their reports concerning the incident, recommended leniency. At this point, a telephone call was received by S. L. Inlow, then the superintendent of schools, from Mrs. Powell's husband, also a teacher at the high school, who reported that he had heard that the third girl involved had been in a fight that evening at a basketball game. Inlow informed the meeting of the news, although he did not mention the name of the girl involved. Mrs. Powell and Waller then withdrew their recommendations of leniency, and the board voted to expel the girls from school for the remainder of the semester, a period of approximately three months.

The board subsequently agreed to hold another meeting on the matter, and one was held approximately two weeks after the first meeting. The girls, their parents, and their counsel attended this session. The board began with a reading of a written statement of facts as it had found them. The girls admitted mixing the malt liquor into the punch with the intent of "spiking" it, but asked the board to forgo its rule punishing such violations by such substantial suspensions. Neither Mrs. Powell nor Waller was present at this meeting. The board voted not to change its policy and, as before, to expel the girls for the remainder of the semester.

II

The District Court instructed the jury that a decision for respondents had to be premised upon a finding that petitioners acted with malice in expelling them and defined "malice" as meaning "ill will against a person—a wrongful act done intentionally without just cause or excuse." In ruling for petitioners after the jury had been unable to agree, the District Court found "as a matter of law" that there was no evidence from which malice could be inferred.

The Court of Appeals, however, viewed both the instruction and the decision of the District Court as being erroneous. Specific intent to harm wrongfully, it held, was not a requirement for the recovery of damages. Instead "[i]t need only be established that the defendants did not, in the light of all the circumstances, act in good faith. The test is an objective, rather than a subjective, one."

Petitioners as members of the school board assert here, as they did below, an absolute immunity from liability under § 1983 and at the very least seek to reinstate the judgment of the District Court. We essentially sustain the position of the Court of Appeals with respect to the immunity issue.

Common-law tradition, recognized in our prior decisions, and strong public-policy reasons lead to a construction of § 1983 extending a qualified good-faith immunity to school board members from liability for damages under that section. Although there have been differing emphases and formulations of the common-law immunity of public school officials in cases of student expulsion or suspension, state courts have generally recognized that such officers should be protected from tort liability under state law for all good-faith, nonmalicious action taken to fulfill their official duties.

Liability for damages for every action which is found subsequently to have been violative of a student's constitutional rights and to have caused compensable injury would unfairly impose upon the school decisionmaker the burden of mistakes made in good faith in the course of exercising his discretion within the scope of his official duties. School board members, among other duties, must judge whether there have been violations of school regulations and, if so, the appropriate sanctions for the violations. Denying any measure of immunity in these circumstances "would contribute not to principled and fearless decision-making but to intimidation." The imposition of monetary costs for mistakes which were not unreasonable in the light of all the circumstances would undoubtedly deter even the most conscientious school decisionmaker from exercising his judgment independently, forcefully, and in a manner best serving the long-term interest of the school and the students. The most capable candidates for school board positions might be deterred from seeking office if heavy burdens upon their private resources from monetary liability were a likely prospect during their tenure.

These considerations have undoubtedly played a prime role in the development by state courts of a qualified immunity protecting school officials from liability for damages in lawsuits claiming improper suspensions or expulsions. But at the same time, the judgment implicit in this common-law development is that absolute immunity would not be justified since it would not sufficiently increase the ability of school officials to exercise their discretion in a forthright manner to warrant the absence of a remedy for students subjected to intentional or otherwise inexcusable deprivations.

We think there must be a degree of immunity if the work of the schools is to go forward; and, however worded, the immunity must be such that public school officials understand that action taken in the good-faith fulfillment of their responsibilities and within the bounds of reason under all the circumstances will not be punished and that they need exercise their discretion with undue timidity.

The disagreement between the Court of Appeals and the District Court over the immunity standard in this case has been put in terms of an "objective" versus a "subjective" test of good faith. As we see it, the appropriate standard necessarily contains elements of both. The official himself must be acting sincerely and with a belief that he is doing right, but an act violating a student's constitutional rights can be no more justified by ignorance or disregard of settled, indisputable law on the part of one entrusted with supervision of students' daily lives than by the presence of actual malice. To be entitled to a special exemption from the categorical remedial language of § 1983 in a case in which his action violated a student's constitutional rights, a school board member, who has voluntarily undertaken the task of supervising the operation of the school and the activities of the students, must be held to a standard of conduct based not only on permissible intentions, but also on knowledge of the basic, unquestioned constitutional rights of his charges. Such a standard imposes neither an unfair burden upon a person assuming a responsible public office requiring a high degree of intelligence and judgment for the proper fulfillment of its duties, nor an unwarranted burden in light of the value which civil rights have in our legal system. Any lesser standard would deny much of the promise of § 1983. Therefore, in the specific context of school discipline, we hold that a school board member is not immune from liability for damages under § 1983 if he knew or reasonably should have known that the action he took within his sphere of official responsibility would violate the constitutional rights of the student affected, or if he took the action with the malicious intention to cause a deprivation of constitutional rights or other injury to the student. That is not to say that school board members are "charged with predicting the future course of constitutional law." A compensatory award will be appropriate only if the school board member has acted with such an impermissible motivation or with such disregard of the student's clearly established constitutional rights that his action cannot reasonably be characterized as being in good faith.

III

The Court of Appeals found that the board had made its decision to expel the girls on the basis of *no* evidence that the school regulation had been violated.

The record reveals that the decision of the Court of Appeals was based upon an erroneous construction of the school regulation in question.

The Court of Appeals interpreted the school regulation prohibiting the use or possession of intoxicating beverages as being linked to the definition of "intoxicating liquor" under Arkansas statutes which restrict the term to beverages with an alcoholic content exceeding 5% by weight. Testimony at the trial, however, established convincingly that the term "intoxicating beverage" in the school regulation was not intended at the time of its adoption in 1967 to be linked to the definition in the state statutes or to any other technical definition of "intoxicating." The adoption of the regulation was at a time when the school board was concerned with a previous beer-drinking episode. In light of this evidence, the Court of Appeals was ill advised to supplant the interpretation of the regulation of those officers who adopted it and are entrusted with its enforcement.

Given the fact that there *was* evidence supporting the charge against respondents, the contrary judgment of the Court of Appeals is improvident. It is not the role of the federal courts to set aside decisions of school administrators which the court may view as lacking a basis in wisdom or compassion. Public high school students do have substantive and procedural rights while at school.

Respondents have argued here that there was a procedural due process violation which also supports the result reached by the Court of Appeals. But because the District Court did not discuss it, and the Court of Appeals did not decide it, it would be preferable to have the Court of Appeals consider the issue in the first instance.

The judgment of the Court of Appeals is vacated and the case remanded for further proceedings consistent with this opinion.

So ordered.

Mr. Justice Powell, with whom The Chief Justice, Mr. Justice Blackmun, and Mr. Justice Rehnquist join, concurring in part and dissenting in part.

I dissent from Part II which appears to impose a higher standard of care upon public school officials, sued under § 1983, than that heretofore required of any other official.

The holding of the Court on the immunity issue would impose personal liability on a school official who acted sincerely and in the utmost good faith, but who was found—after the fact—to have acted in "ignorance . . . of settled, indisputable law." Or, as the Court also puts it, the school official must be held to a standard of conduct based not only on good faith "but also on knowledge of the basic, unquestioned constitutional rights of his charges." Moreover, ignorance of the law is explicitly equated with "actual malice." This harsh standard, requiring knowledge of what is characterized as "settled, indisputable law," leaves little substance to the doctrine of qualified immunity. The Court's decision appears to rest on an unwarranted assumption as to what lay school officials know or can know about the law and constitutional rights. These officials will now act at the peril of some judge or jury subsequently finding that a good-faith belief as to the applicable law was mistaken and hence actionable.

The Court states the standard of required knowledge in two cryptic phrases: "settled, indisputable law" and "unquestioned constitutional rights." Presumably these are intended to mean the same thing, although the meaning of neither phrase is likely to be self-evident to constitutional law scholars—much less the average school board member. One need only look to the decisions of this Court— to our reversals, our recognition of evolving concepts, and our five-to-four splits—to recognize the hazard of even informed prophecy as to what are "unquestioned constitutional rights."

There are some 20,000 school boards, each with five or more members, and thousands of school superintendents and school principals. Most of the school board members are popularly elected, drawn from the citizenry at large, and possess no unique competency in divining the law. Few cities and counties provide any compensation for service on school boards, and often it is difficult to persuade qualified persons to assume the burdens of this important function in our society. Moreover, even if counsel's advice constitutes a defense, it may safely be assumed that few school boards and school officials have ready access to counsel or indeed have deemed it necessary to consult counsel on the countless decisions that necessarily must be made in the operation of our public schools.

In view of today's decision significantly enhancing the possibility of personal liability, one must wonder whether qualified persons will continue in the desired numbers to volunteer for service in public education.

Hoffman v. Board of Education of City of New York
424 N.Y.S. 2d 376 (1979)

Opinion of the Court

The significant issue presented on this appeal is whether considerations of public policy preclude recovery for an alleged failure to properly evaluate the intellectual capacity of a student.

The facts in this case may be briefly stated. Plaintiff Daniel Hoffman entered kindergarten in the New York City school system in September, 1956. Shortly thereafter, plaintiff was examined by Monroe Gottsegen, a certified clinical psychologist in the school system, who determined that plaintiff had an intelligence quotient (IQ) of 74 and recommended that he be placed in a class for Children with Retarded Mental Development (CRMD). Dr. Gottsegen was, however, not certain of his findings. The apparent reason for this uncertainty was that plaintiff suffered from a severe speech defect which had manifested itself long before plaintiff entered the school system. Plaintiff's inability to communicate verbally made it difficult to assess his mental ability by means of the primarily verbal Stanford-Binet Intelligence Test administered by Dr. Gottsegen. As a result, Dr. Gottsegen recommended that plaintiff's intelligence "be re-evaluated within a two-year period so that a more accurate estimation of his abilities can be made."

Pursuant to Dr. Gottsegen's recommendations, plaintiff was placed in a CRMD program. While enrolled in the program, plaintiff's academic progress was constantly monitored through the observation of his teachers and by the use of academic "achievement tests" given twice a year. Although in 1959 and 1960 plaintiff received a "90 percentile" rating as to "reading readiness," indicating that his potential for learning to read was higher than average, the results of his achievement tests consistently indicated that he possessed extremely limited reading and mathematical skills. As a result of plaintiff's poor performance on the standardized achievement tests and, presumably, because his teacher's daily observations confirmed his lack of progress, plaintiff's intelligence was not retested on an examination designed specifically for that purpose.

In 1968, plaintiff was transferred to the Queens Occupational Training Center (OTC), a manual and shop training center for retarded youths. The following year plaintiff's mother requested, for the first time, that plaintiff's intelligence be retested. Plaintiff was administered the Wechsler Intelligence Scale for Adults (WAIS). The results of the test indicated that plaintiff had a "verbal" IQ of 85 and a "performance" IQ of 107 for a "full scale" IQ of 94. In other words, plaintiff's combined score on the WAIS test indicated that he was not retarded. Inasmuch as his course of study at the OTC was designed specifically for retarded youths, plaintiff was no longer qualified to be enrolled. As a result, plaintiff was allowed to complete the spring semester of 1969, but was not allowed to return in the fall.

Thereafter, plaintiff commenced this action against the Board of Education of the City of New York, alleging that the board was negligent in its original assessment of his intellectual ability and that the board negligently failed to retest him pursuant to Dr. Gottsegen's earlier recommendation. Plaintiff claimed that these negligent acts and omissions caused him to be misclassified and improperly enrolled in the CRMD program which allegedly resulted in severe injury to plaintiff's intellectual and emotional well-being and reduced his ability to obtain employment. At trial, the jury awarded plaintiff damages in the amount of $750,000. The Appellate Division affirmed this judgment, two Justices dissenting, as to liability, but would have reversed this judgment and required plaintiff to retry the issue of damages had he not consented to a reduction in the amount of the verdict from $750,000 to $500,000. The Appellate Division predicated its affirmance upon defendants' failure to administer a second intelligence test to plaintiff pursuant to Dr. Gottsegen's recommendation to "re-evaluate" plaintiff's intelligence within two years. The court characterized defendants' failure to retest plaintiff as an affirmative act of negligence, actionable under New York law. There should be a reversal.

[1] At the outset, it should be stated that although plaintiff's complaint does not expressly so state, his cause of action sounds in "educational malpractice". Plaintiff's recitation of specific acts of negligence is, in essence, an attack upon the professional judgment of the board of education grounded upon the board's alleged failure to properly interpret and act upon Dr. Gottsegen's recommendations and its alleged failure to properly assess plaintiff's intellectual status thereafter. As we have recently stated in *Donohue* v. *Copiague Union Free School Dist.*, such a cause of action, although quite possibly cognizable under traditional notions of tort law, should not, as a matter of public policy, be entertained by the courts of this State.

[2] In *Donohue*, this court noted that "[c]ontrol and management of educational affairs is vested in the Board of Regents and the Commissioner of Education. In that case, the court was invited to undertake a review not only of broad educational policy, but of the day-to-day implementation of that policy as well. We declined, however, to accept that invitation and we see no reason to depart from that holding today. We had thought it well settled that the courts of this State may not substitute their judgment, or the judgment of a jury, for the professional judgment of educators and government officials actually engaged in the complex and often delicate process of educating the many thousands of children in our schools. Indeed, we have previously stated that the courts will intervene in the administration of the public school system only in the most exceptional circumstances involving "gross violations of defined public policy." Clearly, no such circumstances are present here. Therefore, in our opinion, this court's decision in *Donohue* is dispositive of this appeal.

The court below distinguished *Donohue* upon the ground that the negligence alleged in that case was a failure to educate properly or nonfeasance, whereas, in that court's view, the present case involves an affirmative act of misfeasance. At the outset, we would note that both *Donohue* and the present case involved allegations of various negligent acts and omissions. Furthermore, even if we were to accept the distinction drawn by the court below, and argued by plaintiff on appeal, we would not reach a contrary result. The policy considerations which prompted our decision in *Donohue* apply with equal force to "educational malpractice" actions based upon allegations of educational misfeasance and nonfeasance.

[3, 4] Our decision in *Donohue* was grounded upon the principle that courts ought not interfere with the professional judgment of those charged by the Constitution and by statute with the responsibility for the administration of the schools of this State. In the present case, the decision of the school officials and educators who classified plaintiff as retarded and continued his enrollment in CRMD classes was based upon the results of a recognized intelligence test administered by a qualified psychologist and the daily observation of plaintiff's teachers. In order to affirm a finding of liability in these circumstances, this court would be required to allow the finder of fact to substitute its judgment for the professional

judgment of the board of education as to the type of psychometric devices to be used and the frequency with which such tests are to be given. Such a decision would also allow a court or a jury to second-guess the determinations of each of plaintiff's teachers. To do so would open the door to an examination of the propriety of each of the procedures used in the education of every student in our school system. Clearly, each and every time a student fails to progress academically, it can be argued that he or she would have done better and received a greater benefit if another educational approach or diagnostic tool had been utilized. Similarly, whenever there was a failure to implement a recommendation made by any person in the school system with respect to the evaluation of a pupil or his or her educational program, it could be said, as here, that liability could be predicated on misfeasance. However, the court system is not the proper forum to test the validity of the educational decision to place a particular student in one of the many educational programs offered by the schools of this State. In our view, any dispute concerning the proper placement of a child in a particular educational program can best be resolved by seeking review of such professional educational judgment through the administrative processes provided by statute.

Accordingly, the order of the Appellate Division should be reversed and the complaint dismissed.

MEYER, JUDGE (dissenting).

I agree with Mr. Justice Irwin Shapiro, on the analysis spelled out in his well-reasoned decision at the Appellate Division, that this case involves not "educational malpractice" as the majority in this court suggests but discernible affirmative negligence on the part of the board of education in failing to carry out the recommendation for re-evaluation within a period of two years which was an integral part of the procedure by which plaintiff was placed in a CRMD class, and thus readily identifiable as the proximate cause of plaintiff's damages. I, therefore dissent.

NOTES

1. Molitor v. Kaneland Community Unit Dist. No. 302, 163 N.E. 2d 89 (1959) at 94–96.
2. Calhoun v. Pasadena Indep. School Dist., 496 S.W. 2d 131 (1973) at 131–32.
3. M. M. McCarthy and N. H. Cambron, *Public School Law* (Boston: Allyn and Bacon, 1981), p. 181.
4. The School Code of Illinois, Chapter 122, Section 24–24, 1984.
5. Kobylanski v. Chicago Board of Education, Chilton v. Cook County School Dist. No. 207, 63 111. 2d 165 (1976) at 171–72.
6. Gerrity v. Beatty, 373 N.E. 2d 1323 (1978) at 1326.
7. Fagan v. Summers, 498 P. 2d 1227 (1972) at 1228–29.
8. Hunter v. Evergreen Presbyterian Vocational School, 338 So. 2d 164 (1976) at 165–66.
9. Conway v. O'Brien, 111 F. 2d 611 (1940) at 612.
10. Segerman v. Jones, 259 A. 2d 794 (1969) at 804.
11. Chapter 42, U.S. Code, Section 1983.
12. Wood v. Strickland, 420 U.S. 308 (1975) at 322.
13. Monell v. N.Y.C. Dept. of Social Services, 436 U.S. 658 (1978) at 694.
14. Owen v. City of Independence, 445 U.S. 622 (1980) at 657.
15. Peter W. v. San Francisco Unified School Dist., 60 C.A. 3d 814 (1976) at 824.

16. Id. at 825.
17. Donohue v. Copiague Union Free School Dist., 407 N.Y.S. 2d 874 (1978) at 881.
18. Id. at 881.
19. Id. at 879.
20. Hoffman v. Board of Educ. of City of New York, 64 A.D. 2d 369 (1978) at 110.
21. Hoffman v. Board of Educ. of City of New York, 424 N.Y.S. 2d 376 (1979) at 379.